Communications in Computer and Information Science 2279

Rationale

The CCIS series is devoted to the publication of proceedings of computer science conferences. Its aim is to efficiently disseminate original research results in informatics in printed and electronic form. While the focus is on publication of peer-reviewed full papers presenting mature work, inclusion of reviewed short papers reporting on work in progress is welcome, too. Besides globally relevant meetings with internationally representative program committees guaranteeing a strict peer-reviewing and paper selection process, conferences run by societies or of high regional or national relevance are also considered for publication.

Topics

The topical scope of CCIS spans the entire spectrum of informatics ranging from foundational topics in the theory of computing to information and communications science and technology and a broad variety of interdisciplinary application fields.

Information for Volume Editors and Authors

Publication in CCIS is free of charge. No royalties are paid, however, we offer registered conference participants temporary free access to the online version of the conference proceedings on SpringerLink (http://link.springer.com) by means of an http referrer from the conference website and/or a number of complimentary printed copies, as specified in the official acceptance email of the event.

CCIS proceedings can be published in time for distribution at conferences or as post-proceedings, and delivered in the form of printed books and/or electronically as USBs and/or e-content licenses for accessing proceedings at SpringerLink. Furthermore, CCIS proceedings are included in the CCIS electronic book series hosted in the SpringerLink digital library at http://link.springer.com/bookseries/7899. Conferences publishing in CCIS are allowed to use Online Conference Service (OCS) for managing the whole proceedings lifecycle (from submission and reviewing to preparing for publication) free of charge.

Publication process

The language of publication is exclusively English. Authors publishing in CCIS have to sign the Springer CCIS copyright transfer form, however, they are free to use their material published in CCIS for substantially changed, more elaborate subsequent publications elsewhere. For the preparation of the camera-ready papers/files, authors have to strictly adhere to the Springer CCIS Authors' Instructions and are strongly encouraged to use the CCIS LaTeX style files or templates.

Abstracting/Indexing

CCIS is abstracted/indexed in DBLP, Google Scholar, EI-Compendex, Mathematical Reviews, SCImago, Scopus. CCIS volumes are also submitted for the inclusion in ISI Proceedings.

How to start

To start the evaluation of your proposal for inclusion in the CCIS series, please send an e-mail to ccis@springer.com.

Yoon Jeon Kim · Zachari Swiecki
Editors

Advances in Quantitative Ethnography

6th International Conference, ICQE 2024
Philadelphia, PA, USA, November 3–7, 2024
Proceedings, Part II

Springer

Editors
Yoon Jeon Kim
University of Wisconsin
Madison, WI, USA

Zachari Swiecki
Monash University
Clayton, VIC, Australia

ISSN 1865-0929 ISSN 1865-0937 (electronic)
Communications in Computer and Information Science
ISBN 978-3-031-76331-1 ISBN 978-3-031-76332-8 (eBook)
https://doi.org/10.1007/978-3-031-76332-8

This Springer imprint is published by the registered company Springer Nature Switzerland AG
The registered company address is: Gewerbestrasse 11, 6330 Cham, Switzerland

Preface

Since its first edition at the University of Wisconsin-Madison in 2019, the International Conference on Quantitative Ethnography (ICQE) has been steadily growing and maturing. This year's submissions demonstrate how quantitative ethnography (QE) has expanded in terms of methods, with many submissions leveraging Large Language Models (LLMs) and AI to enhance the computational elements of QE. We also see an expansion in the contexts where QE is being applied and diverse theoretical developments by incorporating traditions of critical theory and indigenous perspectives. Most importantly, ICQE strives to remain a radically welcoming community, committed to rigorously engaging with the sciences and with each other to converge qualitative and quantitative traditions of science across various disciplines, including policies, education, and health care.

This volume contains the proceedings of the Sixth International Conference on Quantitative Ethnography (ICQE 2024). The conference, alongside the International Society for Quantitative Ethnography (ISQE), has continued to foster an open community, aiming to invite new and returning scholars into discussion around approaches that unify qualitative and quantitative analyses. A core goal of ISQE and the wider community is to foster discussion regarding making meaning from rich datasets.

ICQE 2024 submissions were evaluated by two expert reviewers and a meta-reviewer using a double-blind model. 31 full papers and 10 short papers were accepted from 82 submissions. Accepted posters, Research Agenda Development (RAD) proposals, symposia, and workshops can be found in the ICQE 2024 Conference Proceedings Supplement via the ISQE website.

The diversity of authors, contexts, data, and topics reflects the interdisciplinary nature of the QE community. The authors represent nine countries and over 30 institutions. Analyzed data comes from various sources, including in-person and online learning environments, public discourse, animal conservation sites, and medical care facilities.

These proceedings (split across two volumes) organize papers within three broad themes. 13 papers explore or extend QE *theory and methodology*. Several of these papers investigate the applications of new AI approaches, such as LLMs, to core components of QE methodology, such as coding qualitative data. Continuing the strong tradition of applying QE to educational contexts, 24 papers investigate *teaching and learning*. These papers include investigations of student learning in formal online and in-person settings, informal contexts such as games, and augmented reality–and, in one case, chimpanzees' problem-solving capacities. Teacher knowledge, behaviors, and identities were also explored. Finally, four papers examined *culture and discourse* in diverse contexts, including discussions of polarizing topics, political discourse, and civil discourse.

We would like to thank all the authors and continue to invite new and returning researchers into the QE community. We also thank the reviewers, program committee members, and others in the QE community who have supported the conference. The program chairs acknowledge support from ISQE and the National Science Foundation.

Finally, we are particularly grateful to the local chairs and organizers for their work in planning the conference and welcoming ICQE to Philadephia.

September 2024

Yoon Jeon Kim
Zachari Swiecki

Organization

Program Chair

Y. J. Kim	University of Wisconsin - Madison, USA

Program Co-chair

Zachari Swiecki	Monash University, Australia

Conference Chair

Ryan Baker	University of Pennslyvania, USA

Conference Co-chair

Amanda Barany	University of Pennslyvania, USA

Program Committee

Golnaz Arastoopour Irgens	Vanderbilt University, USA
Ba Shen	Education University of Hong Kong, China
Ryan Baker	University of Pennsylvania, USA
Amanda Barany	University of Pennsylvania, USA
Jennifer Bateman	Clemson University, USA
Yixin Cheng	Monash University, Australia
Brendan Eagan	University of Wisconsin-Madison, USA
Danielle Espino	Pepperdine University, USA
Beatriz Galarza	Purdue University, USA
Rogers Kalisa	University of Oslo, Norway
Simon Knight	University of Technology Sydney, Australia
Mariah Knowles	University of Wisconsin-Madison, USA
Seung Lee	Pepperdine University, USA
Roberto Martinez-Maldonado	Monash University
Y. J. Kim	University of Wisconsin-Madison, USA

Kamila Misiejuk	University of Bergen, Norway
Luc Paquette	University of Illinois at Urbana-Champaign, USA
Vitaly Popov	University of Michigan, USA
Andrew Ruis	University of Wisconsin-Madison, USA
Jennifer Scianna	University of Wisconsin-Madison, USA
Mamta Shah	Elsevier, USA
Jonathon Sun	University of Pennsylvania, USA
Hazel Vega	Clemson University, USA

Conference Committee

Golnaz Arastoopour Irgens	Vanderbilt University, USA
Amalia Dache	University of Pennsylvania, USA
Catherine Davis	University of Wisconsin-Madison, USA
Brendan Eagan	University of Wisconsin-Madison, USA
Aroutis Foster	Drexel University, USA
César Hinojosa	University of Wisconsin-Madison, USA

Additional Reviewers

Adenike Omolare Adefisayo
Ibrahim Adisa
Ruth Akumbu
Tyler Andres–Bray
Zhiqiang Cai
Denis Camou
Brittny Chabalowski
Virginia Clark
Lara Condon
Angela Crumdy
Yuna Dai
Vanessa Dennen
Celeste Francis Esteves
Adina Goldstein
Eric Hamilton
Tianshi Hao
Yusuke Hayashi
Rodrigo Hidalgo
Percy Jardine
Sarah Jerasa
Daisuke Kaneko
Jina Kang
Behdokht Kiafar
Pakon Ko
Letitia Lee
Haiying Li
Huimin Liu
Xiner Liu
Jun Lu
Lisa Lundgren
Yanye Luther
Luis Felipe Martinez-Gomez
Sinead Meehan
Morten Misfeldt
Nidhi Nasiar
Liv Nøhr
Ayano Ohsaki
Ada Onyewuenyi
Jun Oshima
Maciej Pankiewicz
Jade Pratt
Stephanie Rivera-Kumar

Gemma Salazar
Temesgen Samuel
Riku Sayuj
Daniel Spikol
Erk Stenly
Hanall Sung
Yuanru Tan
Adrienne Traxler
Chia-Yu Wang
Ching-Hsing Wang
Yeyu Wang
Liane Weintraub
Brooke Whitworth
David Williamson Shaffer
Moe Woodard
Jianxing Yu
Andres Felipe Zambrano
Jiayi Zhang
Youning Zhao
Szilvia Zörgő

Contents – Part II

Teaching and Learning

Cultural Discourse

Contents – Part I

Theory and Methodology

Teaching and Learning

Different Times, Different Measures: Monitoring Shifting Self-regulation Strategies for Language Learning in Higher Education Across Face-To-Face, Online and Hybrid Instruction

Ward Peeters[1] (✉) and Alexander Ito Maitland[2]

[1] Monash University, Wellington Road, Clayton, VIC 3800, Australia
Ward.Peeters@monash.edu

[2] Kanda University of International Studies, 1 Chome-4-1 Wakaba, Mihama Ward, Chiba 261-0014, Japan
itomaitland-a@kanda.kuis.ac.jp

Abstract. Language learning in higher education has experienced many changes in recent years, most notably in the mode of instruction, with institutions venturing between face-to-face teaching, fully online, and hybrid instruction. As the spaces for teaching and learning evolve, so does learning itself, as well as the support educators have to provide for their students. This study investigates these evolutions, analysing the self-regulation strategies of three groups of English language majors ($N = 250$), enrolled in an effective learning module at a private Japanese University. Data was collected over three academic years: the first year featured face-to-face instruction, the second year shifted to online teaching due to the Covid-19 pandemic, and the third year implemented a hybrid model as students were allowed back on campus. The data includes students' written collaborative discussions and reflections on an online discussion forum, part of their activities for the module. The data were annotated to examine the ways learners address their approaches to learning, the facilities and resources they employ, as well as their performance. This study uses Epistemic Network Analysis to map shifts in self-regulation for language learning among the three student groups, and across different instructional modalities. The results show that the hybrid cohort exhibited strong cognitive and meta-cognitive development, while face-to-face instruction fostered students to engage with more resources. In both the online and hybrid mode, students engaged in language socialisation more frequently, acculturating to the learning environment. This study provides recommendations for adaptive support mechanisms to facilitate effective learning across various instructional modalities.

Keywords: Self-Regulated Learning · Epistemic Network Analysis · Language Learning · Language Awareness · Computer-Supported Collaborative Learning · Peer Interaction · Mode of Instruction

Y. J. Kim and Z. Swiecki (Eds.): icqe 2024, CCIS 2279, pp. 3–18, 2024.
https://doi.org/10.1007/978-3-031-76332-8_1

1 Introduction

Self-regulation for language learning involves learners developing agency in their learning trajectory as they discover, select and apply different learning strategies to plan, monitor, and reflect on their learning and language development [1–3]. However, studies have shown that learners often struggle to fully comprehend and effectively adjust these strategies throughout their studies, which can hinder them in their ability to manage their learning properly, both inside and outside the classroom [4, 5]. Providing support for learners is, therefore, essential to help them navigate their language learning trajectories, ensuring both learning success and successful language acquisition [6].

In order to provide adequate support, educators, learning designers and learning advisors require a thorough understanding of the learning context, which includes knowledge and awareness of experiential and environmental factors that can influence learning [7], the opportunities learners have to develop social capital [8], as well as the modes of instruction they are engaged in [9]. One way of monitoring the impact of these factors is to observe the ways learners interact with the learning content, with resources, and with people around them such as educators and peers [10]. Studies have also shown that these types of interaction can provide researchers and learning analysts with new opportunities to see how language learners provide and handle feedback, how they socialise and explore their language and learner identity, how they experiment with language and practice their proficiency, and how these actions support cognitive functioning as well as metacognitive reflection on language use (see [11] for an overview). In addition, it enables researchers to monitor and map essential aspects of learners' development and progress, such as their self-regulation strategies, and use these analytics to provide personalised assistance and scaffolded support [5, 12].

To better understand the development of self-regulation for language learning, and how contextual factors such as the mode of instruction may affect this process, this study aims to investigate how different groups of language learners in tertiary education navigate and manage their learning by comparing how they discuss and apply language learning strategies across three modes of instruction: face-to-face, online and hybrid. Participants in this study are enrolled in an effective learning module, which prepares them to further develop their awareness, skills and strategies for language learning. Part of the activities for this module include goal-setting, finding useful resources, and drafting learning plans for the future (see [13] for more information). The research questions for this study are as follows:

1. Which self-regulation strategies and meta-strategies do foreign language students apply in a computer-supported collaborative setting for effective learning in higher education?
2. How does the mode of instruction (face-to-face, online, hybrid) influence the selection and application of self-regulation learning strategies and meta-strategies in a computer-supported collaborative setting for effective learning in higher education?

The data for this study consists of students' written collaborative discussions and reflections from an online forum, part of the effective learning module. Epistemic Network Analysis (ENA) was used to examine how learners approach their studies, exchange resources, and discuss their strategies for learning. ENA was used to map the co-occurrence of these themes, as well as any possible changes in self-regulation for language learning across various instructional modes.

2 Literature Review and Background

2.1 The Role of Peer Interaction in Second Language Learning

Peer interaction has a long-standing tradition as a collaborative learning practice within the field of second language acquisition, and can be defined as "any communicative activity carried out between learners, where there is minimal or no participation from the teacher" [14, p. 3]. In research on the topic, learners are often observed to work towards common goals in their collaborative language learning [see 10 for an overview]. However, peer interaction and collaborative dialogue can take many forms, and the needs of learners can vary, ranging from engaging in task-oriented interaction to interaction for socialisation purposes. A common aspect of peer interaction for learning is learners establishing some kind of shared commitment as they pursue their interests [8]. From a teaching and design perspective, within peer interaction spaces, the goal therefore is to have learners actively engage with others while developing "a shared repertoire of resources: experiences, stories, tools, ways of addressing recurring problems—in short a shared practice" [15, p. 2].

Integrating peer interaction opportunities has proven to provide a platform for language learners to develop a community of practice, engage in scaffolded support and knowledge co-construction, and develop self-regulation skills, both in face-to-face classrooms and in hybrid and online spaces [16, 17]. Researching peer interaction to monitor self-regulation for language learning can provide valuable insights into the complex interplay between instances of cognitive and meta-cognitive development, learning management, identity construction and motivation that surface in learner dialogue [17, 18]. In order to account for these dynamics, the present study focused on the various strategies and meta-strategies language learners employ, as described by Oxford [2], and detailed the ways they can be observed in learner interaction.

2.2 Self-regulation for Language Learning

Mapping how various aspects of the self-regulation process materialise in peer interaction, how they interrelate and how this dynamic process unfolds over time, has been the driving force behind recent advances in quantitative and qualitative approaches to researching learning processes, including the field of Quantitative Ethnography [19]. Next to methodological advances, new insights and meta-analyses in the field of Applied Linguistics – most notably by Oxford [2] – have provided more encompassing perspectives and definitions of the self-regulation process. Her account of strategic self-regulation (S2R) for language learning provides a firm basis to map learning strategies, or the "complex, dynamic thoughts and actions, selected and used by learners with some degree of consciousness in specific contexts in order to regulate multiple aspects of themselves (such as cognitive, emotional, and social)" (p. 48). Oxford specifies that, in order to speak of strategies for learning, these thoughts and actions have to have a purpose, e.g., accomplishing language tasks, improving proficiency, regulating emotions or constructing identity. While strategies encompass specific actions, as described above, meta-strategies like planning, monitoring and evaluating help learners better manage their learning journey. In her definition, she emphasises the need to analyse S2R as a dynamic process, since learners will often use different strategies at the same time, meaning that the observable manifestations of these strategies often intertwine.

2.3 A Structured Awareness-Raising Curriculum for Language Learning

A way to foster S2R in language learning is to make it an indissoluble part of the curriculum. Kato and Mynard [20] discuss the building blocks of such a curriculum, which is aimed at helping language learners to better direct and regulate their learning. They advocate a curriculum design that is adaptive and contributes to the development of learner autonomy by focusing on three awareness-raising principles: i) fostering learners' awareness of approaches to learning, which includes explicit and implicit instruction, and creating room for learners to share their individual preferences, ideas, interests, and experiences, ii) scaffolding learners' awareness of the facilities, roles and resources that are available to them, as well as facilities and resources their peers use, and the roles they take up, and iii) harnessing learners' awareness of self, including their acculturation to the learning environment and emotions regarding the learning process.

The present study will analyse how S2R strategies and meta-strategies, as outlined by Oxford [2], manifest in peer interaction spaces part of a structured awareness-raising curriculum (SARC) that instructs learners on the ways they can direct and regulate their learning, and provides ample opportunities for them to discuss their thoughts, actions and progress with peers and with a learning advisor [20]. The aim of this study is to determine whether the dynamic S2R process differs across different modes of instruction, as learners engage in face-to-face, online, and hybrid education, by using the dynamic network models part of an ENA analysis to visualise and analyse data.

3 Methodology

3.1 Context and Data Collection

This study was conducted at a private foreign language university in Chiba, Japan. Just over 4,000 undergraduate students attend the school where they major in various languages through the Department of English, the Department of Asian Languages, or the Department of Spanish and Portuguese. There is also a Department of International Communication in which students focus on English. With the Departments of English and International Communication, over half of the undergraduates focus on English language acquisition. Students are typically motivated learners who are interested in international media and culture, and many aspire to use foreign languages in their future professions. Many participate in a study abroad program during their studies.

The typical undergraduate student is well-motivated, but may lack confidence relating to English communication, and may also encounter difficulties with time management as a new university student [21]. Many enter the university with lower-intermediate English communication ability, and many are also not accustomed to embracing making mistakes in English production when communicating [22].

Participants in this study are first-, second- and third-year English majors from the university's English Department ($N = 250$) who enrolled in the effective learning module offered at the university. The module includes several units designed to enhance learners' self-regulation, planning, resource management, and awareness of learning strategies, requiring weekly written reports and feedback exchanges with learning advisors to foster reflective dialogue and cognitive development. Learners also attend workshops, meet with advisors multiple times during the semester, and submit a final report on their language learning progress. Learners are given the opportunity to discuss their plans and reflections with peers via Google Classroom, an online platform designed for teaching, learning, and collaboration among students and teachers. For the module, no teachers or advisors were present in this peer interaction space. Weekly prompts in the syllabus encouraged online collaboration, with space provided for learners to document their posts and notable comments for feedback to their learning advisors.

This study collected students' posts and comments ($N = 1088$), source IDs, and time stamps over the course of three years. Every year featured a different mode of instruction due to the global Covid-19 pandemic: face-to-face, online and hybrid. Informed consent was obtained from all participants before their data was collected. Text data, which included participants' online conversations on the Google Classroom platform, were collected using an application programming interface (API) scraper tool.

3.2 Data Annotation

The peer interaction process, consisting of posts and comments to the effective learning module's discussion forum, was annotated using a code book based on Oxford's S2R model [2] (as shown in Table 1), also used and validated in previous research on the topic [23]. A team of three coders annotated the data sets, labelling the various strategies and meta-strategies they encountered such as planning, resource management and reflection while keeping record of recurring topics learners addressed. Learners often used multiple strategies and meta-strategies in one post or comment, resulting in one post or comment receiving multiple labels. The coding team went over each other's work and discussed disputed or ambiguous codes until a consensus was reached through the social moderation method [24], ensuring inter-rater agreement on the final annotated data sets.

The code book is divided into three main sections, one addressing learners' awareness of approaches to learning, which focuses on planning, evaluating, and orchestrating strategy use for specific tasks, discussing goals, and reflecting on performance. Another section focuses on awareness of facilities, roles, and resources, and includes obtaining, using, and evaluating relevant resources. The final section, awareness of self, involves monitoring what is being said, expressing emotions and gratitude, sharing personal stories and building learner identity, and generating motivation [20].

3.3 Methods

As a first step, three adjacency matrices were constructed to measure the number of occurrences of different S2R strategies and meta-strategies in the data sets, one per mode of instruction. Second, the ENA Web Tool (version 1.7.0) was used to measure the co-occurrence and links between the S2R strategies and meta-strategies [25–27]. The

Table 1. Code book for self-regulation strategies and meta-strategies in a SARC.

Code	Actions	Strategies & meta-strategies	SARC
A1	Discussing learning goals and objectives	Planning	Awareness of approaches to learning
A2	Discussing planning and timing	Planning	
A3	Identifying possible strategies for learning	Orchestrating strategy use	
A4	Applying strategies for learning	Activating knowledge	
A5	Requesting information on strategies for learning	Orchestrating strategy use	
A6	Reflecting on strategies for learning	Evaluating	
A7	Reflecting on learning performance	Evaluating	
A8	Discussing set-up and motivations for enrolling	Evaluating	
F9	Reflecting on the use of resources	Evaluating	Awareness of facilities, roles, and resources
F10	Discussing the content of resources	Obtaining/using resources	
F11	Sharing resources: people and spaces	Obtaining/using resources	
F12	Sharing resources: university resources	Obtaining/using resources	
F13	Sharing resources: personal resources	Obtaining/using resources	
F14	Requesting (info on) resources	Obtaining/using resources	
F15	Sharing experiences about learning trajectory	Organising learning	
F16	Discussing practical or technical issues	Organising learning	
S17	Expressing emotions on performance	Activating emotions	Awareness of self

(continued)

Table 1. (*continued*)

Code	Actions	Strategies & meta-strategies	SARC
S18	Reflecting on learning trajectory	Monitoring performance	
S19	Asking for acknowledgement/positive reinforcement	Generating motivation	
S20	Providing acknowledgement/positive reinforcement	Generating motivation	
S21	Expressing gratitude	Generating motivation	
S22	Expressing interests	Paying attention	
S23	Leisure talk	Constructing identity	
S24	Discussing personal stories/introductions	Constructing identity	

adjacency matrices were transposed to binary codes to conform with the ENA framework. The units of analysis were defined as all Posts and Comments (Type), the conversations they are part of (SourceID), and time stamps (Time). Strategies and meta-strategies were imported as codes for analysis. The ENA algorithm uses a moving stanza window of 4 to construct a network model for each line in the data, showing how codes in a line are connected to the 3 previous lines within a given conversation. Most conversations did not exceed four turns of talk. The ENA model provides aggregated networks which can then be compared, mapping the co-occurrence of codes in the process of S2R. ENA is particularly well-suited to answer the research questions in this regard as it visualises how these strategies are dynamically interrelated and change over time. ENA networks were normalised before subjecting them to dimensional reduction, normalising the distribution between different units of analysis and the number of coded lines in the data [25]. To measure the differences between Types, a two-sample t-test was applied to each network calculation, assuming unequal variance to the location of points in the projected ENA space for units in 'Posts' and 'Comments'.

4 Results: S2R in a Structured Awareness-Raising Curriculum

4.1 Strategy and Meta-strategy Use Across Modes of Instruction

The first results show that there are some similarities and differences in frequency of use of some of the S2R strategies and meta-strategies when comparing different modes of instruction (Table 2). The most notable similarities across the board can be observed for reflecting on strategies for learning (A6), sharing personal resources (F13) and requesting (info on) resources (F14), which all stay stable in the mid-range frequency category, tending to occur rather frequently, no matter the mode of instruction. Some low-frequency themes that tend to re-occur include discussing planning and timing (A2), applying strategies for learning (A4), reflecting on learning performance (A7), and discussing the content of resources (F10). While their frequency of use is stable, they are not very prominent in the peer interaction process.

Table 2. Frequency of S2R strategies and meta-strategies across modes of instruction.

Code	Actions	Face-to-face	Online	Hybrid
A1	Discussing learning goals and objectives	**8%**	**11%**	**9%**
A2	Discussing planning and timing	**3%**	**1%**	**3%**
A3	Identifying possible strategies for learning	**1%**	**6%**	**10%**
A4	Applying strategies for learning	**3%**	**3%**	**4%**
A5	Requesting information on strategies for learning	**1%**	**0%**	**5%**
A6	Reflecting on strategies for learning	**7%**	**7%**	**6%**
A7	Reflecting on learning performance	**2%**	**1%**	**2%**
A8	Discussing set-up and motivations for enrolling	**1%**	**0%**	**0%**
F9	Reflecting on the use of resources	**1%**	**0%**	**0%**
F10	Discussing the content of resources	**3%**	**1%**	**4%**
F11	Sharing resources: people and spaces	**0%**	**1%**	**3%**
F12	Sharing resources: university resources	**2%**	**0%**	**0%**
F13	Sharing resources: personal resources	**8%**	**9%**	**9%**
F14	Requesting (info on) resources	**9%**	**7%**	**5%**
F15	Sharing experiences about learning trajectory	**6%**	**0%**	**1%**
F16	Discussing practical or technical issues	**0%**	**0%**	**0%**
S17	Expressing emotions on performance	**0%**	**0%**	**1%**
S18	Reflecting on learning trajectory	**3%**	**0%**	**0%**
S19	Asking for acknowledgement / positive reinforcement	**13%**	**13%**	**18%**
S20	Providing acknowledgement / positive reinforcement	**4%**	**2%**	**0%**
S21	Expressing gratitude	**7%**	**7%**	**3%**
S22	Expressing interests	**8%**	**17%**	**9%**
S23	Leisure talk	**6%**	**3%**	**2%**
S24	Discussing personal stories / introductions	**2%**	**8%**	**5%**

Notable differences across the modes of instruction can be found in the peaks and valleys of Table 2. Outliers that stand out are the surge in expressing interests (S22) in the online cohort, and asking for acknowledgement/positive reinforcement (S19) in the hybrid cohort. While there are some minor differences across the frequency of S2R strategies and meta-strategies when considering learners' awareness of approaches to learning (A-section) and awareness of facilities, roles and resources (F-section), awareness of self (S-section) seems to be most impacted by a change in mode of instruction.

4.2 The ENA Perspective

ENA networks were generated to analyse the patterns of association between the different strategies and meta-strategies that were annotated in post and comments of the peer interaction data sets. Separate comparison networks were generated for each student group (Fig. 1), and, for every mode of instruction, ENA networks for post and comment sections were generated (Figs. 2, 3 and 4). Using separate networks allows us to analyse threaded conversations in more detail, accounting for the fact that comment sections often contain a wider variety of S2R strategies and meta-strategies.

For the network in Fig. 1 that shows the student group engaged in face-to-face instruction (left), along the X axis, a two-sample t test assuming unequal variance showed

Fig. 1. Comparison of Posts (red) and Comments (blue) of the three student groups in face-to-face education (left), online education (middle), and hybrid education (right).

that Posts (mean = −0.13, SD = 0.13, N = 177) were statistically significantly different at the alpha = 0.05 level from Comments (mean = 0.28, SD = 0.17, N = 124; t(136.15) = −19.91, p = 0.00, Cohen's d = 2.85). Along the Y axis, a two-sample t test assuming unequal variance showed that Posts (mean = 0.00, SD = 0.27, N = 177) were not statistically significantly different at the alpha = 0.05 level from Comments (mean = 0.00, SD = 0.11, N = 124; t(255.04) = 0.00, p = 1.00, Cohen's d = 0.00). For the network that shows the student group engaged in online instruction (middle), along the X axis, a two-sample t test assuming unequal variance showed that Posts (mean = −0.15, SD = 0.13, N = 361) were statistically significantly different at the alpha = 0.05 level from Comments (mean = 0.58, SD = 0.19, N = 207; t(41.21) = −21.30, p = 0.00, Cohen's d = 5.07). Along the Y axis, a two-sample t test assuming unequal variance showed that Posts (mean = 0.00, SD = 0.34, N = 361) were not statistically significantly different at the alpha = 0.05 level from Comments (mean = 0.00, SD = 0.13, N = 207; t(144.73) = 0.00, p = 1.00, Cohen's d = 0.00). For the network that shows the student group engaged in hybrid instruction (right), along the X axis, a two-sample t test assuming unequal variance showed that Posts (mean = −0.16, SD = 0.13, N = 129) were statistically significantly different at the alpha = 0.05 level from Comments (mean = 0.29, SD = 0.10, N = 90; t(176.35) = −27.02, p = 0.00, Cohen's d = 3.72). Along the Y axis, a two-sample t test assuming unequal variance showed that Posts (mean = 0.00, SD = 0.34, N = 129) were not statistically significantly different at the alpha = 0.05 level from Comments (mean = 0.00, SD = 0.21, N = 90; t(196.58) = 0.00, p = 1.00, Cohen's d = 0.00).

In Posts generated by the group of learners that was engaged in face-to-face instruction (Fig. 2), strong links can be observed between learners discussing learning goals and objectives (A1) while reflecting on some of the strategies they are using (A6), e.g., "My goals is fluency and speaking. So I try to shadow while watching "Full House". I want to listen my recorded voice to evaluate me. But I have no idea how to! Please teach me, who should I ask?". Strategy use also tends to co-occur with asking for information about resources (F14). In the comments, the strongest link can be observed between expressing gratitude (S21) and asking for acknowledgement/positive reinforcement (S19). Both strategies appear frequently in combination with other strategies and meta-strategies, with expressing gratitude co-occurring with expressing interests (S22), talking about pastime (S23) and sharing resources (F13). While the comment section exhibits strong connections with elements that exhibit learners' awareness of self, the posts they generate contain more connections between awareness of approaches to learning and awareness of facilities, roles and resources.

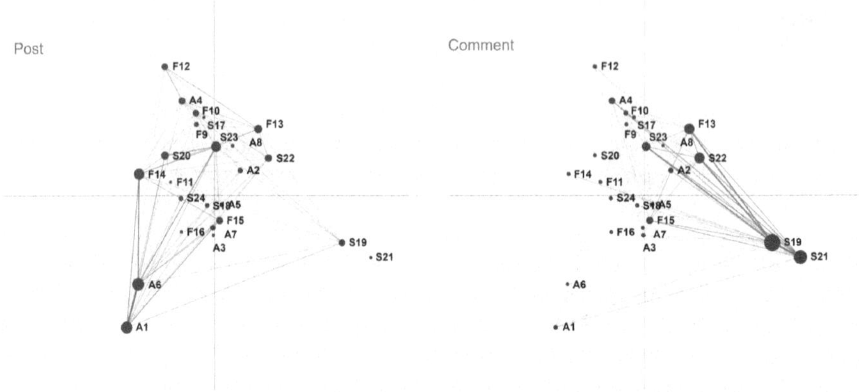

Fig. 2. Posts (red) and Comments (blue) by students engaged in face-to-face education.

In Posts generated by the group of learners that was engaged in online instruction (Fig. 3), a more varied pattern can be observed, linking different aspects of effective learning together. Here, strong links can, again be observed between learners discussing learning goals and objectives (A1) and reflecting on some of the strategies they are using (A6), further enhanced by learners sharing resources (F13) and asking questions about what resources other people are using (F14), e.g., "Hi, I'm [Name]. My goal is to speak English fluently because I always waste time to make perfect sentences in my brain while talking with others. Then I realized I should know native conversation firstly. So now I'm using an app "Hello Talk". But if you know any other good way, please let me know". Compared to the face-to-face cohort, reflecting on strategies (A6) does not tend to co-occur with asking for information about resources (F14) as frequently, but co-occurs more frequently with goal-setting (A1). In this section, strong connections can also be observed between learners expressing their interests (S22), talking about their pastime (S23) and discussing personal stories/introductions (S24), more so than in the face-to-face cohort. In the comments, the strongest link can be observed between expressing gratitude (S21) and asking for acknowledgement/positive reinforcement (S19), which, this time, also tends to include discussions on sharing resources (F13). Learners expressing what they like as they share their interests (S22) and talking about their pastime (S23) also tends to co-occur. In comparison to the face-to-face cohort, the online cohort exhibits more evidence of awareness of approaches to learning and awareness of self in their posts, while the comment section exhibits strong connections between elements that exhibit learners' awareness of self, but, by comparison, contains less variation when it comes to the combination of strategies and meta-strategies.

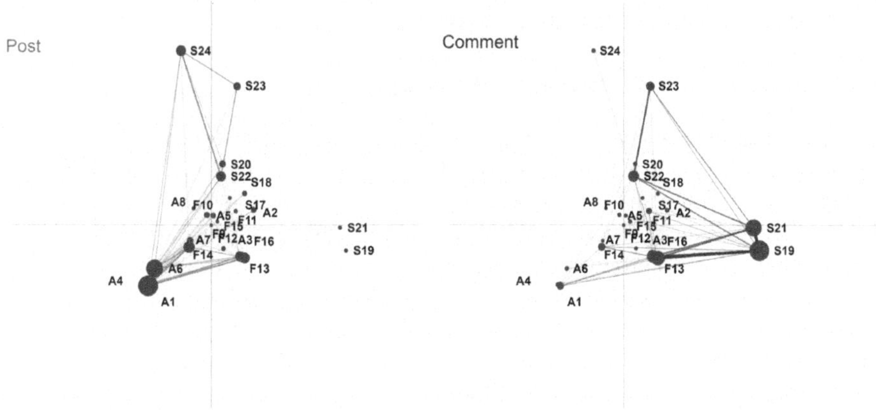

Fig. 3. Posts (red) and Comments (blue) by students engaged in online education.

In Posts generated by the group of learners that was engaged in hybrid instruction (Fig. 4), learners discussing learning goals and objectives (A1) clusters together with identifying possible strategies for learning (A3), applying them (A4), reflecting on the strategies they are using (A6), and sharing resources (F13). In this section, strong connections can also be observed between learners discussing their interests (S22) and discussing personal stories/introductions (S24). In the comments, asking for acknowledgement/positive reinforcement (S19) is the main topic co-occurring with other facets of learning, most notably with identifying possible strategies for learning (A3). While links to other facets of awareness of self are still strong, the link with learners expressing their interests (S22), which was observed in other cohorts, seems to have lost some of its prominence. Much like the online cohort, the hybrid cohort's posts exhibit evidence of awareness of approaches to learning and awareness of self, while the comment section exhibits strong connections with elements that exhibit learners' awareness of self, but revolve strongly around asking for acknowledgement/positive reinforcement from others.

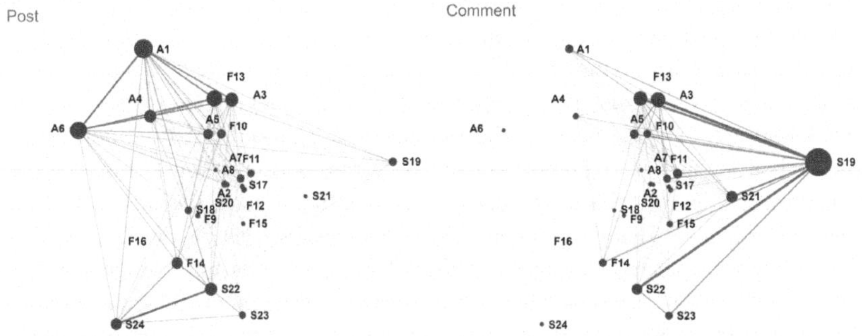

Fig. 4. Posts (red) and Comments (blue) by students engaged in hybrid education.

5 Discussion and Recommendations

5.1 S2R Trends Across Different Modes of Instruction

This study examined which self-regulation strategies and meta-strategies foreign language learners apply in a computer-supported collaborative setting for effective language learning, and asked the question whether the mode of instruction (face-to-face, online, hybrid) influenced their selection and application of self-regulated learning strategies and meta-strategies. All groups fully engaged in the S2R process, as they demonstrated awareness of approaches to learning, awareness of facilities, roles and resources, and awareness of self, which were all facets of language learning that were fostered and scaffolded in the SARC of the effective learning module [20]. In line with previous research, one of the first observations across the different groups is that post and comment sections are distinctly different when it comes to learners' selection of S2R strategies and meta-strategies, and how they tend to co-occur [12, 23]. Posts are often task-oriented, with discussions that feature goal setting, planning and strategy use while comment sections feature learners asking for/providing acknowledgement, sharing personal stories and engaging in resource management. As shown in previous research on language socialisation [28], these dynamics highlight how learners are using language to both contribute to, and flag membership of, a certain community [29].

When comparing the different groups, based on the mode of instruction, it becomes apparent that the face-to-face cohort exhibits the most variety in S2R strategy and meta-strategy use, with fewer outliers to the far negative (never used) or far positive (used extensively) of the scale. Learners engage with more resources, which aligned with their reflections on strategy use (posts) and seeking acknowledgement from others (comments). Access to carefully vetted facilities and resources is what sets this cohort apart, highlighting the environmental factors that distinguish the three groups. For the face-to-face cohort, the three awareness phases tend to co-occur frequently.

The online mode made learners shift gears when it comes to their awareness of self. There were more peaks and valleys to the negative and positive side of the scale, with a notable positive outlier being expressing interests (S22) as learners engaged in conversations about movies, artists or activities they enjoyed. Half of their conversations included strategies and meta-strategies in which they exhibited awareness of self. These tended to cluster together, meaning that identity construction and socialisation often intertwined, as one followed the other. These observations illustrate how learner identity construction within second language acquisition is often "negotiated through language and social interaction" [29, p. 31]. The online cohort carved out time and space to construct a learner and peer identity in the peer interaction process, possibly as an alternative to the opportunities they lacked to engage in language socialisation [8].

In the hybrid mode, learners engaged in conversations that revolved around their awareness of approaches to learning more often than any other group, which also tended to cluster together more often in their posts compared to learners engaged in the other modes of instruction. The comment section seems dominated by a tendency of learners to ask for acknowledgement/positive reinforcement from others (S19) with fewer instances of socialisation, compared to the other groups. Since they occasionally did meet in person, learners might not have felt the need to engage on that level of self in the online environment. They took to the online space to seek confirmation for their strategies and approaches to learning, which the ENA graph showed was well-connected to many other strategies, highlighting how it found its way into a variety of conversations.

The results show that the three groups of learners had different needs that can be traced back to the mode of instruction they engaged in. As in previous ENA research on self-regulation [30], the approach allowed for a targeted comparison between posts, comments, and learner groups. While the face-to-face cohort used the online platform as a repository for resources and a space to share experiences in their learning trajectory, in addition to their in-person meetings with each other, the online cohort engaged in learner identity construction and socialisation as their primary reason for communication, lacking in-person socialisation and access to in-person facilities. The ENA networks for the hybrid cohort show that they, also, have distinct needs that surface in the interaction process. This group sought confirmation for the strategies they apply, as they created room for strategy exchange and discussion, more so than any other cohort. Comparing the learners in the three modes of instruction, the main differences can be found in the face-to-face cohort's focus on resource management, the online cohort's primary engagement with socialisation, and the hybrid cohort's strategy management.

5.2 Recommendations for Practice and Language Learning Design

Recommendations that stem from the results and discussion above focus on language socialisation and learning design, taking into account language learner needs and the different modes of instruction learners in this study were engaged in. These recommendations touch upon issues like S2R development, community, and learner identity [29].

First, interaction prompts can help students get accustomed with a new environment and set the tone. Having students start off with self-introduction posts and sharing their interests, for example, could lower the threshold for interaction and break the ice.

Second, use the community as a resource. Students throughout this study were eager to admit their difficulties and ask for advice. They occasionally shared resources on their own, but often had to be prompted to do so. It is, therefore, necessary to create space for students to develop agency by facilitating their interactions at first and then gradually take away scaffolded support [3]. Educators can facilitate online discourse by setting a weekly topic and a posting schedule, and allow students to share stories of success or failure, of a useful resource, or one of their interests. In the cases of face-to-face or hybrid instruction, where language socialisation may be done in-person, this may be especially important to make sure students can share or pick up strategies and motivation from the group as a whole.

Third, make sure the platform is conducive to interaction. Some posts went unanswered, which may lead to students being reluctant to post again, though in some cases this led to posting the same topic again later. Google Classroom may be partly to blame, as the platform may not be quite as wieldy to navigate as other platforms. Determine which platform is best suited for the purpose of the online learning component [8].

Finally, educators need to be aware of opportunity, learner investment and identity when setting up peer interaction spaces. Too often, there is a tension between the agency we want students to have, and the structure we provide for them to develop and exercise that agency [31]. We, therefore, want to echo some of Friedman's [29] recommendations, who points out that future research and classroom practice should i) take into account the presumed 'cultural differences' between 'Western' and 'non-Western' academic discourse practices, ii) be aware of the influence of different stakeholders and socialising agents in the wider learning environment on students' language socialisation, and iii) evaluate how students in these settings are being prepared to function in contexts where multilingualism and multicompetence are required.

6 Conclusion

This study investigated the dynamics and co-occurrence of self-regulation strategies and meta-strategies of three groups of English language majors, enrolled in an effective learning module at a private Japanese University that was offered in face-to-face, online and in hybrid mode over the course of three years. In line with the first research question, learners applied a range of S2R strategies and meta-strategies, showcasing an awareness of approaches to learning, an awareness of facilities, roles and resources, and an awareness of self. They planned and organised their learning, monitored progress, exchanged best practices, socialised, and constructed learner identity as they were engaging with each other, part of the effective learning module.

To answer the second research question, the results show that within different modes of instruction, language learners modified their S2R interaction with the peer group. Both frequency of use and the co-occurrence of different strategies and meta-strategies in posts and comments have shown that the face-to-face cohort favoured strategy use, resource management, and creating a respectful and constructive environment for exchange. The online cohort also exhibited this behaviour, but supplemented it with a clear socialisation purpose as they spent more time on introductions and expressing their interests, which clustered together in both posts and comment sections. Missing out on opportunities to meet with their peers in class is considered one of the major factors pushing this cohort towards more online socialising behaviour. The hybrid cohort shifted their focus from socialisation to strategy use, making the online peer interaction space into a sounding board for effective learning, explicitly linking it to requests for confirmation on the strategies they were using in their learning journey.

Disclosure of Interests. The authors have no competing interests to declare that are relevant to the content of this article.

References

1. Benson, P.: Language learning and teaching beyond the classroom: An introduction to the field. In: Benson, P., Reinders, H. (eds.) Beyond the language classroom, pp. 7–16. Palgrave Macmillan, Basingstoke (2011)
2. Oxford, R.: Teaching and researching language learning strategies: Self-regulation in context, 2nd edn. Routledge, London (2017)

3. Peeters, W.: Peer interaction and scaffolded support on social media: Exercising learner autonomy. In: Mynard, J., Tamala, M., Peeters, W. (eds.) Supporting learners and educators in developing language learner autonomy, pp. 118–152. Candlin & Mynard, Hong Kong (2020)
4. van de Pol, J., de Bruin, A.B.H., van Loon, M.H., van Gog, T.: Students' and teachers' monitoring and regulation of students' text comprehension: Effects of comprehension cue availability. Contemp. Educ. Psychol. **56**, 236–249 (2019)
5. Peeters, W., Saqr, M., Viberg, O.: Applying learning analytics to map students' self-regulated learning tactics in an academic writing course. In: So, H.-J., Rodrigo, M.M., Mason, J., Mitrovic, A. (eds.) Proceedings of the 28th International Conference on Computers in Education. vol.1, pp. 245–254. Asia-Pacific Society for Computers in Education (2020)
6. Viberg, O., Wasson, B., Kukulska-Hulme, A.: Mobile-assisted language learning through learning analytics for self-regulated learning (MALLAS): A conceptual framework. Australas. J. Educ. Technol. **36**(6), 34–52 (2020)
7. Montrul, S.: How learning context shapes heritage and second language acquisition. In: Dressman, M., Sadler, R.W. (eds.) The handbook of informal language learning, pp. 57–74. Wiley, Hoboken, NJ (2020)
8. Peeters, W., Pretorius, M.: Facebook or fail-book: Exploring "community" in a virtual community of practice. ReCALL **32**(3), 291–306 (2020)
9. Güryay, B.: The relationship between learning modalities and perceived self-regulation levels. Procedia Soc. Behav. Sci. **232**, 389–395 (2016)
10. Tavares, V.: A review of peer interaction and second language learning for ELL students in academic contexts. Canadian Journal for New Scholars in Education/Revue Canadienne des Jeunes Chercheures et Chercheurs en Éducation **10**(2), 113–121 (2019)
11. Adams, R., Oliver, R.: Learning a language with peers: Elevating classroom V-voices. Routledge, London (2023)
12. Peeters, W., Viberg, O., Spikol, D.: Self-regulation in foreign language students' collaborative discourse for academic writing: An explorative study on ENA. In: Filipe, J., Ghosh, A., Prates, R.O., Zhou, L. (eds.) 4th International Conference, ICQE 2022 Copenhagen, Denmark, October 15–19, 2022, Proceedings, pp. 254–269. Springer, Cham (2022)
13. Mynard, J.: Self-access learning and advising: Promoting language learner autonomy beyond the classroom. In: Reinders, H., Ryan, S., Nakamura, S. (eds.) Innovation in language teaching & learning: The case of Japan, pp. 185–209. Palgrave Macmillan, Camden (2019)
14. Philip, J., Adams, R., Iwashita, N.: Peer interaction and second language learning. Routledge, New York, NY (2014)
15. Wenger-Trayner, E., Wenger-Trayner, B.: Communities of practice: A brief introduction (2015). https://www.wenger-trayner.com/wp-content/uploads/2022/06/15-06-Brief-introduction-to-communities-of-practice.pdf
16. Loewen, S., Wolff, D.: Peer interaction in F2F and CMC contexts. In: Sato, M., Ballinger, S. (eds.) Peer interaction and second language learning: Pedagogical implications and research agenda, pp. 163–184. John Benjamins, Amsterdam (2016)
17. Peeters, W.: The peer interaction process on Facebook: A social network analysis of learners' online conversations. Educ. Inf. Technol. **24**(5), 3177–3204 (2019)
18. Hadwin, A.F., Järvelä, S., Miller, M.: Self-regulation, co-regulation and shared regulation in collaborative learning environments. In: Schunk, D., Greene, J. (eds.) Handbook of self regulation of learning and performance, pp. 83–106. Routledge, London (2018)
19. Saint, J., Fan, Y., Gašević, D., Pardo, A.: Temporally-focused analytics of self-regulated learning: A systematic review of literature. Comp. Edu. Artif. Intel. **3**, 100060 (2022)
20. Kato, S., Mynard, J.: Reflective dialogue: Advising in language learning. Routledge, London (2015)
21. Curry, N., Mynard, J., Noguchi, J., Watkins, S.: Evaluating a self-directed language learning course in a Japanese university. Int. J. Self-Directed Learn. **14**(1), 37–57 (2017)

22. Curry, N., Maher, K., Peeters, W.: Identifying emotions and thoughts related to speaking anxiety: laying the groundwork for designing CBT-based support materials for anxious learners. J. Psychol. Lang. Learn. **2**(1), 57–89 (2020)
23. Peeters, W., Mynard, J.: Supporting self-regulated language learning skills online: Awareness raising approaches for computer-supported collaboration. Lang. Aware. **32**(1), 132–152 (2023)
24. Belur, J., Tompson, L., Thornton, A., Simon, M.: Interrater reliability in systematic review methodology: Exploring variation in coder decision-making. Sociol. Meth. Res. **50**(2), 837–865 (2021)
25. Bowman, D., et al.: The mathematical foundations of epistemic network analysis. In: Ruis, A., Lee, S.B. (eds.) Advances in Quantitative Ethnography: Second International Conference, ICQE 2020, Malibu, CA, USA, February 1–3, 2021, Proceedings, pp. 91–105. Springer, Cham (2021)
26. Shaffer, D.W.: Quantitative ethnography. Cathcart Press, Madison, WI (2017)
27. Marquart, C.L., Hinojosa, C., Swiecki, Z., Eagan, B., Shaffer, D.W.: Epistemic network analysis (Version 1.7.0) [Software] (2021). http://app.epistemicnetwork.org
28. Schieffelin, B.B., Ochs, E.: Language socialization. Annu. Rev. Anthropol. **15**, 163–191 (1986)
29. Friedman, D.A.: Language socialization and academic discourse in English as a foreign language contexts: A research agenda. Lang. Teach. **56**(2), 261–275 (2023)
30. Paquette, L., Grant, T., Zhang, Y., Biswas, G., Baker, R.: Using epistemic networks to analyze self-regulated learning in an open-ended problem-solving environment. In: Ruis, A., Lee, S.B. (eds.) Advances in Quantitative Ethnography: Second International Conference, ICQE 2020, Malibu, CA, USA, February 1–3, 2021, Proceedings 2, pp. 185–201. Springer, Cham (2021)
31. Darvin, R., Norton, B.: Investment and motivation in language learning: What's the difference? Lang. Teach. **56**(1), 29–40 (2023)

Investigating Learner Interest and Observation Patterns in a Minecraft Virtual Astronomy Environment

Xiner Liu[1(✉)], Andres Zambrano[1], Amanda Barany[1], Jaclyn Ocumpaugh[1], Jeff Ginger[2], Matt Gadbury[2], H. Chad Lane[2], and Ryan S. Baker[1]

[1] University of Pennsylvania, Philadelphia, PA 19104, USA
xiner@upenn.edu

[2] University of Illinois, Champaign, IL 61820, USA

Abstract. This study explores how student actions in Minecraft-based virtual environments designed to simulate astronomical phenomena shift over time, as their interest in astronomy changes. We analyze observations made by middle school learners participating in the What-if Hypothetical Implementations in Minecraft (WHIMC) project, which adapts the game to immerse learners in scenarios exploring scientific concepts. Combining manual and automated coding techniques, we classify these observations and use epistemic network analysis to investigate how they relate to changes in interest levels as measured by pre- and post-surveys. Our findings show that learners who maintain or increase their astronomy interest produce more complex observational behaviors, such as hypothesis generation and comparisons. Conversely, learners whose interest declines produce more surface-level, factual observations. Results suggest ways to identify and support long-term interest in science education.

Keywords: WHIMC · Automated Coding · Educational Games · STEM Interest

1 Introduction

Ongoing calls for a more STEM-literate workforce [6], coupled with increasing demand for STEM college graduates in astronomy-related fields [25], have prompted educators to seek innovative ways to engage learners and ignite their interest in science. Despite various initiatives, capturing and sustaining student interest remains a significant challenge. One promising approach lies in leveraging popular games and simulated environments [5, 12] like Minecraft [14] to create immersive learning environments that encourage exploration and critical thinking about complex scientific concepts.

Considerable effort has sought to optimize simulations and games to support learner interest [17, 25]. Recently, educators and researchers have investigated ways to leverage the flexibility and immersive nature of simulations in the popular game Minecraft to present learners with STEM-related questions and encourage their overall engagement with scientific content [23, 36, 39]. This study investigates how changes in student interest (from the beginning to the end of a Minecraft learning activity) relate to changes

Y. J. Kim and Z. Swiecki (Eds.): icqe 2024, CCIS 2279, pp. 19–34, 2024.
https://doi.org/10.1007/978-3-031-76332-8_2

in their behavior, using text-based observational data produced by learners in the What-if Hypothetical Implementations in Minecraft (WHIMC) environment [22]. WHIMC is designed to teach learners about astronomy [23]. Therefore, we investigate the research question of how different patterns of in-game observations (made by learners) correlate with changes in learners' interest in astronomy, as measured by the astronomy subscale of Gadbury & Lane's STEM interest survey [11]. By examining these patterns using Quantitative Ethnographic techniques, we hope to identify key factors that contribute to learners maintaining or increasing interest in STEM.

2 Related Works

This study examines the relationship between student interest and their interactions with the WHIMC system. Considerable research indicates that interest positively influences student perceptions, beliefs, attitudes, and willingness to learn more about that topic [15, 19, 32, 33, 38]. Learners with high interest tend to engage more deeply with material, improving their conceptual understanding [3, 31]. Conversely, learners with low interest are typically less likely to persist with the material [26, 35]. As such, interest is often predictive of future academic choices [18].

Early investigations of interest tended to describe it as an emotion [2, 28], but more recent work notes that interest has a longer duration than most emotions, with Renninger and Hidi [32], noting that a purely affective description does not capture interest's cognitive components [33]. Hidi & Renningers' four-phase model of interest development posits that interest emerges as a product of environmental features in its early phases, referred to as situational interest [16]. As learners' knowledge of a topic increases, individual interest emerges as a self-motivating and enduring state.

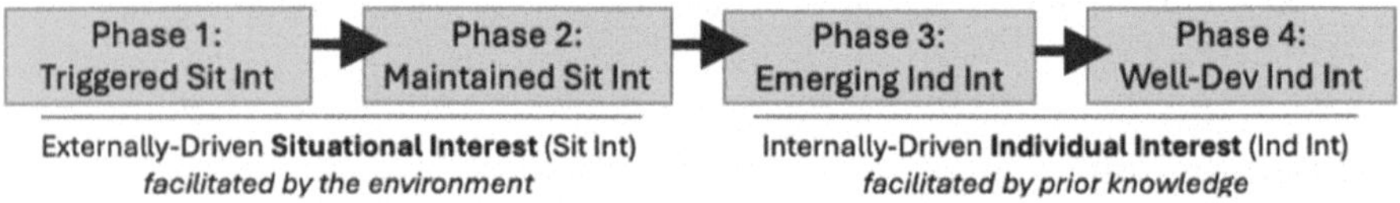

Fig. 1. The Four-Phase Model of Interest [16].

Importantly, research suggests that situational interest is best triggered by novel and attention-getting experiences [13, 30] that lead learners to generate questions [1]. Learners who are in phases 1- 2 are still developing a sense of the value of that content and need support to connect new material to their prior knowledge and skills [29]. As individual interest emerges (phase 3), they become more likely to engage independently, but may see little use in feedback or in the canon of the field; it is not until the interest becomes well-developed that learners effectively manage frustration and actively seek feedback [29].

Eberbach and Crowley emphasize that observational skills develop over time and may require scaffolding [7]. Specific frameworks have been developed to classify and interpret learners' observations in different educational contexts. For example, Yi's framework for coding textual observations made by student includes relevant observations, questions, hypotheses, and texts that might indicate lower engagement with astronomy or the Minecraft platform [42]. Other frameworks consider whether observations made by learners are disengaged [21]. Building on these studies, we expand Yi's system to analyze learners' engagement and learning processes within the WHIMC platform, adding codes relevant to both engagement and off-task behavior [42].

We use Epistemic Network Analysis (ENA) and difference models to compare the connections between different types of observations at the beginning and end of the learning activity. Previous studies have applied ENA specifically in game-based learning environments to analyze player behavior and cognitive skills. For example, Scianna et al. use ENA to visualize player log files and identify variations in how learners responded to game events [37], while Foster et al. explored patterns in learners' identity exploration within play-based environments [9]. Bressler et al. analyzed the conversational discourse of game teams to explore the connections between communication responses, language style, and scientific practice [4].

3 Methods

3.1 Research Context

We conduct this research in the context of WHIMC [23], which exploits the widespread appeal of Minecraft to create scenarios and experiences that stimulate interest in astronomy, Earth science, and other STEM fields related to space exploration. Utilizing Minecraft's Java Edition, WHIMC offers learners simulation environments where they can explore hypothetical astronomy scenarios, addressing *what-if* questions (e.g., *What if Earth had no moon?* or *What if the sun was cooler?*). During informal learning settings (e.g., summer camps), learners are guided by pedagogical agents and human facilitators to make scientific observations that assess each world's potential for human habitation.

In addition to these hypothetical worlds, the WHIMC server features a NASA-inspired launch site, a lunar base, a space station, a Mars map based on real Martian terrain data, several known exoplanets, and phenomena such as black holes and quasars. Learners can access various science tools that support their investigations, enabling them to measure critical habitability factors (i.e., temperature, air pressure, radiation, gravity, and atmospheric composition). Learners are taught to use these measures as evidence by making descriptive, comparative, and inferential observations that underpin testable hypotheses. As part of their game exploration, players record their observations on wooden signs that are displayed to other players and collected with our data.

Previous WHIMC research used association rule mining to examine the ways in which a more limited range of learner behaviors is correlated with learner interest [10], as the open-ended nature of this environment provides many opportunities for supporting student STEM interest development [41]. This study analyzes data collected in 2022 from 76 learners (49 male, 20 female, and 7 who either reported a third option or preferred not to answer) across 5 locations in 3 states. Participants were drawn from populations rural, suburban and urban populations and represented a wide range of racial backgrounds (12 Black/African American, 3 American Indian, 2 Asian/Pacific Islander, 10 Hispanic/Latino, 22 White/Caucasian, 1 multiple categories, 6 other, and 19 who preferred not to answer). Socio-economic backgrounds varied considerably between locations, with nearly half of the learners coming from two of the wealthiest counties in the US and the remainder coming from mixed or lower income areas. Disability status was not consistently captured, but some learners reported receiving accommodations. Data was collected during 12–15-h informal learning camps hosted at planetariums, libraries and community centers. Recruitment was run with community partners as part of their regular programming, with sign-ups occurring online. Participation in the research was entirely optional. Written consent was obtained from all parents, and participants assented on the first day.

3.2 Codebook Development

This study expands on Yi's initial efforts to code the observations learners make while exploring WHIMC (Table 1) [42]. Yi's work classified observations into only 4 codes (Noun, Measure/Descriptive, Comparison, Hypothesis), which were designed to capture observations that closely align with WHIMC's learning goals [42]. We augment this framework using an inductive thematic analysis approach to select themes [40]. This process involved identifying and iteratively refining topics that emerged from an open-ended review and discussion of the data. New codes include several constructs that reflect other forms of game-related interactions that were not fully captured by the coding schemes used in [42] and social communication. Finally, codes reflecting non-game interactions (i.e., random characters, unrelated content, or off-topic conversations) were coded separately (to facilitate accurate automatic coding) but then collapsed because they all appear to reflect off-task conversations. As codes are not mutually exclusive, observations may be labeled more than once.

Two researchers independently coded 200 lines of data for the presence or absence of each construct using these definitions. After each researcher coded approximately 100 lines, interrater reliability (IRR) was checked; those constructs that did not reach sufficient Kappa were discussed before additional data were coded and interrater reliability was re-checked. All discrepancies between the two human coders were resolved using social moderation before evaluating the performance of the automated coding models.

3.3 Automated Coding of Observation Data

To effectively scale the coding of this data for real-time analysis, we automated our codebook using Python scripts and GPT-4 [27]. Table 2 also provides Kappa between the 2 human coders before resolving disagreements, and the performance metrics for each code, including Kappa, Precision, and Recall scores between GPT and human coding. Kappas between GPT and human coders ranged between 0.72 to 0.95, and Shaffer's rho was sufficient for all codes ($p \leq 0.05$) [8].

Coding Using GPT-4. We used gpt-4-turbo-2024-04-09, which was the latest available version, through OpenAI's application programming interface (API). We adhered to default hyperparameter settings throughout our analysis, except for setting the temperature hyperparameter to 0 to ensure the consistency of the output. Because the stochastic nature of GPT models can produce variable outputs even with temperature set to 0, we replicated each input configuration three times during model evaluation.

Table 1. Inductive Themes/Constructs Derived from Observations Made by Learners

Code Name	Definition/Example
Noun	**Def**: Stating nouns without any elaborations. (Previously labeled as "factual" in [42]). **Ex**: "I see trees"
Measure/ Descriptive (Meas)	**Def**: Related to measures of physical attributes that learners are encouraged to take in each of the different planets and moons they visit, including color, temperature, quantity, weight or size, radiation, temperature, airflow, pressure, altitude, etc. [42]. **Ex**: "the temp is −20.6 C, −5.1 F, 252,5 K"
Comparison (Comp)	**Def**: Observations that compare/contrast conditions either (a) among in-game worlds (e.g., 2 planets they've explored) or (b) their real-life experiences on Earth to the in-game worlds. Also inc. Examples that suggest their expectations were violated [42]. **Ex**: "the grass is greener in the habitable strip."
Hypothesis (Hypo)	**Def**: Making hypotheses or guesses, showing speculative thinking, forming conjectures, or making predictions or explanations [42]. **Ex**: "this world is probably closer to the sun"
Questioning (Quest)	**Def**: Asking questions about game mechanics or world elements; Seeking to understand the game better, showing curiosity. **Ex**: "Why is there no grass?"
Exclamations (Exc)	**Def**: Pure exclamations without any accompanying explanation of observations, including exclamatory grammatical markers or words. **Ex**: "Wow!"
Continuing Discussion (ContDisc)	**Def**: The same user's observations are not syntactically exact, but they represent the continuation of discussion around a specific topic. **Ex**: "Can't find [NAME]," "[NAME] where are you?"
Repetition (Rep)	**Def**: A student repeats the exact same observations 3 or more times w/o respect to case sensitivity. **Ex**: "temperature," "temperature," "temperature."
Social Communication (Soc)	**Def**: Interactions with other players through observations: communication or shared exploration. **Ex**: "[NAME] Hello!"
Non-game: True Nonsense	**Def**: A sequence of characters, emojis, or symbols repeated excessively, including random numbers or letters without associated explanations or observations. **Ex**: "AAAAAAAAAAAAAAAAAAAAAAA"

(*continued*)

Table 1. *(continued)*

Code Name	Definition/Example
Non-game: Unrelated Phrases	**Def**: Sentences or phrases unrelated to the purpose of making observations during Minecraft gameplay. **Ex**: "this will expire in a week"
Non-game: Out-of-Context Ref	**Def**: References to movies, books, celebrities, etc., without relevance to the game. **Ex**: "Subscribe to Mr.Beast Gaming"

Table 2. Performance Metrics for Each Automated Model

Construct	Freq	Method	Hum-Hum Kappa	Hum-GPT Kappa	Prec	Recall
Noun	17%	Zero-shot	0.85	0.84	0.88	0.83
Measure/Descriptive (Meas)	36%	Few-shot	0.80	0.78	0.88	0.83
Comparison (Comp)	14%	Few-shot	0.73	0.74	0.73	0.79
Questioning (Quest)	9%	Zero-shot	0.96	0.95	0.9	1.00
Hypotheses (Hypo)	6%	Zero-shot	0.73	0.77	0.81	0.76
Exclamation (Exc)	6%	Zero-shot	0.95	0.86	0.81	0.96
Continuing Discussion (ContDisc)	13%	Embed	0.88	0.93	0.97	0.95
Repetition (Rep)	9%	Python	1.00	1.00	1.00	1.00
Social (Soc)	3%	Python	0.95	0.94	1.00	0.9
NonGam: True Nonsense	4%	Zero-shot	0.97	0.95	0.94	0.97
NonGam: Unrelated Phrases	7%	Few-shot	0.75	0.77	0.82	0.91
NonGam: Out-of-context Reference	3%	Few-shot	0.88	0.86	0.93	0.81

Coding with Zero-Shot Prompting. In the zero-shot prompting approach, we present the GPT-4 model with definitions of each construct without examples and query the model to code across the full 200-line dataset. This approach achieved good IRR for constructs with well-defined definitions that could not be readily associated with keywords.

Coding with Few-Shot Prompting. This method builds on the foundation laid by zero-shot prompting but adds illustrative examples to improve the model. This approach performs better than zero-shot for more nuanced constructs that may require more sophisticated contextual interpretations. To ensure generalizability, we limit training examples to instances that model is not asked to code during the validation process.

Coding with Embedding Models. Embedding is a process that converts words, phrases, or larger texts into numerical vectors that can be compared. We used OpenAI's text embedding model ext-embedding-3-small to code the construct Continuing Discussion, which identifies observations that are not syntactically identical but represent the ongoing discussion of a specific topic. In this method, each observation is first converted into embeddings using OpenAI's text embedding model. Next, we compute the cosine similarity in the spatial domain between the current observation's embedding and the embedding of the previous line. Similarity scores greater than 0.6 (selected based on experimental performance) are coded as '1'; otherwise, it is coded as '0'.

Coding with Python Programs. Two constructs—Social and Repetition—are coded using Python, due to their specific coding criteria. For the Social construct, coding involves identifying keywords such as identity pronouns or other players' username. The Repetition construct requires a systematically defined rule; it is coded when the same student in the same context repeats the same observation more than three times.

3.4 Analysis of Student Interest

This study analyzes existing data on astronomy interest, using a subscale of Gadbury & Lane's STEM interest survey [11]. Gadbury & Lane's [11] subscale contains items that closely reflect the learner characteristics of Hidi & Renninger's [16] stage 3 of interest development—emerging individual interest (as described in [29]). As such, this subscale differentiates those with emerging individual interest from those more likely to need support in developing astronomy interest.

We first validated Gadbury & Lane's STEM survey using a confirmatory factor analysis (CFA) using the data from all 76 learners in the study [11]. Item loadings demonstrated that the items reflect the same latent variable: emerging individual interest in astronomy (pre-survey loadings: 0.57–0.83; post-survey loadings: 0.64–0.84). This survey utilizes a Likert scale (1 = *not at all interested*, 5 = *extremely interested*). We use a 5-item subscale to assess learners' interest in astronomy (e.g., *I search for information about space in my free time*) with questions that are compatible with emerging individual interests [29]. We then classify learners into 4 groups based on their relative interest in the pre and post surveys (above/below median for each).

3.5 Epistemic Network Analysis

Epistemic networks were generated with the ENA Web Tool [24]. Specifically, we use difference models to compare learners who started with a similar level of astronomy interest but who finished the camp with a different interest gain (HiHi vs HiLo, and LoHi vs LoLo). For these difference models, observations made by each learner were coded temporally, with observations split into thirds. Difference models compare learners with different interests during the initial and final third of each student's observations. Doing so offers a detailed view of how initial and final interest levels interact with game elements and how these interactions might influence the development of astronomical interest.

To analyze the observations for each learner in the order they were produced, data was sorted by world (i.e., the order used in camps), username, and timestamp. Data was segmented by both user and world because the last observation a learner makes in one world is unlikely to influence the first observation made in the next. Several moving stanza window sizes were tested before selecting 4. This decision was made by randomly selecting 20 lines from the observation data to determine how far back connections extended (i.e., 3 was the most common number). ENA models were generated from all 10 codes, with smaller line weights (LW ≤ 0.04) excluded for visual clarity.

4 Results

This study groups leaners by pre and post measures of interest to explores how astronomy interest reflects changes in learner observations within the WHIMC learning system. ENA difference models are then used to compare the networks of these different groups between the first third and last third of the observation period, looking for patterns that might signal the need for interventions.

4.1 Descriptive Statistics

This study explores the differences between groups that began with relatively similar levels of interest but diverged in their final level of interest. Therefore, our difference models (Sects. 4.2–4.3) compare the LoLo group to the LoHi group, and the HiHi group to the HiLo group. Table 3 shows the descriptive statistics for the interest surveys for each of the four groups of learners: (a) those who started and ended with astronomy interest that was above the median (HiHi), (b) those who started above but ended below the median (HiLo), (c) those who started below but ended above the median (LoHi), and (d) those who started and ended below the median (LoLo). Table 4 shows frequency statistics for each code across the 4 groups of learners for the initial and final third of their observations. As this shows, Measurement is the most common code across all groups and times (23–49%), but Nongame codes are surprisingly high among the early gameplay of the HiHi group (24%). Comparison codes also emerge relatively often across this data (12–15%).

Other codes vary more between groups or across time. Exc codes are considerably more common in the initial third of the HiHi group's observations (11%) than they are in the final third (5%) or for any other group/time combination (0–6%). Conversely, the Noun codes are relatively infrequent for the initial third of the HiHi group's observations (7%) compared to all other group/time combinations (18–25%), including their own. Moreover, Meas codes increase sharply for the HiLo group from 28% to 49%, which shows a more pronounced shift towards making observations involving quantitative measures for learners in this group towards the later part of the game. Notably, Quest

Table 3. Pre- and Post-Interest Scores and Gains for Each Interest Groups

Interest Group	N	Pre, Med. (Std)	Post, Med. (Std)	Gains, Med. (Std)
High-High (HiHi)	15	4.00 (0.45)	4.20 (0.50)	0.00 (0.43)
High-Low (HiLo)	13	3.40 (0.34)	3.00 (0.35)	−0.40 (0.38)
Low-High (LoHi)	12	3.00 (0.23)	3.40 (0.48)	0.50 (0.44)
Low-Low (LoLo)	12	2.30 (0.48)	2.20 (0.38)	0.00 (0.33)

Table 4. Frequencies of Codes Across Learner Groups

Code	Initial Third of Observation						Final Third of Observation					
	HiHi	HiLo	Diff	LoHi	LoLo	Diff	HiHi	HiLo	Diff	LoHi	LoLo	Diff
Total (N)	168	93	**75**	149	123	**26**	152	100	**62**	128	123	**5**
Quest	4%	1%	**3%**	12%	12%	**0%**	23%	5%	**18%**	12%	11%	**1%**
Hypo	4%	6%	**−2%**	2%	6%	**−4%**	9%	2%	**7%**	4%	6%	**−2%**
Soc	5%	3%	**3%**	2%	16%	**−14%**	0%	0%	**0%**	0%	0%	**0%**
Noun	7%	25%	**−18%**	18%	17%	**1%**	22%	21%	**2%**	17%	14%	**3%**
Rep	7%	0%	**7%**	0%	3%	**−3%**	8%	3%	**5%**	3%	2%	**1%**
ContDisc	9%	6%	**3%**	7%	6%	**1%**	11%	3%	**8%**	11%	3%	**7%**
Exc	11%	0%	**11%**	6%	2%	**5%**	5%	3%	**3%**	6%	1%	**5%**
Comp	12%	19%	**−7%**	12%	13%	**0%**	15%	14%	**2%**	9%	9%	**1%**
Meas	23%	28%	**−5%**	32%	28%	**4%**	32%	49%	**−17%**	42%	39%	**3%**
NonGam	23%	8%	**17%**	10%	7%	**3%**	4%	5%	**−1%**	13%	3%	**10%**

codes rise 4% to 23% for the HiHi group and 1% to 5% in the HiLo group, but remain stable across time for both the LoHi and LoLo groups (11–12%). Social codes are infrequent overall, but the LoHi group decrease sharply (16% initial to 0% final).

4.2 Temporal Changes in the Difference Models for HiHi and HiLo Groups

Figure 1 shows the difference models for learners who started with high astronomy interest, and Table 5 shows the corresponding line weights for these models. Both difference models compare learners who start and end with high interest (HiHi) to those who starts high but ends low (HiLo). Figure 2a (left) shows the observations that were made early in the learners' game play, while Fig. 2b (right) shows the same learners' observations later in the game. For both models, a Mann-Whitney test shows a significant difference between the two groups along the X-axis (initial: $U = 141.00$, $p < 0.01$, effect size of $r = -0.68$ at $\alpha = 0.05$; final: $U = 23.50$, $p < 0.01$, effect size of $r = 0.76$ at $\alpha = 0.05$). That is, the two groups start and end their gameplay with differences in their observation patterns.

In the initial third of observations, both HiHi and HiLo groups start with connections between a wide, evenly-distributed range of observational categories. However, HiLo

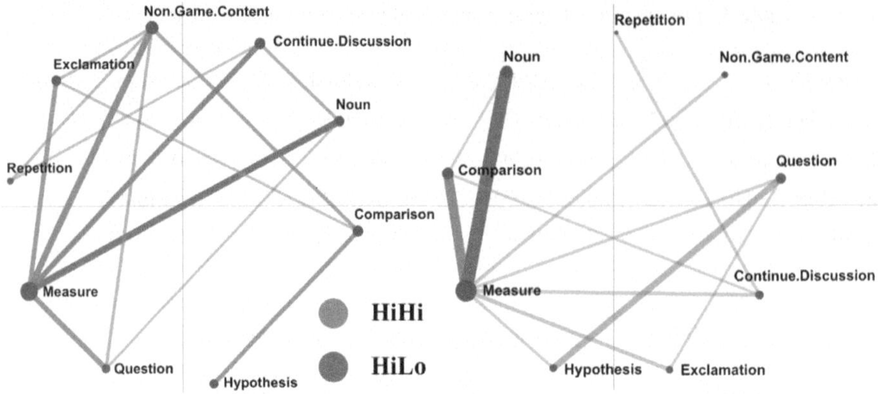

a. Initial third of observations b. Final third of observations

Fig. 2. Difference models for the HiHi group (blue) and the HiLo group (red).

Table 5. Line Weights for Epistemic Visualization in Fig. 1.

	Initial Third of Observation			Final Third of Observation		
Transition	**HiHi**	**HiLo**	**Diff**	**HiHi**	**HiLo**	**Diff**
Meas ↔ Noun	0.14	**0.25**	**-0.11**	0.10	**0.35**	**-0.25**
Meas ↔ ContDisc	0.09	**0.18**	**-0.09**	**0.07**	-	**0.07**
Comp ↔ Hypo	0.01	**0.08**	**-0.07**	**0.03**	-	**0.03**
Noun ↔ ContDisc	0.02	**0.08**	**-0.06**	0.03	0.03	-
Comp ↔ NonGam	0.02	**0.08**	**-0.06**	**0.04**	0.03	**0.01**
Meas ↔ Comp	0.19	**0.23**	**-0.04**	0.2	**0.38**	**-0.18**
Meas ↔ Hypo	0.08	**0.11**	**-0.03**	**0.07**	0.02	**0.05**
Noun ↔ Comp	0.04	**0.08**	**-0.03**	-	**0.05**	**-0.05**
Comp ↔ ContDisc	0.01	**0.04**	**-0.03**	**0.05**	-	**0.05**
Exc ↔ Quest	-	-	-	**0.05**	-	**0.05**
Hypo ↔ Quest	**0.02**	0.01	**0.01**	**0.12**	-	**0.12**
Exc ↔ NonGam	**0.05**	-	**0.05**	**0.02**	-	**0.02**
Comp ↔ Exc	**0.05**	-	**0.05**	**0.02**	-	**0.02**
Rep ↔ NonGam	**0.05**	-	**0.05**	**0.03**	-	**0.03**
Noun ↔ Quest	**0.05**	-	**0.05**	0.05	**0.08**	**-0.03**
Rep ↔ ContDisc	**0.05**	-	**0.05**	**0.10**	0.03	**0.07**
Quest ↔ NonGam	**0.06**	-	**0.06**	**0.03**	-	**0.03**
Meas ↔ Exc	**0.08**	-	**0.08**	**0.08**	-	**0.08**
Meas ↔ Quest	**0.11**	0.02	**0.09**	**0.12**	0.06	**0.06**
Meas ↔ NonGam	**0.17**	0.06	**0.11**	0.03	**0.10**	**-0.07**

learners increasingly produce 2 specific connections (Meas ↔ Comp and Meas ↔ Noun), which rise in the final third of observations. This shift suggests that HiLo learners' engagement pattern becomes more focused and potentially less exploratory.

HiLo learners also show more connections between continuous discussions and other types of content-related observations in the initial third of their observations, as indicated by higher line weights associated with this construct (i.e., Meas $\leftrightarrow$ ContDisc, Noun $\leftrightarrow$ ContDisc, and Comp $\leftrightarrow$ ContDisc). However, these connections decreased in the final third and became more prevalent for the HiHi group. This decline suggests that sustaining these discussions might be an important factor for maintaining a high level of interest among learners started with high astronomy interest.

Interestingly, instead of predominantly making meaningful observations, the HiHi group shows higher levels of excitement (i.e., Meas $\leftrightarrow$ Exc, Exc $\leftrightarrow$ NonGam) and curiosity (i.e., Meas $\leftrightarrow$ Quest, Quest $\leftrightarrow$ NonGam) in their observations about the game throughout the study. They also occasionally go off-task to discuss topics unrelated to the game (i.e., Meas $\leftrightarrow$ NonGam, Quest $\leftrightarrow$ NonGam). These findings highlight that sustained interest in astronomy may be linked to a more enthusiastic and inquisitive approach to observations, rather than just making the most meaningful observations.

4.3 Temporal Changes in the Difference Models for LoHi and LoLo Groups

As the difference models in Fig. 3 show, the observation patterns of players in the LoHi and LoLo groups are noticeably different in both the initial and final thirds of observations. For both models, a Mann-Whitney test shows significant differences along the X-axis (initial third: $U = 24$, $p = 0.01$, effect size of $r = 0.64$ at $\alpha = 0.05$; final third: $U = 109$, $p = 0.03$, effect size of $r = -0.51$ at $\alpha = 0.05$). Like the HiHi and HiLo groups, the LoHi and LoLo groups start and end their gameplay with different patterns of observations.

During the initial third of the observations, the LoLo group shows more connections involving social communication (i.e., Quest $\leftrightarrow$ Soc; Meas $\leftrightarrow$ Soc), which may indicate a tendency to focus more on interactions with others than on the game content itself (though note exception, Comp $\leftrightarrow$ Soc). Conversely, the LoHi group shows more connections involving exclamations (i.e., Exc $\leftrightarrow$ NonGam, Noun $\leftrightarrow$ Exc) than the LoLo group, implying higher initial levels of excitement and perhaps greater interest.

In the initial set of observations, the LoLo group also shows stronger connections between Noun $\leftrightarrow$ Hypo and Hypo $\leftrightarrow$ Quest than the LoHI, but this difference diminishes in the final third of their observations. This early link between questions and hypothesis generation might suggest that situational interest is not being properly supported.

We also observed that, in the final third of observations, the LoLo group shows a markedly less diverse interaction network, characterized by fewer connections and lower interaction intensity compared to the LoHi group. Conversely, the LoHi group demonstrates substantial growth in network density and interaction diversity from the initial to the final third of observations. As illustrated in Table 6, only two connections in the LoLo group are stronger than those in the LoHi group during the final third of observations. The observation data also shows that in the final third of observations made by players in the LoLo group, more than 8% of these observations were non-game-related exclamations (e.g., "TECHNOBLADE NEVER DIES!").

These findings indicate that players in the LoHi group not only increase their frequency of interactions but also diversify the types of interactions they engage in. This diversification may be contributing to the increase in their interest levels. In contrast,

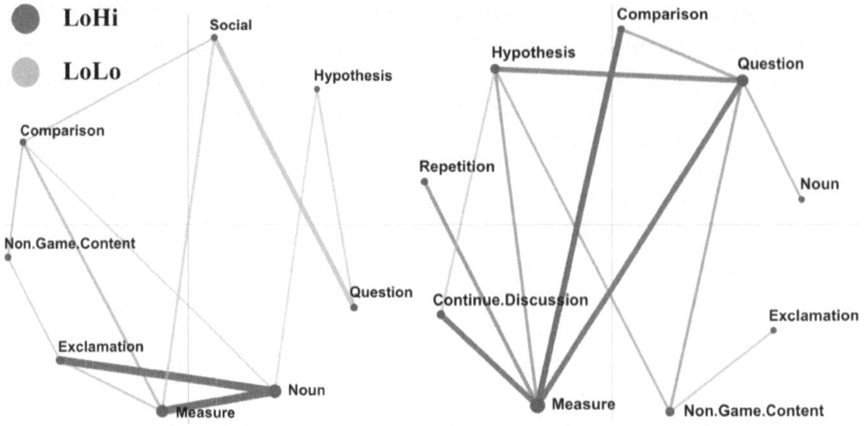

a. Initial third of observations b. Final third of observations

Fig. 3. Difference networks for the LoHi group (purple) and the LoLo group (orange).

Table 6. Line Weights for Epistemic Visualization in Fig. 3.

	Initial Third of Observation			Final Third of Observation		
Transition	**LoHi**	**LoLo**	**Diff**	**LoHi**	**LoLo**	**Diff**
Quest ↔ Soc	-	0.11	**-0.11**	-	-	-
Meas ↔ Soc	0.04	0.10	**-0.06**	-	-	-
Hypo ↔ Quest	-	**0.06**	**-0.06**	**0.08**	-	**0.08**
Noun ↔ Comp	0.04	**0.09**	**-0.05**	0.03	0.03	-
Noun ↔ Hypo	0.02	**0.07**	**-0.05**	-	**0.01**	**0.01**
Meas ↔ Rep	-	**0.04**	**-0.04**	**0.07**	-	**0.07**
Meas ↔ Hypo	0.03	**0.06**	**-0.03**	**0.07**	0.01	**0.06**
Hypo ↔ NonGam	0.01	**0.03**	**-0.02**	**0.05**	-	**0.05**
Noun ↔ Quest	0.08	**0.09**	**-0.01**	**0.07**	0.02	**0.05**
Hypo ↔ ContDisc	-	**0.01**	**-0.01**	**0.04**	-	**0.04**
Quest ↔ NonGam	0.07	0.07	**0**	**0.05**	-	**0.05**
Meas ↔ ContDisc	**0.15**	0.14	**0.01**	**0.13**	0.04	**0.09**
Comp ↔ Quest	**0.02**	0.01	**0.01**	**0.06**	-	**0.06**
Meas ↔ Quest	**0.07**	0.05	**0.02**	**0.18**	0.09	**0.09**
Comp ↔ Soc	**0.04**	-	**0.04**	-	-	-
Exc ↔ NonGam	**0.05**	-	**0.05**	-	**0.05**	**-0.05**
Comp ↔ NonGam	**0.05**	-	**0.05**	-	-	-
Meas ↔ Comp	**0.2**	0.13	**0.07**	**0.23**	0.13	**0.1**
Meas ↔ Noun	**0.31**	0.14	**0.17**	**0.35**	0.33	**0.02**
Noun ↔ Exc	**0.17**	-	**0.17**	0.03	-	**0.03**

the LoLo group shows minimal change in observation patterns, and may benefit from interventions that encourage more diverse and interactive observations.

5 Discussion and Conclusion

This study used ENA difference models to explore how learners with varying levels of interest interact with an online learning system early and late in their usage of a Minecraft learning activity. The goal was to identify how qualitative characteristics related to students' text-based observations--may be used to identify learners who are in need of additional support. By identifying the initial observation patterns of learners with low interest, we hope to provide actionable insights for educators and facilitators to design targeted interventions and effective education programs.

Interest was measured using a scale that approximated stage three in Hidi & Reninger's four-stage model. To analyze the observational data, a group of researchers reviewed the data to distill themes inductively, and we then used automated methods with GPT-4 and Python to qualitatively code the large amount of data. To study how these patterns evolved, we divided the data into temporal thirds and compared the initial and final thirds.

ENA results reveal distinct patterns of observation connections among different interest groups. More specifically, learners who maintained or increased their interest (HiHi and LoHi) tended to make a wider range of types of observations and more frequently posed questions, formed hypotheses, and expressed excitement. These learners showed higher levels of exploratory behavior and curiosity-driven interactions. These findings suggest that fostering an environment that encourages curiosity and diverse observations might help in maintaining or even increasing interest among players.

Conversely, learners whose interest declined or stayed low (the HiLo and LoLo groups) showed a narrower range of observations in their later activity, increasingly transitioning between specific observations that involve measurement and comparisons (i.e., Meas ↔ Comp, Meas ↔ Noun). This shift may indicate that they are still working to obtain the basic knowledge required to move into more advanced stages of interest, and may require additional scaffolding to facilitate this process. Alternatively, perhaps they were compliant but not genuinely interested, and needed activities better tailored to their interests to capture their attention. Interestingly, the HiHi group showed not only meaningful observations but also moments of excitement (i.e., Meas ↔ Exc) and curiosity (i.e., Meas ↔ Quest), with occasional off-task behavior throughout the game. These trends were also observed in the LoHi group. Future research should investigate the specific triggers of these learners' exclamations to better understand what captured their interest. Since this excitement seems to reflect a more developed individual interest, it may indicate that learners are connecting to prior knowledge. Future research should consider the degree to which these explanations are doing so, and should explore the extent to which helping learners with less-developed knowledge and interest might increase the apparent excitement of those learners who start with lower survey scores.

Meanwhile, these findings also suggest that sustained interest in astronomy might be linked to balancing structured scientific observations with spontaneous or off-task moments (e.g., Meas ↔ NonGam, Exc ↔ NonGam). It is possible that learners may be regulating their emotions using off-task behavior (e.g., [34]) or that these non-game observations are showing some sort of social function [20]. Future research could interview learners who are showing these observation patterns; fostering their enthusiasm and curiosity could play a significant role in maintaining or improving interest.

That said, observations that appear to be more social in nature do not always correspond with higher interest. For example, the LoLo group had more social interactions during the initial third of their observations (16% vs. 3–5%). This suggests that for learners with consistently low interest, social interactions may be more distraction than a support. However, it is possible that the learners regulate this tendency, as these occurrences disappear uniformly in the final third of the observations. Facilitators might consider interventions that refocus these learners on individual exploration or otherwise encourage them to record and analyze their own observations and insights, but be alert to ensure that eliminating these experiences does not reduce situational interest.

Some limitations impact what conclusions can be drawn from this study. With fewer than 15 participants per group, the generalizability of our findings is limited. The small sample size also limits our ability to account for demographic differences (and the cultural factors that may align with them), which can sometimes be associated with limited opportunities for learners to interact with these concepts. Because these opportunity gaps may affect the knowledge development that is critical to the transition between situational interest and maintained individual interest [16], future research should examine the degree to which these results may replicate in other populations.

Another limitation is the use of measurements related to individual interest—a more advanced level of interest found among learners who have preexisting domain knowledge. Augmenting this analysis with surveys of situational interest would highlight how learner observations change as they acquire such knowledge, which would likely help us to better understand our LoLo and LoHi.

This study uses ENA provides insights into the ways different interaction patterns within a digital learning environment like WHIMC may relate to shifts in learner interest. We identified key patterns that can guide targeted interventions, though future research is still needed to improve our understanding of some of these patterns. Overall, these findings identify indicators that could help us to develop strategies for interventions that can support the development and maintenance of student interest in STEM.

References

1. Ainley, M., Ainley, J.: Early science learning experiences: Triggered and maintained interest. In: Renninger, K.A., Nieswandt, M., Hidi, S. (eds.) Interest in Mathematics and Science Learning, pp. 17–31. American Educational Research Association (2015)
2. Ainley, M.: Being and feeling interested. Emotion in Ed., pp. 147–163. Elsevier (2007)
3. Andre, T., Windschitl, M.: Interest, epistemological belief, and intentional conceptual change. In: Sinatra, G., Pintrich, P. (eds.) Intentional Conceptual Change, pp. 179–203. Routledge (2003)
4. Bressler, D., Bodzin, A., Eagan, B., Tabatabai, S.: Using epistemic network analysis to examine discourse and scientific practice during a collaborative game. J. Sci. Ed. & Tech. **28**, 553–566 (2019)
5. Crider, A.: Astronomy education in virtual worlds and virtual reality. In: Astronomy Education, V2: Best Practices for Online Learning Environments. IOP Pub. Ltd. (2020)
6. Deitz, S., Freyman, C.: The state of U.S. science & engineering 2024. Nat. Sci. Foundation, Nat. Sci. Board, Nat. Center for Sci. & Eng. Statistics, Alexandria, VA (2024)
7. Eberbach, C., Crowley, K.: From everyday to scientific observation: how children learn to observe the biologist's world. Rev. Educ. Res. **79**(1), 39–68 (2009)

8. Eagan, B., Brohinsky, J., Wang, J., Shaffer, D.: Testing the reliability of inter-rater reliability. In: Proc. 10th Int. Conf. on Learning Analytics & Knowledge, pp. 454–461 (2020)
9. Foster, A., Shah, M., Barany, A., Talafian, H.: Tracing identity exploration trajectories with quantitative ethnographic techniques: a case study. In: Inter. Conf. Quant. Ethnography, pp. 77–88 (2019)
10. Gadbury, M., Lane, H.: Mining for STEM interest behaviors in Minecraft. In: 23rd Artificial Intell. in Ed. Conf., Durham, UK, vol. 13356, pp. 236–239. Springer Int. Pub. (2022)
11. Gadbury, M., Lane, H.: A bayesian analysis of adolescent STEM interest using Minecraft. In: Int. Conf. on Art. Intell. in Ed., pp. 384–389 (2023)
12. Gee, J.: What video games have to teach us about learning and literacy. Computational Entertain. **1**(1), 20 (2003)
13. Harackiewicz, J., Smith, J., Priniski, S.: Interest matters: the importance of promoting interest in education. Policy Insights fr. the Behav. & Brain Sciences **3**(2), 220–227 (2016)
14. Hewett, K., Zeng, G., Pletcher, B.: The acquisition of 21st-century skills through video games: Minecraft design process models and their web of class roles. Simul. Gaming **51**(3), 336–364 (2020)
15. Hidi, S., Harackiewicz, J.M.: Motivating the academically unmotivated: a critical issue for the 21st century. Rev. Edu. Res. **70**(2), 151–179 (2000)
16. Hidi, S., Renninger, K.A.: The four-phase model of interest development. Educational Psychologist **41**(2), 111–127 (2006)
17. Ishak, S., Din, R., Hasran, U.: Beyond play: Conceptualising the capability of a good digital game to stimulate interest in STEM. Int. J. of Learning, Teaching & Ed. Res. **20**(10) (2021)
18. Knogler, M., Harackiewicz, J., Gegenfurtner, A., Lewalter, D.: How situational is situational interest? Investigating the longitudinal structure of situational interest. Contemp. Educ. Psychol. **43**, 39–50 (2015)
19. Krapp, A.: Interest, motivation and learning: An educational-psychological perspective. Eur. J. Psychol. Educ. **14**(1), 23–40 (1999)
20. Kreijns, K.: Sociable CSCL environments: Social affordances, sociability, and social presence. Unpublished MA Thesis, Open U., Heerlen, The Netherlands (2004)
21. Langer-Osuna, J.M., Gargroetzi, E., Munson, J., Chavez, R.: Exploring the role of off-task activity on students' collaborative dynamics. J. of Ed. Psych. **112**(3), 514 (2020)
22. Lane, H.C., et al.: Triggering STEM interest with Minecraft in a hybrid summer camp. Technology, Mind, & Behavior **3**(4) (2022)
23. Lane, H.C., Yi, S., Guerrero, B., Comins, N.F.: Minecraft as a sandbox for STEM interest development: Preliminary results. In: Proc. 25th Int. Conf. on Computers in Ed. (2017)
24. Marquart, C.L., Hinojosa, C., Swiecki, Z., Eagan, B., Shaffer, D.W.: Epistemic network analysis (Ver. 1.7.0) [Software] (2021). http://app.epistemicnetwork.org
25. National Science & Tech. Council, Office of Science & Tech. Policy: Interagency roadmap to support space-related STEM education & workforce (2022)
26. Nieswandt, M.: Student affect and conceptual understanding in learning chemistry. J. Res. Science Teaching **44**(7), 908–937 (2007)
27. OpenAI.: GPT-4-turbo (Version GPT-4-turbo-2024-04-09) [Large language model]. OpenAI (2024). https://www.openai.com
28. Reeve, J., Jang, H., Hardre, P., Omura, M.: Providing a rationale in an autonomy-supportive way as a strategy to motivate others during an uninteresting activity. Motiv. Emot. **26**, 183–207 (2002)
29. Renninger, K.A.: Interest and identity development in instruction: An inductive model. Educational Psychologist **44**(2), 105–118 (2009)
30. Renninger, K., Bachrach, J.: Studying triggers for interest and engagement using observational methods. Educational Psychologist **50**(1), 58–69 (2015)

31. Renninger, K., Hidi, S., Krapp, A.: The role of interest in learning & development. Routledge. https://doi.org/10.4324/9781315807430 (1992)
32. Renninger, K., Hidi, S.: The power of interest for motivation and engagement. Routledge (2015). https://doi.org/10.4324/9781315771045
33. Renninger, K., Nieswandt, M., Hidi, S.: Interest in mathematics and science learning. American Educational Research Association (2015)
34. Sabourin, J., Rowe, J., Mott, B., Lester, J.: When off-task is on-task: The affective role of off-task behavior in narrative-centered learning environments. In: 15th Int. Conf. Art. Intell. in Ed., Auckland, NZ, vol. 15, pp. 534–536 (2011)
35. Sansone, C., Fraughton, T., Zachary, J., Butner, J., Heiner, C.: Self-regulation of motivation when learning online: The importance of who, why and how. Ed. Tech. Res. & Dev. **59**, 199–212 (2011)
36. Saricam, U., Yildirim, M.: The effects of digital game-based STEM activities on students' interests in STEM fields and scientific creativity: Minecraft case. Int. J. Technol. Edu. Sci. **5**(2), 166–192 (2021)
37. Scianna, J., Gagnon, D., Knowles, B.: Counting the game: Visualizing changes in play by incorporating game events. In: Inter. Conf. Quant. Ethnography, pp 218–231 (2021)
38. Silvia, P.J.: Exploring the psychology of interest. Oxford University Press (2006)
39. Tablatin, C.L.S., Casano, J.D., Rodrigo, M.M.T.: Using Minecraft to cultivate student interest in STEM. In: Frontiers in Education, vol. 8, p. 1127984. Frontiers Media SA (2023)
40. Thornberg, R., Charmaz, K.: Grounded theory and theoretical coding. The SAGE Handbook of Qualitative Data Analysis **5**, 153–169 (2014)
41. Yi, S., Gadbury, M., Lane, H.: Identifying and coding STEM interest triggers in a summer camp. In: Proc. 15th Int. Conf. Learning Sciences, pp. 915–916 (2021)
42. Yi, S., Gadbury, M., Lane, H.: Coding and analyzing scientific observations from middle school students in Minecraft. In: 14th Int. Conf. Learning Sciences (2020)
43. Zambrano, A., et al.: Cracking the code of learning gains: Using ordered network analysis to understand the influence of prior knowledge. In: Inter. Conf. Quant. Ethnography, pp. 18–33 (2023)

Quantitative Ethnography Reveals Behavioral Elements Associated with Problem-Solving in Wild Chimpanzee Tool-Use

Tyler C. Andres-Bray[1,2(✉)] and Mary Katherine Gonder[2,3]

[1] Department of Biological Sciences, Drexel University, Philadelphia, PA 19104, USA
tca38@drexel.edu

[2] Cameroon Biodiversity Protection Program, Yaoundé, CM, Cameroon

[3] Department of Ecology and Conservation Biology, Texas A&M University, College Station, TX 77843, USA

Abstract. This work uses quantitative ethnography to explore problem-solving in wild chimpanzees in a real-world context. Chimpanzees are the closest living relatives to humans and are known for their behavioral diversity. Tool use is a behavior exhibited by chimpanzees where an environmental material is modified to access embedded resources like social insects or nuts. Given that this is a cognitively complex skill involving elements of choice (e.g., material selection) and flexible combination of many individual behavioral elements, it serves as a visible expression of the problem-solving process. In this study, we use Ordered Network Analysis (ONA) to compare patterns of elements between successful and unsuccessful bouts of a particular type of chimpanzee tool use called termite fishing in a community of Nigeria-Cameroon chimpanzees (*Pan troglodytes ellioti*) in central Cameroon. We coded 382 videos of chimpanzees from between 2019 and 2022, representing over 5 h of observation time of 17 individual chimpanzees. Networks revealed significant differences in the combinations of termite fishing behavioral elements between periods of successful and unsuccessful termite fishing, pointing to certain behavioral elements that appear to be responses to lack of success. Further, non-parametric Wilcoxon signed-rank tests suggest that incorporation of certain elements does not significantly increase overall chances of termite fishing success, which implies chimpanzees are responding to specific situations by choosing to incorporate elements that may improve success in a particular context. The findings provide insight into the problem-solving process in chimpanzees and highlight the value of using quantitative ethnography in studies of non-human animal cognition.

Keywords: Nigeria-Cameroon Chimpanzee · Termite Fishing · Cognition · Problem Solving · Ordered Network Analysis

Y. J. Kim and Z. Swiecki (Eds.): icqe 2024, CCIS 2279, pp. 35–49, 2024.
https://doi.org/10.1007/978-3-031-76332-8_3

1 Introduction

1.1 Chimpanzee Tool Use and Problem Solving

Tool use is a cognitively complex behavior that often allows chimpanzees to access high-value embedded resources [1–4]. Tool use is broadly defined as the modification/manipulation of an object to attain a specific goal [5]. Chimpanzees use tools to acquire a number of potentially valuable diet items, such as social insects (e.g., termites and ants), nuts, and honey [6]. For example, research has shown that chimpanzees can achieve their daily vitamin B12 requirements from termites alone [6]. Further, social insects are high in iron and manganese, and may have more biologically relevant proteins for chimpanzees compared to plants [7, 8]. These tool-using behaviors are highly flexible and comprised of distinct behavioral elements that are combined into meaningful, task-oriented combinations that may vary based on individuals and context [1, 3, 9].

Termite fishing is a widespread and well-documented chimpanzee tool use behavior [1, 4]. It involves inserting a modified plant probe into termite nests and extracting termite soldiers by exploiting their defensive biting behaviors [3, 5]. The ways that chimpanzees fish for termites varies considerably within and between communities in terms of the type and combinations of behavioral elements [1, 3]. This variation is shaped in part by local ecological variation, which implies that some community-specific termite fishing elements may arise as innovative responses to environmental factors [10–12]. In this context, variation in termite fishing tool use can serve as a unique way to explore the act of problem-solving in a natural, wild setting.

Tool use is an excellent candidate for exploring problem-solving in wild chimpanzees. In this case, a problem is defined as some aspect of a situation that prevents the achievement of a goal [13]. Food is a core need for all animals, and tool use allows certain animals to acquire otherwise inaccessible food items [13]. Unlike artificial captive experiments, the goal of tool-use behaviors is clear to both the experimenter and the chimpanzees, thus by watching wild tool use it can be assumed that the chimpanzee is currently motivated to achieve this goal [14]. Previous research on chimpanzee tool use has found evidence of planning, a particular type of problem-solving that implies consideration of a future problem and taking an appropriate course of action to address it in the present [14]. Chimpanzees have been known to bring materials from over one mile to a site for use, suggesting both that they are selective about tool materials and that they are planning to use these tools to achieve a particular goal [14, 15]. As chimpanzees are our closest relatives, understanding their cognitive abilities can inform us about our own evolution. Tool use is often innovative, and greater innovative ability has been associated with larger brain size and greater cognitive ability [16]. Further, tool use behaviors vary culturally between communities, and culture has been hypothesized to be linked to increased encephalization in early hominins in order to contain a community's entire cultural repertoire [17].

1.2 Ordered Network Analysis

Ordered Network Analysis (ONA) is an extension of Epistemic Network Analysis (ENA) that provides additional interpretable information about patterns of cognitive/behavioral elements [18]. Based on the concept of epistemic frames, ENA and ONA are quantitative ethnographic methods that statistically and visually compare patterns of large-scale coded data, with a particular focus on the associations between elements [19]. Cognitive/behavioral elements are represented as present or absent in rows of coded data and are associated based on their occurrence in recent temporal context [19, 20]. ENA and ONA use these associations to plot rotated, weighted network models along orthogonal dimensions that maximize the explained variance of the data [21]. Networks are generated based on assigned unit variables representing metadata relevant to the questions being explored, and these can be compared based on shape, the strength of their associations, or the position of their unit means in 2-dimensional space [19]. While ENA indicates the strength of associations between pairs of elements via line thickness, ONA goes a step further and provides the direction of association. Line thickness at each node represents how often that element comes sequentially after the other, with an arrow showing the more common direction of use [18].

Both ENA and ONA have been predominantly used in the learning sciences, however they have recently begun expanding into other fields, including health science [21, 22] and animal behavior [9] The way that these methods represent sequential connections in behaviors fits well with the elemental framework to explore chimpanzee tool use [9, 23]. Further, ENA has been used in the past to explore problem solving in humans [24], but it has not been used to explore non-human animal problem solving.

1.3 Research Question

In this study, we use ONA to ask: How do chimpanzees flexibly adjust their behavior in response to unsuccessful termite fishing? Based on previous research on chimpanzees planning [14], we expect that ONA will be able to identify patterns of behavior that represent chimpanzee's attempts to improve likelihood of obtaining termites.

2 Methods

2.1 Study Site

This study was conducted at Ganga Research Station, located in the north-eastern portion of Mbam & Djerem National Park (MDNP) in central Cameroon. MDNP is a 4,165 km^2 protected area established in 2000 that serves as an important conservation site for *P. t. ellioti* [25, 26]. MDNP is in the transition zone where three major biomes (the Guinean and Congolian rainforests, and the Sudania Sahel) intersect, creating a complex mosaic of forest and savanna that has impacted chimpanzee behavior [25, 26]. Ganga Research Station has been conducting chimpanzee biomonitoring in MDNP since 2016 and is the only currently active field study of *P. t. ellioti*.

2.2 Video Collection and Coding

We used motion-activated camera traps placed at eight termite mounds located along 10 2-km long parallel transects near Ganga Research Station to collect videos of chimpanzees participating in termite fishing. Cameras were secured 2–3 m off the ground on trees 5–10 m from the mound using rigger belts and were angled to capture the entire mound. One camera was active during May 2019 for a pilot study, and all eight cameras were continuously monitoring these termite mounds from February 2020 to May 2022. Termite fishing in this chimpanzee community is a highly seasonal behavior, occurring predominantly between April and June, which means this period captures videos from 4 separate termite fishing seasons [12]. Altogether, these cameras captured 15,305 videos of 42 unique species, including 900 videos total of chimpanzees at these termite mounds. Videos that were shorter than 5 s long, low-quality, or where chimpanzee behaviors were not observable were excluded, leaving a remaining 382 high-quality videos of chimpanzee termite fishing that amounts to 5 h 45 m 54 s of observation time. These videos include 17 unique chimpanzee tool users (Adult: $n = 11$, Juvenile: $n = 3$, Infant: $n = 3$) (male: $n = 4$, female: $n = 8$, unknown: $n = 5$).

Videos were coded for behavioral elements, defined in this study as the individual actions that when combined in sequence comprise termite fishing behavior, using a comprehensive ethogram of 71 chimpanzee behavioral elements [1, 27]. Each row of data represents a single behavioral element per chimpanzee per video and includes information on the start time of the behavior within the video (to the nearest quarter second), body position, hand used, and success. These behavioral elements were considered mutually exclusive, so the start time of one behavioral element also represents the end time of the preceding element, leading to a temporal sequence of behavioral elements that captures the flexible technical combinations used by chimpanzees to fish for termites. Chimpanzee subjects overall used between 20 and 60 behavioral elements per minute, with adults more often using more elements in a shorter time frame [9]. Finally, success was determined broadly at the video level by the presence of a behavioral element named "Eat from Tool", which denotes the chimpanzee consuming a termite from the tool itself. Thus, an entire video was labeled as "Successful" if there was at least one occurrence of the "Eat from Tool" element, and if that element did not occur in a video, the entire video was labeled "Unsuccessful". While this broad determination of success may miss the more immediate, fine-scale responses of chimpanzees to an unsuccessful termite fishing bout, the larger time frame may provide greater insight into the planning/problem-solving process. As the videos are on average 1-min long, an entire video where there is not successful termite fishing implies a comparably larger problem to solve compared to one or two unsuccessful bouts within an otherwise successful period of termite fishing. A greater barrier to termite fishing that requires longer time to address can thus provide more information about the flexible ways in which chimpanzees attempt to improve termite fishing success.

All videos were coded by T. Andres-Bray and a team of six undergraduate research assistants from Texas A&M University and Drexel University. T. Andres-Bray is experienced in chimpanzee behavioral coding, and prior to coding videos for data collection, the six undergraduate research assistants underwent a period of training via co-coding practice with T. Andres-Bray, followed by interrater reliability tests on 20 independently coded practice videos. We used Cohen's k to assess interrater reliability, and each undergraduate research assistant achieved $k \geq 0.6$, which is considered good agreement in animal behavior research, prior to coding independently [28].

2.3 Ordered Network Analysis

We used Ordered Network Analysis (ONA) in the ENA Web Tool (version 1.7.0) to generate a model visualizing combinations of behavioral elements between videos with successful and unsuccessful termite fishing [18, 29]. Units were defined in this model as all lines of data associated with successful vs. unsuccessful termite fishing subset by chimpanzee age class, subject ID, and sequence number. Of note, sequence number refers to a unique number code given to a period of termite fishing at a single mound in a single day. For example, Sequence 1 denotes 109 separate 1-min videos that were taken at Mound I on 5/18/2019, of which each individual video could be denoted either "Successful" or "Unsuccessful".

We used a moving stanza window set to 4 to construct network model. This means that for each line in the data, the moving stanza window connected the behavioral element coded in that line to the 3 previous lines within a conversation. This is in line with previous work that indicates that termite fishing comprises 3–6 behavioral elements on average [3]. We defined the conversation for this model as all lines of data for a given subject in a given video, which limits the window to only drawing associations by behavioral elements that were observed to occur in sequence. The resulting networks are aggregated networks using a binary summation for all units of analysis.

We performed ONA using the 13 behavioral elements most commonly observed during termite fishing (Table 1). Two behavioral elements are Tool Making elements, reflecting actions taken to alter the shape or structure of tool. Four behavioral elements are Tool Use elements, denoting actions taken during termite fishing when the probe is inserted into the termite mound. Two behavioral elements are Non-Tool Use elements, which includes one action ("Scratch Ground") which may serve a preparatory function for termite fishing, and a second action ("Pick") which is a non-tool use method for acquiring termites and thus may be used as an alternative means for eating termites. Finally, the remaining five behavioral elements are tool-directed behaviors that are not involved in termite fishing, such as dropping or retrieving a tool from the ground or moving to a new location with the tool.

The ONA model normalizes each network across all units of analysis prior to dimensional reduction, which allows for comparison between units that may have different amounts of coded data [21]. Singular value decomposition was used to reduce the dimensions in the data to two orthogonal dimensions, and because we are comparing only two networks ("Successful" and "Unsuccessful"), we used a means rotation to maximize the variance along the first dimension [21]. The resulting network graphs include nodes (behavioral elements) and edges (connections). The edges in this context represent the relative frequency of co-occurrence between two behavioral elements using the moving stanza window [19]. In ONA, the primary direction of the association in sequence is also shown using an arrow inside the edge [18]. The positions of the network graph nodes are determined based on minimizing the difference between the plotted points and their corresponding network centroids in the models. The co-registration correlations for our model were 0.96 (Pearson) and 0.96 (Spearman) for the first dimension, indicating that there is a strong goodness of fit between the visualization and the original model. These networks were then shown as a unit circle, which removes the ability to interpret the positions of the nodes and the unit means in space but makes comparing the connections represented by the edges easier.

Table 1. Ethogram listing the type, names, and descriptions of termite fishing behavioral elements assessed using ONA in this study.

Behavior Type	Behavior	Description
Tool Making	Fray Bite	Bite tool on the to-be-inserted extremity before inserting
	Reshape	Pulls tool through hands to straighten fibers for insertion
Tool Use	Probe 1 h	Use only one hand to insert the stick fishing for termites
	Oscillate	Subject moves tool repeatedly in-and-out before extraction
	Wrist Help	Place wrist of free hand under tool when extracted
	Extract 1 h	Use only one hand to pull the stick out of the mound
Non-Tool Use	Pick	Subject removes termites from ground with hand
	Scratch Ground	Uses fingernail to scratch at the ground/termite mound
Other	Drop Tool	Subject releases tool on the ground and does not retrieve
	Retrieve Tool	Chimpanzee picks up existing tool from the ground
	Smell Tool	Brings tool to nose to smell the to-be-inserted extremity
	Switch Tool	Subject switches tool between hands or mouth
	Transport Tool	Subject travels along the ground with tool

2.4 Functional Groups of Behavioral Elements

Behavioral elements used in functional combination with probing and extracting the tool from the termite mound were divided into four categories: 1) Maintenance ("Fray Bite" and "Reshape"), which involves elements associated with altering tool form, 2) Shake ("Oscillate"), which involves shaking an inserted tool, 3) Preparation ("Scratch Ground"), which involves preparing the surface of the mound for probing, and 4) Assist ("Wrist Help"), which involves the using the opposite arm to remove the tool and bring it to the mouth. We used Python to programmatically quantify all combinations of these elements with "Probe 1 h" and "Extract 1 h" that did (successful) and did not (unsuccessful) conclude with "Eat from Tool". We then used pairwise Wilcoxon signed-rank tests to determine if the inclusion of behavioral elements from any of these four functional groups influenced rates of tool use success [30].

This analysis was done to provide context for the ONA results by exploring whether the use of certain types of behavioral elements led to consistently higher success rates. If any of these categories does not lead to overall greater success in termite fishing, this could suggest that the use of the behavioral elements within that category are contextually relevant to specific ecological/situational contexts.

3 Results

3.1 Ordered Network Comparisons

Figure 1 shows the positions of all units in the ONA model. Each circle represents a single chimpanzee in a single sequence, color coded by network, and the squares represent the unit means for the "Successful" (green) and "Unsuccessful" networks (red). Each unit mean is bounded by a box which represents a confidence interval for the location of the unit mean in the x- and y-directions.

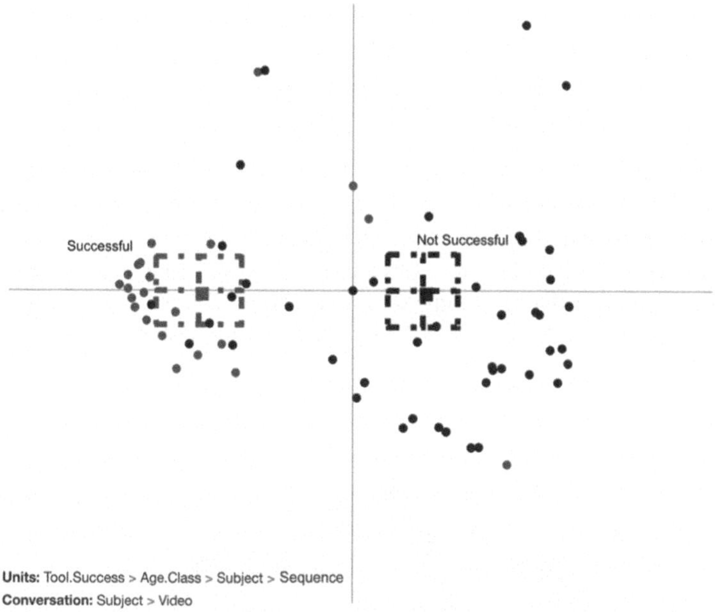

Fig. 1. Epistemic network of chimpanzee subjects across all videos. Circles represent individual chimpanzees in individual sequence. Squares represent unit means for periods of successful (green) and unsuccessful (red) periods of termite fishing, with 95% confidence intervals around the means in both the x- and y-dimensions. Because there are only two groups, this model uses means rotations to maximize variation along the x-dimension.

As this model was made using a means rotation, only the x-direction is pertinent, and Fig. 1 shows that unit means are significantly separated along this dimension ($t(49.69) = -8.31$, $p = 0.00$***, effect size: $d = 1.96$). This indicates that there are significant differences in the ways that the 13 behavioral elements included in the model are being combined between periods of successful and unsuccessful termite fishing. Of note here, the individual plotted points in the "Successful" network are much more clustered in space compared to those in the "Unsuccessful" network (Fig. 1). This suggests that there is low variation in the ways Ganga chimpanzees successfully fish for termites, but that there is greater variation in the ways they seek to address periods of unsuccessful termite fishing. This may represent either inter-individual variation in responses as they attempt to solve the problem that is preventing successful fishing, or potentially variation in the types of problems that may impede termite fishing.

Figures 2, 3 and 4 show the network models for "Successful" and "Unsuccessful" termite fishing in a unit circle. Figures 2 and 3 show the individual networks for both units, while Fig. 4 is a comparison model, where the strength of the connections in the "Unsuccessful" network have been subtracted from the "Successful" network. This means that any connection that is green is stronger in the "Successful" network while any connection that is red is stronger in the "Unsuccessful" network. All 13 behavioral elements included in this model appear in both "Successful" and "Unsuccessful" termite fishing contexts, with the exception of the "Smell Tool" element, which was only present in the "Unsuccessful" network (Figs. 2 and 3). This behavioral element involves a chimpanzee smelling the distal end of the tool and may be an attempt to detect whether termites were present in the mound opening currently being fished. In addition to "Smell Tool", there were three other behavioral elements whose connections were all stronger in the "Unsuccessful" network compared to the "Successful" network: "Fray Bite", "Scratch Ground", and "Transport Tool" (Fig. 4). This suggests three non-exclusive possible responses by the chimpanzees to periods of unsuccessful termite fishing. First, chimpanzees may seek to improve the efficacy of the tool through maintenance behaviors like. Second, chimpanzees may seek to uncover or create novel mound openings to fish. Third, chimpanzees may carry the tool to a different part of the mound to seek new areas to fish. Both the second and third responses may be a reaction

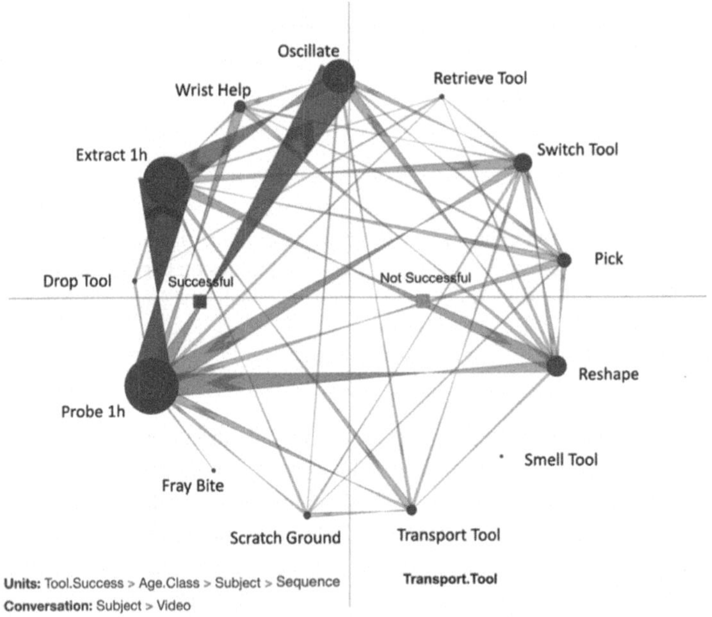

Fig. 2. Ordered networks of successful termite fishing. This figure shows the ordered connections between behavioral elements (circles) representing successful termite fishing.

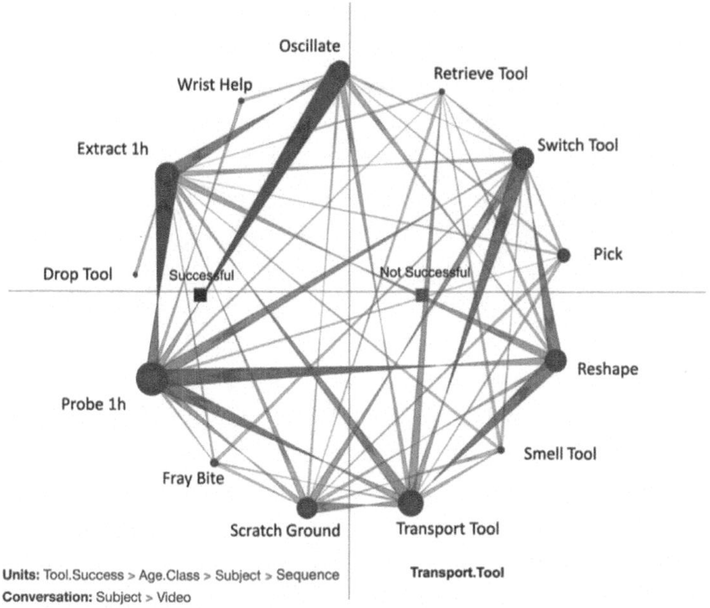

Fig. 3. Ordered networks of unsuccessful termite fishing. This figure shows the ordered connections between behavioral elements representing unsuccessful termite fishing.

to decreased termite presence in a particular area of the mound, either as a result of overfishing or possibly a termite behavioral response to prolonged fishing.

Three behavioral elements had some connections that were stronger in the "Unsuccessful" network and some in the "Successful" network: "Retrieve Tool", "Switch Tool", and "Reshape" (Fig. 4). These may be particularly interesting as they could represent a shift from unsuccessful to successful termite fishing. "Retrieve Tool" more often preceded "Probe 1 h" in the "Successful" network, as well as "Transport Tool" and "Smell Tool" in the "Unsuccessful" network, and more often followed "Scratch Ground" in the "Unsuccessful" network. This suggests that acquiring a new, already-crafted tool from the surface of the mound is done frequently with attempts to create or find new mound openings to fish. Further, the combination with "Smell Tool" suggests that when choosing a previously used tools, chimpanzees may look for evidence that the tool has succeeded before (e.g., smelling evidence of termites on the tool). This may also be coupled with seeking out new mound openings to fish as "Smell Tool" was also connected to "Scratch Ground" in the "Unsuccessful" network, meaning chimpanzees choose to fish near the location where a previously successful tool was found. "Switch Tool" was connected to a number of other behavioral elements, but most frequently used second in sequence. In particular, it has stronger connections following "Scratch Ground" and "Transport Tool" in the "Unsuccessful" network, which could indicate the chimpanzees is attempting to free up a hand for performing other actions rather than switching the hand to improve tool success. Finally, the "Reshape" behavior frequently followed Tool Use behavioral elements in the "Successful" network and more strongly preceded "Transport Tool" and

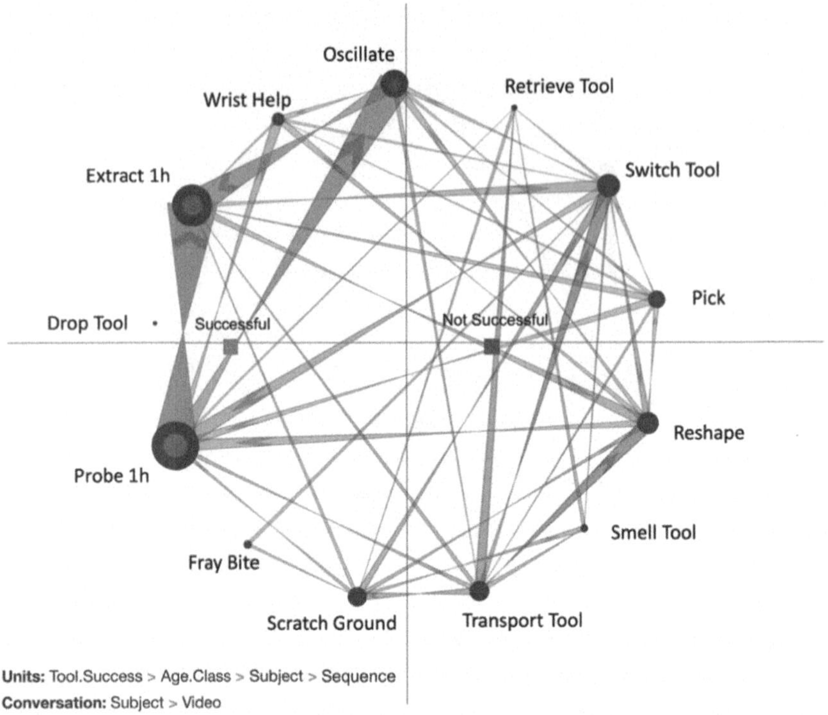

Fig. 4. Comparison of ordered networks of successful and unsuccessful termite fishing. This figure shows the difference in ordered connections between behavioral elements (circles) representing successful and unsuccessful periods of termite fishing. Associations that are green are seen more during successful periods of termite fishing while associations that are red are seen more during unsuccessful periods of termite fishing.

"Switch Tool" in the "Unsuccessful" network. This suggests that straightening the brush fibers of the tool after repeated fishing bouts may be important for successful fishing, either as a means of attracting termites to bite or simply to facilitate insertion of the tool into the mound.

Finally, the "Pick" element possessed stronger connections to other elements, particularly Tool Use elements, in the "Successful" network. This suggests that "Pick" is not being used as an alternative to tool use during periods of unsuccessful termite fishing but is being employed frequently in conjunction during periods of successful tool use. Anecdotally, several adult subjects who are adept tool users were seen picking up termites with one hand while simultaneously oscillating the tool in the mound with the other hand. It may be that in defense of the mound, termite soldiers respond to the invasive tool use by swarming the surface of the mound and practiced tool users will take advantage of this to increase the number of termites they acquire.

3.2 Functional Groups of Behavioral Elements

Pairwise Wilcoxon sign rank tests found that inclusion of four functional categories of elements (Maintenance, Shaking, Preparation, and Assistance) did not significantly impact success (Maintenance: $p = 0.43$; Shaking: $p = 0.27$; Preparation: $p = 0.82$; Assistance: $p = 0.43$) (Fig. 5). This, coupled with the results of the ONA, is evidence that these elements are being incorporated contextually in response to specific ecological/situational problems.

4 Discussions

Problem-solving is a complex cognitive task that can provide valuable adaptive benefits. It is costly both in terms energy, as complex cognition requires overall larger brains, and in terms of risk, as problem-solving often involves inherent risk via access to new/unknown resources or from wasted time spent on potentially non-profitable goals [13]. However, there is evidence that cognitive abilities like problem-solving and innovation have contributed to increased brain size and increased reproductive success, suggesting the benefits of complex cognition may outweigh the costs in certain contexts [16, 31, 32]. Tool use represents a complex behavior that provides opportunity to explore problem-solving in chimpanzees, as the action has a clear goal, and aspects such as tool material choice and tool making imply forethought and thus make the problem-solving process more "visible" [14].

In this study, we found evidence of problem-solving in the context of wild chimpanzee termite fishing. While the specific problems being addressed in each context are unknown, the chimpanzees in this study responded to broad problem of unsuccessful termite fishing through the increased incorporation of several behavioral elements associated with tool maintenance or seeking evidence of greater termite abundance. Chimpanzees more frequently employed the tool-making element "Fray Bite" during periods of unsuccessful termite fishing, suggesting attempts to improve the efficacy of the tool. There was also increased use of the "Retrieve Tool" element, suggesting that some chimpanzees choose instead to look for another ready-made tool. This was sometimes combined with the "Smell Tool" element, which may indicate chimpanzees are looking for evidence that a tool has been successful in acquiring termites prior to using it. Further, chimpanzees scratched at the ground or would move to another location on the mound more frequently during unsuccessful termite fishing, which may represent an attempt to find areas of the mound with greater termite abundance. Finally, the flexible incorporation of various behavioral elements in the termite fishing process (e.g., maintaining the tool, shaking the inserted tool, etc.) did not increase the chances of successfully acquiring termites. This may suggest that these elements are unnecessary for successful termite fishing and may be cultural variants of termite fishing that are socially learned, however many subjects in this study used a variety of termite fishing techniques that did and did not include these behavioral elements. This could indicate that these behavioral elements are contextually useful, and thus experienced termite fishing chimpanzees use existing knowledge to employ these elements when they would be effective. More detailed information about the context of use of these elements could clarify if this is the case.

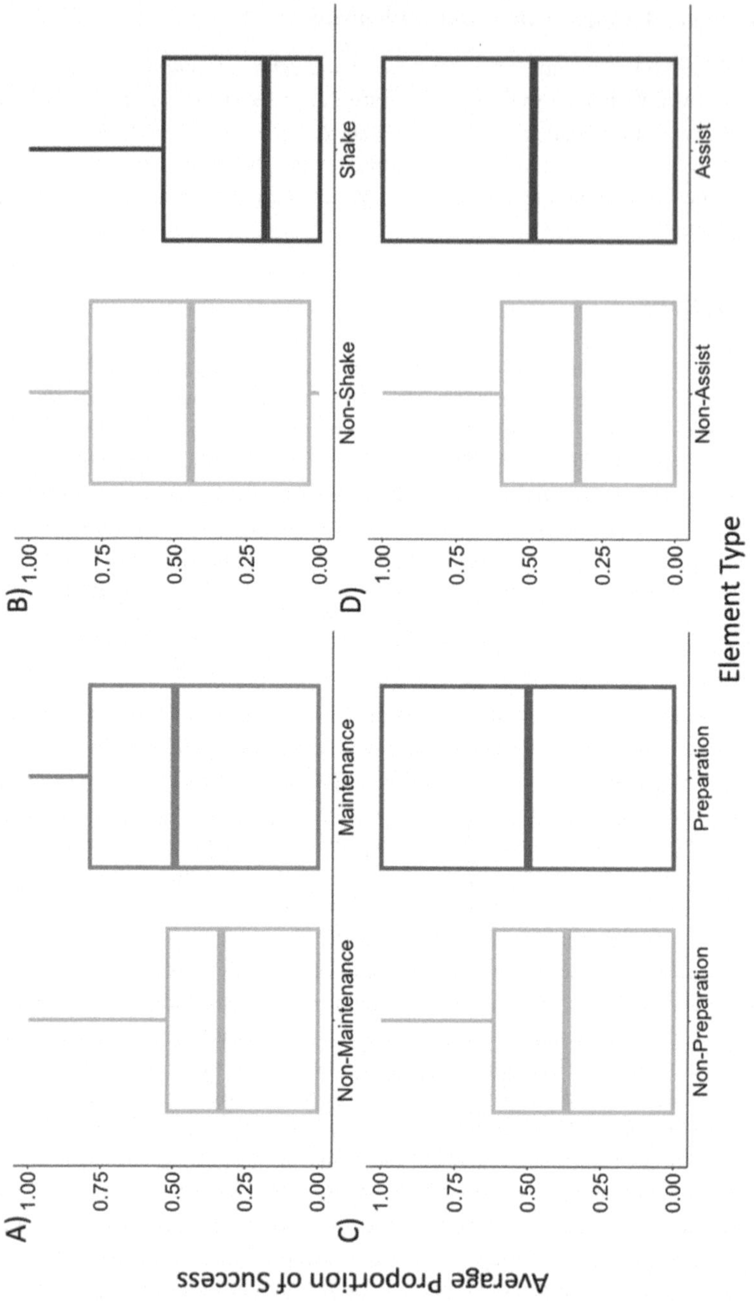

Fig. 5. Average proportion of technique success relative to the presence or absence of four different types of behavioral elements: A) Maintenance elements ("Fray Bite", "Fray Pull", "Reshape", "Reduce"), B) Shake elements ("Oscillate", "Shake Side"), C) Preparation elements ("Shake Ground"), and D) Assistance elements ("Wrist Help", "Forearm Help"). Horizontal lines within the boxes represent median values, the tops/bottoms of the boxes represent first and third quartile, and vertical lines represent 2.5% and 97.5% quantiles.

These findings suggest a high level of flexibility present in chimpanzee tool use, and this flexible inclusion of a diverse set of behavioral elements is likely shaped by a combination of social learning, responses to environmental context, and experience. There is evidence that environmental complexity can lead to increased cognitive ability in some animal species, but this remains largely unexplored for many species, including chimpanzees [16]. Recently, there has been some argument for an integrated approach to animal cognition known as "Cognitive Ecology", which emphasizes exploring animal cognition as part of a complex web of associations between environment and neurobiology by viewing complex cognitive abilities as adaptations to ecological challenges [33]. This study fits well within this framework, as it identifies flexible parts of chimpanzee behavior that are potential responses to local environmental barriers to termite fishing success. Further, quantitative ethnography is particularly well-suited for exploring hypotheses within Cognitive Ecology, as it provides information on patterns of use of cognitive/behavioral elements between different contexts. Future studies can use quantitative ethnographic methods in conjunction with detailed ecological surveys to explore fine-scale differences in behavior between individual chimpanzees, the same chimpanzees at different insect nests, or between nests of different insect species. These data could provide insight into how ecological factors like soil characteristics, insect species characteristics, or social dynamics within a chimpanzee community shape differences in behavior. Further, broader scale comparisons between entire chimpanzee communities would also be able to link ecological context with behavioral differences and potentially cognitive differences.

References

1. Boesch, C., et al.: Chimpanzee ethnography reveals unexpected cultural diversity. Nature Human Behaviour **4**(9), 910–916 (2020)
2. Fox, E.A., Sitompul, A.F., van Schaik, C.P.: Intelligent tool use in wild Sumatran orangutans. In: Parker, S.T., Mitchell, R.W., Miles, H.L. (eds.) The Mentalities of Gorillas and Orangutans, pp. 99–116. Cambridge University Press, UK (1999)
3. Sanz, C.M., Morgan, D.B.: Elemental variation in the termite fishing of wild chimpanzees (*Pan troglodytes*). Biol. Let. **7**(4), 634–637 (2011)
4. Whiten, A., et al.: Cultures in chimpanzees. Nature **399**, 682-685 (1999)
5. Goodall, J.: Tool-using and aimed throwing in a community of free-living chimpanzees. Nature **201**(4926), 1264–1266 (1964)
6. Deblauwe, I., Janssens, G.P.: New insights in insect prey choice by chimpanzees and gorillas in southeast Cameroon: the role of nutritional value. Am. J. Phys. Anthropol. **135**(1), 42–55 (2008)
7. Hladik, C.M.: Chimpanzees of Gabon and chimpanzees of Gombe: some comparative data on the diet. Primate ecology: Studies of feeding and ranging behaviour in lemurs, monkeys, and apes, 81–501 (1977)
8. Barker, D., Fitzpatrick, M.P., Dierenfeld, E.S.: Nutrient composition of sleected whole invertebrates. Zoo Biol. **17**(2), 123–134 (1998)
9. Andres-Bray, T., Barany, A., Gonder, M.K.: Using epistemic network analysis to explore flexibility and development of termite fishing techniques in nigeria-cameroon chimpanzees (*Pan troglodytes ellioti*). In: International Conference on Quantitative Ethnography 2023, pp. 155–169. Springer Nature Switzerland, Cham (2023)

10. Sanz, C.M., Morgan, D.B.: Ecological and social correlates of chimpanzee tool use. Philos. Trans. R. Soc. B **368**, 20120416 (2013)
11. Dutton, P., Chapman, H.: New tools suggest local variation in tool use by a montane community of the rare Nigeria-Cameroon chimpanzee, *Pan troglodytes ellioti*. Nigeria. Primates **56**, 89–100 (2015)
12. Andres-Bray, T.C., Smith, J., Nichols, I., Abwe, E.E., Gonder, M.K.: Ecological correlates of chimpanzee termite fishing behavior in Mbam & Djerem National Park. Cameroon. Ecology and Evolution **14**(7), e70080 (2024)
13. Seed, A.M., Call, J.: Problem-solving in tool-using and non-tool-using animals. Encyclopedia of Animal Behavior **2**, 778–785 (2010)
14. Byrne, R.W., Sanz, C.M., Morgan, D.B.: Chimpanzees plan their tool use. Tool Use in Animals, 48–64 (2013)
15. Boesch, C., Boesch, H.: Tool use and tool making in wild chimpanzees. Folia Primatol. **54**(1–2), 86–99 (1990)
16. Lefebvre, L., Reader, S.M., Sol, D.: Brains, innovations and evolution in birds and primates. Brain Behav. Evol. **63**(4), 233–246 (2004)
17. Muthukrishna, M., Doebeli, M., Chudek, M., Henrich, J.: The Cultural Brain Hypothesis: How culture drives brain expansion, sociality, and life history. PLoS Comput. Biol. **14**(11), e1006504 (2018)
18. Tan, Y., et al.: Ordered network analysis. In: 2022 International Conference on Quantitative Ethnography (2022)
19. Shaffer, D.W.: Quantitative Ethnography. Cathcart Press, Madison, WI (2017)
20. Barany, A., Shah, M., Foster, A.: Connecting curricular design and student identity change: an epistemic network analysis. In: Ruis, A.R., Lee, S.B. (eds.) Advances in Quantitative Ethnography. ICQE 2021. Communications in Computer and Information Science, vol 1312. Springer, Cham (2021)
21. Sullivan, S.A., et al.: Using epistemic network analysis to identify targets for educational interventions in trauma team communication. Surgery **163**(4), 938–943 (2017)
22. Ruis, A.R., Rosser, A.A., Quandt-Walle, C., Nathwani, J.N., Shaffer, D.W., Pugh, C.M.: The hands and head of a surgeon: Modeling operative competency with multimodal epistemic network analysis. Am. J. Surg. **216**(5), 835–840 (2018)
23. Byrne, R.W.: Culture in great apes: using intricate complexity in feeding skills to trace the evolutionary origin of human technical prowess. Philosophical Trans. Royal Soc. B: Biological Sci. **362**(1480), 577–585 (2007)
24. Zhang, S., et al.: Understanding student teachers' collaborative problem solving: Insights from an epistemic network analysis (ENA). Comput. Educ. **183**, 104485 (2022)
25. Abwe, E.E. : Linking behavioral diversity with genetic and ecological variation in the Nigeria-Camerioon chimpanzee. Dissertation: Drexel University, USA (2018)
26. Maisels, F.: Mbam Djerem National Park. Conservation status. In: Large mammals and human impact: Final report. WCS-Cameroon (2003)
27. Nishida, T., Kano, T., Goodall, J., McGrew, W.C., Nakamura, M.: Ethogram and Ethnography of Mahale Chimpanzees. Anthropol. Sci. **107**(2), 141–188 (1999)
28. Fleiss, J.L.: Statistical Methods for Rates and Proportions. Wiley, New York, NY (1981)
29. Marquart, C.L., Hinojosa, C., Swiecki, Z., Eagan, B., Shaffer, D.W.: Epistemic Network Analysis (Version 1.7.0) [Software] (2018). http://app.epistemicnetwork.org
30. Woolson, R.F.: Wilcoxon signed-rank test. Wiley Encyclopedia of Clinical Trials, 1–3 (2007)
31. Wetzel, D.P.: Problem-solving skills are linked to parental care and offspring survival in wild house sparrows. Ethology **123**(6–7), 475–483 (2017)

32. Huebner, F., Fichtel, C., Kappeler, P.M.: Linking cognition with fitness in a wild primate: fitness correlates of problem-solving performance and spatial learning ability. Philosophical Trans. Royal Soc. B: Biological Sci. **373**(1756), 20170295 (2018)
33. Mettke-Hofmann, C.: Cognitive ecology: ecological factors, life-styles, and cognition. Wiley Interdisciplinary Reviews: Cognitive Science **5**(3), 345–360 (2014)

"My Inquiry Question is ...": How Novice Social Studies Educators in Mixed Video Groups Explore Their Teacher Role Identities

Lindsey Graham(✉)

University of Pennsylvania, Philadelphia, PA 19104, USA
lrgraham@upenn.edu

Abstract. This paper investigates how pre-service (PST) and in-service teachers (IST) in mixed video groups in a Methods class explore and develop their role identities as social studies teachers during weekly meetings over the course of the semester. Ordered Network Analyses of the video group protocol and video group discourse suggest that the video group protocol heavily influenced novice social studies teachers' identity exploration by promoting discussion of ontological beliefs and action possibilities, resulting in highly similar connections between identity components for PSTs and ISTs. However, the protocol was not determinative and significant differences were found between the ISTs and PSTs' identity exploration and development, with ISTs making relatively stronger connections between self-perceptions, dilemmas and other components of their identity systems than PSTs.

Keywords: Identity Formation · Initial Teacher Education · Teaching Dilemmas

1 Introduction

Teacher education programs face the challenge of bridging the gap between the university, where they are typically situated, and the classroom, where instruction is enacted [1]. The ubiquity of videorecording technology in the 21st century offers a potential avenue for teachers to bring recordings of their practice into teacher education spaces to engage with and reflect on their practice more directly [2]. Methods courses, where secondary social studies teachers are typically supported in developing their pedagogical content knowledge in teacher education programs, may be a rich site for a video-supported communities of practice. However, we must investigate the substance of discourse within video groups to better understand how they can help novice teachers develop their identities as social studies teachers.

The data explored here was collected as part of a larger ethnographic year-long study exploring how participants in a Social Studies Methods course develop their identities as social studies teachers. This paper focuses on discourse in a particular space developed in the second semester of the year-long Methods course: three-to-four-person weekly video groups where novice teachers who were pre-service teachers (PSTs) and in-service

Y. J. Kim and Z. Swiecki (Eds.): icqe 2024, CCIS 2279, pp. 50–58, 2024.
https://doi.org/10.1007/978-3-031-76332-8_4

teachers (ISTs) were asked to record their teaching and follow a video group protocol to discuss their teaching dilemmas. Due to the proliferation of alternative certification pathways, in-service teachers are a growing population in teacher education programs [3], and teacher educators must better understand how IST and PST exploration development differs.

This paper explores the questions: In what ways do pre-service and in-service social studies teachers in a shared disciplinary Methods class utilize video groups to explore and develop their role identities as social studies teachers? To what extent is this identity exploration shaped by the video group protocol? In what ways is this identity exploration similar or different across PST and IST identities?

2 Review of Literature

Investigations of social studies teacher identity have historically focused on narrow components of a social studies teacher's identity, such as Methods course participants' uptake of a belief in using "student-centered" approaches [4]. In a recent scoping study of literature on social studies teacher identity covering the period 2000 to 2021, four central themes emerge in how social studies teachers' identity has been studied: beliefs and self-perceptions (n = 41), civic self-definitions (n = 31), personal and collective identifications (i.e. ethnic, cultural, sexual orientation and gender identities)(n = 23), and content-driven identities (n = 19) [5]. The authors point to the lack of integration of the facets of identity in previous studies and propose a complex dynamic systems approach to social studies teacher identity that stresses the interdependence, emergence and contextualism of teachers' role identity [5].

Community of practice (CoP) qualitative literature has traditionally focused on communities comprised of in-service teachers [6–8]. While CoP were originally conceived of as "newcomers" learning from "old-timers" through an apprenticeship of observation [9], CoP composed solely of novice teachers and a facilitator have been shown to surface concerns of novice teachers and allow them to work through problems of practice [7, 8]. In video-based virtual inquiry groups where novice math teachers watched peers' videos and provided written feedback, they became more reflective in their feedback and took up a focus on "responsive teaching" practices over time [2].

3 Methods

3.1 Theoretical Framework

This study applies the Dynamic Systems Model of Role Identity (DSMRI) [12] to explore novice social studies teachers' role identity development in video group discourse. The DSMRI holds that identity is a complex, dynamic system, and one's actions are understood to be situated within a specific role (i.e. social studies teacher). One's actions in a role are a result of interactions between the four main components of one's role identity: self-perception, ontological and epistemological beliefs, action possibilities, and goals [10]. Tensions between and among these components drive an individual's role identity development, as an individual is motivated to resolve these tensions and seek a state of harmony in their role identity system [10].

3.2 Study Design, Setting and Participants

The study was conducted in a year-long Social Studies Teaching Methods course in a historically White-serving research university that placed teachers in the surrounding urban school district, predominately teaching Black students. In the second semester of the course, the Methods instructor sorted the novice teachers into video groups that met once a week with one another outside of class on Zoom. In preparation for these meetings, participants recorded 5-15-min segments from their school placements. During the meetings, participants viewed the videos together using a protocol that asked: 1) video presenter provide an "overview" of their school context, goals and inquiry question 2) watch the video, pausing for the feedback-givers to engage in "descriptive review" of their observations of what happened in the video, and the presenter to provide a "stimulated-recall" [11] of what that teaching moment was like for them and 3) have the feedback-givers provide feedback ("glows and grows") and for the presenter respond to this feedback. Each meeting ranged from 16–68 min. At the end of each meeting, participants were asked to journal for five minutes in a group document, which I treated as a continuation of the conversation for that meeting.

For the purposes of this study, I sampled two video groups that contained both PSTs and ISTs who were teachers who taught social studies subjects and consented to be in the study. Between these two groups there were three ISTs (Amy, Liam, and Jada) and two PSTs (Jacky, Joan) who opted into the study. Participants in video groups who were not in the study (one PST) or were not followed in the second half of the semester due to a change in video group composition (one PST and one IST), inform the ONA model but are not included in my presentation of participants. From the eight video group meetings each video group engaged in, I took a subsample of two meetings from the first half (meetings 2 and 3) and two meetings from the second half (6 and 7).

3.3 Data Collection and Organization Techniques

For the Ordered Network Analysis (ONA) of the video group discourse, the Zoom meeting recordings were transcribed using Otter.ai, and segments of discussions that focused on meeting logistics were deleted and treated as breaks in the conversation thread. At the end of each video group meeting, the journal entries the participants wrote were copied into the data analysis spreadsheet and treated as a continuation of the meeting, with separate conversation threads for each post. Data was organized chronologically by meeting. The Video Group Protocol was used to guide segmentation decisions of all turns (i.e. sharing "glows" was separated from "grows" because they were separate bullet points in the protocol.) Within each meeting, data was organized into conversation threads, with breaks where participants watched new video clips.

For the ONA of the Video Group Protocol, the in-person "Meeting Protocol" was collected and segmented into lines according to the structure of the protocol, multiplying the lines where each feedback-giver would speak as if there were three people in the feedback-giver role in the meeting. This allowed for the construction of a model that simulates the epistemic frames that the protocol is eliciting in the meeting, and their order. As in the organization of the video transcript data, the data was organized into conversation threads, with breaks where participants watched novel video clips.

3.4 Data Analysis Techniques

Code Development and Coding Procedures. Data was coded using binary coding (0,1) of deductive codes adapted from the Dynamic Systems Model of Role Identity (DSMRI) Codebook (ontological beliefs, action possibilities, self-perception and self-definition, and purpose and goals) [12]. All codes were only applied if they referenced the social studies teacher role identity. Ontological Beliefs (OB) are beliefs relating to teaching (ex: "I realize that actively participating in a discussion is a skill that requires a lot of scaffolding but is rarely taught and practiced in schools.") Action Possibilities (AP) are statements that include references to teaching behaviors, whether carried out or imagined (ex: "It reminded me of like a Do Now or something like kind of a quick activity, a Turn-and-talk.") Self-Perception & Self-Definition (SP) are statements that indicate how an individual views themselves as a teacher, including their perceived ability or self-efficacy as teachers (ex: "I don't really have the bandwidth at this stage in my career to script things out verbatim.") Purpose and Goals (G) are statements that indicate the purpose behind one's actions as a teacher, or goals as a teacher, whether applied to oneself or another teacher (ex: "Your objective wasn't in that moment for them to like, be creating stuff. But it was more like the content… background knowledge stuff.") All exemplar quotes here are drawn from the data.

In addition, the DSMRI Code Book was further utilized to indo-deductively construct the "Dilemma" (Dil.) code [12]. "Dilemma" is an emic term utilized by the Methods course instructors and reflected in the language of the protocol and participants, and maps onto the way in which "tension" is conceived of in the DSMRI framework. A "Dilemma" is an explicit tension that arises when two components of the DSMRI conflict (i.e. an individual holds two contradictory goals, a goal and a conflicting action possibility, two contradictory beliefs, etc.) and can be explicit or implicit (ex: "It was a little bit chaotic, as you guys probably saw. And that was - my dilemma, because it can get so chaotic, I think I kind of come down harsher, or can be more regimented, where I'm like, we're raising our hands and I'm calling on you. But ideally, I would love to have them call on each other.").

Test-Retest Single Rater Reliability. My positionality as a participant-observer of the year-long Methods course provides an emic perspective of the teacher education community of practice, helping me establish the fairness of codes to the community as an insider [13]. To test my reliability as a single rater, after I completed a first round of coding the data, I calculated Cohen's kappa by sampling the first 10% of lines I coded (60 lines), recoding them, and testing my consistency. A Cohen's kappa threshold of 0.70 was reached for the ontological beliefs, action possibilities, self-perceptions, and dilemma codes in this first round (OB $\kappa = 0.9$; AP $\kappa = 0.8$; SP $\kappa = 0.7$, Dil. $\kappa = 0.9$). For the purpose and goals code, Cohen's kappa threshold of 0.7 was met on the second round of test-retest coding, which I completed utilizing the next 10% of lines (G $\kappa = 0.7$).

Ordered Network Analysis. For the ONA of the video group discourse, data was segmented by the conversation variables of the video group (1 or 2), meeting number (meeting 2,3, 6 or 7) and conversation thread (1–65). Unit variables used for analysis include the program the participants are in (PST or IST), the time in the semester (first half or second half), the meeting number (2,3,6 or 7) and the individual participants, to account for individual and group variation. A moving stanza window of 4 was used, based on randomly sampling ten points in the data and calculating the average lines of previous discourse the line connected to. The ONA of the video group protocol was structured similarly to the ONA of the video groups: the conversation variables included the protocol number (1), part of the protocol (overview, descriptive review, inquiry question and feedback, and journaling) and conversation thread. Unit variables included the protocol number and part of protocol, which allowed the model to show how the different parts of the protocol elicited different role identity components. The same codes were applied in both ONAs. The substance of the protocol and teacher discourse is used to close the interpretive loop by illustrating how the identity components relate to one another as individuals explore their identities.

Models normalized the networks to account for different amount of coded lines [14]. Nonparametric Mann-Whitney U tests (assuming non-normality) were conducted to test whether differences between pre-service and in-service teacher discourse were statistically significant along the X-axis, as a means rotation was used to maximize variance along one axis.

4 Results and Discussion

4.1 Video Group Protocol Ordered Network Analysis

The structure of the video group protocol encourages teachers to emphasize and connect their beliefs related to teaching, discussion of the action possibilities of teachers, and their dilemmas, but does not encourage teachers to connect goals or self-perception to other elements of the identity system or their dilemmas (see Fig. 1).

Fig. 1. ONA Model of Video Group Protocol

In the protocol, the co-occurrence of ontological beliefs with ontological beliefs (lw = 0.54) is nearly twice as strong the next largest connection of action possibilities to ontological beliefs (lw = 0.29). The "Overview" section of the protocol, where the video presenter shares relevant information about the lesson, their students and school-placement and the feedback-givers ask clarification questions, pulls teachers towards expressing these ontological beliefs. The "Descriptive Review" section of the protocol pulls teachers towards conveying action possibilities and ontological beliefs, for example by asking them to report, "What did you hear/see the teacher doing/saying in this clip?" a question that orients teachers towards the presenting teacher's actions and surfaces beliefs about their teaching. Structurally, by asking each of the feedback-givers to engage in descriptive review before moving into the "Inquiry Question and Feedback" section the protocol works to intensify these connections. Lastly, the protocol prompts teachers to connect beliefs about teaching to their dilemmas of practice and dilemmas of practice to beliefs about teaching. The "Journaling" section of the protocol is especially important to pulling teachers towards connecting their dilemmas to other elements of their identity systems.

The protocol does not prompt teachers to engage as much in self-perception or goals-oriented speech, because it only asks video group presenters to relate these components one time each. This resulted in comparatively few co-occurrences with goals or self-perceptions, with the highest co-occurrences involving goals or self-perceptions being from goals to ontological beliefs (lw = 0.8) and self-perceptions to ontological beliefs (lw = 0.2).

4.2 Comparison of Pre-Service Teachers' (PST) and In-Service Teachers' (IST) Identity Structure and Dilemma-Co-Occurrences in Video Group Discourse

The overall structure of the connections within the Pre-Service Teacher (PST) model and the connections within the In-Service Teacher (IST) identity structure models are largely similar (see Fig. 2). Like the ONA of the video group protocol, both the PST and IST models have the strongest connections between action possibilities and ontological beliefs and their self-referential connections, and weaker connections to goals, self-perceptions and dilemmas.

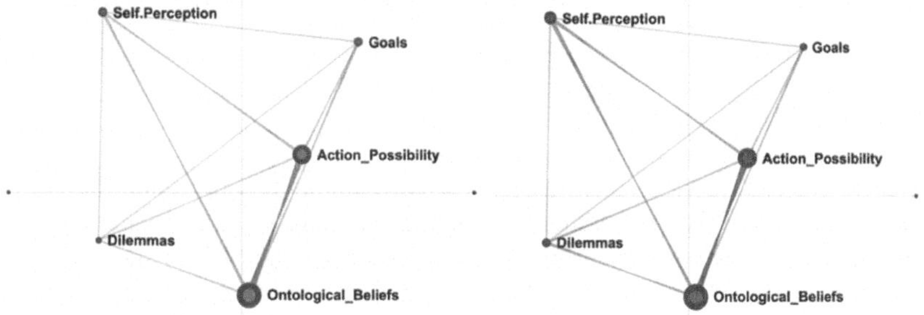

Fig. 2. ONA Models of Pre-Service Teachers' Identity Structure (left) and In-Service Teachers' Identity Structure (right)

While we cannot directly compare the relative line weights of the connections in the teacher video group discourse with the line weights in the video group protocol model because of the underlying differences in the structure of the data, the similarities of the relative weights *within* each model suggest that the tool likely plays a large role in shaping the teachers' discourse. However, the protocol does not appear to be determinative, because the relative strength of connections differs between the teachers and the protocol, and between PSTs and ISTs. From the ONA of the video group protocol, we might expect to see a lower rate of connections between goals, self-perceptions and other parts of the identity system compared to the rate of connections between ontological beliefs and ontological beliefs. In addition, from the video protocol we might expect that teachers have a higher co-occurrence of dilemmas-ontological beliefs relative to the co-occurrence of self-referential ontological beliefs than they do in the discourse. Instead, teachers in the video groups made relatively more connections to their self-perceptions and goals, and relatively fewer connections to their dilemmas, than we might expect from the video group protocol ONA.

A comparison ONA model of ISTs and PSTs shows that ISTs drew more connections to self-perceptions and dilemmas than PSTs. The most significant differences in the model are ISTs' stronger connections between self-perceptions and ontological beliefs (lw = 0.09 in favor of ISTs) and self-perceptions and actions (lw = 0.07 in favor of ISTs). ISTs' positionality as practicing teachers may prompt them to engage in defining themselves as teachers more often than PSTs, for whom many classroom decisions are restricted by their classroom mentor teachers' systems and structures, and whose comparatively small amount of time lead-teaching may not have given them a chance to develop their self-perceptions as teachers. In addition, the ISTs' stronger connections than PSTs from dilemmas to their actions (lw = 0.06 in favor of ISTs) and dilemmas to their ontological beliefs (lw = 0.07 in favor of ISTs), may similarly reflect a more developed sense of dilemmas that emerges from ISTs' positionality, though it is important to note that there is no difference in the co-occurrence of dilemmas-goals.

Model Metrics. For the comparison model of PSTs and ISTs the Pearson's Goodness of Fit was 0.95 along the X-axis and 0.99 along the Y-axis. Along the X axis (MR1), a Mann-Whitney test showed that Pre-Service Teacher Ed. Program (Mdn = 0.11, N = 13) was statistically significantly different at the alpha = 0.05 level from In-Service Teacher Ed. Program (Mdn = −0.08, N = 14 U = 31.00, p = 0.00, r = 0.66).

5 Conclusion

While previous studies have investigated how teachers operate in asynchronous video groups that are relatively unstructured [2] or only serve in-service novice teachers [7, 8], this study suggests that synchronous video groups can help elicit specific types of identity exploration and are utilized differently in mixed video groups according to a novice teacher's positionality (pre-service or in-service.) For researchers, the influence of the protocol on the discourse highlights the importance of considering the situated nature and mediating tools of any interaction that we seek to analyze with quantitative ethnographic methods. For teacher educators, this study suggests that video groups can be a way to help novice teachers explore their identities as teachers, but that, if one adopts a video protocol similar to the one investigated here, there is outstanding work to be done to scaffold teachers' identity exploration to help them: 1) connect their goals and self-perceptions to their actions and beliefs, and 2) articulate their dilemmas. Teacher educators may also need to be sensitive to the positionality of the novice teachers they are working with. For example, pre-service teachers using a similar video group protocol may need more support articulating their self-perceptions and self-definitions as a teacher separate from their mentor teacher.

Further research might explore how different protocols may help novice teachers explore their social studies teacher role identities in more balanced ways and resolve tensions in their identity systems (i.e. their dilemmas), and how the substance of their dilemmas and identity systems differs between in-service and pre-service teachers.

Acknowledgments. Dr. Amanda Barany supported the conceptualization and structuring of the ONA and served as a first reader.

Disclosure of Interests. The author has no competing interests to declare that are relevant to the content of this article.

References

1. Feiman-Nemser, S., Buchmann, M.: Pitfalls of experience in teacher preparation. Teach. Coll. Rec. **87**(1), 53–65 (1985)
2. Ebby, C.B., Remillard, J.T., Goldsmith-Markey, L.T.: Learning to teach responsively through asynchronous collaborative discourse around video records of practice. J. Teach. Educ. **74**(5), 451–466 (2023)
3. Grossman, P., Loeb, S.: Introduction. In: Grossman, P., Loeb, S. (eds.) Alternative Routes to Teaching. Harvard Education Press (2008)
4. Doppen, F.H.: The influence of a teacher preparation program on preservice social studies teachers' beliefs: a case study. The J. Social Stud. Res. **31**(1), 54–64 (2007)
5. Patterson, T., Bridgelal, I., Kaplan, A.: Becoming a social studies teacher: An integrative systems perspective on identity content, structure, and processes. Teach. Teach. Educ. **120**, 1–17 (2022)
6. Horn, I.S., Little, J.W.: Attending to problems of practice: routines and resources for professional learning in teachers' workplace interactions. Am. Educ. Res. J. **47**(1), 181–217 (2010)
7. Cuddapah, J.L., Clayton, C.D.: Using wenger's communities of practice to explore a new teacher cohort. J. Teach. Educ. **62**(1), 62–75 (2011)
8. Meyer, T.: Novice teacher learning communities: an alternative to one-on-one mentoring. Am. Second. Educ. **31**(1), 27–42 (2002)
9. Lave, J.: Situating learning in communities of practice. In: Resnick, L.B., Levine, J., Teasley, S.D. (eds.) Perspectives on Socially Shared Cognition, pp. 63–83. American Psychological Association, Washington, D.C. (1991)
10. Kaplan, A., Garner, J.K.: A complex dynamic systems perspective on identity and its development: the dynamic systems model of role identity. Developmental Psychology **53**(11), 2036–2051 (2017)
11. Lyle, J.: Stimulated recall: a report on its use in naturalistic research. Br. Edu. Res. J. **29**(6), 861–878 (2003)
12. Kaplan, A., Garner, J.K.: Dynamic Systems Model of Role Identity (DSMRI): Analysis guide and codebook: Version 3. Temple University & Old Dominion University (2020)

13. Shaffer, D.W., Ruis, A.R.: How we code. In: Ruis, A.R., Lee, S.B. (eds.) ICQE2021.CCIS, vol. 1312, pp. 62–77. Springer, Cham (2021)
14. Shaffer, D.W., Collier, W., Ruis, A.R.: A tutorial on epistemic network analysis: analyzing the structure of interactions in cognitive, social and interaction data. J. Learn. Analy. **3**(3), 9–45 (2006)

Enhancing Student Interest and Motivation Through Cultural Integration in an Online Global Science, Technology, Engineering and Mathematics Community

Ruth Vitsemmo Akumbu(✉)

Pepperdine University, Los Angeles, CA, USA
ruthakumbu@gmail.com

Abstract. This study investigates the interplay between cultural integration and student interest or motivation in Science, Technology, Engineering, and Mathematics (STEM) within the Asset Based Learning Environment (ABLE) online global community. Findings highlight the importance of integrating cultural elements into STEM education to enhance its effectiveness and appeal. U.S. learners modeled all cultural constructs comprehensively, while Ghanaian learners showed strong links between culture, cultural sensitivity, and STEM. These insights emphasize the need for culturally tailored educational approaches to foster interest and motivation in STEM, accounting for local contextual differences promoting a nuanced understanding of STEM principles.

Keywords: Cultural integration · STEM · Interest · Motivation · Online learning · Diversity

1 Introduction

The Asset Based Learning Environment (ABLE) project provides a culturally diverse learning environment for students aged 12–18 to explore their Science, Technology, Engineering, and Mathematics (STEM) interests. Building on insights from the Synergies Project [1], this study examines how cultural elements influence youth interest in STEM within a global learning environment aimed at nurturing and sustaining learners' STEM interests over time. The study explores the relationship between cultural elements and students' interests/motivation to pursue STEM subjects within the ABLE Project. Reporting on findings from the first year of the study (2023), the paper identifies cultural elements and other factors that support learners' STEM interests. Understanding how culture influences STEM engagement for students from the U.S.A., Mexico, Brazil, Ghana, and Kenya can help educators and policymakers develop strategies to attract and retain a diverse student population in STEM, thereby promoting diversity in STEM education.

Y. J. Kim and Z. Swiecki (Eds.): icqe 2024, CCIS 2279, pp. 59–69, 2024.
https://doi.org/10.1007/978-3-031-76332-8_5

1.1 Cultural Elements in STEM Education

Integrating cultural elements into STEM education significantly enhances student engagement and achievement, particularly for those from diverse backgrounds [2, 3]. Aligning STEM curricula with students' cultural contexts makes learning more relevant, fostering greater interest and enjoyment [1, 3, 4]. By incorporating students' cultural backgrounds, educators validate their identities and bridge the gap between home and school, encouraging sustained participation in STEM [3, 5]. Culturally responsive STEM curricula are essential, especially in underserved communities, where traditional approaches may fall short [3–5]. This aligns with Local STEM (LSTEM), which emphasizes grounding STEM education in local contexts and addressing real-world issues that resonate with students' lives, making STEM subjects more accessible and engaging, and promoting a more inclusive global STEM environment.

The Cultural Integration and Augmentation (CIA) framework, rooted in postcolonial theory, emphasizes prioritizing local cultures in education, particularly in African contexts [5, 6]. Based on ethnographic research in the Kisii K–12 education system, the CIA framework identifies nine cultural elements for integration, including language, heritage, oral traditions, beliefs, values, and local STEM (LSTEM) [5]. Complementing this, the Transfer and Adoption/Adaptation of Universal Principles (TAUP) Model highlights the relationship between learners, teachers, and local culture in knowledge transmission, adoption/adaptation, or construction, offering a comprehensive approach to culturally informed STEM education.

1.2 Interest-Driven Creator Theory

This study is grounded in Chan et al.'s [7] Interest-Driven Creator (IDC) Theory and Hidi and Renninger's [8] Four-Phase Model of Interest Development. The IDC theory asserts that learning outcomes and skill development are maximized when learners pursue their interests, fostering lifelong learning through interest, creation, and habit loops [7, 9]. The Four-Phase Model describes stages of interest development: triggered situational interest (short-term interest sparked by external factors), maintained situational interest (sustained focus through meaningful tasks), emerging individual interest (recurring engagement driven by curiosity), and well-developed individual interest (deep, long-term engagement fueled by intrinsic motivation) [8].

Falk et al. [1] applied this model in the Synergies project, showing increased interest in science and technology among adolescents. The study found that situational interest, initially sparked by external factors, can develop into lasting individual interest through enhanced knowledge, subject value, and feedback. Research further supports that deepening understanding and enjoyment of science boosts STEM interest [1, 3, 4]. We argued that integrating cultural elements into STEM education, aligned with the CIA framework and TAUP model, can create more engaging and relatable learning experiences, fostering intrinsic interest in STEM [1–4, 10]. This approach tailors education to diverse cultural backgrounds, promoting a more inclusive STEM community where all students feel inspired, valued, and empowered to pursue their interests and contribute meaningfully to the field.

2 Methods

The dataset consists of transcribed recordings from 15 global meet-up breakout sessions held between September and December 2023, involving 28 adolescent participants from Brazil (4), Ghana (2), Kenya (5), and the United States (17). Transcriptions were conducted using Trint software, segmented by speaker turns, and then amalgamated into a qualitative data table coded according to the CIA and TAUP frameworks. A codebook was generated containing 6 constructs (Table 1). Cultural elements like beliefs, values, practices, heritage, and oral traditions were combined into one construct named Culture_Combined due to overlapping definitions and low coding frequency (beliefs 1.6%, values 2.4%, practices 2.5%, heritage 29%, oral traditions 1.2%) across the 510 lines of data [2, 10–13]. Each interview was independently coded by two raters using the codebook, followed by social moderation as described by Herrenkohl and Cornelius [14] to ensure consistency and reduce bias. Coding used a binary system, with 1 indicating the presence of a construct and 0 its absence.

The coded transcripts were then analyzed using the Epistemic Network Analysis (ENA) web tool, following Shaffer's methodology [15], to visualize discourse patterns by identifying co-occurrences among constructs. The dataset, comprising 510 lines of student utterances, excluded any input from mentors or adults. The ENA algorithm employed a dynamic window mechanism to create a network model for each data line, illustrating connections between codes in the current line and those occurring previously [16, 17]. Networks were aggregated for each unit of analysis using binary summation, reflecting the presence or absence of code co-occurrence. Conversations were defined by all lines associated with a specific MeetingID, such as MeetingID 2023.09.23_Food_Room.

3 Results

The ENA network models (Figs. 1, 2, 3, 4 and 5) reveal interview patterns by country and student participants, with visualizations showing the strength of connections through line thickness and saturation. Co-registration correlations were 0.95 (Pearson) and 0.95 (Spearman) for the first dimension, and 0.92 (Pearson) and 0.95 (Spearman) for the second. Strong connections between culture_combined, interest_motivation, and local STEM are evident in Figs. 1, 2 and 3, with slight differences in cultural elements across country models. The quadrant positions of codes in Figs. 2, 3 and 4 generally align with Fig. 1, except for a few unconnected codes.

3.1 United States

Figure 1 places local STEM in the lower left, identity recognition and cultural sensitivity in the upper left, culture_combined and interest_motivation in the lower right, and sense of belonging in the upper right quadrant. The strongest connections are between culture_combined and interest_motivation, with notable links between local STEM and both interest_motivation and culture_combined.

Table 1. ABLE Participant Analysis Codebook

Code	Definition & Sample Utterance	
Interest/Motivation	Definition:	What the individual likes, loves, or recognizes as important
	Sample:	I picked the topic because I feel like, where I'm from, there's a lot of different cultures there and a lot of different things that you can do here, and they're interesting
Culture Combined	Definition:	Cultural elements such as values, ways of being, heritage, and practices (norms or customs), including factors such as food, locations, history, songs, proverbs, stories, music, and dance
	Sample:	"And also, because it's cultural food and definitely food you've never tried before."
Cultural Sensitivity	Definition:	Awareness, knowledge, respect for the other, and understanding
	Sample:	"There's definitely some things that you want to try, but you just can't get over here in the US, or at least not like the proper dishes."
Local STEM	Definition:	Local ways of thinking about STEM or local resources and material
	Sample:	"I love to know more about other people's culture. And I as well see, like some places where we don't have water, there are people who lack water."
Sense of Belonging	Definition:	Feeling of security, support, or sense of acceptance, inclusion, and identity
	Sample:	"Yeah, I think it would go well. I feel like it's nice having a smaller group, though, because you have like. I feel like you can have a bit better communication."
Identity/Recognition	Definition:	Acknowledgment, acceptance, validating identity
	Sample:	"The three words that could describe me, is tolerant, patient, and a listener. I like things."

3.2 Brazil

In Fig. 2, representing Brazil, connections to the constructs cultural sensitivity and identity recognition seemed absent. Stong lines of triangulated connections are noted between culture_combined, interest_motivation, and local STEM. Medium lines of saturation are noted between the constructs Local STEM and sense of belonging.

Strong connections between culture_combined and local STEM and interest_motivation also show that the students from Brazil's interests and motivation in selecting a STEM topic as a group project were influenced by several factors, including culture. A Brazilian student states, "Uh, yes, of course. I was trying to find a group interested in math because I'm working with math in my job…I think I can, uh, can contribute." Another Brazilian student indicated a strong interest in pizza and the desire

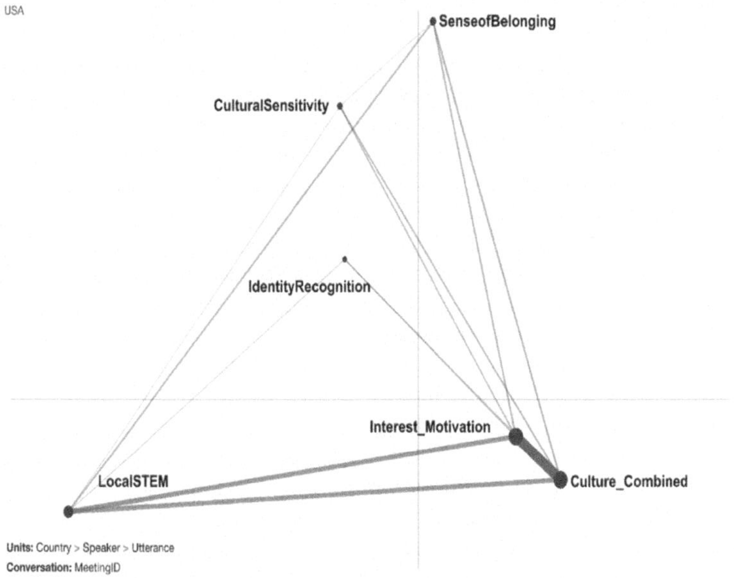

Fig. 1. ENA network model for United States participants.

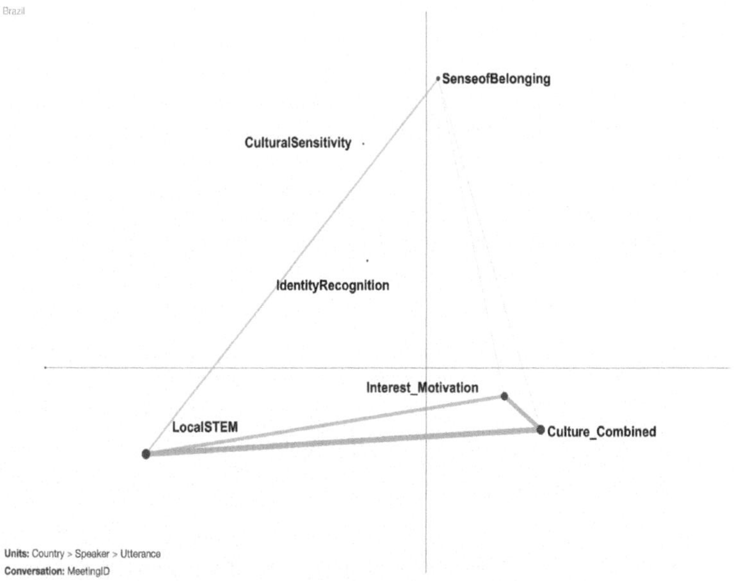

Fig. 2. ENA network model for Brazilian participants.

to visit Korea but not to live: "I like to go to, what would it be, is Korea. Just to visit. I don't like to live, but I like to visit."

3.3 Kenya

In Fig. 3 patterns of discourse and strong connections are noted within the triangulation of constructs culture_combined, interest_motivation, and local STEM among Kenyan learners.

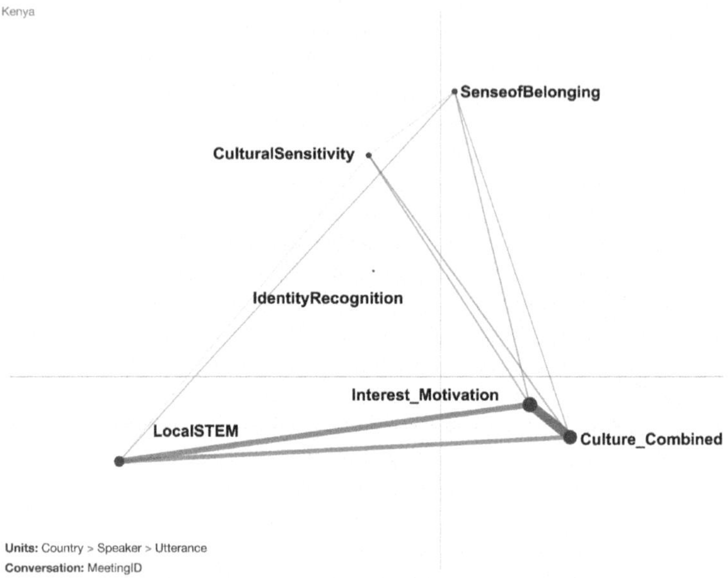

Fig. 3. ENA network model for Kenyan participants.

Kenyan students show a strong interest in learning about food and visiting other countries. A student notes: "I think I chose food 'cause I think there are different cultures with different types of foods and different things that they enjoy." The students noted that they think it is important to know about cultural foods of other communities:

> "I was thinking, because I'm in Kenya and we have different tribes, and different communities. I'd really prefer… We know more about other people's community, what they eat, what they do, and then we combine all of them to know what specific food they eat, what are their traditions? What are their fortunes? Yeah, apart from [looking at Kenya in general], we do specific communities". -Kenyan Student.

Connecting culture to STEM, a Kenyan learner notes that they posted their finding on Slack, the technology tool for sharing projects: "I did local foods in Kenya, I did a rice dish, I posted on Slack." Another learner sought to understand the cultural meaning of holidays: "We can also talk about the meanings of the holidays to the cultures."

3.4 Ghana

Discourse between Ghanaian participants are noted in Fig. 4. While little to no connections include the construct identity recognition, strong lines of saturation are seen between culture_combined and cultural sensitivity as well as interest_motivation and Local STEM, interest motivation and culture combined, as well as interest motivation and cultural sensitivity.

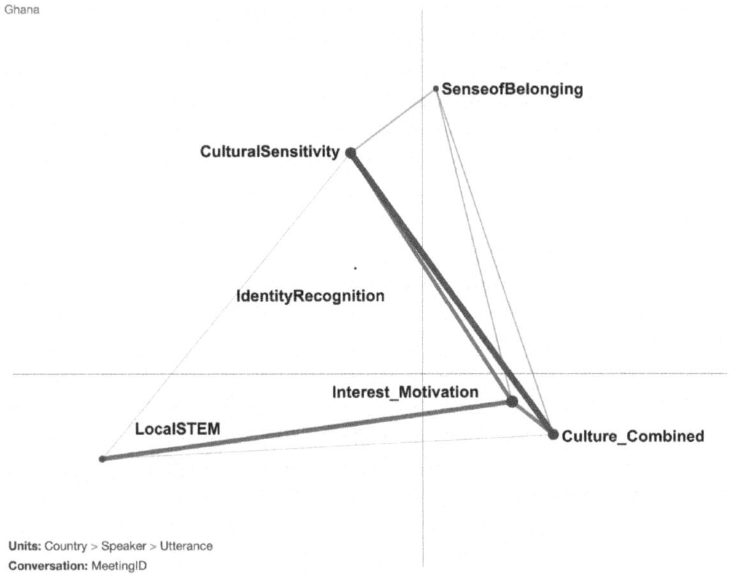

Fig. 4. ENA network model for Ghanaian participants.

Students from Ghana made strong connections between the node culture combined & cultural sensitivity. As a student noted, "I chose as everyone says, who doesn't like food? Everyone likes food." Indicating a sense of belonging and a desire to "eat food from different countries, eating from different cultures." This interest may potentially result in established in cultural sensitivity and awareness as learners gain an understanding of their peers' cultures and experience through foods from other cultures:

> And it will be good to So learning how to each other people's food is a very good idea. I think there's a reason behind why I chose this. And I hope by the end of our discussion, I'll be able to know each and everyone kind of food they like and maybe here I will just prepare it. -Ghanaian Student.

Many Ghanaian conversations contribute to cultural sensitivity and awareness. The Ghanaian learners are engaging in the contextualized transfer of universal principles of geography, defying a common understanding that all West African countries are hot and that it does not snow in the region.

3.5 U.S.A. And Ghana

Figure 5 models the discourse of learners from the U.S.A. and Ghana and is represented as a subtracted graph. Strong connections or salient differences are noted among

USA learners between culture_combined and interest_motivation as well as connections among Ghanaian learners culture_combined and cultural_sensitivity, showing the main differences between learners from these two countries.

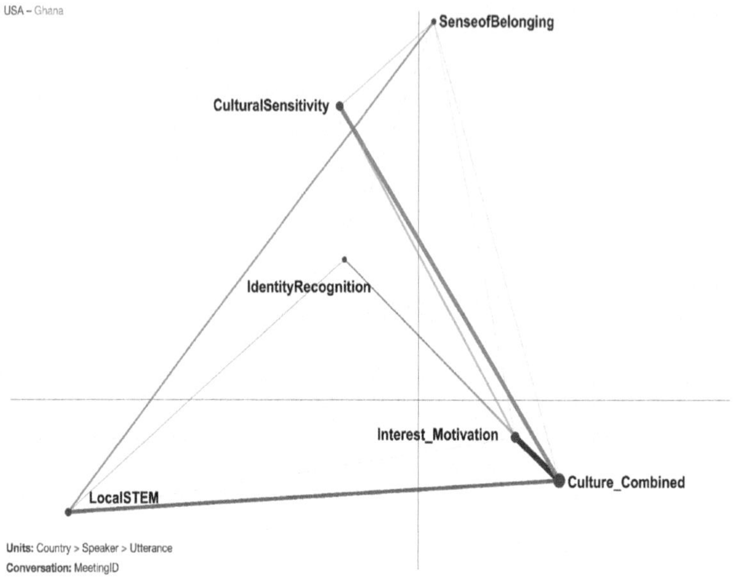

Fig. 5. ENA network model subtracted graph between USA and Ghanaian participants.

A learner from Ghana shared insights about Ghana's climate diversity and tourist attractions, which provided a broader perspective on their country's unique characteristics. A US student noted that as regards travel, "I've never left the state or not even the what's it called, the continent."

> "I feel like there's a lot of Asian issues that I think are really fascinating as well as African, African dishes as well…There's definitely some things that you want to try, but you just can't get over here in the US, or at least not like the proper dishes. It's definitely, you know, integrated with a lot of US kind of things like already. Like I've heard of recently, I went to a restaurant and I heard something that like called a burrito with fries inside it. So yeah, it's definitely not just one culture, it's definitely a mixture of like the melting pot we have here. So yeah, I think just going to the place where this food was kind of originated would be really cool. -USA Learner.

The students in the US-Ghana group are very invested in learning about peers' unique cultures and STEM. US learners highlighted personality factors such as curiosity that motivate them to explore new experiences.

4 Discussion

In the early phase of the project, triggered situational interest [8], the discourse reveals various cultural motivations among the participants. These include an interest in exploring cultural heritage, such as traditional foods and countries they wish to visit. Additional motivations are driven by the desire to learn and contribute meaningfully to their teams. Most notably, learners demonstrated a strong interest in STEM subjects, particularly in math and biology. This indicates a blend of cultural curiosity and academic enthusiasm driving their engagement.

In regard to the relationship between constructs, this study finds a strong relationship between culture and interest or motivation as it relates to the initial breakout sessions of the ABLE project. Underpinning these results are demonstrations of cultural elements that seem to shape the way learners engage in topics related to STEM within an online global community. The strong relationship between culture and interest/motivation among students of diverse cultural backgrounds highlights the importance of integrating cultural elements into STEM education to make it more engaging or effective [3, 18]. All groups except for Ghana indicated strong connections between culture, interest/motivation, and STEM. Constructs from the Ghana group showed strong connections between culture, cultural sensitivity, and STEM. The U.S.A. group modeled connections between all constructs more comprehensively compared to Ghana, Kenya, and Brazil. The unique patterns observed, such as the strong connections between culture and cultural sensitivity in the Ghana group and the comprehensive modeling of all constructs in the U.S.A. group, provide insights into how tailored educational approaches can address diverse cultural backgrounds, ultimately fostering greater interest and motivation in STEM learning. Contextualized cultural integration also allows space for a nuanced understanding, transmission, and adoption/adaptation of STEM principles [2, 11, 12]. This contextualized cultural integration and understanding also indicates that the learners are aware of subtle STEM differences observed in their local contexts, such as climate, weather patterns, or temperatures, compared to others as observe in conversations by the students from Ghana.

5 Conclusion

The study reveals that cultural integration in STEM education boosts student interest and motivation, as well as engagement. The research provides insight into the factors driving the interests and motivations of learners from diverse cultural backgrounds in a STEM learning community. Educators and policymakers are encouraged to tailor educational strategies to diverse cultural backgrounds in other to fosters engagement and effectiveness in STEM learning, as evidenced by varying patterns among the U.S.A., Kenyan, Ghanaian, and Brazilian learners. Continued research throughout the ABLE project is essential to assess the remaining phases of The Four-Phase Model of Interest Development: maintained situational interest, emerging individual interest, and well-developed individual interest [8].

Acknowledgements. The authors also gratefully acknowledge funding support from the U.S. National Science Foundation (#2215613) for the work this paper reports. The views in this paper do not reflect those of the funding agency.

References

1. Falk, J.H., Staus, N., Dierking, L.D., Penuel, W., Wyld, J., Bailey, D.: Understanding youth STEM interest pathways within a single community: The Synergies project. Int. J. Sci. Edu. Part B: Comm. Pub. Engage. **6**(4), 369–384 (2016). https://doi.org/10.1080/21548455.2015.1093670
2. Akumbu, R.V., Lux, K., Schulz, D., Espino, D., Hamilton, E.: Cultural Impact on a Global Virtual STEM Project. In: Arastoopour Irgens, G., Knight, S. (eds.) Advances in Quantitative Ethnography. ICQE 2023. Communications in Computer and Information Science, vol 1895. Springer, Cham (2023). https://doi.org/10.1007/978-3-031-47014-1_7
3. Gay, G.: The what, why, and how of culturally responsive teaching: international mandates, challenges, and opportunities. Multicultural Education Review **7**(3), 123–139 (2015). https://doi.org/10.1080/2005615x.2015.1072079
4. Thevenot, Y.: Culturally responsive and sustaining STEM curriculum as a problem-based science approach to supporting student achievement for Black and Latinx students. VUE (Voices in Urban Education) **50**(1), 61 (2021). https://doi.org/10.33682/bhr8-6z56
5. Akumbu, R.V.: Culturally relevant elements for K–12 education in Kisii. (Order No. 29323485) [Doctoral dissertation, Pepperdine University]. ProQuest Dissertations Publishing (2022)
6. Poloma, A.W., Szelényi, K.: Coloniality of knowledge, hybridisation, and indigenous survival: Exploring transnational higher education development in Africa from the 1920s to the 1960s. Compare: A Journal of Comparative and International Education **49**(4), 635–653 (2019). https://doi.org/10.1080/03057925.2018.1445962
7. Chan, T., et al.: IDC theory: Creation and the creation loop. Res. Pract. Technol. Enhanc. Learn. **14**(1), 1–29 (2019). https://doi.org/10.1186/s41039-019-0120-5
8. Hidi, S., Renninger, K.A.: The four-phase model of interest development. Educational Psychologist **41**(2), 111–127 (2006). https://doi.org/10.1207/s15326985ep4102_4
9. Chen, W., et al.: IDC theory: Habit and the habit loop. Res. Pract. Technol. Enhanc. Learn. **15**(1), 1–19 (2020). https://doi.org/10.1186/s41039-020-00127-7
10. Hite, R., Taylor, D.: Fostering interest in and motivation for STEM: An illustrative case study of middle grade students' experiences in out-of-school time STEM activities. Journal of Interdisciplinary Teacher Leadership **5**(1), 1–23 (2021). https://doi.org/10.46767/kfp.2016-0035
11. Kelley, T.R., Knowles, J.G.: A conceptual framework for integrated STEM education. International Journal of STEM Education **3**(1), 1–11 (2016). https://doi.org/10.1186/s40594-016-0046-z
12. Kennedy, T.J., Odell, M.R.: Engaging students in STEM education. Science Education International **25**(3), 246–258 (2014). https://files.eric.ed.gov/fulltext/EJ1044508.pdf
13. Staus, N.L., et al.: Interested, disinterested, or neutral: Exploring STEM interest profiles and pathways in a low-income urban community. EURASIA Journal of Mathematics, Science and Technology Education **16**(6), 1–4 (2020). https://doi.org/10.29333/ejmste/7927
14. Herrenkohl, L.R., Cornelius, L.: Investigating elementary students' scientific and historical argumentation. J. Learn. Sci. **22**(3), 413–461 (2013). https://doi.org/10.1080/10508406.2013.799475

15. Shaffer, D.W.: Quantitative ethnography. Cathcart Press, Madison, WI (2017)
16. Ruiz, M.S., et al.: Using interrupted time series analysis to measure the impact of legalized syringe exchange on HIV diagnoses in Baltimore And Philadelphia. J. Acquired Immune Deficiency Syndromes (1999) **82**(Suppl 2(2)), S148–S154 (2019). https://doi.org/10.1097/QAI.0000000000002176
17. Siebert-Evenstone, A.L., et al.: In search of conversational grain size: Modeling semantic structure using moving stanza windows. Journal of Learning Analytics **4**(3), 123–139 (2017). https://doi.org/10.18608/jla.2017.43.7
18. Jackson, C., et al.: Equity-oriented conceptual framework for K-12 STEM literacy. Int. J. STEM Edu. **8**(38), 1–16 (2021). https://doi.org/10.1186/s40594-021-00294-z

Navigating Usability Challenges in Collaborative Learning with Augmented Reality

Rodrigo Hidalgo(✉) and Jina Kang

University of IL Urbana–Champaign, Champaign, Illinois, USA
{rh24,jinakang}@illinois.edu

Abstract. This study investigates how augmented reality (AR) significantly enhances collaborative activities, aiding students in grasping complex STEM concepts. Using Epistemic Network Analysis (ENA), we analyzed conversations between student pairs exploring Kepler's laws of planetary motion with an AR simulation. The results from both ENA analyses and pre-/post-assessments indicate that AR promotes effective collaboration through dynamic communication and problem-solving strategies and has a profound positive impact on collaborative learning. Despite technical challenges, such as AR software and hardware issues, the overall impact on collaborative learning was positive. AR's interactive elements encouraged active participation, more profound comprehension of the content, and positive attitude changes toward science. This research underscores AR's potential in enhancing STEM education while highlighting the need to address technical and usability issues in AR applications. The encouraging results of this study should inspire and motivate further exploration and development of AR in education.

Keywords: Augmented Reality · Immersive Learning · STEM Education · Usability · Collaborative Problem-Solving · Computer-Supported Collaborative Learning

1 Introduction

1.1 Background

Augmented Reality (AR) offers interactive and immersive learning experiences that are particularly effective for comprehending complex STEM concepts (Psycharis et al., 2023; Sırakaya et al., 2020; Radu, 2019; Moro et al., 2023). It enhances scientific investigation, hands-on learning, learning emotions, conceptual comprehension, and spatial skills, all crucial in STEM education. Additionally, AR's unique capabilities, such as facilitating human-to-human interaction through see-through technology, are increasingly recognized for their specific benefits. These capabilities enable the overlay of virtual objects onto physical ones, creating seamless interactions and supporting collaborative problem-solving with peers (e.g., Marques et al., 2022). However, integrating immersive technologies poses new challenges, making it essential to prioritize user-friendliness and accessibility and consider potential side effects like technical difficulties

Y. J. Kim and Z. Swiecki (Eds.): icqe 2024, CCIS 2279, pp. 70–78, 2024.
https://doi.org/10.1007/978-3-031-76332-8_6

and cognitive overload when implementing them for educational purposes (Moro et al., 2023). User feedback gathered from epistemic empirical analysis studies plays a crucial role in enhancing user experiences and deepening our understanding of the impact of AR on learning outcomes. Further research is required to merge user experience considerations to successfully adopt AR in education (Law and Heintz, 2021) while avoiding usability and learning pitfalls.

This exploratory study utilizing AR in collaborative learning scenarios aims to observe and inform iterative design processes, ensuring that AR applications provide positive user experiences, ultimately fostering understanding, engagement, and collaboration among students. By employing ENA, we aim to investigate collaborative dynamics and usability problems that arise when pairs of students participate in collaborative AR tasks. We aspire to answer the following research questions (RQs):

- RQ1: How does AR-supported immersive collaborative learning impact the students' attitudes and learning outcomes?
- RQ2: How do collaboration dynamics differ between pairs engaged in AR-supported collaborative learning activities, and what specific usability challenges do they encounter?

1.2 Theoretical Framework

The present study is grounded in the literature on collaborative problem-solving (CPS) and existing CPS frameworks (e.g., Nelson, 1999), which underscore the importance of establishing shared knowledge and coordinating team efforts to address complex problems effectively. Our focus centers on the collaboration competency model proposed by Sun et al. (2020), highlighting the intricate interplay of ideas, skills, and knowledge that yield outcomes greater than individuals can achieve separately. They advocate for structured communication and strategic alignment of resources and expertise, which are crucial for collaboration's structural and dynamic aspects. While this model primarily addresses human-human interaction, it lays a foundational understanding for exploring how advanced technologies can enhance collaborative processes.

This study examines the role of technologies through the lens of distributed cognition theory (Hollan et al., 2000). This theory posits that knowledge and cognitive processes are distributed across the system, encompassing educational content, learners, and technology such as AR. AR tools actively transform the cognitive landscape by altering how learners interact with content, enhancing cognitive efficiency. As learners manipulate AR content, they distribute the cognitive workload between themselves and the technology, using the augmented environment to scaffold complex problem-solving tasks. Recent studies (e.g., Hoppenstedt et al., 2021) examine AR's specific educational contributions, demonstrating that AR can mitigate collaborative challenges through dynamic 3D visualizations and improved sensory information access. These capabilities foster a deeper understanding and retention of complex concepts compared to traditional non-AR environments. Building upon the CPS literature and the theory of distributed cognition, this study aims to provide a nuanced understanding of collaboration within AR-enhanced STEM education, focusing on the dynamics where students collaborate with digital objects.

2 Methods

We developed an immersive learning application called *HoloOrbits* to teach Kepler's laws of planetary motion using a Microsoft HoloLens2 headset. The app immerses students in an exoplanetary system, allowing them to visualize and collect data to understand orbital systems and Kepler's laws. The research involved six pairs of students in a one-hour session, including a pre-survey, a tutorial on using HoloLens2, a series of structured CPS tasks, a post-survey, and a semi-structured interview. The following tasks were designed to scaffold the learning experience, integrating individual and collaborative interactions with the AR simulation:

- **Task 1:** Introduced students to the fundamental concepts of an ellipse and its elliptical orbit through a mission statement and a pen-and-paper activity.
- **Task 2:** Transitioned students to the AR application, applying and visualizing the elliptical concepts within a simulated exoplanetary system.
- **Task 3:** Involved a strategic planning phase where students discussed their findings from Task 2 and prepared for a data measurement activity within the AR application. This stage was crucial for fostering collaborative skills and setting the stage for more advanced applications of their newly acquired knowledge.
- **Task 4:** Required participants to take measurements in the simulation to gather data, which they then used to calculate and collaboratively verify whether the system adhered to Kepler's first law of planetary motion. This task culminated in collaborative learning activities, integrating the skills and knowledge developed in the earlier tasks.

This paper focuses on analyzing Task 4 as it is designed to culminate collaborative learning activities, requiring complex interactions between students and will make them interact with the AR mechanics after getting used to them.

The study involved 12 participants (6 pairs; 42% female) from a Midwestern university, consisting of 11 graduate students and one undergraduate student. Participants were recruited through email and flyers targeting various student associations. The demographic breakdown included eight participants from STEM fields and four from non-STEM fields, providing a diverse sample for the study.

We collected quantitative and qualitative data: (1) quantitative data: pre- and post-surveys with four demographic questions, six subject matter questions, and eleven sentiment questions; (2) qualitative data: audio and video recordings of the participants' collaborative activities and interviews. We employed a mixed-methods approach. First, we applied thematic analysis (Braun et al., 2006) to analyze the pairs' conversation transcripts extracted during the collaborative activities. We divided the transcribed audio data into individual sentences to avoid excessive overlapping of codes in the same utterance. As shown in Table 1, our coding scheme categorized participants' discourse around collaboration based on the Sun et al. (2020) CPS framework and usability problems identified by Law and Heintz (2021). Two coders applied the coding scheme to ensure consistency, achieving a high inter-rater reliability score of 0.92 using Cohen's Kappa.

We then utilized the ENA Web Tool (version 1.7.0) to organize the coded data into 'conversations,' defined as the complete session for each pair. Within these conversations, we further divided the data into stanzas, averaging four utterances per stanza to maintain

Table 1. Coding Scheme

Facet	Sub facet	Description
Constructing Shared Knowledge	• Build on other ideas to improve solutions	• Builds on others' ideas to improve solutions • Talks about specific topics/concepts and ideas on problem-solving • Proposes specific solutions • Talks about the givens and constraints of a specific task
	• Validate knowledge	• Recognizes and verifies understanding of others' ideas • Confirms understanding by asking questions/paraphrasing • Repairs misunderstandings
Executing Team Solutions/ Negotiation	• Disagreement	• Interrupts or talks over others • Does not respond when spoken to • Is rude to others • Refusal of statement or concept
	• Agreement	• Relates to 'Responds to others' questions/ideas • Involves discussing and agreeing on shared goals and actively engaging in team coordination • Provides reasons to support/refute a potential solution • Talks about results • Agreement on shared objectives, roles, and goals
Maintaining Team Functions	• Proactive monitoring	• Continuous monitoring and regulation of team progress • Adjusting actions as necessary to meet objectives
	• Taking initiative	• Takes initiatives to advance collaboration processes
	• Positive socio-affective behavior	• Compliments or encourages others

(continued)

Table 1. (*continued*)

Facet	Sub facet	Description
Challenges	• UI and interactivity problems	• Problems with control and manipulation • Problems, and inconsistencies in UI/UX
	• Technical challenges of the device	• Overheating, Frame Rate • Difficulties in interacting with the device

coherence. The ideal window size for our ENA was determined to be four utterances, effectively capturing the dynamic flow of conversation within the structured sessions.

3 Results and Discussion

3.1 RQ1

To address RQ1, we examined the average learning outcomes for students participating in the AR-supported activity. During the pre-and post-test, the participants were evaluated on their performance with a maximum possible score of 12. All the students showed improvement, but there was some variation among them. The results indicated a range of normalized learning gains, suggesting differences in the amount of students' progress. Specifically, Pair 1 showed a small improvement with a normalized gain of 0.250. In contrast, Pair 2 and Pair 4 achieved the highest possible normalized gain of 1.000, indicating that they had reached the maximum improvement based on their pretest scores. Pair 3 and Pair 5 showed normalized gains of 0.625 and 0.750, respectively. Lastly, Pair 6 demonstrated a moderate normalized gain of 0.500.

The participants' interests in astronomy and their perceptions regarding science also showed improvement. The results indicate improvement in participants' ability to explain Kepler's laws, as evidenced by the increase in the mean score from 2.25 (pre-survey) to 3.75 (post-survey). Additionally, there was a positive shift in participants' enjoyment of learning new scientific concepts, with the average response increasing from 4.00 to 4.25. Attitudes toward the inclusiveness of science, as reflected in responses to "Science is only for smart people," also showed a positive change, decreasing from a mean of 1.67 to 1.33, suggesting a reduced agreement with the statement. Regarding the self-perception as potential scientists, participants showed slight improvements. The mean score for "I could be a good scientist" increased from 3.92 to 4.08. Notably, there were no significant changes in participants' preferences for learning through activities (mean = 4.25), and their perception of the relevance of astronomy remained consistent (mean = 3.75).

It is worth noting that although all participants showed improvement, the variation in normalized learning gains necessitates caution in interpreting our results, particularly in attributing educational outcomes solely to the AR-supported environment. Our findings show the shifts in students' interest in astronomy and self-perceptions of science. For instance, the increase in the enjoyment of learning new concepts and changes in the perception of science and astronomy indicate their positive learning experiences with AR (Holland et al., 2000; Ibáñez and Delgado-Kloos, 2018; Kerawalla et al., 2006). Moreover, the findings indicate the potential of AR technology in enhancing understanding through more tangible interactions with scientific concepts.

3.2 RQ2

To address RQ2, we used ENA to explore the specific aspects of AR technology that either facilitate or hinder effective collaboration. Figure 1 reveals the collaborative strategies employed by each student pair through visually distinctive elements (Marquart et al., 2018; Shaffer et al., 2016). Each colored square, alongside its corresponding dotted line, represents the frequent co-occurrence of specific nodes for a particular pair. This visual differentiation offers key insights into the interaction patterns. For instance, Pair 1 exhibits a methodical style of collaboration, characterized by their regular and systematic engagement with the task elements. This suggests that Pair 1 likely employs a controlled and thorough approach to collaboration, regularly regulating and monitoring their interactions to ensure consistent progress. In contrast, Pair 2's proximity to consensus-driven nodes indicates a collaborative approach that prioritizes group agreement and shared decision-making. This inference is drawn from their frequent engagements with nodes involving collective input and mutual understanding, suggesting that their collaboration style leans towards achieving consensus among members before making decisions.

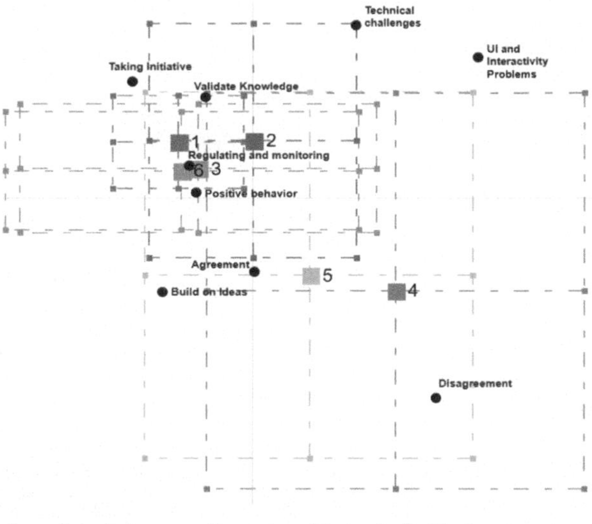

Fig. 1. A projection plot of the overall session (Tasks 1–4). Each colored square represents a student pair. Each node represents a code of our coding scheme.

We then compared the networks across the pairs. We found interesting patterns of collaborative behaviors in an AR learning environment, including ideation, consensus building, technical challenge navigation, engagement with disagreement, self-regulation, monitoring, and proactive problem-solving. For example, Pair 1 and Pair 5 (Fig. 2) show a strong connection between the 'Build on Ideas' and 'Agreement' nodes, indicating a process where participants engage in a harmonious negotiation process to construct shared knowledge. Pairs exhibit a synergy where new ideas are welcomed and critically evaluated, as seen in the connection to 'Validate Knowledge.' Pair 1 has a conservative approach, while Pair 5 shows a more dynamic interaction with a blend of agreement and moderate disagreements. Both groups showed positive socio-affective behavior and are separate from central nodes. Positive social behavior was likely present but not at the forefront or closely connected to the other aspects of the problem-solving process.

As such, CPS fosters significant improvements in students' understanding through effective team collaboration, where establishing a shared understanding and pursuing joint actions are crucial (Graesser et al., 2018). Our findings suggest that CPS deepens students' comprehension of complex subjects like astronomy and enhances their problem-solving abilities. Supporting this, Strijbos et al. (2004) emphasize the importance of assigning functional roles within teams, improving coordination, and leading to more effective collaboration, particularly in understanding complex scientific concepts such as Kepler's laws. Together, this calls for future studies of assigning and examining the roles of group members and their impact on improving learning outcomes and fostering deeper engagement in an AR-supported learning environment.

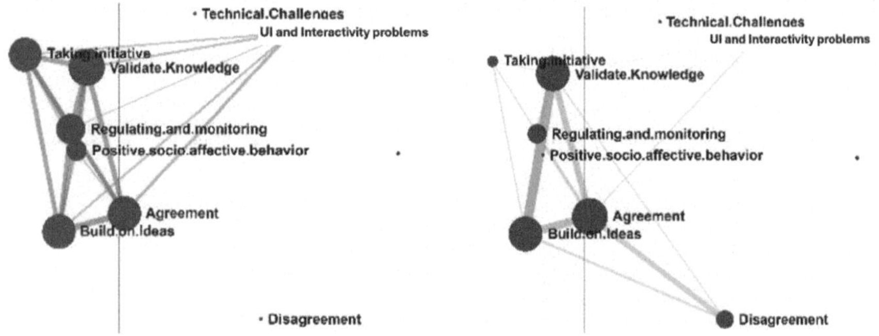

Fig. 2. Comparison of Pair 1 (left) and Pair 5 (right) ENA plots for Task 4

4 Conclusion

Integrating AR into educational settings enhances learning by providing tangible and interactive experiences within real-world contexts. ENA maps and analyzes these interactions, offering a quantitative complement to qualitative observations. Key findings reveal distinct collaboration strategies, effective consensus-building, adept handling of technical challenges, and improved learning outcomes. However, despite positive impacts, technical and usability issues were also identified, emphasizing the importance of addressing these factors to optimize the educational benefits of immersive technologies like AR. As such, our approach is crucial, particularly for providing insights into AR's implementation and design and fostering an inclusive and engaging learning environment. Further research with larger samples and diverse settings is necessary to generalize these findings and refine AR educational strategies.

References

1. Braun, V., Clarke, V.: Using thematic analysis in psychology. Qual. Res. Psychol. **3**(2), 77–101 (2006). https://doi.org/10.1191/1478088706qp063oa
2. Hollan, J., Hutchins, E., Kirsh, D.: Distributed Cognition: Toward a New Foundation for Human-Computer Interaction Research. ACM Transactions on Computer-Human-Interaction **7**, 174–196 (2000). https://doi.org/10.1145/353485.353487
3. Hoppenstedt, E., Radu, I., Joy, T., Schneider, B.: Augmented reality in collaborative problem solving: a qualitative study of challenges and solutions. International Conference on Computer Supported Collaborative Learning (2021). https://par.nsf.gov/biblio/10276295
4. Law, E.L.-C., Heintz, M.: Systematic review and validation of the Usability Problem Inspector (UPI): A tool for the identification of usability problems. International Journal of Human-Computer Studies **149**, 102601 (2021). https://doi.org/10.1016/j.ijhcs.2021.102601
5. Marquart, C.L., Hinojosa, C., Swiecki, Z., Eagan, B., Shaffer, D.W.: Epistemic Network Analysis (Version 1.5.2) [Software] (2018). http://app.epistemicnetwork.org
6. Marques, B., Silva, S., Alves, J., Araujo, T., Dias, P., Santos, B.S.: A conceptual model and taxonomy for collaborative augmented reality. IEEE Trans. Visual Comput. Graphics **28**(12), 5113–5133 (2021)
7. Moro, C., Phelps, C., Redmond, P., Stromberga, Z.: HoloLens and mobile augmented reality in medical and health science education: A randomized controlled trial. Br. J. Edu. Technol. **52**(2), 680–694 (2021). https://doi.org/10.1111/bjet.13049
8. Papadakis, S., Kalogiannakis, M.: Editorial: The impact of smart screen technologies and accompanied apps on young children learning and developmental outcomes, volume 2. Front. Educ. **8**, 1249116 (2023). https://doi.org/10.3389/feduc.2023.1249116
9. Psycharis, S., Sdravopoulou, K., Botsari, E.: Augmented reality in STEM education: Mapping out the future. In: Lecture Notes in Networks and Systems, Vol. 767, pp. 677–688. Presented at TLIC 2023: The Learning Ideas Conference (2023)
10. Radu, I., Schneider, B.: What Can We Learn from Augmented Reality (AR) Benefits and Drawbacks of AR for Inquiry-based Learning of Physics. In: Proceedings of the 2019 CHI Conference on Human Factors in Computing Systems (CHI '19), pp. 1–12. Association for Computing Machinery (2019). https://doi.org/10.1145/3290605.3300774
11. Ruis, A.R., Lee, C.H., Shaffer, D.W.: Toward a framework for assessing complex collaborative problem solving in online environments. Journal of the Learning Sciences **29**(1), 107–131 (2020). https://doi.org/10.1080/10508406.2019.1707677
12. Ruis, A.R., Siebert-Evenstone, A.L., Pozen, R., Eagan, B.R., Shaffer, D.W.: Finding common ground: a method for measuring recent temporal context in analyses of complex, collaborative thinking. In: Lund, K., Niccolai, G., Lavoué, E., Hmelo-Silver, C., Gweon, G., Baker, M. (eds.) A wide lens: Combining embodied, enactive, extended, and embedded learning in collaborative settings: 13^(th) International Conference on Computer-Supported Collaborative Learning (CSCL), Vol. I, pp. 136–143 (2019)
13. Ruis, A.R., Rosser, A.A., Quandt-Walle, C., Nathwani, J.N., Shaffer, D.W., Pugh, C.M.: The hands and head of a surgeon: modeling operative competency with multimodal epistemic network analysis. Am. J. Surg. **216**(5), 835–840 (2018)
14. Shaffer, D.W.: Quantitative ethnography. Cathcart Press, Madison, WI (2017)

15. Shaffer, D.W., Collier, W., Ruis, A.R.: A tutorial on epistemic network analysis: Analyzing the structure of connections in cognitive, social, and interaction data. Journal of Learning Analytics **3**(3), 9–45 (2016)
16. Shaffer, D.W., Ruis, A.R.: Epistemic network analysis: A worked example of theory-based learning analytics. In: Lang, C., Siemens, G., Wise, A.F., Gasevic, D. (eds.) Handbook of learning analytics, pp. 175–187. Society for Learning Analytics Research (2017)
17. Siebert-Evenstone, A., et al.: In search of conversational grain size: Modelling semantic structure using moving stanza windows. Journal of Learning Analytics **4**(3), 123–139 (2017). https://doi.org/10.18608/jla.2017.43.7
18. Sirakaya, M., Alsancak Sirakaya, D.: Augmented reality in STEM education: a systematic review. Interact. Learn. Environ. **30**(8), 1556–1569 (2020). https://doi.org/10.1080/10494820.2020.1722713
19. Sun, C., Shute, V.J., Stewart, A., Yonehiro, J., Duran, N., D'Mello, S.: Towards a generalized competency model of collaborative problem solving. Comput. Educ. **143**, 103672 (2020). https://doi.org/10.1016/j.compedu.2019.103672

Understanding the Impact of Observer Effects on Student Affect

Xiner Liu[1(✉)], Ashish Gurung[2], Ryan S. Baker[1], and Amanda Barany[1]

[1] University of Pennsylvania, Philadelphia, PA 19104, USA
xiner@upenn.edu

[2] Carnegie Mellon University, Pittsburgh, PA 15213, USA

Abstract. The measurement of affect presents a challenge for researchers in quantitative ethnography and related communities, as each of the several possible methods for obtaining ground truth have downsides and often disagree with each other. One common method is field observations; some accounts have raised concerns about observer effects, but further research is needed to understand how much observer effect is present and exactly how observer effects manifest. In this study, we attempt to quantify and detail observer effects in classroom data collected using the Baker Rodrigo Ocumpaugh Monitoring Protocol (BROMP). We leveraged prediction models developed in prior work to assess students' affect and disengaged behavior, during periods where observers were present or not present. Statistical analyses revealed differences in both affective states and behaviors on days when field observations were conducted. When observers were present, students showed increases in concentration and decreases in frustration, off-task behavior, and gaming the system. Findings suggest that the collection of observation data changes the proportion of behavior and affect observed, which should be taken into account when designing, implementing, and analyzing observation-based research. We discuss implications of this finding for quantitative ethnography, when observation data is systematized, visualized, and compared. Our findings do not suggest that the individual observations of specific affective states or behaviors are invalid but offer insights for QE scholars to consider when collecting and analyzing observation data.

Keywords: Observer Effect · Quantifying Observer Effect · BROMP · Affect · Classroom Observation · Field Observation

1 Introduction

Quantitative Ethnographic (QE) research is defined by the formal and systematic examination of data in context to maximize understanding of complex processes while minimizing bias [52]. As such, QE research exploring concepts such as affect (the experience of emotion; emotion in context) and disengagement has continued to expand [34]. Scholars studying affect in the QE community and neighboring communities have employed a variety of techniques to structure or "quantify" data after collection by segmenting it into lines or segments that have interpretable meaning, coding for the presence of that

Y. J. Kim and Z. Swiecki (Eds.): icqe 2024, CCIS 2279, pp. 79–94, 2024.
https://doi.org/10.1007/978-3-031-76332-8_7

meaning, and grouping coded lines for the purpose of visualization or comparison. Two key issues that impact the interpretability of these results must be addressed, however. First, datasets must be "thick" enough in detail and contextual information for results to reliably represent subtle phenomena such as affect or disengagement. This poses a particular challenge in some cases, as data sources are often incomplete secondhand records of an experience (e.g., transcripts), or are perspectival (e.g. self-report data). Second, the process of systematizing the data positions researchers as the primary "instrument" of knowledge creation [5], which increases the likelihood of issues around fairness and validity, particularly when interpreting secondhand and perspectival data. While practices exist to help address issues of fairness and validity that emerge during these post hoc processes (e.g., inter-rater reliability metrics), they too have been critiqued as inconsistent at best and prone to error at worst [24, 53].

One possible solution to these issues is to conduct field observations [18], in which trained researchers can view and systematically annotate affect in real time. This approach has potential to maximize the contextual information available to the interpreting researcher and helps to ensure that coding and systematization are embedded in the context being studied. Once an ethnographer enters the research context, however, the potential for observer effects (in this case, shifts in the way student affect manifests as a result of being observed) emerges [30]. Observer effects have been recognized as potentially impactful on QE research [52], but further exploration is needed to determine the extent of observer effects and the ways in which they manifest, so that we better understand the impacts they have on the complex behavior and latent constructs such as affect that we are studying. In this study, we attempt to quantify and describe the observer effects that emerged in classroom observation data collected using the Baker Rodrigo Ocumpaugh Monitoring Protocol (BROMP), widely used in other research communities. We use a different method, automated detectors of affect (themselves originally developed using BROMP, but with separate data), to compare students' affect and disengaged behavior during periods when observers were present and when they were not. Our research question is: What are the impacts of observer effects in classroom observation data on how affect and disengagement manifest?

2 Observation Research in QE

The underpinning of QE is high quality data [52]. While the majority of QE research has involved textual data (e.g., [5, 34]) other research in our community has relied upon computer interaction log data [37], observational data [2], and sensor data [4].

However, all data collection introduces distortion [28] as the very act of collecting data impacts the phenomena being studied. For example, placing a camera in a public location can change the behavior of individuals in that location [56], interviews can provoke changes in the participant's thinking [15, 40], and self-report in questionnaires can influence an individuals' emotions (cf. in [9]) and physiological reactions [35].

There has been considerable recent interest in phenomena surrounding affect and disengagement during learning [20, 21, 38], including within the QE community [3, 36]. Research on these constructs predominantly relies on two sources for acquiring coded data for analysis: self-report data (e.g., [32]) and external observations (e.g., [23]). Self-report data offers the advantage of obtaining direct insights from students themselves regarding their learning experiences. However, it is prone to response biases stemming from limited self-awareness [57] or social desirability/demand [39], potentially compromising the accuracy and reliability of the collected information.

External expert judgments can address these limitations, offering more standardized evaluations of students' affective states and behaviors [54]. There are several types of external judgment, each conferring unique benefits and limitations. For instance, text replays, which consist of segments of actions in log data that are reviewed and coded for specific behaviors, have been found to be 2–6 times faster than other labeling methods [8]; but may overlook crucial non-verbal cues such as facial expressions and body movements. By contrast, video replays enable more comprehensive reviews of students' actions and interactions, allowing for convenient rewatches at any given time [50]. However, the processing and coding of substantial video data can be time-consuming and resource-intensive, and the presence of cameras can change behavior [22, 33].

Field observations afford observers an even more in-depth view of students' experiences during learning. During field observations, trained observers, following a specific annotation scheme (cf. [50]), physically attend classroom sessions and systematically record students' affective states and behaviors in real-time. This approach provides observers highly authentic information about students' learning [18], but the presence of observers in the classrooms may lead to observer effects, where students' affective states and behaviors might be influenced due to their awareness of being observed [30].

However, the impact of observer effects has been much more widely reported in an informal fashion than explicitly studied [55] although some exceptions exist. The studies that have attempted to identify explicit quantitative observer effects have in many cases failed to obtain any observer effect at all. For example, Crofoot et al. use radio telemetry to argue that monkey behavior is not different during observations, once monkeys have habituated [19]. Hagel et al. also found that human observers did not change handwashing behavior compared to behavior measured through logs in automated dispensers [31]. On the other hand, notifying individuals that their social media posts are being monitored appears to substantially change their posting behavior [51]. In addition, the research attempting to quantify observer effects seems to largely focus on straightforward behaviors rather than the more complex behaviors or latent constructs (such as emotions, affect, self-regulation) typically investigated in the QE community.

In this paper, we therefore empirically investigate whether observer effects occur for field observations conducted to study complex behavior and latent constructs. We do so in the context of BROMP (the Baker Rodrigo Ocumpaugh Monitoring Protocol; [12]), one of the most widely used approaches for classroom observation of complex behavior and emotion. In this paper, we investigate the observer effect associated with BROMP through an analysis of interaction log files sourced from the widely used ASSISTments learning platform. We compare the same students both when they were being observed during BROMP and when they were not being observed with BROMP (both earlier and later in the school year). We use previously validated prediction models (themselves initially developed using BROMP) to assess students' affect and disengaged behaviors during these periods – the same constructs being assessed by BROMP, to see if those constructs are impacted by observer effects. Then, we conducted statistical tests comparing the same group of students between the observed and non-observed periods to assess whether the presence of observers influenced the prevalence of emotional or behavioral displays among students. We also investigate whether these differences are consistent across students in urban, rural, and suburban settings.

By developing methods for understanding the impact of observer effects, we can determine the degree to which an observational method produces data which is a reliable indicator of the authentic (unobserved) manifestation of the constructs being studied, and fair to the lived experiences of research subjects [52, 53].

3 The BROMP Protocol

BROMP is a widely used protocol for conducting observations of student affect and complex behavior in educational settings [12]. BROMP utilizes a momentary time sampling approach to code students' behavior and affect, one student at a time, in a predetermined order, in order to ensure a representative sample and avoid focusing on extreme events. During observations, the observers focus on one student until visible affect or behavior is identified or 20 s have elapsed, after which they proceed to the next student. The observers make a comprehensive and holistic evaluation of the students' affect and behavior, considering their facial expression, posture, utterances, activity, and other factors. Observations are typically recorded using a custom-built application called HART (Human Affect Recording Tool; [45]), which provides precise time stamps of each observation to facilitate unobtrusive data collection.

The influence of BROMP is not limited to the United States alone [12]. With over 150 certified coders in 7 countries, BROMP has been applied to study a wide range of phenomena, such as learners' cognition [42], on-task reflection [29], teachers' proactive remediation [41], affect sequences [36], and the effect of engagement interventions [7]. BROMP has been used in several studies to generate training labels for the development of automated detectors, including detectors of affective states [16] and disengaged behaviors such as gaming the system [10], off-task behavior [17], and wheel-spinning [46]. These detectors, in turn, have been used for a number of purposes, including to inform and contextualize interviews [3, 11] and also to study phenomena such as participation in stem-related careers [1]. Overall, BROMP has generated data which has been extensively used in many research communities, including QE [3, 36].

BROMP's design integrates several strategies to mitigate the observer effect [12]. Before sessions, observers coordinate with teachers to minimize extra interaction and clarify their role to students if needed. During observations, observers maintain a neutral and unobtrusive disposition to minimize disruptions, including avoiding eye contact, not looking directly at the student being observed, dressing in bland colors, and moving slowly ("mosey don't walk"). If a student becomes aware of being observed, the data for that particular observation is discarded to ensure the integrity of the data. Furthermore, the HART app allows labeling with small handheld devices, which are relatively unobtrusive and hard for students to see. However, it is not clear whether these measures have been successful at addressing observer effects.

4 Context

In this study, we investigated the potential observer effect of conducting BROMP observations within the ASSISTments platform, an online learning system that is primarily focused on mathematics. With a user base of around 500,000 students and 20,000 teachers, ASSISTments is widely used, primarily in the United States but also in over 20 other countries [26]. The platform breaks down problems into steps, provides hints at each stage, and offers the answer through a "bottom-out hint" when requested. The assessment process offers assistance, scaffolding, and feedback to students, while equipping teachers with detailed information about students' knowledge and performance for targeted assistance. Several randomized controlled studies have shown significant learning gains for students who regularly engage with the platform [25, 27, 43].

4.1 Dataset and Population

ASSISTments provides substantial support for external researchers by offering publicly available datasets that include rich interaction log data, along with field observation data and longitudinal student outcomes. To investigate the potential impact of classroom observers on students' affective experiences and behaviors during online learning, we used both the interaction log data and the data on field observations conducted during the same years, obtaining the field observation data from the ASSISTments webpage (https://sites.google.com/site/assistmentsdata/) and other data from the same year directly from the ASSISTments team, by request. The field observation data were systematically collected by human observers during in-class computer lab sessions [44]. During observations, the handheld devices for affect labeling were synchronized to the educational software logging server. Leveraging the time stamp and user ID in the interaction log file, we were able to select students who were part of the field observations and discern whether specific actions by the student occurred within or outside the days when observation occurred.

Our secondary analysis involves a sample of middle school students from three distinct populations in the Northeastern region of the United States, with data originally reported in a prior study by [44]. The first group, drawn from two schools in Maine, consists of predominantly white students from a rural background with low socioeconomic status, over 50% of whom receive free or reduced-price lunch (which is commonly used as an indicator of poverty in the United States). The second group, drawn from three suburban schools in Massachusetts, consists mainly of mid-to-high socioeconomic-status White and East-Asian students, with less than 20% receiving free or reduced-price lunches. The third group of students came from an urban setting in Massachusetts and comprises primarily lower-income Latinos/students of Puerto Rican origin, with English as their first language, as well as African American and Balkan students, over half of whom received free or reduced-price lunch. Inclusion of these distinct populations in the study sample enables us to comprehensively investigate potential differential impacts of human observers on various student populations.

5 Method

5.1 Inferring Students' Affective States

The primary goal of this study was to quantify observer effects and study their magnitude during classroom observations, focusing on potential changes in the frequency of students' affective states and disengaged behaviors. To accomplish this goal, we derived students' affective experiences and behavioral responses during both the observation and non-observation periods; the same constructs being studied using BROMP.

We inferred students' affective states (i.e., boredom, engaged concentration, frustration, and confusion) using the interaction log files data from ASSISTments. The interaction log files were pre-processed and run through the ASSISTments affect detectors from [16], which utilized the Long-Short Term Memory (LSTM) algorithm. Evaluated through a rigorous 5-fold cross-validation procedure at the student level, these detectors achieved an average AUC ROC of 0.77 across four affective states (AUC ROC is the most relevant metric for our current analyses, since our analyses aggregate across detector confidences), as shown in Table 1. It is worth noting that these detectors were originally developed using BROMP observations (on other data) as ground truth. This choice enables us to avoid confounds if ground truth obtained in other fashions (such as self-report) lead to the constructs of interest being defined subtly differently.

The source code of these models was made available to us by the ASSISTments team. This code computes the confidence scores for each affective state at the level of 20-s clips. For example, if the engaged concentration detector gives an output of 0.67, it signifies a moderate level of confidence, indicating that the detector believes that there is a 67% probability that the student is experiencing engaged concentration based on their actions. To ensure comparability among the affect detectors, we implemented a normalization procedure. This involved subtracting the minimum value from each score and dividing it by the difference between the maximum and minimum confidence values for that state (across all data). Within each clip, we then averaged across all clips in a problem to identify the most prevalent affective state for each problem.

5.2 Inferring Students' Disengaged Behaviors

We used the same interaction log data for identifying students' disengaged behaviors, consisting of instances of being off-task and gaming the system. Although machine-learned detectors of gaming the system and off-task behavior have been developed for ASSISTments [49], these detectors are not currently available from the ASSISTments platform. Therefore, we used different models of gaming the system (e.g. [48]) and off-task behavior [6]. These predictions were also generated at the clip level. However, a different clip size was used for these detectors, based on the way the gaming detector in [48] was developed. In ASSISTments, when students are presented with an "original" problem, they are expected to provide the answer without needing to detail individual steps, as long as they solve the problem correctly on their initial attempt. However, if students fail to provide the correct answer, they may need to answer "scaffolding questions" correctly in order to successfully complete the problem. As a result, a clip was defined as the sequence of actions starting from the first action on an original unscaffolded problem to the last attempt before the subsequent original unscaffolded problem. This definition implies that a clip can consist of just one action or more than 50 actions. [48] developed a cognitive model leveraging knowledge engineering to discern instances of gaming behavior. In our study, we applied this detector to the current data set to obtain predictions at the same clip level as previously defined.

For off-task behavior, we use a model proposed by [6] and also used as a feature in the machine-learned ASSISTments model [49]. [6] compared a machine-learned detector of off-task behavior to a simpler approach that used a fixed time cutoff of 80 s. While the sophisticated model outperformed the cutoff model in distinguishing between on-task and off-task behavior, the cutoff model still exhibited a reasonable correlation of 0.46 with classroom observations of off-task behavior. Given the unavailability of the machine learned model for our current data set, we used this cutoff model to identify students' off-task behavior, classifying clips as involving off-task behavior if any action within the clip exceeded 80 s.

5.3 Data Aggregation

The data were filtered to include clips from active student users who were present both before, during, and after the observations. We then created a time period variable based on the timestamps, which had a value of 1 if the students were using the system during the field observations (same day) and 0 otherwise. Using these filtered datasets, we constructed two pivot tables to calculate the clip-level percentages of learners' affective states or behaviors for both periods. For affective states, the dataset was grouped based on user ID, and periods. Then, four separate columns were created to represent different affect categories: boredom, concentration, frustration, and confusion. The same approach was employed for summarizing off-task and gaming behaviors. Within each period, we calculated the occurrence count for each affective state/behavior and expressed it as a percentage relative to the total number of clips.

5.4 Statistical Analysis and Benjamini-Hochberg Procedure

Prior to conducting the statistical test, we examined the normality assumption of affect/behavior percentages through visual inspections of histograms and normal probability plots. The outcomes indicated notable deviations from a normal distribution. Concentration appeared to be highly left-skewed, while boredom, frustration, and confusion showed highly right-skewed distributions. These findings are consistent with the observations reported by [16]. Off-task percentages displayed a relatively uniform distribution ranging from 0 to 1 for both observed and non-observed periods. The percentages of gaming the system behaviors, on the other hand, displayed right-skewness for both periods, aligning with the findings of [48].

To further validate the results, we performed the Shapiro-Wilk test to assess the normality assumptions; results reaffirmed that the percentages do not follow a normal distribution ($p < 0.01$). Therefore, given the structure of the data and the presence of paired students across the observed and non-observed periods, we proceeded with using the Wilcoxon Matched-Pairs Signed-Ranks Test, which is suitable for non-parametric data analysis and dependent samples, without relying on the assumption of normality.

In assessing our findings, we employed the Benjamini-Hochberg procedure (B&H; [14]) which is designed to control the false discovery rate (FDR) when multiple tests are conducted. Benjamini-Hochberg was used instead of Benjamini-Yekutieli due to the lack of positive regression dependency between tests. When applying B&H, we identified statistically significant findings while maintaining control over the overall occurrence of false positives. The procedure involves arranging the obtained p-values in ascending order and comparing them to critical thresholds that are adjusted based on the number of tests conducted (i.e., adjusted alpha value). These critical thresholds guarantee that the expected proportion of false discoveries among all rejected hypotheses remains below the predetermined FDR level (0.05). Specifically, the first p-value is compared to a threshold of (0.05 divided by the number of tests), the second p-value is compared to (0.05 divided by the number of tests minus 1), and so forth, until the last p-value is compared to 0.05. If a p-value is less than or equal to its corresponding critical threshold, it indicates statistical significance at the chosen FDR level. Alternatively, a p-value greater than the critical threshold but less than twice that threshold indicated marginal significance at the chosen level. In our study, we investigated the potential observer effect on four affective states and two learning behaviors, leading to 6 statistical tests across all regions and 18 statistical tests across the three subregions. We compared the obtained p-values from tests conducted on all regions or subregions to their adjusted alpha values based on 6 and 18 tests, respectively.

6 Results

6.1 Observer Effect on Learners' Affective States

Table 2 presents the statistical results for affect percentages during and not during observations. We first consider boredom. Overall, no significant differences in boredom percentages were observed among all students considered together. When analyzing students from specific subregions, boredom levels did not significantly differ for students from suburban and urban areas. Students in rural regions appeared to be less bored during the observations than outside of them ($p = 0.036$), but this difference becomes only marginally significant after applying the B&H post-hoc correction ($\alpha = 0.035$). By contrast, the results revealed an increase in concentration percentages during observations when all regions are considered together ($p = 0.049$), which remained marginally significant after the B&H correction ($\alpha_{adjusted} = 0.067$). The results indicated that the presence of observers in the classroom seemed to be associated with higher levels of student concentration. However, there were no significant differences in concentration levels between periods within rural and suburban regions, and the apparent decrease in confidence observed in urban regions did not retain significance after the correction ($p = 0.029$, $\alpha = 0.014$).

A significant difference was also found in frustration levels between observed and non-observed periods when all regions were considered together ($p = 0.019$). Specifically, distribution plots (Fig. 1) revealed that students experienced lower levels of frustration during observations compared to when they were not being observed. In specific, the mean during the observation period was 0.004, whereas the mean outside the observation period was 0.008. When examining the results for individual regions, only the

Table 1. Statistical Results for Affect Percentages During and Not During Observations

Affective States	Region	Sample Size	W Statistics	p-value	Median Not During	Median During
	All	202	15262	0.792	0.04	0.05
Boredom	Rural	10	16	0.036	0.05	0.02
	Suburban	125	5368	0.781	0.03	0.04
	Urban	67	1841	0.626	0.07	0.08
	All	202	16258	0.049*	0.83	0.86
Engaged	Rural	10	34	0.151	0.88	0.90
Concentration	Suburban	125	6409	0.475	0.81	0.87
	Urban	67	1782	0.029	0.85	0.86
	All	202	766	0.019**	0.00	0.00
Frustration	Rural	14	7	0.462	0.00	0.00
	Suburban	155	119	0.004**	0.00	0.00
	Urban	79	199	0.927	0.00	0.00
	All	202	12782	0.097	0.06	0.06
Confusion	Rural	10	33	0.363	0.04	0.06
	Suburban	125	5798	0.866	0.06	0.07
	Urban	67	918	0.007**	0.06	0.05

* Marginally Significant after B&H correction.
** Significant after B&H correction

suburban region showed a significant difference in frustration levels ($p = 0.004$). For suburban learners, the mean during the observation period was 0.003, whereas the mean outside the observation period was 0.007. This finding is shown in the distribution plot on the right side of Fig. 1.

No significant differences were observed in confusion levels between observed and non-observed periods when all regions were considered together. This was also seen in rural and suburban schools. However, a significant decrease in confusion level was observed during the observation period within students in urban regions ($p = 0.007$).

6.2 Observer Effect on Learners' Behaviors

We next present the statistical results for disengaged behavior percentages during and not during observations in Table 3. The analysis of off-task behavior revealed significantly less off-task behavior for all regions were considered together when observers were present in the classroom ($p < 0.001$), a finding also seen in the urban region ($p = 0.005$) but not in rural and suburban regions.

A significant though small decrease in gaming the system behavior occurred during observations when all regions were considered together ($p < 0.001$). The mean amount

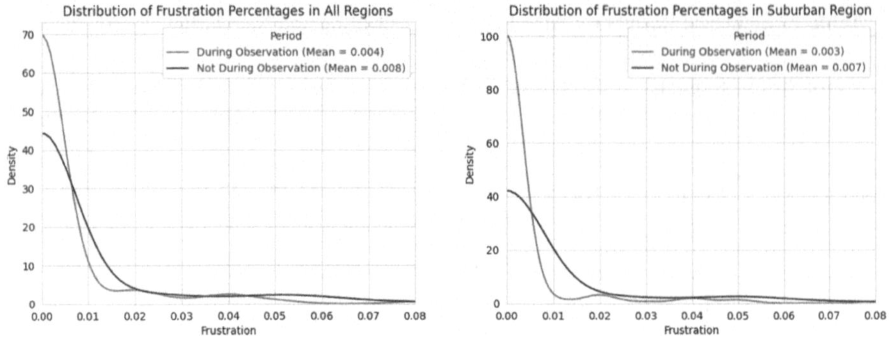

Fig. 1. Distribution of Frustration Percentages in All regions (*left*) and Suburban Region (*right*)

Table 2. Statistical Results for Behavior Percentages During and Not During Observations

Affective States	Region	Sample Size	W Statistics	p-value	Median Not During	Median During
	All	717	106151	0.000**	0.299	0.270
Off-task	Rural	100	1885	0.143	0.276	0.231
	Suburban	288	17832	0.083	0.227	0.220
	Urban	329	22336	0.005**	0.400	0.333
	All	717	17029	0.000**	0.000	0.000
Gaming	Rural	100	275	0.000**	0.005	0.000
the System	Suburban	288	925	0.249	0.000	0.000
	Urban	329	6831	0.047	0.000	0.000

* Marginally Significant after B&H correction.
** Significant after B&H correction

of gaming during the observation period was 0.02, while the mean amount of gaming outside the observation period was 0.03. This decrease was also seen in rural areas ($p < 0.001$), while no significant difference was observed for urban and suburban schools.

7 Discussion and Conclusion

Within quantitative ethnography, our methods draw conclusions that are shaped by the codes that we obtain and the structure we set. The quality of those choices has a significant impact on the validity of the conclusions we can draw, and whether they are fair to phenomena and individuals being studied [53]. All active measurements impact the subjects being studied in some way, but the impact of measurements on the phenomena being studied are themselves under-studied. We attempted to quantify the degree to which classroom observations conducting using the Baker Rodrigo Ocumpaugh Monitoring Protocol (BROMP) have observer effects, and how the observer effect impacts the prevalence of different affective experiences and behaviors observed among students. Our findings revealed significant observer effects: a noticeable increase in engaged concentration, as well as a decrease in frustration, off-task behavior, and gaming the system when human observers were present in the classroom. Some differences in observer effects were found between demographic cohorts of students – better understanding these differences might require interviews of students during or after observations.

The existence of an observer effect raises important questions about the meaning and validity of codes collected through BROMP and similar methods. One possible interpretation is that the presence of human observers has actually changed the distribution of affective states and behavior among students. For example, the presence of more adults in the room might prompt students to focus more on the learning task, producing all the effects seen. In other words, students might genuinely be gaming the system less and taking the learning task more seriously. If this is the case, then BROMP observation is not changing how behaviors and affect manifest but is instead changing how much (and perhaps when) behaviors and affect occur. This would not substantially impact the validity of automated detectors trained using these codes but might impact the validity of conclusions drawn from analyzing BROMP data directly in QE research.

If the observer effect only alters the proportion of observed affect and behavior in a dataset, the impact on visual and statistical analyses of the data is likely to produce consistent findings, particularly for epistemic networks, which are normalized to account for different unit sizes. However, if observer effects instead lead to changes in how the same affect and behavior manifest, it could lead to more serious consequences for reliability and validity. For example, our results could also be due to students consciously concealing or feigning different affect than what they are genuinely experiencing. In this case, even though the students may appear to be more focused or less frustrated during observation, their expressions may stem solely from self-presentation considerations. Consequently, merely observing the students may fail to provide an accurate reflection of their true emotional and behavioral dynamics, as their external reactions no longer authentically represent their inner experiences. The labels collected through these observations would not truly represent the learners' states and conditions. If this were the case, it becomes relevant to ask what the previous correlations between BROMP-derived detectors and other measures means. Is engaged concentration genuinely associated with better learning (e.g., [49])? Or is a combination of genuine engaged concentration and the situational awareness to fake it what is actually predictive?

While our study provides evidence for an observer effect, it is unclear whether BROMP observation alters the proportion of affect and behavior or whether BROMP is modifying their externally visible manifestations. Still, if BROMP is being used to compare the proportion of different affect or disengaged behaviors between systems or contexts, it can only safely be compared to data also collected using BROMP or very similar methods. This recommendation aligns with QE analysis best practices, where only datasets from similar sources and of similar structure can be reliably compared.

However, our findings do not yet indicate that there is risk involved in using BROMP to develop detectors of affect, as we have yet not seen evidence that BROMP changes how behaviors and affect manifest in log data. To investigate that foundational question, further research and triangulation will be necessary. This may involve finding a method with highly similar operationalizations but without such an observer effect. For example, retrospective hand-labeling of interaction data has been extensively used to identify some disengaged behaviors (e.g. [47]). At the moment, we are not aware of an approach for affect coding that lacks such limitations, as self-report produces demand effects, video observation also produces observer effects [13] and observing students through video without their awareness would generally be considered unethical.

In addition, while data collected using BROMP showed evidence of observer effects, there is no evidence that observer effects using BROMP are higher than the distortions that might be produced by competing methods, such as video, other classroom observation methods, and self-report. For all we know, BROMP may be less impacted than other approaches; determining this requires evaluating the impact of alternative label collection methods on the same types of constructs within the same types of settings. The comparison would benefit the QE field by determining how significant the observer effects are for a range of data collection methods that can be used by the community.

However, while the precise nature and extent of the observer effect in BROMP and other methods remains uncertain, our findings indicate that greater attention to this phenomenon is necessary. While it is improbable that we can eliminate observer effects, greater consideration of this challenge may enable us to better understand the limitations of our current data and findings, and over time, may help us to increase the validity of our methods and the quality of our data. In turn, this will help to guarantee that quantitative ethnography analyses meet their goals for fairness and validity.

Acknowledgement. We express our sincere appreciation to the ASSISTments team for providing us with the interaction log data, BROMP data, and source code for the affect detectors. Thank you to Dr. Luc Paquette for sharing the source code of the gaming system detector transferred to the ASSISTments platform and for assisting with its application. We are grateful to Stefan Slater for conducting a thorough code review for this project.

References

1. Almeda, M.V., Baker, R.S.: Predicting student participation in STEM careers: the role of affect and engagement during middle school. J. Educ. Data Min. **12**(2), 33–47 (2020)
2. Andres-Bray, T., Barany, A., Gonder, M.K.: Using epistemic network analysis to explore flexibility and development of termite fishing techniques in nigeria-cameroon chimpanzees (pan troglodytes ellioti). In: Irgens, G.A., Knight, S. (eds.) Advances in Quantitative Ethnography: 5th International Conference, ICQE 2023, Melbourne, VIC, Australia, 8–12 Oct 2023, Proceedings, pp. 155–169. Springer Nature Switzerland, Cham (2023). https://doi.org/10.1007/978-3-031-47014-1_11
3. Andres, J.M.A.L., Hutt, S., Ocumpaugh, J., Baker, R.S., Nasiar, N., Porter, C.: How Anxiety affects affect: A quantitative ethnographic investigation using affect detectors and data-targeted interviews. In: Wasson, B., Zörgő, S. (eds.) Advances in Quantitative Ethnography: Third International Conference, ICQE 2021, Virtual Event, November 6–11, 2021, Proceedings, pp. 268–283. Springer International Publishing, Cham (2022). https://doi.org/10.1007/978-3-030-93859-8_18
4. Andrist, S., Collier, W., Gleicher, M., Mutlu, B., Shaffer, D.: Look together: analyzing gaze coordination with epistemic network analysis. Front. Psychol. **6**, 144911 (2015)

5. Irgens, G.A., Eagan, B.: The foundations and fundamentals of quantitative ethnography. In: Damşa, C., Barany, A. (eds.) Advances in Quantitative Ethnography: 4th International Conference, ICQE 2022, Copenhagen, Denmark, 15–19 Oct 2022, Proceedings, pp. 3–16. Springer Nature Switzerland, Cham (2023). https://doi.org/10.1007/978-3-031-31726-2_1
6. Baker, R.S.: Modeling and understanding students' off-task behavior in intelligent tutoring systems. In: Proceedingsof the ACM SIGCHI Conference, pp. 1059–1068 (2007)
7. Baker, R.S., Beck, J.: Adapting to when students game an intelligent tutoring system. In: Proceedings of the 8th International Conference on Intelligent Tutoring Systems, pp. 392–401 (2006)
8. Baker, R.S., Corbett, A.T., Wagner, A.Z.: Human classification of low-fidelity replays of student actions. In: Proceedings of the Educational Data Mining Workshop at the 8th International Conference on Intelligent Tutoring Systems, vol. 2002, pp. 29–36 (2006)
9. Baker, R.S., D'Mello, S.K., Rodrigo, M.M.T., Graesser, A.C.: Better to be frustrated than bored: the incidence, persistence, and impact of learners' cognitive-affective states during interactions with three different computer-based learning environments. Int'l J. Human-Comput. Stud. **68**(4), 223–241 (2010)
10. Baker, R.S., Corbett, A.T., Koedinger, K.R.: Detecting student misuse of intelligent tutoring systems. In: Proceedings of the 7th International Conference on Intelligent Tutoring Systems, pp. 531–540 (2004)
11. Baker, R.S., et al.: Detector-driven classroom interviewing: Focusing qualitative researcher time by selecting cases in situ. To appear in Educational Technology Research & Development (in press)
12. Baker, R.S., Ocumpaugh, J.L., Andres, J.M.A.L.: BROMP quantitative field observations: A review. Learning Science: Theory, Research, and Practice, pp. 127–156 (2020)
13. Becker, T.E., Marique, G.: Observer effects without demand characteristics: an inductive investigation of video monitoring and performance. J. Bus. Psychol. **29**, 541–553 (2014)
14. Benjamini, Y., Hochberg, Y.: Controlling the false discovery rate: a practical and powerful approach to multiple testing. J. Roy. Stat. Soc.: Ser. B (Methodol.) **57**(1), 289–300 (1995)
15. Bosch, N., Zhang, Y., Paquette, L., Baker, R., Ocumpaugh, J., Biswas, G.: Students' verbalized metacognition during computerized learning. In: Proceedings of the 2021 ACM SIGCHI Conf. on Human Factors in Computing Systems, pp. 1–12 (2021)
16. Botelho, A.F., Baker, R.S., Heffernan, N.T.: Improving sensor-free affect detection using deep learning. In: André, E., Baker, R., Hu, X., Mercedes, M., Rodrigo, T., du Boulay, B. (eds.) Artificial Intelligence in Education, pp. 40–51. Springer International Publishing, Cham (2017). https://doi.org/10.1007/978-3-319-61425-0_4
17. Carpenter, D., et al.: Detecting off-task behavior from student dialogue in game-based collaborative learning. In: Bittencourt, I.I., Cukurova, M., Muldner, K., Luckin, R., Millán, E. (eds.) Artificial Intelligence in Education: 21st International Conference, AIED 2020, Ifrane, Morocco, 6–10 July 2020, Proceedings, Part I, pp. 55–66. Springer International Publishing, Cham (2020). https://doi.org/10.1007/978-3-030-52237-7_5
18. Cleary, T.J., Platten, P.: Examining the correspondence between self-regulated learning and academic achievement: A case study analysis. Educ. Res. Int. **2013**, 1–18 (2013). https://doi.org/10.1155/2013/272560
19. Crofoot, M.C., Lambert, T.D., Kays, R., Wikelski, M.C.: Does watching a monkey change its behaviour? Quantifying observer effects in habituated wild primates using automated radiotelemetry. Anim. Behav. **80**(3), 475–480 (2010)
20. D'Mello, S.K., Moulder, R.G., Jensen, E.: Momentary measures of emotions during technology-enhanced learning prospectively predict standardized test scores in two large samples. Learn. Instr. **90**, 101872 (2024)

21. de Morais, F., Jaques, P.A..: Dinâmica de afetos dos alunos em um sistema tutor inteligente de matemática no contexto brasileiro. In: Anais do XXXII Simpósio Brasileiro de Informática na Educação, pp. 691–704 (2021)
22. Derry, S.J., et al.: Conducting video research in the learning sciences: guidance on selection, analysis, technology, and ethics. J. Learn. Sci. **19**(1), 3–53 (2010)
23. Dragon, T., Arroyo, I., Woolf, B.P., Burleson, W., el Kaliouby, R., Eydgahi, H.: Viewing student affect and learning through classroom observation and physical sensors. In: Woolf, B.P., Aïmeur, E., Nkambou, R., Lajoie, S. (eds.) Intelligent Tutoring Systems: 9th International Conference, ITS 2008, Montreal, Canada, June 23-27, 2008 Proceedings, pp. 29–39. Springer Berlin Heidelberg, Berlin, Heidelberg (2008). https://doi.org/10.1007/978-3-540-69132-7_8
24. Eagan, B., Brohinsky, J., Wang, J., Shaffer, D.W.: Testing the reliability of inter-rater reliability. In: Proceedings of the International Conference on Learning Analytics and Knowledge (2020)
25. Fairman, J., Porter, M., Fisher, S.: Principals discuss early implementation of the ASSISTments online homework tutor for mathematics. ASSISTments Efficacy Study Report 2 (2015)
26. Feng, M., Heffernan, N., Collins, K., Heffernan, C., Murphy, R.F.: Implementing and evaluating ASSISTments online math homework support at large scale over two years: Findings and lessons learned. In: Wang, N., Rebolledo-Mendez, G., Matsuda, N., Santos, O.C., Dimitrova, V. (eds.) Artificial Intelligence in Education: 24th International Conference, AIED 2023, Tokyo, Japan, July 3–7, 2023, Proceedings, pp. 28–40. Springer Nature Switzerland, Cham (2023). https://doi.org/10.1007/978-3-031-36272-9_3
27. Feng, M., Roschelle, J., Heffernan, N., Fairman, J., Murphy, R.: Implementation of an intelligent tutoring system for online homework support in an efficacy trial. In: Proceedings of the 12th International Conference on Intelligent Tutoring Systems, pp. 561–566 (2014)
28. Geertz, C.: The interpretation of cultures (Vol. 5019). Basic books (1973)
29. Grawemeyer, B., Mavrikis, M., Holmes, W., Gutiérrez-Santos, S., Wiedmann, M., Rummel, N.: Affective learning: improving engagement and enhancing learning with affect-aware feedback. User Model. User-Adap. Inter. **27**, 119–158 (2017)
30. Gupta, A., D'Cunha, A., Awasthi, K., Balasubramanian, V.: Daisee: Towards user engagement recognition in the wild. arXiv preprint arXiv:1609.01885 (2016)
31. Hagel, S., et al.: Quantifying the hawthorne effect in hand hygiene compliance through comparing direct observation with automated hand hygiene monitoring. Infect. Control Hospital Epidemiol. **36**(8), 957–962 (2015)
32. Hutt, S., Grafsgaard, J.F., D'Mello, S.K.: Time to scale: Generalizable affect detection for tens of thousands of students across an entire school year. In: Proceedings of the 2019 CHI Conf. on Human Factors in Computing Systems, pp. 1–14 (2019)
33. Jansen, A.M., Giebels, E., Van Rompay, T.J., Junger, M.: The influence of the presentation of camera surveillance on cheating and pro-social behavior. Front. Psychol. **9**, 302214 (2018)
34. Kaliisa, R., Misiejuk, K., Irgens, G.A., Misfeldt, M.: Scoping the emerging field of quantitative ethnography: opportunities, challenges and future directions. In: Proceedings of the International Conference on Quantitative Ethnography, pp. 3–17 (2021)
35. Kassam, K.S., Mendes, W.B.: The effects of measuring emotion: physiological reactions to emotional situations depend on whether someone is asking. PLoS ONE **8**(6), e64959 (2013)
36. Karumbaiah, S., Baker, R.S.: Studying affect dynamics using epistemic networks. In: Proceedings of the International Conference on Quantitative Ethnography, pp. 362–374 (2021)
37. Karumbaiah, S., Baker, R.S., Barany, A., Shute, V.: Using epistemic networks with automated codes to understand why players quit levels in a learning game. In: Eagan, B., Misfeldt, M., Siebert-Evenstone, A. (eds.) ICQE 2019. CCIS, vol. 1112, pp. 106–116. Springer, Cham (2019). https://doi.org/10.1007/978-3-030-33232-7_9

38. Karumbaiah, S., Baker, R.S., Ocumpaugh, J., Andres, J.M.A.L.: A re-analysis and synthesis of data on affect dynamics in learning. IEEE Trans. Affect. Comput. **14**(2), 1696–1710 (2021)
39. Krumpal, I.: Determinants of social desirability bias in sensitive surveys: a literature review. Qual. Quant. **47**(4), 2025–2047 (2013)
40. Kvale, S.: Inter Views: An Introduction to Qualitative Research Interviewing. Sage, Thousand Oaks, CA (1996)
41. Miller, W.L., Baker, R., Labrum, M., Petsche, K., Liu, Y-H., Wagner, A.: Automated detection of proactive remediation by teachers in reasoning mind classrooms. In: Proceedings of the 5th Internatinal Learning Analytics and Knowledge Conference, pp. 290–294 (2015)
42. Munshi, A., Rajendran, R., Ocumpaugh, J., Biswas, G., Baker, R.S., Paquette, L.: Modeling learners' cognitive and affective states to scaffold SRL in open-ended learning environments. In: Proceedings of the 26th Conference on User Modeling, Adaptation, and Personalization (2018)
43. Murphy, R., Roschelle, J., Feng, M., Mason, C.A.: Investigating efficacy, moderators and mediators for an online mathematics homework intervention. J. Res. Educ. Effect. **13**(2), 235–270 (2020)
44. Ocumpaugh, J., Baker, R., Gowda, S., Heffernan, N., Heffernan, C.: Population validity for educational data mining models: a case study in affect detection. Br. J. Edu. Technol. **45**(3), 487–501 (2014)
45. Ocumpaugh, J., Baker, R.S., Rodrigo, M.M.T., Salvi, A. van Velsen, M., Aghababyan, A., Martin, T.: HART: The human affect recording tool. In: Proceedings of the ACM Special Interest Group on the Design of Communication (SIGDOC) (2015)
46. Palaoag, T.D., et al.: Wheel-spinning in a game-based learning environment for physics. In: Micarelli, A., Stamper, J., Panourgia, K. (eds.) Intelligent Tutoring Systems, pp. 234–239. Springer International Publishing, Cham (2016). https://doi.org/10.1007/978-3-319-39583-8_23
47. Paquette, L., Baker, R.S.: Comparing machine learning to knowledge engineering for student behavior modeling: a case study in gaming the system. Interact. Learn. Environ. **27**(5–6), 585–597 (2019)
48. Paquette, L., Baker, R.S., De Carvalho, A., Ocumpaugh, J.: Cross-system transfer of machine learned and knowledge engineered models of gaming the system. In: Proceedings of the 22nd Conference on User Modeling, Adaptation, and Personalization, pp. 183–194 (2015)
49. Pardos, Z.A., Baker, R.S.J.d., San Pedro, M.O.C.Z., Gowda, S.M., Gowda, S.M.: Affective states and state tests: investigating how affect and engagement during the school year predict end-of-year learning outcomes. J. Learn. Anal. **1**(1), 107–128 (2014)
50. Porayska-Pomsta, K., Mavrikis, M., D'Mello, S., Conati, C., Baker, R.S.: Knowledge elicitation methods for affect modelling in education. Int. J. Artif. Intell. Educ. **22**(3), 107–140 (2013)
51. Saha, K., Gupta, P., Mark, G., Kıcıman, E., De Choudhury, M.: Observer Effect in Social Media Use. Unpublished manuscript. https://www.researchsquare.com/article/rs-2492994/v3 (2024). Retrieved 2 May 2024
52. Shaffer, D. W.: Quantitative ethnography. Lulu. com (2017)
53. Shaffer, D.W., Ruis, A.R.: How we code. In: Ruis, A.R., Lee, S.B. (eds.) ICQE 2021. CCIS, vol. 1312, pp. 62–77. Springer, Cham (2021). https://doi.org/10.1007/978-3-030-67788-6_5
54. Spencer, C., et al.: Assessing the use of physiological signals and facial behaviour to gauge drivers' emotions as a UX metric in automotive user studies. In: 12th Int'l Conference on Automotive User Interfaces and Interactive Vehicular Applications, pp. 78–81 (2020)
55. Sporrong, S.K., Kalleberg, B.G., Mathiesen, L., Andersson, Y., Rognan, S.E., Svensberg, K.: Understanding and addressing the observer effect in observation studies. In: Contemporary Research Methods in Pharmacy and Health Services, pp. 261–270. Elsevier (2022). https://doi.org/10.1016/B978-0-323-91888-6.00008-9

56. Van Rompay, T.J., Vonk, D.J., Fransen, M.L.: The eye of the camera: effects of security cameras on prosocial behavior. Environ. Behav. **41**(1), 60–74 (2009)
57. Widen, S.C., Russell, J.A.: Children acquire emotion categories gradually. Cogn. Dev. **23**(2), 291–312 (2008)

Ordered Network Analysis of Prompted Student Discourse in a Collaborative Learning Context

Seung B. Lee(✉), Danielle P. Espino, and Eric Hamilton

Pepperdine University, Malibu, CA 90263, USA
seung.lee@pepperdine.edu

Abstract. Prompting serves an important role in collaborative learning processes by promoting engagement and facilitating the sharing of ideas and information. Prompts can support learning by eliciting critical thinking and guiding deeper inquiry through questions, hints, suggestions and feedback. Studies have shown that both prompting by adults and peers can contribute to student learning and engagement in collaborative settings. This paper examines patterns of directed connections among salient constructs in prompted discourse of students in an online collaborative STEM learning environment. In particular, the study analyzes adult- versus peer-prompted discourse and how they evolve over the course of a collaborative learning session.

Keywords: Collaborative Learning · Prompted Discourse · Ordered Network Analysis

1 Introduction

Collaborative learning involves the exchange and co-construction of knowledge and experiences through a dynamically evolving process of social interaction among participants. Working together, students gain listening skills, learn how to provide and receive assistance and clarification, and create shared understanding while developing relationships that strengthen group cohesion and help build trust and confidence [1].

Prompting serves an important role in collaborative learning processes by promoting engagement and facilitating the sharing of ideas and information. Prompts can support learning by eliciting critical thinking and guiding deeper inquiry through questions, hints, suggestions and feedback [2, 3]. Research has shown that use of prompting in instruction can lead to enhancements in cognitive development as well in strengthening pro-social behaviors [4–6]. In collaborative STEM learning environments, prompting can be used to encourage shifts in the interactive discourse of the participants to foster enhanced scientific thinking and reasoning.

Given that the quality and depth of student discussion during collaborative learning processes determine how beneficial their engagement will be, it is important to examine the influence of prompts on subsequent student discourse. This requires investigating which elements of the discourse were used in the prompting as well as the responses given by the students to the prompts. In this process, the directional nature of prompting

Y. J. Kim and Z. Swiecki (Eds.): icqe 2024, CCIS 2279, pp. 95–103, 2024.
https://doi.org/10.1007/978-3-031-76332-8_8

(i.e. which prompts elicit which responses) needs to be taken into account. This paper seeks to study the patterns of prompting and responses in collaborative learning discourse through the application of ordered network analysis (ONA), focusing on an examination of adult- and peer-prompted student utterances.

1.1 Prompting by Adults and Peers

Studies have shown that both prompting by adults and peers can contribute to learning and engagement in collaborative settings. Adults, including teachers and facilitators, play a critical role in fostering student development in higher order reasoning, argumentation and reflection through interaction and exchange with others [1, 7]. Research on peer-prompting has highlighted the prosocial benefits of peer interaction, particularly in enhancing social competence and inclusive disposition of students [8–10].

A study examining patterns of peer and teacher-guided discussions on science-related topics found that teacher-facilitated groups were more efficient (in fewer turns) in reaching more advanced levels of thinking through the questioning and probing on the part of the teachers [11]. Discourse in the peer groups, while more scattered, were more favorable to idea generation, elaboration and justification. It was further observed that more sophisticated reasoning was reached when participants were able to expound on each other's ideas [11].

Exploring the impact of facilitator and peer prompting in computer-supported collaborative learning environments, it was found that consensus building was enhanced for peer prompting groups [12]. Given that greater perceived consensus is likely to be associated with higher levels of commitment to tasks emerging from the collaborative process, it was noted that teachers wishing to promote group consensus may want to encourage students to play the role of prompters. Furthermore, lower levels of discomfort in the group learning process were also reported for peer prompting groups as well as higher levels of explanations, justifications, recognitions, and challenges [12]. Research has also demonstrated that students exposed to prompting strategies by adult facilitators can learn and implement similar approaches with their peers to foster productive discourse [13].

1.2 Purpose of the Study

This paper examines patterns in adult- versus peer-prompted student discourse and how they evolve over the course of a collaborative learning session. This paper builds on an earlier analysis applying epistemic network analysis (ENA) on the same data that explored the patterns of student discourse according to whether it was prompted, who was the prompter, and what type of prompt was utilized [14]. The previous study found that prompting fosters connections related to STEM content in the collaborative discourse, with the prompting being mostly modeled by the adults and mirrored by the students. Peer prompting was more frequently associated with media production and information sharing, whereas the adult prompting resulted in connections to social disposition [14]. Through the analysis of the directed connections in the prompted student discourse, this paper seeks to uncover additional insights about the effects of prompting in collaborative learning contexts.

2 Methods

2.1 Dataset

This paper analyzes data from a study involving adolescent learners who collaborate on STEM-related digital media projects as part of an online, global network of after-school clubs in several countries across four continents. Participants regularly engage in synchronous video conference calls, referred to as global online "meet-ups," that bring together middle and high school students from multiple clubs. Adult facilitators and observers also join the meet-ups to provide support for the discussions. The data for this analysis comes from two meet-ups held in 2018 and 2019 with participants from Kenya and the United States. The group discussions from the two meet-ups were recorded and transcribed, then segmented by turn of talk, or utterance, to represent a single line of data.

2.2 Coding

The codebook was developed based on a grounded analysis of the data. The codes identified for this analysis are as follows: Collaborative Disposition, Content Focus, Curiosity, Feedback, Information Sharing, Media Production, Participatory Teaching and Social Disposition (refer to [14] for full codebook). In addition, each utterance was examined to identify whether it had been prompted by another line. The response provided by a participant to a specific question or directed request for feedback, for example, were classified as prompted utterances. For each prompted utterance, it was also determined whether it had been prompted by a facilitator/observer (adult) or another student (peer). Following the independent coding of each utterance by two raters, the final coding was determined through a process of social moderation [15].

2.3 Ordered Network Analysis (ONA)

This paper utilizes ONA to examine the patterns of directed connections between discourse codes in the prompted student utterances. ONA is a technique in quantitative ethnography that expands on ENA to account for the order of events occurring over time [16]. By incorporating directionality into the co-temporal models, ONA allows for researchers to consider the influence that information from the common ground has on the subsequent response.

ONA was applied to investigate the prompted student utterances at two levels. The first level compares the patterns of directed connections between adult- and peer-prompted student utterances. The second level disaggregates the networks by when they occurred during the meet-up. Each meet-up was divided into three segments, each consisting of one third of the meet-up's total number of utterances. The three segments therefore correspond to the early (1), middle (2) and late (3) portions of each meet-up's discussion. For this analysis, a participant was defined as the unit of analysis, and each meet-up was determined to be a conversation to which the connections were limited. A moving window of five lines was applied to produce ONA models representing the co-occurrence of codes between the given line and four preceding lines in the conversation.

3 Results

3.1 Student Utterances Prompted by Adults and Peers

The mean ONA networks for the student utterances prompted by adults and peers are presented in Fig. 1. For the adult-prompted utterances, Information Sharing, Social Disposition and Feedback are the dominant responses to Content Focus, while Content Focus is a prominent response code to Curiosity. Furthermore, Media Production is a strong response to Social Disposition.

In the peer-prompted discourse, Content Focus can be seen as a prominent response to Collaborative Disposition, Curiosity and Media Production. In addition, Feedback and Media Production are dominant responses to Social Disposition, whereas Information Sharing and Participatory Teaching are frequent responses to Content Focus.

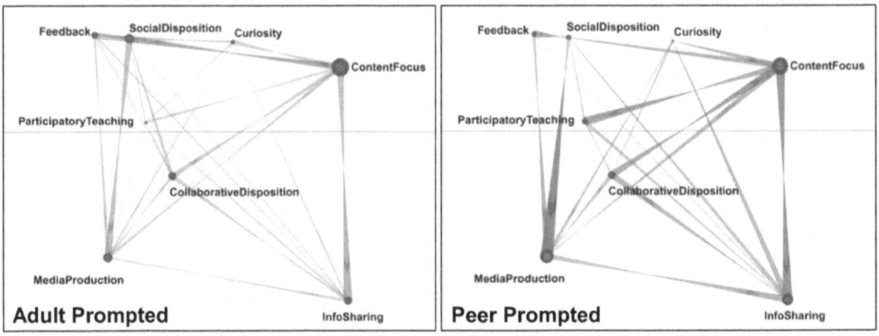

(a) (b)

Fig. 1. ONA networks for student utterances prompted by (a) adults and (b) peers

3.2 Student Utterances Prompted by Adults and Peers in Meet-Up Segments

The ONA networks for the adult- and peer-prompted student utterances disaggregated by meet-up segments are provided in Fig. 2. In meet-up segment 1, the two networks exhibit distinct patterns of directed associations in the prompted student utterances. Adult-prompted student discourse displays prominent connections from Content Focus to Information Sharing, from Media Production to Content Focus, and from Social Disposition to Collaborative Disposition. In contrast, the peer-prompted utterances show stronger connections to Participatory Teaching from Social Disposition, and Feedback from Social Disposition.

In meet-up segment 2, a prominent response of Social Disposition and Curiosity from Content Focus, and Feedback from Social Disposition can be seen in the adult-prompted discourse. Peer-prompted utterances have Information Sharing as a strong response to Content Focus, Curiosity, Social Disposition and Media Production. Additionally, the peer-prompted discourse displays a prominent response of Media Production from Social

Disposition, Curiosity, and Information Sharing. Content Focus also represents a strong response to Media Production, Social Disposition and Curiosity.

Looking to meet-up segment 3, adult-prompted utterances exhibit strong responses of Feedback from Social Disposition as well as Content Focus from Feedback. In the peer-prompted discourse, strong responses of Participatory Teaching from Content Focus, Content Focus from Collaborative Disposition, followed by Information Sharing from Content Focus and Media Production are present.

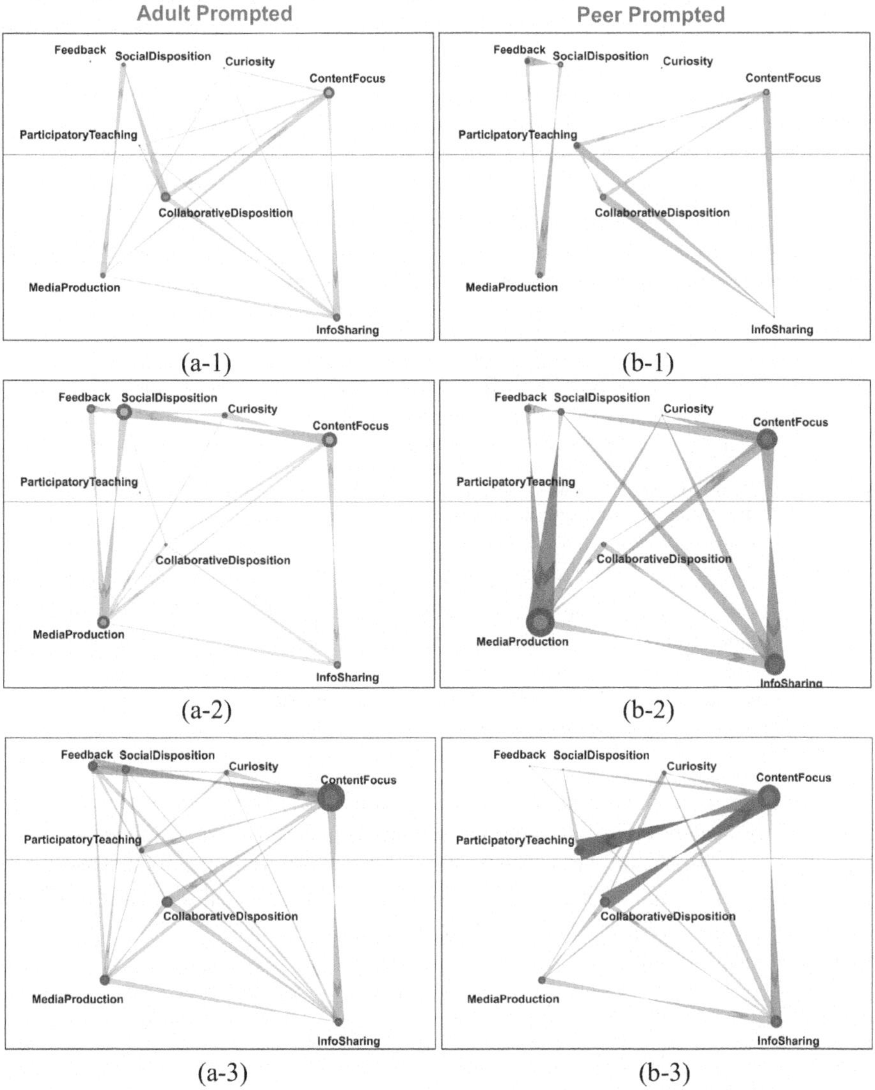

Fig. 2. ONA networks for student utterances prompted by adults (a) and peers (b) disaggregated by the meet-up segment (1, 2, 3)

4 Discussion

This paper presents an analysis of the directional connections of prompted student utterances, focusing on the patterns of prompts and responses for adult- and peer-prompted discourse. Disaggregating the student discourse into those prompted by adults and peers offers insights into how the prompts are used by individuals in each group as well as how students respond to these prompts.

For the adult-prompted utterances, connections from Social Disposition to Media Production and from Content Focus to Information Sharing were relatively more prominent. This is reflective of the role that adult facilitators play in collaborative learning contexts, in which they seek to encourage engagement, offer suggestions and elicit meaningful responses from the students. The Social Disposition to Media Production connection is representative of the facilitator's responsibilities to provide acknowledgement and validation while ensuring continuous progress in the meet-up. The Content Focus to Information Sharing connection also reflects this role, as students receiving content-related prompts from adults often share pertinent information in their responses. The excerpt below demonstrates this as the adult facilitator shares praise for one student then calls on the next student to describe their STEM-related media project.

Speaker	Utterance	Code
Student_1	There has to be a dominant side in that story or video, if you really want people to be more engaged with it. Obviously having a versus video was the real motive for that	Media Production
Adult_1	Wow, that was so great actually. So maybe we can take a look at the next project and before you share your project, give us an overview	Social Disposition
Student_2	So my video is basically about like things you can learn from computer science. It's not really computer science related as in like how to code or something, but it's more about like career skills you learn from it. In fact, the title of the video is called For Career Skills you can learn from computer science so that's basically the gist of the video	Content Focus Media Production Information Sharing

For the peer-prompted student discourse, connections from Curiosity and Media Production to Content Focus are quite prominent. This is reflective of the tendency for peers to pose questions out of curiosity to seek content-related information. The excerpt below demonstrates an instance where one student shares a compliment on a video showcasing another student's Rube Goldberg machine then asks a follow-up question about its intended function.

Speaker	Utterance	Code
Student_3	As for me, I enjoyed the video but I have a question. So, what do [you get to] work on that machine?	Social Disposition Curiosity

(*continued*)

(*continued*)

Speaker	Utterance	Code
Student_4	Um, basically, you sort of have an object at the beginning and it goes through a long obstacle course sort of. And at the end, the purpose of the one in the video was to hit the bell, but a lot of other people make it to do maybe close a door or something. There's like a bunch of purposes that it can fulfill. You should try one	Content Focus Information Sharing

The networks for the prompted student utterances in the three meet-up segments shed light on how the patterns of the student responses evolve over the course of the discussion. While differences in the prompted discourse are visible in the networks for the early part of the meet-up (segment 1), a general mirroring pattern can be observed between the adult- and peer-prompted student discourses at later stages. In segment 2, the adult-prompted network displays directed connections primarily between Media Production, Content Focus and Social Disposition. Building on this pattern, the peer-prompted discourse exhibits stronger responses with the codes Media Production, Content Focus and Information Sharing. It is evident from this network that the students are prompting each other to speak about STEM and media-related content. This mirroring effect may be attributed to the adoption of adult prompting behaviors by the students into their peer prompting actions, which is in line with previous research findings. In segment 3, the modeling role of the adult continues with a focus on providing supportive comments (Social Disposition) and feedback on STEM content. At the same time, the adult-prompted discourse points to the activation of Participatory Teaching and Collaborative Disposition as response codes. It can then be seen that these two codes along with Content Focus form strong directed connections in the peer-prompted student utterances in segment 3.

The following excerpt from the middle segment of one meet-up demonstrates the mirroring dynamic. Soon after the adult facilitator provides feedback on a project, one of the students follows suit by offering encouragement and asking a content-related question.

Speaker	Utterance	Code
Adult_2	You know…I'm wondering if maybe somebody here in one of the other sites might you do a mini prototype of what you're saying, like a quick video for you to incorporate into your project. You're saying that's very simple materials, right?	Content Focus Feedback
Student_5	I made a prototype in the video you can see	Content Focus
Student_6	Wow, that's really cool. You think I can build a prototype right now?	Content Focus Social Disposition
Adult_2	Can you? Do you have the materials? Wait…	
Student_5	Yes. (laughter)	

(*continued*)

(*continued*)

Speaker	Utterance	Code
Student_6	Right now. What makes you think that inspires you right now? Well, I mean like he said you can use household items. I'm assuming you have most of them home. I didn't know you could build like some kind of gravity machine with household items. I think that's really interesting	Content Focus Social Disposition

While preliminary in nature, the findings of this analysis point to the potential for applying ONA to further examine the prompt-response dynamics within collaborative learning discourse.

Acknowledgements. The authors gratefully acknowledge funding support from the US National Science Foundation for the work this paper reports. Views appearing in this paper do not reflect those of the funding agency.

References

1. Gillies, R.M.: Promoting academically productive student dialogue during collaborative learning. Int. J. Educ. Res. **97**, 200–209 (2019)
2. Hammond, T.C., Manfra, M.M.: Giving, prompting, making: Aligning technology and pedagogy within TPACK for social studies instruction. Contemp. Issues Technol. Teacher Educ. **9**(2), 160–185 (2009)
3. Harney, O., Hogan, M., Broome, B., Hall, T., Ryan, C.: Investigating the effects of prompts on argumentation style, consensus and perceived efficacy in collaborative learning. Int. J. Comput.-Support. Collab. Learn. **10**(4), 367–394 (2015)
4. Layous, K., Katherine Nelson, S., Oberle, E., Schonert-Reichl, K.A., Lyubomirsky, S.: Kindness counts: Prompting prosocial behavior in preadolescents boosts peer acceptance and well-being. PLoS ONE **7**(12), e51380 (2012). https://doi.org/10.1371/journal.pone.0051380
5. Vogt, A., Babel, F., Hock, P., Baumann, M., Seufert, T.: Prompting in-depth learning in immersive virtual reality: impact of an elaboration prompt on developing a mental model. Comput. Educ. **171**, 104235 (2021)
6. Yarrow, F., Topping, K.J.: Collaborative writing: the effects of metacognitive prompting and structured peer interaction. Br. J. Educ. Psychol. **71**(2), 261–282 (2001)
7. Ge, X., Land, S.M.: A conceptual framework for scaffolding III-structured problem-solving processes using question prompts and peer interactions. Educ. Tech. Res. Dev. **52**(2), 5–22 (2004)
8. Ackerman, K.B., Spriggs, A.D., Rhodes, A.L.: Peer mediators' use of prompting to increase social communication in students with disabilities. Commun. Disord. Q. **43**(1), 42–50 (2021)
9. Arendale, D.R., Hane, A.R.: Holistic growth of college peer study group participants: prompting academic and personal development. Res. Teach. Dev. Educ. **31**(1), 7–29 (2014)
10. Velez, M.S., Barton, E.E., Yoder, P.J., Wright, J.C.: Systematic prompting of peer-related social behaviors in a small group academic instructional context. Behav. Disord. **46**(2), 67–79 (2020)
11. Hogan, K., Nastasi, B.K., Pressley, M.: Discourse patterns and collaborative scientific reasoning in peer and teacher-guided discussions. Cogn. Instr. **17**(4), 379–432 (1999)

12. Harney, O.M., Hogan, M.J., Quinn, S.: Investigating the effects of peer to peer prompts on collaborative argumentation, consensus and perceived efficacy in collaborative learning. Int. J. Comput.-Support. Collab. Learn. **12**(3), 307–336 (2017)
13. Rosenshine, B., Meister, C., Chapman, S.: Teaching students to generate questions: a review of the intervention studies. Rev. Educ. Res. **66**(2), 181–221 (1996)
14. Espino, D., Lee, S.B., Hokama, M., Hamilton, E.: Examining prompted discourse patterns in an informal, online, global collaborative learning environment. In: Weinberger, A., Chen, W., Hernández-Leo, D., Chen, B. (eds.) Proceedings of the 15th International Conference on Computer-Supported Collaborative Learning – CSCL. International Society of the Learning Sciences, Hiroshima, Japan (2022)
15. Herrenkohl, L.R., Cornelius, L.: Investigating elementary students' scientific and historical argumentation. J. Learn. Sci. **22**(3), 413–461 (2013)
16. Tan, Y., Ruis, A. R., Marquart, C., Cai, Z., Knowles, M.A., Shaffer, D.W.: Ordered network analysis. In: Advances in Quantitative Ethnography: 4th International Conference on Quantitative Ethnography, pp. 101–116. Springer, Cham (2022)

Impact of Text Structures on Student Language in High- and Low-Quality Summaries

Haiying Li[1](✉) and Fanshuo Cheng[2]

[1] University of Pennsylvania, Philadelphia, PA 19014, USA
haiyli@upenn.edu
[2] University of Iowa, Iowa City, IA 52242, USA
fanshuo-cheng@iowa.edu

Abstract. This study explores the impact of text structures of source texts on student language in high- and low-quality summaries written by adult learners in AutoTutor ARC (Adult Reading Comprehension). We used the Coh-Metrix-ENA (Epistemic Network Analysis) approach to visualize the structure of language connections across five Coh-Metrix dimensions: non-narrativity, word abstractness, syntactic complexity, referential cohesion, and deep cohesion. The ENA networks detected differences in language connection structures between high- and low-quality summaries when source texts were causation rather than comparison texts. Specifically, in causation texts, the connections between word abstractness and referential cohesion, and between word abstractness and deep cohesion were stronger in the high-quality summary networks compared to the low-quality summary networks. Moreover, the connections between syntactic complexity and non-narrativity, and between syntactic complexity and deep cohesion were weaker in the high-quality summary networks compared to the low-quality summary networks. Implications are discussed for the design of summary writing interventions and instructions for academic writing.

Keywords: AutoTutor ARC · Causation · Coh-Metrix · Comparison · Epistemic Network Analysis · Summary writing · Text Structure

1 Introduction

Summary writing is a crucial skill that connects reading and writing activities, and is used to assess students' deep reading comprehension and understanding through their writing [31]. It also enhances students' background knowledge through reading and improves overall writing performance [2]. From undergraduate students to professionals, writing a good summary is essential for academic success [11] and career success [7]. For example, in research contexts, summary writing requires students or researchers to restate the main ideas from the source text in their own words, excluding personal opinions [21] and unimportant information [1]. Summary writing interventions have been implemented through varied computer-assisted language learning (CALL) tools, such as intelligent tutoring systems (ITS), mobile technologies, and virtual text and graphics on interactive

Y. J. Kim and Z. Swiecki (Eds.): icqe 2024, CCIS 2279, pp. 104–119, 2024.
https://doi.org/10.1007/978-3-031-76332-8_9

multimedia to enhance students' engagement, self-efficacy, and learning outcomes for students across K-12 to undergraduate, graduate students, and adult learners [16, 24, 31]. These interventions contain components of prior knowledge activation, provide summarization strategy instruction (e.g., deletion, selection, generalization, invention), offer personalized feedback and scaffolding, detect students' metacognitive and motivational processes, or raise students' awareness of text structures of source texts.

However, the evaluation in these interventions focuses on summary quality based on analytic rubrics, which assess the inclusion of topic sentences and/or main ideas, exclusion of unimportant details, the use of one's own words, content accuracy, and grammar and mechanics [4, 18]. Only a few studies have examined student language use in written summaries [15], and designed language interventions that focus on signal words across different text structures [18]. To date, no interventions have specifically addressed language use in summaries or compared student language use between high- and low-quality summaries. In this study, we will use the Coh-Metrix-ENA approach to examine the patterns of student language use in high- and low-quality written summaries, where the source texts have comparison and causation text structures.

This study contributes to summary writing research for three main reasons. First, it provides insights for instructors and researchers on the differences in language use between high- and low-quality summaries depending on the text structures of source texts. This will raise their awareness of the importance of language use skills and encourage them to include these language skills in summary writing interventions. Second, the study reveals the patterns of language use between comparison and causation source texts—two frequently studied structures [3, 5, 27] to enhance the design of adaptive language use interventions tailored to different text structures. Third, the Coh-Metrix-ENA approach advances language research by shifting the focus from individual language features in isolation to the interaction of these features across multiple text levels. This approach acknowledges and considers that language comprises multiple levels, and they interactively contribute to writing.

1.1 Summary Writing

Summary writing is frequently used to evaluate students' reading comprehension and understanding through writing. Unlike traditional reading comprehension measures such as multiple-choice tests, summary writing allows for a more integrated and accurate assessment of a student's ability to identify and articulate the main ideas of a text [6, 10]. Summary writing is established on the Construction-Integration (CI) model of text comprehension [14, 30] and the developmental model of writing [12]. Summary writing requires comprehending the source text and accurately representing its ideas using academic language [6, 28]. Academic language is pre-planned, well-organized, precise, and coherent. It is used in both spoken and written communication within academic and professional communities [8, 18]. In contrast, everyday language is spontaneous, disorganized, and disjointed, often relying on context or shared understanding among participants.

Summary writing requires various language skills, ranging from decoding the text at the word and syntactic level to language comprehension at the textbase level, as well as higher-order skills of synthesis and reproduction. Summary writing requires generalizing ideas from source texts, and using academic language affects the performance in summarizing scientific expository texts [6, 15]. For instance, writers with higher writing skills, either native English learners or proficient language learners, tend to use more syntactic complexity and adversative connectors in their written summaries than those with lower writing skills. Moreover, the occurrence between syntactic complexity and connectives has also been found in summary writing [15]. Conversely, language learners often demonstrated more elaborate phrases and diverse vocabulary [28]. However, how text structures of source texts impact the role of language use in high- and low-quality summaries has not been investigated, which is within the scope of the present study.

1.2 Text Structures of Source Texts

Meyer and Ray [25] categorized six major text structures: description (e.g., categorization), enumeration (e.g., list), sequence (e.g., chronological description), comparison, causation, and problem/solution. Each text structure represents a unique organization to delineate the logical connections and hierarchical relationships among ideas [22]. For example, comparison text structures discuss similarities and/or differences between ideas, things, or events, while causation text structures describe how one event impacts another through causal links [3, 26]. According to structure strategy theory, students who are structure-aware recall more information and main ideas than those who are not structure-aware for two reasons. First, structure-aware students are more likely to use a text structure strategy for encoding and retrieving textual ideas during text processing, linking large chunks of information into a cohesive whole [22, 27]. Second, they build a coherent mental representation of the text at both micro and macro levels, creating a textbase comprehension and integrating textbase information with prior knowledge to make inferences and elaboration, in line with Kintsch's CI model [13].

Instruction on text structure strategies positively impacts learners' comprehension and retention of information across various age groups [26]. However, a recent meta-analysis found that text structure instruction had positive immediate effects on reading comprehension for students in grades 4–6, but not at delayed posttests [3]. Additionally, students find it easier to recall information from comparison and causation texts than from other text structures [23]. However, students tend to have a high awareness of comparison structures but a low awareness of causation structures [27]. Meyer and Ray [24] state that comparison and causation texts are the easiest to comprehend, whereas Englert and Hiebert [5] argue that comparison texts are the hardest to learn. These two structures impact students' comprehension. Will they also impact their writing?

Only one study has examined the impact of text structures on student language use in summaries [17], while most studies on text structure have focused on content-related features, such as paragraph-level organization, active construction of graphic organizers, and rule-based summarization techniques [3]. The Coh-Metrix-ENA approach revealed the differences in language connections that the Coh-Metrix approach alone did not detect [15] (see 1.3 for details). Specifically, for both causation and comparison texts, informal agent language prompted students to use more abstract words in non-narrative summaries. Additionally, informal agent language elicited a weaker language association between syntactic complexity and referential cohesion in comparison texts. When writing summaries for expository texts, students, particularly less proficient ones, tended to rely heavily on the source texts, whereas more proficient students utilized less exact copying of the source texts than less proficient students [19]. However, no studies have examined the impact of the text structures of source texts on students' language use between high- and low-proficient students, a gap addressed in the present study.

1.3 Coh-Metrix-ENA Approach

The Coh-Metrix-ENA approach integrates Coh-Metrix language and discourse components with ENA to uncover nuanced distinctions in language associations across various language levels, including non-narrativity, word abstractness, syntactic complexity, referential cohesion, and deep cohesion. Coh-Metrix, an automated text analysis tool, is developed based on a pragmatics-based framework and a multilevel theoretical framework that encompasses the textbase of the word and syntactic structures, situation model, genre, and rhetorical structure, and pragmatic communication [9, 30]. It computes approximately a hundred language features outlined in the pragmatic-based framework. Coh-Metrix extracts five primary components through a principal components analysis, using a corpus of texts from kindergarten to early college [8].

These five major Coh-Metrix components align with the first five levels of the multilevel framework, each representing either ease or difficulty of comprehension as follows: (1) **Word concreteness** (inversed: word abstractness): This dimension measures the meaningfulness of concrete words (e.g., rainbow) that evoke mental images for easier comprehension, in contrast to abstract words (e.g., evaporation). (2) **Syntactic simplicity** (inversed: syntactic complexity): This dimension measures the ease of sentence processing and comprehension, characterized by simple and familiar syntactic structures with short sentence lengths, as opposed to complex sentence structures with multiple clauses and modifiers for noun and verb phrases. (3) **Referential cohesion**: This dimension evaluates the overlap of words and ideas across sentences, paragraphs, and the entire text, contributing to cohesive threads that link to the explicit textbase. (4) **Deep cohesion**: This dimension involves using causal (e.g., influence), intentional (e.g., plan), temporal (e.g., subsequently), or other connectives or conceptual ideas to construct a more coherent and deeper comprehension at the situation model level. (5) **Narrativity** (inverse: non-narrativity): This dimension indicates the presence of a familiar storytelling style or everyday oral conversational style, closely linked to characters, events, places, and objects. Its opposite is a non-narrative or informational style.

Components 1, 2, and 5 represent text ease, while components 3 and 4 denote text difficulty. To maintain consistency, the ease-oriented components were inverted into difficulty by multiplying them by -1. Thus, the five dimensions that scale academic language are non-narrativity, word abstractness, syntactic complexity, referential cohesion, and deep cohesion [15, 17]. A text using more academic language indicates an increase in more abstract words, complex syntax, referential cohesion, deep cohesion, and non-narrative style.

The majority of research on student language has analyzed individual linguistic and discourse features in isolation. While this method can reveal certain differences in language use, it fails to fully capture the intricacies of real language use in writing. A holistic approach that considers the interactive levels of language is demanding. The Coh-Metrix-ENA approach emphasizes the interaction among language features through visualization and a series of statistical analyses, representing language connections through nodes and co-occurrences through lines [15, 17]. The size of the nodes indicates the strength of language associations, while the darkness and thickness of lines denote the strength of co-occurrence between language features. Additionally, superimposed and subtracted networks explicitly illustrate the dynamic changes in language connections across different situations. While statistical analyses involve multiple comparisons and require Bonferroni corrections, this approach proves more effective in discerning disparities in the structure of language associations and uncovering subtle differences that individual language features in isolation or when using the ENA approach alone, might fail to identify. The Coh-Metrix-ENA approach surpasses the Coh-Metrix approach or the ENA approach in detecting discrepancies in language patterns [15, 17].

This study investigates differences in language connections between high- and low-quality summaries when source texts are comparison and causation structures. Specifically, we employed the Coh-Metrix-ENA approach to examine the disparities in language connection structures between high-quality and low-quality summaries written by adult learners utilizing the AutoTutor ARC (Adult Reading Comprehension) system. Our research is guided by the following question: *How does the text structure of source texts impact the language patterns in high- and low-quality summaries?* We hypothesize that variations in the text structure of the source text will lead to different patterns of language use between high- and low-quality summaries due to the distinct characteristics of source texts and disparities in writing proficiency.

2 Method

2.1 Participants and Summary Data

Participants were recruited from Amazon Mechanical Turk (AMT) with the expectation of improving their English summary writing skills. A total of 164 participants completed a three-hour summary intervention, receiving a compensation of $30. The participants had an average age of 33.46 ($SD = 8.81$), with 42.7% female participants. Among them, 89.0% were language learners. 56.7% were from India, 11.0% from China, 11.0% from the U.S., and the rest from 25 other countries. On average, the language learners had studied English for 16.55 years ($SD = 8.85$) and had spent 1.60 years ($SD = 0.49$) in a foreign country. Among the participants, 36.0% held a master's or higher degree, 45.7% had a bachelor's degree, and 18.3% had less than four years of higher education.

In this study, we examined two text structures of source texts: comparison and causation. These structures were chosen because they are frequently studied [3, 5, 27], yet research has yielded inconsistent findings regarding their ease of learning [5, 27], recall [23], and structure awareness [27]. We aim to investigate whether these two text structures will impact student language use differently. Participants wrote the summary for each of the eight texts in this study: four comparison texts and four causation texts. The average text length was 260.13 words each ($SD = 63.47$). The comparison texts included *Walking and Running*, *Kobe and Jordan*, *Butterfly & Moth*, and *Hurricane*, while the causation texts included *Effects of Exercising*, *Diabetes*, *Floods*, and *Job Market*. These texts were randomly chosen using a balanced 4×4 Latin-square design to control for the order effect. The texts had a difficulty level suitable for upper middle school students and high school students [18]. Participants were instructed to summarize each text using their own words, containing signal words and topic sentences to capture the main ideas and significant supporting details. The total number of summaries was 1,295, with 648 summaries for comparison texts and 647 summaries for causation texts.

2.2 Measures for Summary Quality and Summary Language

The rubric of summary grading comprised four components: (1) topic sentences, (2) content inclusion and exclusion, (3) grammar and mechanics, and (4) signal words of text structures [18]. Each component was rated on a scale of 0–2 points: 0 indicating the absence of target knowledge, 1 indicating partial knowledge, and 2 indicating complete knowledge. Four native English speakers (1 male and 3 females) with expertise in discourse analysis participated in training for grading summaries. At the beginning of the training, they collectively reviewed each component in the rubric and graded three summaries of high, medium, and low quality, respectively. Subsequently, the raters underwent three rounds of training. In each round, they graded 32 randomly selected summaries from eight texts and then resolved any discrepancies until an agreement was reached. The average interrater reliability for the three training sets met the threshold (Cronbach $\alpha = .82$). After training, each rater graded summaries for two source texts, totaling 1,295 summaries. The average summary score was 4.89 ($SD = 1.73$).

To examine whether the language in student-written summaries differs between high-quality and low-quality summaries, we selected summaries with scores 1 standard deviation (SD) above the mean as high-quality and those with scores 1 SD below the mean as low-quality. The t-test results showed a significant difference between these two groups, $t(171.30) = 56.48$, $p < 0.001$, Cohen's $d = 8.04$. Specifically, the mean scores were significantly higher in high-quality summaries ($M = 7.38$, $SD = 0.49$) than in low-quality summaries ($M = 2.50$, $SD = 0.72$). This finding indicates that these two groups represent distinct quality levels of summaries. The final summary data for the Coh-Metrix-ENA analyses consist of 167 summaries for causation texts ($N_{High} = 82$, $N_{Low} = 85$) and 153 summaries for comparison texts ($N_{High} = 70$, $N_{Low} = 83$), ensuring a within-subject design.

We used Coh-Metrix version 3.0 to compute five primary Coh-Metrix components with percentile scores from the written summaries: narrativity, word concreteness, syntactic simplicity, referential cohesion, and deep cohesion. To maintain consistency in measuring academic language, the scores for the first three Coh-Metrix components were inverted into non-narrativity, word abstractness, and syntactic complexity by multiplying by -1. Finally, these five components with percentile scores were standardized using z-scores for the final Coh-Metrix-ENA analysis.

3 Results

We utilized the *rENA* package [20] in *R* (version 4.3.1; RStudio version: 2023.09.1) to conduct ENA analyses on five Coh-Metrix components to answer our research question: *How does the text structure of source texts impact the language patterns in high- and low-quality summaries?* We generated ENA language networks within a one-moving summary window and examined the variation in language connections among the five Coh-Metrix components: non-narrativity, word abstractness, syntactic complexity, referential cohesion, and deep cohesion.

The units of analyses and conversations were summary quality (high vs. low), text structures of source texts (comparison vs. causation), and individual students. The ENA model was generated using endpoints of 10 co-occurrences among the five Coh-Metrix components, weighted by the square root. The rotation direction was set from low-quality summaries to high-quality summaries, maximizing the variance between the means of the two summary quality groups. In the ENA plots, the left side represents a strong co-occurrence of language features in low-quality summaries, and the right side represents a strong co-occurrence of language features in high-quality summaries.

The ENA plots display two networks of high- and low-quality summaries, superimposed and subtracted networks. In the plot, nodes are placed in fixed positions, allowing for meaningful comparisons of language connection patterns and interpretation of the projection space [29]. The size of each node indicates the strength of the connections of one Coh-Metrix component with other Coh-Metrix components, with lines representing the co-occurrence of these components. Darker, thicker lines indicate stronger connections, whereas lighter, thinner lines indicate weaker connections. Each dot represents an individual learner: red dots for learners who wrote low-quality summaries and blue dots for those who wrote high-quality summaries. The square at the center of each coordinate represents the means, and the dotted line represents the 95% confidence interval (Conf. Int.).

Figures 1a and b illustrate the superimposed and subtracted networks in both high- and low-quality summaries written for comparison texts. The visualizations display a difference in the structure of language connections, mainly a stronger connection between word abstractness and deep cohesion and between word abstractness and referential cohesion in the comparison network. The blue lines representing these connections are stronger in the high-quality summaries, indicating that the high-quality summaries in comparison text structures exhibit these two stronger language connections.

Figures 1c and d illustrate the superimposed and subtracted networks for high- and low-quality summaries written for causation texts. The visualization reveals a consistent pattern of language connections: in high-quality summaries, there is a stronger connection between word abstractness and deep cohesion, as well as between word abstractness and referential cohesion, with both blue lines appearing thicker than those in the comparison networks. Additionally, the ENA network for causation texts indicates another strong language connection in high-quality summaries between word abstractness and non-narrativity. Conversely, the networks display two thick red lines between syntactic complexity and deep cohesion, and between syntactic complexity and non-narrativity, highlighting these stronger language connections in low-quality summaries.

3.1 Language Connections in Comparison Texts

The ENA network projections reveal both similarities and differences in language connection structures between high- and low-quality summaries in comparison and causation texts. However, determining the statistical significance based on the visualization is challenging, as the thickness of the lines representing language connections does not distinctly indicate statistical significance. Therefore, we performed a *t*-test on the rotation of the means of language features between high- and low-quality summaries in comparison texts to test for statistical significance. The results showed a significant effect of summary quality on student language in comparison texts, $t(137.07) = 2.28$, $p = 0.024$, Cohen's $d = 0.38$. Specifically, the mean scores were significantly higher in high-quality summaries ($M = -0.03$, $SD = 0.29$) than in low-quality summaries ($M = -0.13$, $SD = 0.25$) in the comparison texts. The finding implies that high-quality summaries exhibited different language usage compared to low-quality summaries.

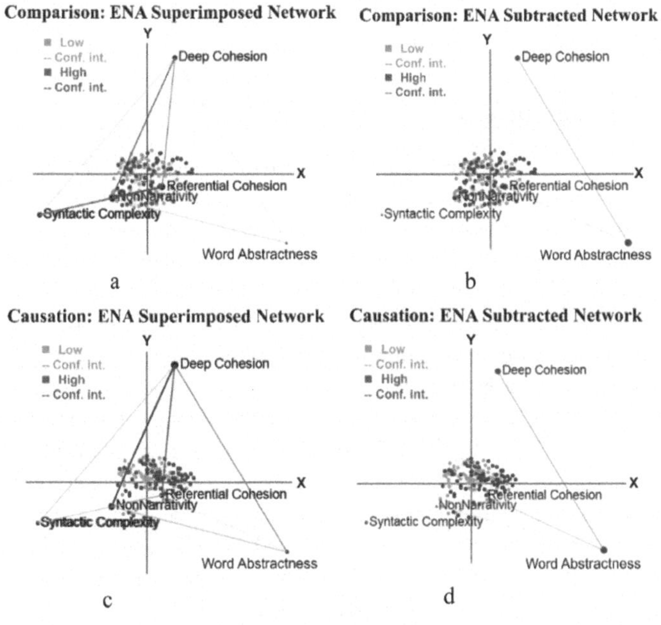

Fig. 1. Superimposed and subtracted networks.

To identify which language connections are significantly different, we performed 10 *t*-test analyses on 10-line weights in ENA networks that represented the language connections between each two out of five Coh-Metrix components in comparison texts (see Table 1). Thus, the significance criteria were adjusted using the Bonferroni correction, setting 0.010 for the marginal significance and 0.005 for the significance (see Note for Table 1). However, we reported significantly different language connections both before and after the Bonferroni correction to demonstrate the differences between visualization and statistical analyses.

The t-test results confirmed part of the findings revealed from ENA visualizations: two language connections related to word abstractness were significantly different. Specifically, the language connection between word abstractness and referential cohesion was significantly higher in high-quality summaries ($M = 0.18$, $SD = 0.14$) than in low-quality summaries ($M = 0.13$, $SD = 0.12$) with a small effect size, $t(134.72) = 2.18$, $p = 0.031$, Cohen's $d = 0.36$. However, a p-value of 0.031 was not significantly different after the Bonferroni correction.

Moreover, the language connection between word abstractness and deep cohesion was significantly higher in high-quality summaries ($M = 0.19$, $SD = 0.19$) than in low-quality summaries ($M = 0.12$, $SD = 0.15$) with a small effect size, $t(128.99) = 2.56$, $p = 0.012$, Cohen's $d = 0.42$. However, a p-value of 0.012 was not significantly different after the Bonferroni correction.

These findings confirmed that the ENA visualization revealed language connection differences. However, after applying the Bonferroni correction for multiple comparisons, the differences shown by the visualization may not be statistically different. This discrepancy highlights the importance of statistical analysis in further confirming the differences indicated by ENA visualizations.

3.2 Language Connections in Causation Texts

We used the same procedure to perform the t-test on the rotation of the means of language features between high- and low-quality summaries in causation texts to test for statistical significance. The results showed a significant effect of summary quality on student language in causation texts, $t(162.91) = 4.61$, $p < 0.0001$, Cohen's $d = 0.72$. Specifically, the mean scores were significantly higher in high-quality summaries ($M = 0.17$, $SD = 0.28$) than in low-quality summaries ($M = -0.02$, $SD = 0.25$) in the causation texts. The finding implies high-quality summaries exhibited different language usage than low-quality ones in causation texts.

We used the same method to test the significance of language connections in causation texts (see Table 1 causation). The t-test results also confirmed part of the findings revealed from ENA visualizations. Specifically, the language connection between non-narrativity and word abstractness was significantly higher in high-quality summaries ($M = 0.27$, $SD = 0.18$) than in low-quality summaries ($M = 0.21$, $SD = 0.17$) with a small effect size, $t(163.35) = 2.16$, $p = 0.032$, Cohen's $d = 0.33$. However, a p-value of 0.032 was not significantly different after the Bonferroni correction.

Conversely, the language connection between non-narrativity and syntactic complexity was significantly lower in high-quality summaries ($M = 0.20$, $SD = 0.16$) than in low-quality summaries ($M = 0.28$, $SD = 0.18$) with a small effect size, both before and after the Bonferroni correction, $t(162.59) = -2.90$, $p = 0.0043$, Cohen's $d = 0.45$. This finding implies that in high-quality summaries, when students tended to write more informational summaries rather than narrative summaries, they used simpler sentence structures to facilitate the information delivery.

Furthermore, the language connection between word abstractness and referential cohesion was significantly higher in high-quality summaries ($M = 0.21$, $SD = 0.12$) than in low-quality summaries ($M = 0.12$, $SD = 0.12$), with a medium effect size, both before and after the Bonferroni correction, $t(164.55) = 4.55$, $p < 0.0001$, Cohen's $d =$

Table 1. Descriptives and *t*-test results of language connections

Language	Quality	Comparison				Causation			
		M	*SD*	*t (df)*	*d*	*M*	*SD*	*t (df)*	*d*
Non-Narrativity * Word Abstractness	High	0.22	0.18	0.69 (150.87)	0.11	0.27	0.18	2.16 (163.35)	0.33
	Low	0.20	0.22			0.21	0.17		
Non-Narrativity * Syntactic Complexity	**High**	0.33	0.20	−0.88 (137.53)	−0.14	**0.20**	**0.16**	**−2.90*** **(162.59)**	**−0.45**
	Low	0.36	0.17			**0.28**	**0.18**		
Non-Narrativity * Referential Cohesion	High	0.38	0.17	−0.98 (148.63)	−0.16	0.29	0.15	0.74 (164.97)	0.11
	Low	0.41	0.18			0.27	0.16		
Non-Narrativity * Deep Cohesion	High	0.32	0.18	1.09 (150.57)	0.18	0.40	0.18	−1.30 (158.03)	−0.20
	Low	0.29	0.21			0.45	0.23		
Word Abstractness * Syntactic Complexity	High	0.14	0.11	0.38 (149.29)	0.06	0.14	0.12	1.09 (159.62)	0.17
	Low	0.13	0.12			0.12	0.10		
Word Abstractness * Referential Cohesion	**High**	0.18	0.14	2.18 (134.72)	0.36	**0.21**	**0.12**	**4.55*** **(164.55)**	**0.70**
	Low	0.13	0.12			**0.12**	**0.12**		
Word Abstractness * Deep Cohesion	**High**	0.19	0.19	2.56 (128.99)	0.42	**0.32**	**0.21**	**3.64** (157.17)**	**0.57**
	Low	0.12	0.15			**0.21**	**0.17**		
Syntactic Complexity * Referential Cohesion	High	0.29	0.19	−1.44 (149.29)	−0.23	0.19	0.16	−1.69 (163.03)	−0.26
	Low	0.33	0.20			0.24	0.19		
Syntactic Complexity * Deep Cohesion	**High**	0.20	0.14	−0.30 (148.90)	−0.05	**0.22**	**0.15**	**−2.83† (162.71)**	**−0.44**
	Low	0.21	0.15			**0.29**	**0.17**		
Referential Cohesion * Deep Cohesion	High	0.29	0.2	0.38 (146.45)	0.06	0.35	0.18	1.34 (164.94)	0.21
	Low	0.28	0.2			0.31	0.19		

Note. ***, $p < .0001$; **, $p < .001$; *, $p < .005$; †, $p < .01$. *M* = Mean, *SD* = Standard Deviation, *t* = *t*-test statistics, *df* = degree of freedom, *d* = Cohen's *d*.

0.70. This finding implies that in high-quality summaries, when students tended to use more abstract words rather than concrete words in high-quality summaries, they also used the same words or expressions to enhance text cohesion, facilitating understanding by reducing the efforts required from readers.

Similarly, the language connection between word abstractness and deep cohesion was significantly higher in high-quality summaries ($M = 0.32$, $SD = 0.21$) than in low-quality summaries ($M = 0.21$, $SD = 0.17$), with a medium effect size, both before and after the Bonferroni correction, $t(157.17) = 3.64$, $p = 0.0004$, Cohen's $d = 0.57$. This finding implies that in high-quality summaries, when students tended to use more abstract words, they also used more connectives to enhance text cohesion, facilitating understanding by reducing the efforts required from readers.

Conversely, the language connection between syntactic complexity and deep cohesion was significantly lower in high-quality summaries ($M = 0.22$, $SD = 0.15$) than in low-quality summaries ($M = 0.29$, $SD = 0.17$) with a small effect size, $t(162.71) = -2.83$, $p = 0.005$, Cohen's $d = 0.44$. While a p-value of 0.005 was marginally significantly different after the Bonferroni correction, these findings suggest that in high-quality summaries, students tended to balance the usage of complex sentence structures and logical and causal relationship words compared to low-quality summaries. Specifically, if students used more complex sentences, they also added logical and causal connectives to facilitate understanding in high-quality summaries, reducing the difficulty of information understanding.

These findings further confirm that the language connection differences revealed by ENA visualization may not be statistically significant after applying the Bonferroni correction for multiple comparisons in the statistical analysis. Thus, it is crucial to conduct statistical analysis to confirm the differences indicated by visualizations.

4 Discussions and Conclusions

This study explores how the text structures of the source texts impact student language in their written summaries using the Coh-Metrix-ENA approach. The ENA network visualization and t-test analyses for language connections revealed differences in language connection structures between the high- and low-quality summaries within comparison and causation texts. Specifically, in comparison texts, no language connections showed significant differences after Bonferroni corrections. However, high-quality summaries generated from causation texts exhibited more differences in language connections than those from comparison texts after Bonferroni corrections. Specifically, in causation texts, language connections between word abstractness and referential cohesion and between word abstractness and deep cohesion co-occurred more strongly in high-quality summaries than in low-quality summaries. However, two language connections—syntactic complexity and non-narrativity, and syntactic complexity and deep cohesion—were found to be weaker in high-quality summaries than in low-quality ones. We utilized examples to illustrate the differences in language connection structures between high- and low-quality summary networks in causation texts.

4.1 More Abstract Words, High Referential Cohesion and Deep Cohesion

This study found that in causation texts, high-quality summaries exhibited the co-occurrence of abstract words with referential cohesion and deep cohesion. Specifically, when students used more abstract words in their written summaries, high-quality summaries tended to exhibit higher referential cohesion and deep cohesion. These cohesive devices, such as content word overlapping and logical and causal connectives, facilitate understanding by increasing the inter-connectedness between sentences. To better explain the phenomena, we provided two student summaries as examples: one high-quality summary with a score of 7 out of 8 points and one low-quality summary with a score of 2. Both examples contained abstract words (underlined with a single line), such as "insulin" and "production," to summarize the important information about diabetes presented in the source text. However, Example 1, a high-quality summary, repeatedly used the noun "diabetes" or the pronoun "It" to refer to the same concept. In this way, each sentence delivers additional information about diabetes to enhance understanding with the least cognitive effort to construct coherence of information. Moreover, this summary included more causal words (underlined with doubled lines), such as "due to," "because," and "causes," to present logical and causal relationships between information explicitly.

Example 2, a low-quality summary, also contained many abstract words to introduce diabetes. However, this summary had lower referential and deep cohesion, which failed to explicitly show the cohesion and coherence between sentences, making it very challenging to understand. Specifically, in the third and fourth sentences, the noun "cells" and the demonstrative pronoun "this" suddenly appeared without an explicit relationship to the previous information about diabetes, making it difficult to connect the information to the previous content. Furthermore, this low-quality summary failed to accurately use logical or causal words to convey the flow of meaning, let alone proper grammar, which further increases the difficulty in understanding the summary.

Example 1 (High-quality: Summary Score = 7):
Word Abstractness = 0.97, Referential Cohesion = 0.87, Deep Cohesion = 1.00.

Diabetes is a chronic disease and a diabetic person has higher amount of sugar in his blood. It is due to abnormal production of Insulin by Pancreas gland. Excess thirst, weight loss, fatigue etc are some symptoms of Diabetes. Type 1 diabetes is more serious than type 2. Because type 1 diabetes cannot be prevented. Whereas Type 2 diabetes can be prevented by healthy lifestyle. Diabetes causes so many health complications.

Example 2 (Low-quality: Summary Score = 2):
Word Abstractness = 0.95, Referential Cohesion = 0.13, Deep Cohesion = 0.02.

Diabetes is one one of the major lifestyle disease nowadays. There are type 1 and type two diabetes were in both insulin production in pancreas is affected. The cells cannot pass glucose molecules. This in turn lead to may serious health issues. This disease should be treated to avoid complications in later life.

4.2 More Complex Sentences, Low Non-Narrativity and Deep Cohesion

Conversely, this study also found that in causation texts, high-quality summaries demonstrated weaker co-occurrence of syntactic complexity with non-narrativity and deep cohesion. Specifically, when students used more complex sentences (see underlined sentences), they tended to use a more familiar narrative writing style rather than an informational style and moderate deep cohesion to balance the difficulty of these two usages. Examples 3 and 4 contained complex sentences, featuring multiple clauses and varied sentence structures. In the high-quality summary, the student contained some narrative elements, such as familiar sentence structures, "there were," like telling a story, which makes it easily understood, even though it had many clauses. Moreover, the moderate use of causal phrases, "as a result" and "led to," and the connectives, "also," "another", and "all of these things," explicitly convey the meaning further.

Conversely, in Example 4, the combination of complex sentences and abundant factual information makes the summary difficult to comprehend. The excessive use of causal words resulted in poor grammar (see the first sentence), departing from the main purpose of the text (see the second sentence). The source text introduces different natural and human factors contributing to floods, while the summary repeatedly emphasizes the damage caused by floods. Additionally, the source text suggests that while scientists may not always predict exactly when floods will occur, they have knowledge about the signs indicating the likelihood of floods. However, this summary misinterprets the intention of the source text by solely focusing on damages caused by floods.

Example 3 (High-quality: Summary Score = 7):
Syntactic Complexity = 0.98, Non-Narrativity = 0.75, Deep Cohesion = 0.41.

There were many factors that contributed to the decline of the middle of the labor market. As a result of a higher number of workers entering the labor pool in the 1970's, there were fewer jobs available. Also, as more things became increasingly automated as a result of better machines, fewer people have been needed to do many jobs. Another factor is the outsourcing of US jobs to countries where wages are much lower than America. All of these things have led to fewer jobs and decreased wages.

Example 4 (Low-quality: Summary Score = 2):
Syntactic Complexity = 0.99, Non-Narrativity = 0.99, Deep Cohesion = 0.94.

Natural disasters are the worst enemy of man kind, of this one of the main is Floods, Flood cause devastation of lives to properties around the world. Even the scientists cannot predict when and where a flood will happen because this is a natural disaster that creates havoc in the world. Many floods are caused by humans intervention with nature only.

4.3 Contributions, Implications, and Future Directions

In summary, these findings suggest that text structures significantly impact language use in high- and low-quality summaries. While there was no significant difference in language connections between high- and low-quality summaries in comparison texts, causation texts revealed distinct patterns after the Bonferroni corrections. High-quality summaries in causation texts demonstrated a strong co-occurrence of abstract words with referential cohesion and deep cohesion, as well as a weak co-occurrence of syntactic complexity with non-narrativity and deep cohesion. These results highlight the importance of balancing academic language at different language levels to facilitate effective information delivery in summary writing.

Future studies should include additional text structures, such as problem-solution, sequence, and description, to investigate how patterns vary among these different structures. By examining these structures, future research can provide a more comprehensive understanding of the role of language connections between high- and low-quality summaries among various text structures. Moreover, further investigation is needed to determine whether interventions for academic language would improve the quality of summary writing.

These findings have significant implications for researchers and educators in designing interventions or instructions for summary writing that align with the goals of academic writing instruction. Understanding the patterns of language connections in high- and low-quality summaries across different text structures can help educators and researchers develop more effective teaching strategies for summary writing and ultimately enhance students' writing abilities.

Acknowledgment. This research was supported by the Institute of Education Sciences (IES) Grant (#R305C120001). The opinions expressed in this paper are those of the authors and not of the IES.

References

1. Abdi, S.A., Idris, N.: An analysis on student-written summaries: automatic assessment of summary writing. Int. J. Eng. Sci. Technol. **3**(1), 466–472 (2014)
2. Asaro-Saddler, K., Muir-Knox, H., Meredith, H.: The effects of a summary writing strategy on the literacy skills of adolescents with disabilities. Exceptionality **26**(2), 106–118 (2018)
3. Bogaerds-Hazenberg, S.T.M., Evers-Vermeul, J., Bergh, H.: A meta-analysis on the effects of text structure instruction on reading comprehension in the upper elementary grades. Read. Res. Q. **56**(3), 435–462 (2021)
4. Chew, C., Wu, W.W., Idris, N., Loh, E.F., Chua, Y.P.: Enhancing summary writing of ESL learners via a theory-based online tool: system development and evaluation. J. Educ. Comput. Res. **58**(2), 398–432 (2020)
5. Englert, C.S., Hiebert, E.H.: Children's developing awareness of text structures in expository materials. J. Educ. Psychol. **76**(1), 65–74 (1984)
6. Galloway, E.P., Uccelli, P.: Beyond reading comprehension: exploring the additional contribution of core academic language skills to early adolescents' written summaries. Read. Writ. **32**(3), 729–759 (2019)
7. Gayathri, V.S.: What are the benefits of summarization? https://www.linkedin.com/pulse/what-benefits-summarization-dr-v-s-gayathri/ (2023)
8. Graesser, A.C., McNamara, D.S., Cai, Z., Conley, M., Li, H., Pennebaker, J.: Coh-Metrix measures text characteristics at multiple levels of language and discourse. Elem. Sch. J. **115**(2), 210–229 (2014). https://doi.org/10.1086/678293
9. Graesser, A.C., McNamara, D.S.: Computational analyses of multilevel discourse comprehension. Top. Cogn. Sci. **3**(2), 371–398 (2011)
10. Graham, S., Harris, K.R.: Common core state standards and writing: introduction to the special issue. Elem. Sch. J. **115**(4), 457–463 (2015). https://doi.org/10.1086/681963

11. Kim, S.: Characteristics of EFL readers' summary writing: a study with Korean university students. Foreign Lang. Ann. **34**(6), 569–581 (2001)
12. Kim, Y.S.G., Schatschneider, C.: Expanding the developmental models of writing: a direct and indirect effects model of developmental writing (DIEW). J. Educ. Psychol. **109**(1), 35–50 (2017). https://doi.org/10.1037/edu0000129
13. Kintsch, W.: Comprehension: A Paradigm for Cognition. Cambridge University Press, New York (1998)
14. Kintsch, W.: Text comprehension, memory, and learning. Am. Psychol. **49**(4), 294–303 (1994)
15. Li, H., Cai, Z., Wang, G., Cheng, F., Marquart, C.: Impact of agent language on student language in the structures of language connections. In: Irgens, G.A., Knight, S. (eds.) Advances in Quantitative Ethnography. ICQE 2023. Communications in Computer and Information Science, vol. 1895, pp. 49–65. Springer, Cham (2023)
16. Li, H., Cheng, F., Wang, G., Graeser, A.: The Impact of conversational agents' language on self-efficacy and summary writing. In: Rodrigo, M.M., Matsuda, N., Cristea, A.I., Dimitrova, V. (eds.) Artificial Intelligence in Education: 23rd International Conference, AIED 2022, Durham, UK, July 27–31, 2022, Proceedings, Part I, pp. 553–559. Springer International Publishing, Cham (2022). https://doi.org/10.1007/978-3-031-11644-5_48
17. Li, H., Cheng, F., Wang, G., Cai, Z., Graeser, A.: The impact of conversational agent language and text structure on student language. In: Sifaleras, A., Lin, F. (eds.) Generative Intelligence and Intelligent Tutoring Systems. ITS 2024. Lecture Notes in Computer Science, vol.14798, pp. 217–231. Springer, Cham (2024)
18. Li, H., Graesser, A.C.: The impact of conversational agents' language on summary writing. J. Res. Technol. Educ. **53**(1), 44–66 (2021)
19. Li, J.: Examining EFL learners' source text use in summary writing. Lang. Teach. Res. (2021). https://doi.org/10.1177/13621688211055887
20. Marquart, C.L., Zachar, S., Collier, W., Eagan, B., Woodward, R., Shaffer, D.W.: rENA: Epistemic Network Analysis (2018). https://cran.rproject.org/web/packages/rENA/index.html
21. McAnulty, S.J.: Paraphrase, summary, precis: advantages, definitions, models. Teaching Engl. Two-Year College **8**(1), 47–51 (1981)
22. Meyer, B.J.F., Brandt, D.M., Bluth, G.J.: Use of top-level structure in text: key for reading comprehension of ninth-grade students. Read. Res. Q. **16**(1), 72–103 (1980)
23. Meyer, B.J.F., Freedle, R.O.: Effects of discourse type on recall. Am. Educ. Res. J. **21**(1), 121–143 (1984)
24. Meyer, B.J.F., Wijekumar, K., Lei, P.: Comparative signaling generated for expository texts by 4th–8th graders: variations by text structure strategy instruction, comprehension skill, and signal word. Read. Writ. **31**(9), 1937–1968 (2018)
25. Meyer, B.J.F., Ray, M.N.: Structure strategy interventions: increasing reading comprehension of expository text. Int. Electron. J. Elem. Educ. **4**(1), 127–152 (2011)
26. Pyle, N., et al.: Effects of expository text structure interventions on comprehension: A meta-analysis. Read. Res. Q. **52**(4), 469–501 (2017)
27. Richgels, D.J., McGee, L.M., Lomax, R.G., Sheard, C.: Awareness of four text structures: effects on recall of expository text. Read. Res. Q. **22**(2), 177–196 (1987)
28. Rivard, L.P., Gueye, N.R.: Syntactic complexity and connector use in the summary writing of L1 and L2 Canadian students. J. Fr. Lang. Stud. **33**(2), 1–30 (2023)
29. Shaffer, D.W., Collier, W., Ruis, A.R.: A tutorial on epistemic network analysis: analyzing the structure of connections in cognitive, social, and interaction data. J. Learn. Anal. **3**(3), 9–45 (2016). https://doi.org/10.18608/jla.2016.33.3

30. Van Dijk, T.A., Kintsch, W.: Strategies of Discourse Comprehension, pp. 11–12. Academic Press, New York (1983)
31. Yohana, E., Anugerahwati, M.: Researching summary writing through computer-assisted language learning (CALL): a systematic review. Mextesol J. **47**(3), 1–9 (2023). https://doi.org/10.61871/mj.v47n3-20

Examining the Contribution of Adult Mentor Interactions in Project-Based Adolescent Peer Group Cohesion

Danielle P. Espino[1(✉)], Kristina Lux[1], Lu Liang[1], Chuyue Shan[1], Julia S. Gibson[1], Seung B. Lee[1], Dante Schulz[1], Nastassia Jones[2], and Eric Hamilton[1]

[1] Pepperdine University, Malibu, CA 90263, USA
danielle.espino@pepperdine.edu

[2] Southern University and A&M College, Baton Rouge, LA 70807, USA

Abstract. This paper explores how adult mentors impact the conversational dynamics of two adolescent peer groups in a global, collaborative informal STEM learning community. Each group had a different mentor approach: the rocketry project group had mentors as content experts, while the life science project group had mentors as facilitators focused on engagement. Examination of the discourse from meeting recordings revealed that the rocketry group, guided by content experts, demonstrated strong cohesion with connections between Adult STEM Explanation and STEM Curiosity, then shift to Collaborative Orientation and Task Negotiation. In contrast, the life science group initially focused on Independent Orientation and Task Negotiation, then shifted to Collaborative Orientation with Task Accountability and Negotiation. While both groups got to collaborative orientation, the life science group initially had connections to Awkwardness and Adult Intervention, indicating less cohesion. This suggests that mentors best support student group cohesion by acting as resources than active facilitators, allowing for natural socially shared regulation among students.

Keywords: Project-based learning · collaborative learning · STEM · group dynamics · group interactions · youth · adult mentors · adult interactions

1 Introduction

The cohesion of a group can impact progress towards a task, especially in project-based efforts. Kreijns et al. (2013) emphasize the importance of social aspects of computer-supported collaborative learning (CSCL) environments [1]. They elaborate on the concept of how well a learning environment creates a sound social space through socioemotional interaction. The development of a sound social space is identified by strong interpersonal relationships, trust, and a sense of cohesion, which in turn creates an optimal social context for collaborative learning [1].

Ongoing research exists in examining the various dimensions of interactions in collaborative learning in computer-supported environments, including peer to peer (among students) and teacher to students [2]. Most studies related to this work are in formal

Y. J. Kim and Z. Swiecki (Eds.): icqe 2024, CCIS 2279, pp. 120–128, 2024.
https://doi.org/10.1007/978-3-031-76332-8_10

learning or higher education settings, and such findings generally identify the importance of the teacher's role in carefully planned execution, supervising and facilitating, while also offering support and feedback [3, 4]. Such interaction framing accounts for adults in the formal educator or teacher role, but does not examine less formal roles, such as extracurricular or club advisors. In informal learning settings, adults do not necessarily carry the expectation of leading the learning process as teachers do. Instead, they are supporters of the learning experience for students. Consideration for the impact of non-teacher, adult contributions in the context of informal project-based environments for adolescent learners is explored in this analysis.

1.1 Project Context

This paper examines a project involving adolescent learners from Brazil, Canada, Ghana, Kenya, Mexico, and the United States engaged in informal, project-based STEM learning and media creation. Collaboration is fostered among students through virtual engagement outside the classroom, emphasizing the unique contributions of each participant. Students interact through weekly "global meet-ups" on Zoom, co-creating and discussing STEM-related projects to share at the bi-annual showcase.In the first iteration, the process of regulating collective activity within the project group, or socially shared regulation [5], was led by the students, without intentional adult facilitation. In the second half of the school year, teacher mentors were introduced as content experts, with students choosing projects from six categories: Coding, Life Science, Mathematics, Physics, Robotics, and Rocketry. Project groups met three Saturdays a month on their projects for the bi-annual showcase. While all groups had mentors for content expertise, their roles varied. The Rocketry group's mentors maintained a resource role, while the Life Science group's mentors heavily mediated discussions. This paper examines how the adult mentors for these two project groups contributed to the group cohesiveness across two meeting dates by looking at the conversation dynamics of recorded meetings.

2 Methods

This study analyzed conversations of two project groups, Rocketry and Life Science. Two conversations for each group were recorded. A comprehensive list of participants and adult mentors for the dataset is seen in Table 1. The Life Science room had an overlap in USA participants, Kenyan learner and adult mentor between the dates.

The four recorded Zoom conversations were transcribed and reviewed for accuracy. A codebook containing 12 constructs was developed through an iterative grounded analysis of the data (Table 2). The transcriptions were coded independently by two raters to determine construct presence or absence for each line of data, segmented by turn of talk, and came together in a process of social moderation to reach agreement.

After a final determination of coding the data was reached, visualization models for each group meeting were generated using the epistemic network analysis (ENA) webtool. ENA, an approach within quantitative ethnography, creates visualization of data through the patterns of connections between constructs [6]. The speaker was the unit of analysis and each group meeting the conversations in which connections were limited. The edge weights were scaled to 1.5 to better visualize the connections.

Table 1. Participant Demographic Information

Group	Date	Participants
Rocketry	February 2024	3 Brazilian learners, 1 USA learner, 2 USA adults
	March 2024	2 Brazilian learners, 1 USA learner, 1 Kenyan learner, 1 USA adult
Life Science	February 2024	5 Ghanan learners, 1 Kenyan learner, 4 USA learners, 1 Ghanan adult, 1 Kenyan adult, 5 USA adults
	March 2024	2 Kenyan learners, 3 USA learners, 1 Kenyan adult, 2 USA adults

Table 2. Codebook used for analysis

Code	Definition & Example Utterances	
Task Negotiation	Definition:	Steering the conversation toward completing a task related to the project, asking questions and negotiating/discussing what is needed for the task
	Example:	*…so if we can have meetings during the week before then to update each other on our projects, that would be great on how we can move forward*
Task Accountability	Definition:	Checking if anyone has completed their task related to the project
	Example:	*Yeah, that sounds great... Did you already share that in slack?*
STEM Curiosity	Definition:	Asking question(s) related to understanding STEM content
	Example:	*So are you just using the Lego EV3 and using different parts, or are you making this hand of like actual Legos?*
Adult Intervening	Definition:	Extended silence or pause intervened by the adult mentor
	Example:	*[Silence]... Can we have everyone to go around... introduce themselves and say their interest? Maybe that might make it a little bit easier*
Global/Cultural Awareness	Definition:	Recognition of differences based on culture; a global perspective
	Sample:	*What you want to do allows you to put on a time zone to make it easier for others*

(*continued*)

Table 2. (*continued*)

Code	Definition & Example Utterances	
Collaborative Orientation	Definition:	Recognition of needing others to accomplish something, including a desire to work with others
	Sample:	*So we're... a group. So I'm working on the coding. I believe [Name] are going to work on the coding. I believe you [Name] are doing the 3D part*
Independent Orientation	Definition:	Reliance of self rather than others in the accomplishment of something, self-reliant disposition
	Sample:	*I have [not talked with anyone, but instead] been reading everyone's comments, and their like facts about the water filtration*
Awkwardness	Definition:	Statements not responded to after a long pause (more than 15 s), sharp topic changes, or explicit mentions of awkwardness
	Sample:	*(After a one minute pause) [Name] and [Name]. Do you guys have something to say from [Name]? What, what she was asking about?*
Learner STEM Explanation	Definition:	Elaboration from a learner on a STEM topic
	Sample:	*I know that hydroponic plants can help plants grow faster than using soil. So if we use [them] ...then we wouldn't have to use pesticides*
Adult STEM Explanation	Definition:	Elaboration from an adult or mentor on a STEM topic
	Sample:	*Niobium and titanium are the two that are used in conjunction to make sure if it holds pressure very well... it's a very used material here in the US*
Encountering Challenge	Definition:	Describing challenges in teamwork or communication
	Sample:	*I think I would like to join the robotic hand, although I don't really know much about robotics, so I think I would need a lot of help to be able to do it*

3 Results

The resulting ENA network models for the Rocketry and Life Science groups for February 2024 and March 2024 are below. The dots represent coded constructs and edges (lines) represent the weighted connections between the constructs. Thicker lines indicate stronger connections, while thinner lines indicate weaker connections.

3.1 Rocketry Project Group ENA Model

The Rocketry group model for February 2024, March 2024 and subtracted are below (Fig. 1). For both there are connections between Task Negotiation with Collaborative Orientation and Learner STEM Explanation. No connections to Independent Orientation, Adult Intervening, or Awkwardness. In February, most prominent connections are between STEM Curiosity and Adult STEM Explanation and Learner STEM Explanation. March has a stronger connection between Task Negotiation, Encountering Challenge and Collaborative Orientation. A Mann-Whitney test along the Y axis found February 2024 (Mdn = 0.38, N = 6) was statistically significantly different at the alpha = 0.05 level from March 2024 (Mdn = 0.18, N = 5 U = 28.00, p = 0.02, r = -0.87).

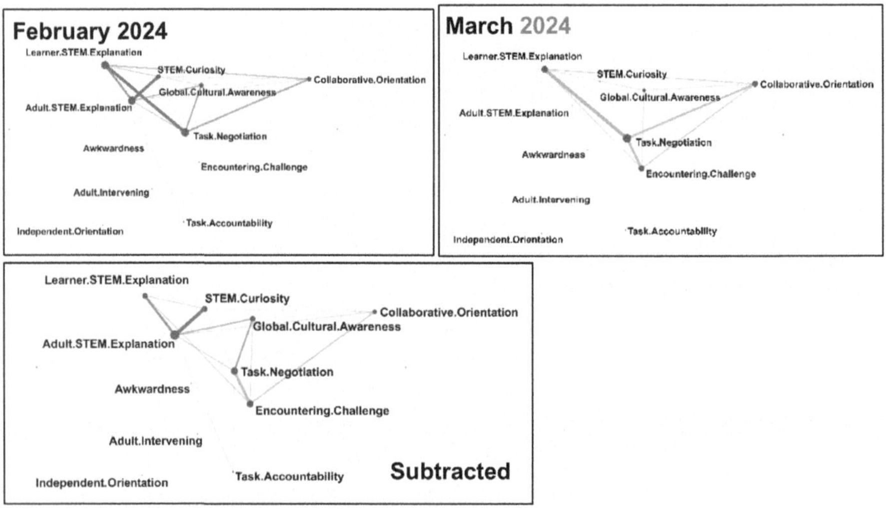

Fig. 1. ENA network models for the Rocketry group in February 2024 (upper left, red), March 2024 (upper right, green) and subtracted network from February and March 2024 (bottom).

3.2 Life Science Project Group ENA Model

The ENA model for the Life Science project group from February 2024, March 2024 and subtracted are seen below in Fig. 2. Across the two dates, similarities are seen in connections to Awkwardness, Adult Intervening, and lack of connection to Global Cultural Awareness. In February 2024, the strongest connections are between Task Orientation with Independent Orientation and Learner STEM Explanation. For March 2024, the strongest connections a triangle between Collaborative Orientation, Task Accountability and Task Negotiation. A Mann-Whitney test along the X axis which showed that February 2024 (Mdn = 0.31, N = 12) was statistically significantly different from March 2024 (Mdn = -0.47, N = 5 U = 60.00, p = 0.00, r = -1.00).

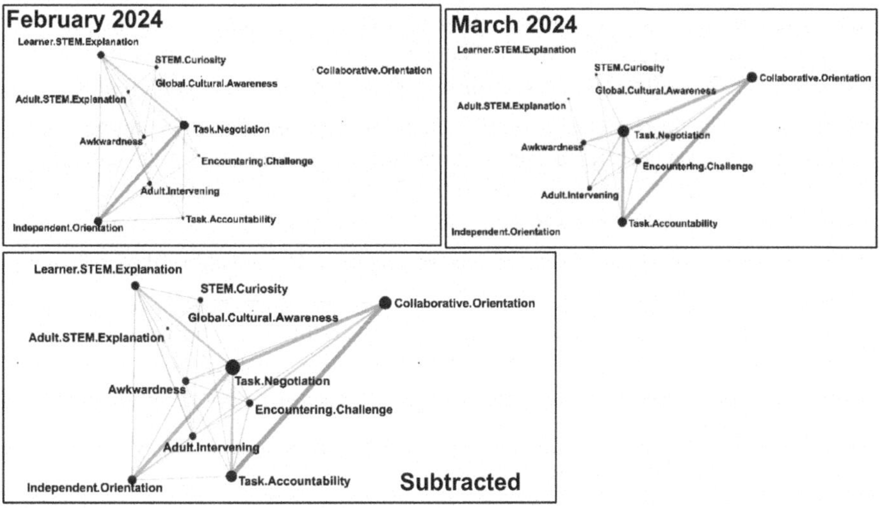

Fig. 2. ENA network models for the Life Science group in February 2024 (upper left, blue), March 2024 (upper right, orange) and subtracted network model from February and March 2024 (bottom).

4 Discussion

The examination of these two project groups show different dynamics in how discourse progressed for each group, both within the group across two months but also between the two groups. For the Rocketry project group, they initially (in February 2024) had strong engagement with their adult mentors (Adult STEM Explanation and STEM Curiosity), which was not prominent in the Life Science project group. The cohesiveness of the group working together by March 2024 is solidified by a triangle of Task Negotiation, Encountering Challenge, and Collaborative Orientation. The Life Science project group was reliant on Independent Orientation and Task Orientation in February 2024, with no connection to Collaboration. In March 2024 we see a distinct triangle of connections between Task Accountability, Collaborative Orientation, and Task Negotiation. The next sections complement observations from the network models with further qualitative examination of the characteristics of each project group's dynamics with respect to their adult mentor involvement and group cohesion.

4.1 Examining the Rocketry Project Group

The Rocketry group was comprised of students from Brazil, Kenya and the United States and adult mentors from the United States. As a rocket scientist, one of the adult mentors was a content expert in the field, while the other mentor had familiarity from classroom experience. During the February 2024, the strong connection between STEM Curiosity and Adult STEM Explanation exemplified the eagerness of the students to ask questions from their content expert. A response from the mentor seemed to elicit more questions from the students, which resulted in a rich exchange for a good portion of the conversation.

USA Student 1: I have a question. So would there be a thing where instead of using like, gas, you feel like your fuel could change? Like they're using gas? The power of the ship with electricity count as a good power source, you know.

Mentor 1: So the thing with electricity is, in order to get the amount of combustible power that you can get from a chemical reaction versus an electrical reaction, the rocket will probably have to weigh 10 to 15 times more. [Lengthy explanation continues]

USA Student 1: Yeah, okay, that makes some sense. But wouldn't they be used solar panels? To make it.

Mentor 1: So we actually use solar panels for satellites to keep them in orbit. The thing is that the amount of energy that comes from a solar panel is fractional compared to what you would get from a, a gas combustion engine, right? [Lengthy explanation continues]

USA Student 1: Okay, that makes sense.

The conversation had no lull (evidenced by no connections to Awkwardness and Adult Intervening) and the students worked towards using their knowledge (Learner STEM Explanation) and moving the project along (Task Negotiation). In the March 2024 meeting, the content expert mentor was not present, however the group had already acted on their knowledge and worked towards building preliminary bottle rockets. This resulted in the students discussing their challenges with one another:

Brazil Student 1: So I'm not sure if this one will count… well, this one the rocket that has the wings in the nosecone. The other rockets didn't have any of those, but it went vertical…

USA Student 1: So we, we built, a rocket, 3D printed fins and cones…But for our large winds and large cones, they can't we can't work out with those because the large fins can't be printed…

Kenya Student 1: Hi, apparently [my rocket] was destroyed by someone. I had to start all over again. But I haven't had that time… But by the time, when I get home, I think I'll be able to [start again].

While the group encountered challenges, they rallied to document their efforts and ways to improve on them and include this in their final video about their project. This is evidenced by the connection between Collaborative Orientation with Task Negotiation and with Encountering Challenge. In this group, the remaining mentor listened and checked in but did not prominently dominate or heavily facilitate the conversation, allowing the process of socially shared regulation to naturally occur, as the students determined suggestions and collaboratively determine the next steps of their project. Across both meeting dates, there was no connection to Awkwardness, Adult Intervening, and Independent Orientation, indicating the cohesiveness of the group.

4.2 Examining the Life Science Project Group

The Life Science group, consisting of students from Ghana, Kenya, and the United States, had mentors who were experienced life science educators but not experts in the students' specific projects. Consequently, students took on the responsibility of directing their research, with mentors acting more as facilitators than content experts. This dynamic led to an individualized approach, as observed in the February 2024 meeting, where strong connections between Independent Orientation and Task Negotiation emerged. Students primarily worked with local peers and only shared information when prompted by mentors. As mentors shifted to project management roles, students began to disengage, leading to moments of silence, reflected in connections with Awkwardness and Adult Intervening. By March 2024, while issues of Awkwardness and Adult Intervening persisted, there was a noticeable shift towards Collaborative Orientation, with less emphasis on Independent Orientation. This connection of Task Negotiation and Collaborative Orientation is expressed by one student:

> ***USA Student C:*** I think what we're trying to do is once everybody just has other information put together and they have pictures and videos because we took pictures and videos while we were doing everything through every step…we could just put it all together at the end and…hopefully get fabulous.

While this shift towards collaboration took place among students, the conversation was still heavily facilitated by the adult mentors. As seen by the lack of connection to Learner STEM Explanation and instead on Task Negotiation in the March 2024 network model, rather than focusing on challenges related to the content of their project, most of the discussion was around how to produce the video about their group project. While the group was not necessarily cohesive in trying to learn together, their shared goal to create a video about their project kept the students focused on collaboration.

4.3 Closing Thoughts

The Rocketry project group displayed balanced interactions among students and mentors, strong social cohesion, and consistent student engagement. The presence of a content expert mentor contributed to the group's cohesion by encouraging students to ask questions, reinforcing their interest and fostering natural socially shared regulation. In contrast, the Life Science group exhibited weaker cohesion, characterized by stronger independent orientation and reliance on their mentor as a facilitator, leading to a dynamic resembling formal learning with less spontaneous student participation.

While this analysis cannot definitively attribute group interactions solely to the mentors, the impact of having a content expert versus a facilitator is evident. A content expert mentor can sustain student interest and promote collaborative disposition, enhancing group cohesion and allowing for socially shared regulation. Over-reliance on a facilitator may weaken student commitment, as seen in the Life Science group's awkward pauses and lack of engagement. Despite these differences, both groups successfully produced final videos of their projects. Whether challenged by problems with the project itself or with the group's cohesion, students demonstrated commitment to finishing their projects and later reflected on how they learned about others and themselves about the experience in post-experience assessments. This speaks to the larger aim of the project community, and how international, informal STEM learning environments can help foster the development of STEM learning.

Acknowledgements. The authors gratefully acknowledge funding support from the National Science Foundation (#2215613) for the work this paper reports. Views appearing in this paper do not reflect those of the funding agency.

References

1. Kreijns, K., Kirschner, P.A., Vermeulen, M.: Social aspects of CSCL environments: A research framework. Educ. Psychol. **48**(4), 229–242 (2013)
2. Hernández-Sellés, N., Muñoz-Carril, P.C., González-Sanmamed, M.: Interaction in computer supported collaborative learning: an analysis of the implementation phase. Int. J. Educ. Technol. High. Educ. **17**(1), 23 (2020)
3. Molinillo, S., Aguilar-Illescas, R., Anaya-Sánchez, R., Vallespín-Arán, M.: Exploring the impacts of interactions, social presence and emotional engagement on active collaborative learning in a social web-based environment. Comput. Educ. **123**, 41–52 (2018)
4. Kuo, Y.-C., Walker, A.E., Schroder, K.E.E., Belland, B.R.: Interaction, internet self-efficacy, and self-regulated learning as predictors of student satisfaction in online education course. Internet High. Educ. **20**, 35–50 (2014). https://doi.org/10.1016/j.iheduc.2013.10.001
5. Järvelä, S., Järvenoja, H., Malmberg, J., Hadwin, A.F.: Exploring socially shared regulation in the context of collaboration. J. Cogn. Educ. Psychol. **12**(3), 267–286 (2013)
6. Shaffer, D.W.: Quantitative Ethnography. Cathcart Press, Madison, WI (2017)

Exploring Teacher Positioning Through Curriculum Materials: A Quantitative Ethnographic Study Comparing Two Educational Systems

Riku Sayuj[1(✉)], Amanda Barany[2], and Janine Remillard[1]

[1] University of Pennsylvania, Philadelphia, PA 19104, USA
Sayuj7@upenn.edu
[2] Drexel University, Philadelphia, PA 19104, USA

Abstract. This study examines the variance in teacher positioning within and between popular math curriculum programs in the United States and Finland, using Epistemic Network Analysis (ENA) for comparative analysis to map the discourse patterns against a Teacher Positioning Matrix derived from positioning theory and current research on teacher development. This matrix supported examinations along the dual dimensions of professionalism and expertise, to understand how different educational contexts and curriculum development practices influence teacher roles. Through epistemic network analysis, some trends emerged: American programs, despite their variability, demonstrate a consistent approach in teacher positioning, suggesting a template-driven and potentially deliberate approach to achieving homogeneity in positioning. Finnish programs exhibit a uniform positioning that consistently aligns teachers as professional experts, potentially reflecting the deeper cultural and pedagogical values embedded within Finnish educational policy and practice. Findings highlight the unique impacts of systemic educational structures on teacher autonomy and professional identity and raise questions about the implications of rigid templates in curriculum design.

Keywords: Teacher Positioning · Curriculum Materials · Epistemic Network Analysis · Positioning Theory

1 Introduction

The enactment of curriculum plays a crucial role in shaping educational outcomes, with teachers at the heart of this process. Teachers are not only implementers of curriculum, but are also active interpreters and agents within their educational settings [1]. There is broad academic consensus that the agency and identity of teachers are crucial in how they engage with and perform these roles during curriculum enactment [2]. This agency is particularly significant as the drive towards professionalization in teaching has seen a growing focus on enhancing teacher expertise and autonomy within the classroom [3]. Effective professional development, which cultivates teacher agency, significantly

Y. J. Kim and Z. Swiecki (Eds.): icqe 2024, CCIS 2279, pp. 129–143, 2024.
https://doi.org/10.1007/978-3-031-76332-8_11

contributes to teacher effectiveness through the promotion of self-efficacy and strategic goal-setting that adapt to contextual challenges [4]. In addition to professionalization and teacher agency, teacher expertise [5], defined as a blend of pedagogical knowledge, classroom management skills, and the ability to adapt teaching strategies to meet student needs, is another aspect that has been emphasized as crucial to teacher effectiveness [6].

Within this context, examining how teachers are positioned by curriculum materials along the dimensions of being both professionals and experts could prove useful, as these materials often serve as the primary tools for both teaching and reform agendas [7]. Research indicates that curriculum materials play a pivotal role as mediators of educational practice, affecting how teachers perceive and enact their professional roles [8]. The positioning embedded within these materials can significantly influence a teacher's identity and performance, affecting not only their day-to-day actions but also their long-term professional trajectories [9]. Positioning theory explains how individuals are defined within the narratives of social interactions and practices. It posits that the consistent portrayal of teachers in particular roles can shape their professional identities and influence their perceptions of agency and autonomy [9].

If teacher identity and effectiveness are influenced by curriculum materials, then understanding the positioning embedded within them becomes essential. With this aim in mind, this work applies positioning theory to explore how teachers are depicted along the dimensions of professionalism and expertise across two distinct international educational contexts as evidenced by their popular curriculum materials. The USA and Finland provide contrasting backdrops for this investigation due to their divergent approaches to educational policy and curriculum development. While the USA has traditionally emphasized more standardized outcome-based educational frameworks, reflecting a trend towards uniformity and measurable benchmarks in education [10], Finland is noted for its bottom-up, teacher-led approach, which has been linked to high performance on international assessments like PISA (Programme for International Student Assessment) [11]. These differing approaches provide a rich contrast for examining how curricular materials across varied educational environments position teachers.

The following research questions are investigated to examine these contrasts:

1. How do curriculum materials position teachers as professionals and experts?
2. How does teacher positioning by curriculum materials vary across and within different educational contexts (USA & Finland)?

2 Literature Review

2.1 Teacher Curriculum Interaction

Existing literature on teacher-curriculum interaction frames our understanding of the complex dynamics between educational materials and teachers. Within this discourse, the Instructional Tetrahedron, as modified from Rezat and Straesser's work [12] provides a useful conceptual framework for understanding the interactions between curriculum, teachers, students, and mathematics. We assume that active agents in this model (Teacher, Students, and Curriculum materials) actively position each other within this tetrahedron and aim to investigate the Curricular positioning of teachers. Teachers interact with curriculum materials [13] not just as implementers but also as interpreters, suggesting that the relationship takes the shape of an instructional discourse between these two nodes of the tetrahedron. Such discourse [14] is a significant factor in the development of teacher identity, impacting how teachers perceive and engage with curriculum materials through various knowledge-making processes and social practices. Teacher identity and the professional roles they assume within the curriculum enactment process are thus expected to be influenced by the nature of the curriculum materials they engage with.

The concept of teacher agency in curriculum enactment is also central to understanding how teachers adapt and modify curriculum materials in practice. Teacher decisions and interactions with curriculum materials significantly affect the implementation of educational reforms and the instructional changes they are meant to inspire [7]. These interactions can reinforce or reshape the educational trajectories within classrooms and by extension, influence educational outcomes. The professionalization of teachers, particularly through frameworks that emphasize standards and outcomes, has been extensively documented [3]. These frameworks often aim to define what teachers should know and be able to do, thus contributing to shaping the professional identities of teachers by positioning them within specific pedagogical narratives.

Our study builds on previous research that examined five mathematics curriculum programs used in the USA [15]. That analysis, conducted under the ICUBiT project (Improving Curriculum Use for Better Teaching), includes an examination of how mathematical support is communicated to teachers and how this shapes instructional practices. This foundational work informs the primary codes used in our study, modified to align with the instructional tetrahedron and positioning theory framework. Thus, this study aims to extend the ICUBiT curriculum analysis further by applying ENA and positioning theory to understand the dynamic interactions between curriculum materials and teacher positioning.

Positioning theory [9] provides a robust theoretical framework for analyzing these dynamics. It suggests that the roles teachers are assigned in curriculum materials are not just instructional prescriptions but are also indicative of deeper societal and cultural narratives about teaching and professionalism. These roles contribute to the ongoing construction of teacher identities within the educational discourse, influencing how teachers perceive their autonomy, expertise, and professional growth. In positioning theory, "rights and duties" are key elements that determine individuals' social positions, made visible through the discourse that surrounds them [16]. Deriving from this, in this study, we interpret the "rights and duties" of teachers through the guidance provided in curriculum materials [15]. By focusing on different types of guidance—directive and educative—we can better understand how these materials position teachers and the implications for their professional roles [17]. Additionally, the authority and power dynamics embedded in this guidance reflect broader educational and societal values, illustrating how teachers are expected to conform to certain norms and practices within their cultural contexts [18]. This approach aims to provide insights into how curriculum materials influence teacher positioning, shaping their professional identity and autonomy in practice.

Synthesized from our review of existing research, we leverage the following teacher positioning matrix to characterize teacher positioning along two dimensions—professional perception and level of expertise (See Fig. 1). This matrix categorizes positions based on the balance between Educative and Directive Guidance, alongside the level of Instructional Autonomy provided and support for Reflective Practice and uses ENA as a tool to achieve these categorizations as detailed in the methods section below.

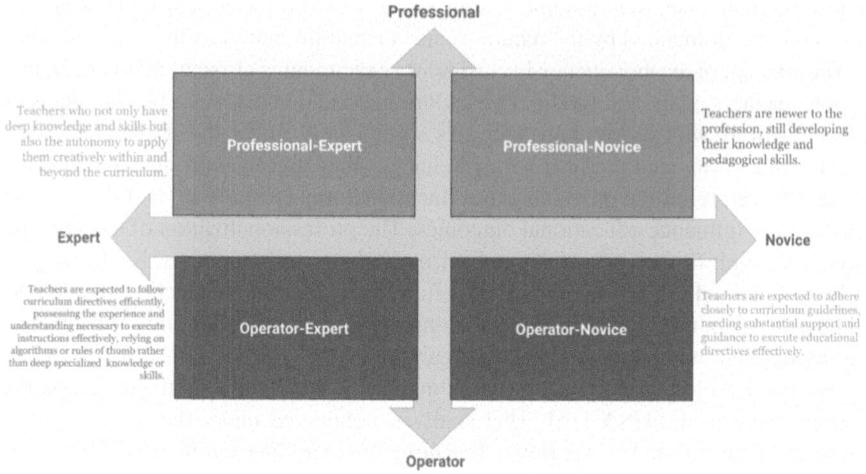

Fig. 1. Teacher Positioning Matrix

2.2 Comparing Educational Systems

In contrasting educational systems such as those in the USA and Finland, curriculum materials play differing roles in shaping teacher professionalism and expertise. Research on teaching practices indicates that instructional systems are embedded within cultural systems, reflecting an "implicit cultural logic" [19]. In Finland, instructional practices are based predominantly on trust and agency [20], and emphasizes a strong belief in schooling, respect for teachers, and trust in schools [21]. The national core curriculum provides broad guidelines without national testing, giving teachers considerable autonomy to design their lessons and foster student agency, promoting active engagement with learning materials [22]. This approach reflects a cultural ethos that values pedagogical freedom and professional judgment [23].

In contrast, the United States places greater emphasis on control and structured support in its educational practices [19]. The focus on standards and accountability has shifted to standardized-test results and value-added measures, creating a culture of performativity that employs judgments and comparisons for control and change [24]. Administrators often dictate curriculum resources and lesson sequencing, with state standards outlining specific learning outcomes measured by high-stakes assessments [25]. Teachers' guides provide substantial guidance, expecting teachers to follow closely scripted lessons, which can limit pedagogical freedom and innovation [15].

Studies have shown that where teachers feel supported by curriculum frameworks that respect and enhance their professional judgment, there is a corresponding improvement in teaching quality and student outcomes [26]. Conversely, overly prescriptive curriculum models that limit teacher creativity and professional discretion can lead to disengagement and a lack of innovation in teaching practices. In the USA, the push towards standardization in curriculum design is often seen as a move to ensure consistency and accountability in educational outcomes [10]. The Finnish educational system is characterized by a higher degree of teacher autonomy, with curriculum frameworks designed to support teacher-driven interpretations and innovations [27]. This approach not only highlights different educational philosophies but also underscores the significant role that cultural and policy contexts play in shaping how teachers are positioned by curriculum materials.

3 Methods

This study employed a comparative research design to study the curriculum programs across the USA and Finland. The data selected for this study included mathematics curriculum materials from two leading programs among each country's top ten programs, as indicated by their market shares [28, 29] and indicated usage in teacher surveys [30]. The selected programs were EngageNY/Eureka Math (EN) and Illustrative Mathematics (IM) from the USA, and Tuhattaituri (TT) and Laskutaito (LT) from Finland to form a sample size of 8 TGs (2 TGs each from grades 3 and 5) and 24 lessons (3 lessons from each TG). Only the Teacher Guides (TGs) were coded, as they directly address teachers, unlike other curriculum materials that primarily target students. The teacher guides were coded at the paragraph level because meaningful segments of information suitable for structured coding were presented only at that level.

The codebook used for this study was developed from existing research on teacher professionalism, teacher expertise, and educative guidance. This research builds on the data and findings from the ICUBiT project [15], which examined the communication about mathematics in elementary curriculum materials, focusing on the types of support provided to teachers. They identified various forms of mathematical guidance, such as direct explanations, anticipated student strategies, and the embedding of mathematical ideas in teacher actions. This analysis informed the primary codes in our study. For example, the code for "Directive Guidance" was adapted from the types of explicit mathematical support identified in that analysis [15], while the code for "Educative Guidance" was based on their findings related to pedagogical rationale and support for understanding student strategies. The "Instructional Autonomy" and "Reflective Practice" codes were further developed to capture teacher agency and professional growth, extending the original codebook to meet the specific requirements of this study. These adaptations enabled the application of Epistemic Network Analysis (ENA) and positioning theory to explore how curriculum materials influence teacher positioning, providing deeper insights into their professional identity and autonomy in various educational contexts.

Each primary code was further subdivided into corresponding subcodes to align with the dimensions of the instructional tetrahedron, allowing for an analysis of how each primary code operates across these dimensions (See Table 1). This ensured that the codebook adhered closely to the positioning theory framework while addressing literature on teacher guidance, autonomy, and the relationship model emphasized by the Instructional Tetrahedron model. Inter-rater reliability was assessed using Cohen's kappa, with all codes reaching a threshold of 0.8, indicating substantial agreement among the coders.

Table 1. Codebook with definitions and code hierarchy.

#	Code Name	Definition
1	Directive Guidance (DG)	Explicit, detailed instructions on teaching methods
1.1	Content Coverage	Guidelines on topics, and the order and extent of coverage
1.2	Directing Action	Detailed, procedural steps for lesson execution
1.3	Classroom Management Directions	Guidance on managing the classroom environment during instruction
2	Educative Guidance (EG)	Guidance aimed at deepening teachers' content knowledge and enhancing their pedagogical skills
2.1	Attending to Math	For better understanding of mathematical concepts
2.2	Pedagogical Rationale	Guidance on teaching techniques, tasks, representations, teacher moves, or activities and their rationale
2.3	Curriculum Design	Explanation of lesson structure, goals, aims, etc
2.4	Mathematical Goals	Communication and rationale about goals
2.5	Classroom Management Tips	Suggestions with explanation of classroom management strategies
2.6	Attending to Student Thinking	Addresses student understanding: what students should know or be able to do, ways they may respond, etc
3	Instructional Autonomy (IA)	Encouragement for teachers to adapt lessons based on professional judgment
3.1	Adaptation Opportunities	Suggestions to modify lessons to suit contextual needs
3.2	Contextual Decision-Making	Freedom to alter instruction based on classroom dynamics and individual student needs
4	Reflective Practice (RP)	Suggestions to reflect on teaching effectiveness
4.1	Effectiveness Questions	Prompts that encourage evaluation of teaching methods

(*continued*)

Table 1. (*continued*)

#	Code Name	Definition
4.2	Student Feedback Reflection	Utilizing student feedback to inform instructional adjustments
5	Referential Information	Includes information on material or vocabulary, references to standards, other pages or resources, solutions, etc

In this study, epistemic network analysis [31] was applied to the data using the ENA Web Tool (version 1.7.0). ENA can be used to compare units of analysis in terms of their plotted point positions, individual networks, or network difference graphs. The ENA algorithm uses a moving window to construct a network model for each line in the data, showing how codes in the current line are connected to codes that occurred previously [32], here defined as 4 lines (each line plus the 3 previous lines) within a given conversation. This window length was arrived at through iteration and represents approximately half a page of the teacher guides and typically tends to deal with instructional activity (See Fig. 2). The resulting networks are aggregated for all lines for each unit of analysis in the model. Our ENA model included all the codes listed in Table 1.

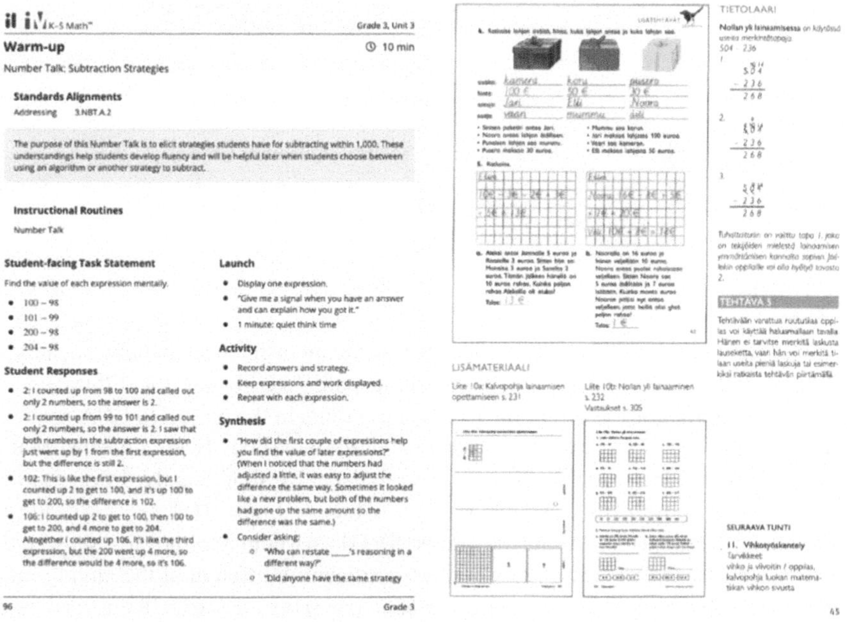

Fig. 2. Sample TG Page USA (IM) & Sample TG Page Finland (TT)

ENA was useful to analyze the frequency and interconnectedness of these codes across different programs and thus characterize the programs. Programs are allocated to the four quadrants of the Teacher Positioning Matrix (Fig. 1)—Professional-Expert, Professional-Novice, Operator-Expert, and Operator-Novice—based on the frequency and interconnectedness of specific codes—DG, EG, IA, RP, and their sub-codes, with specific criteria for quadrant placement (See Fig. 3). This approach allowed the placement of programs based on observed patterns of autonomy and guidance. To further deepen the analysis, Narrative Exposition was employed to articulate the contextual narratives found within the data for a more comprehensive understanding of how curriculum materials construct teacher identities and roles [33].

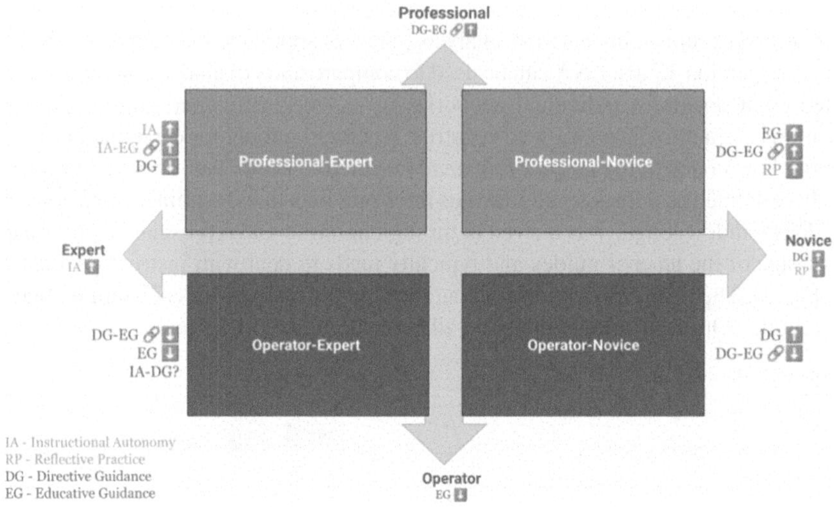

Fig. 3. 1Teacher Positioning Matrix - Quadrant Criteria

4 Results

Epistemic Network Analysis helped uncover significant differences in how teachers are positioned within U.S. and Finnish curriculum materials. To test for differences we applied a Mann-Whitney U test to the location of points in the projected ENA space for units in Finland and USA, which showed that along the x-axis (with a means rotation applied) Finland (Mdn = -0.30, N = 8) was statistically significantly different at the alpha = 0.05 level from USA (Mdn = 0.35, N = 8 U = 0, p = 0.00, r = 1.00). For the second model (within USA), along the x-axis (SVD1), a Mann-Whitney test showed that IM (Mdn = 0.07, N = 14) was statistically significantly different at the alpha = 0.05 level from EN (Mdn = −0.22, N = 24 U = 66.00, p = 0.00, r = 0.61). In the third model (within FIN), along the x-axis (SVD1), a Mann-Whitney test showed that LT (Mdn = 0, N = 15) was not statistically significantly different at the alpha = 0.05 level from TT (Mdn = 0, N = 15 U = 101.50, p = 0.66, r = 0.10). For model 1, we defined the units of analysis as all lines of data associated with a single value of Context subsetted by Program.Name and Lesson. For models 2 and 3, we defined the units of analysis as all lines of data associated with a single value of Program.Name subsetted by Lesson and Lesson.Part. The co-registration correlations for all models were consistently high, indicating a strong goodness of fit: 1 (Pearson) and 1 (Spearman) for the first dimension, and 0.99-1 (Pearson) and 0.98-1 (Spearman) for the second.

In the United States, Network Graph 1 below (See Fig. 4) revealed that the American curriculum programs commonly exhibit strong ties to DG, which is associated with a more structured, less autonomous approach. For example, in the EN program, the lesson structure is explicitly prescribed, such as in 'Relate Division and Multiplication' where the lesson is segmented into distinct time-allocated parts: Fluency Practice [12 min], Application Problem [5 min], Concept Development [33 min], and Student Debrief [10 min], indicating minimal flexibility for teacher adaptation. They thus exhibit a consistent positioning away from the 'professional-expert' quadrant and towards a more guided and templated discourse with teachers, reflecting the directive nature of the curriculum materials which limit pedagogical freedom. In contrast, Finnish programs show robust links between IA and EG, consistently positioning teachers in the 'Professional-Expert' quadrant, indicative of an educational environment that values and promotes teacher autonomy and expertise. For example, in the TT program lesson on Sequential Borrowing, the guidance provided to teachers details steps such as borrowing one from the higher place when subtracting from the ones, and marking the borrowing and the remaining ones, which helps teachers understand the methodology and rationale behind each step. Additionally, the TG states that "teachers can modify these examples as needed to fit their classroom context," providing explicit autonomy for teachers to adapt and change the instructional approach.

The predominance of 'Directive Guidance' in the USA materials may reflect a narrative that positions teachers in roles where they have certain duties to deliver the curriculum in a specific manner, aligning with the 'Professional-Novice' quadrant where there is an expectation of following structured yet Educative guidance, as was illustrated in the detailed lesson plan structure (IM) that gives the rationale for the segments but still expects the teacher to follow the rigid time-bound structure. The positioning of 'Instructional Autonomy' closer to the USA might indicate that even within a structured curriculum, there are opportunities for teachers to make professional judgments. However, the lack of interconnectedness with other nodes suggests these opportunities are not deeply integrated into the curriculum's discourse. The strong association of 'Educative Guidance' with the Finnish context suggests a view of teachers as professionals who are expected to understand the content, resonating with the 'Professional-Expert' quadrant. For instance, Finnish materials provide detailed notes on how to engage students in deeper thinking, such as in the instruction to "Have students discuss how they can make sure the middle mark shows half of the liquid". Referential Information' being less interconnected in the Finnish context can be seen as consistent with a paradigm that trusts teachers to source and integrate such information independently, as one would expect from the 'Professional-Expert' quadrant. For example, the note stating, "You can save the fraction strips students create during this lesson for use in future lessons", highlights the expectation for teachers to use their judgment in utilizing resources over time. These patterns were used to place the programs within the Teacher Positioning Matrix (Fig. 5) based on the criteria illustrated in Fig. 3.

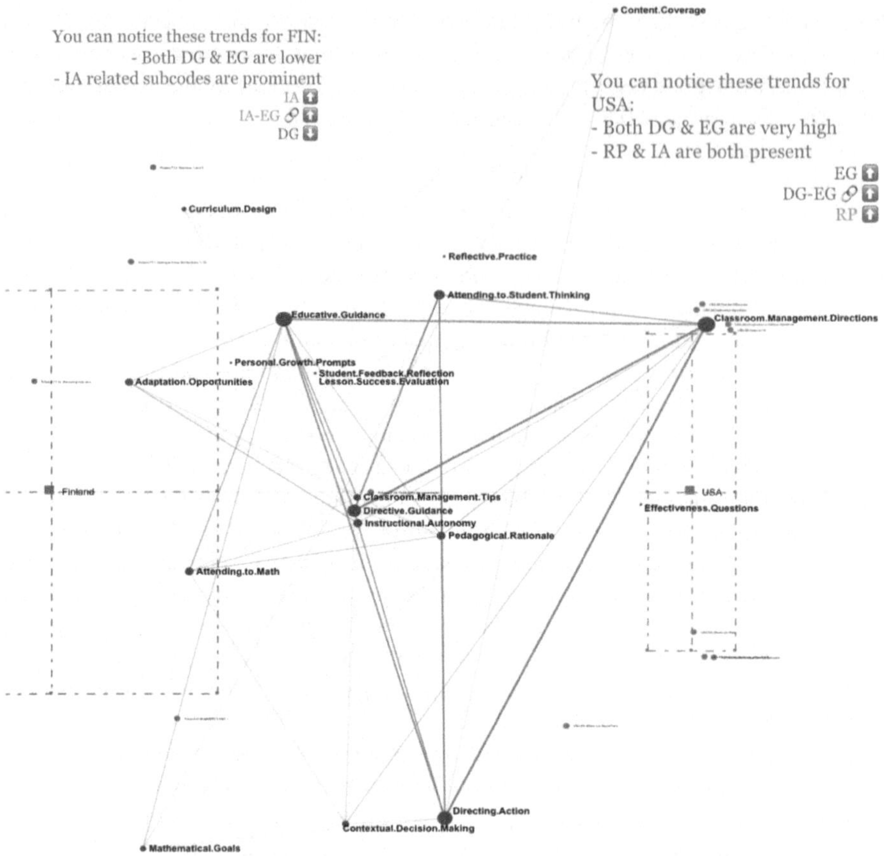

Fig. 4. Network Graph 1: FIN-USA Network Difference Graph

Graphs 2 and 3 (Figs. 6 and 7), which compare different programs within the United States and within Finland respectively, showcase some more interesting trends. American programs exhibit significant variance from one another, but always maintaining their positioning away from the 'professional-expert' quadrant. This suggests a prevalent use of curricular templates in the USA that direct teacher behavior and potentially restricts teacher autonomy by enforcing standardized instructional practices. This was something researchers observed repeatedly while reading through the teacher guides as part of the data collection and cleaning process.

Finnish programs demonstrate a consistent approach of empowering teachers, aligning closely with the professional expertise quadrant. The analysis showed that Finnish curriculum materials rarely prescribe rigid instructional pathways but rather, encourage pedagogical freedom and innovation, thus supporting the professional growth and autonomy of teachers. For instance, in a typical TT program lesson on numbers, teachers are encouraged to explore numerical relationships by investigating everyday objects available to them in the classroom, to represent zero and one.

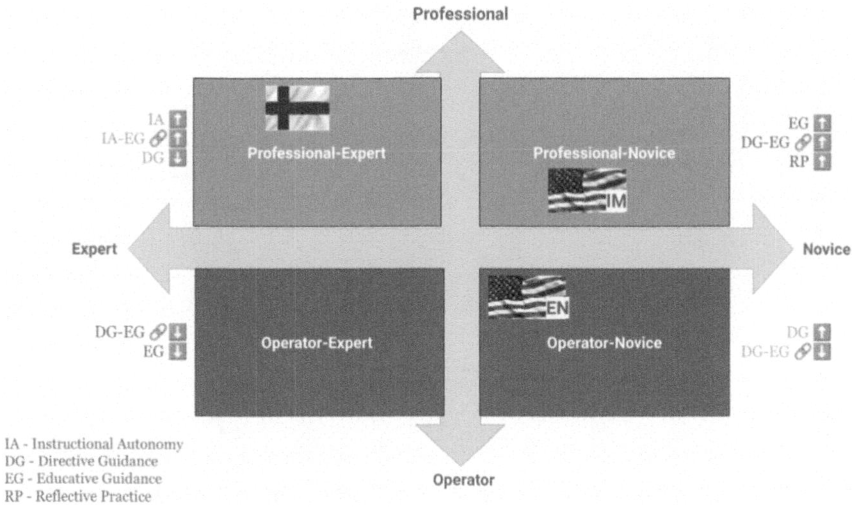

Fig. 5. Teacher Positioning Matrix with all programs mapped into the quadrants

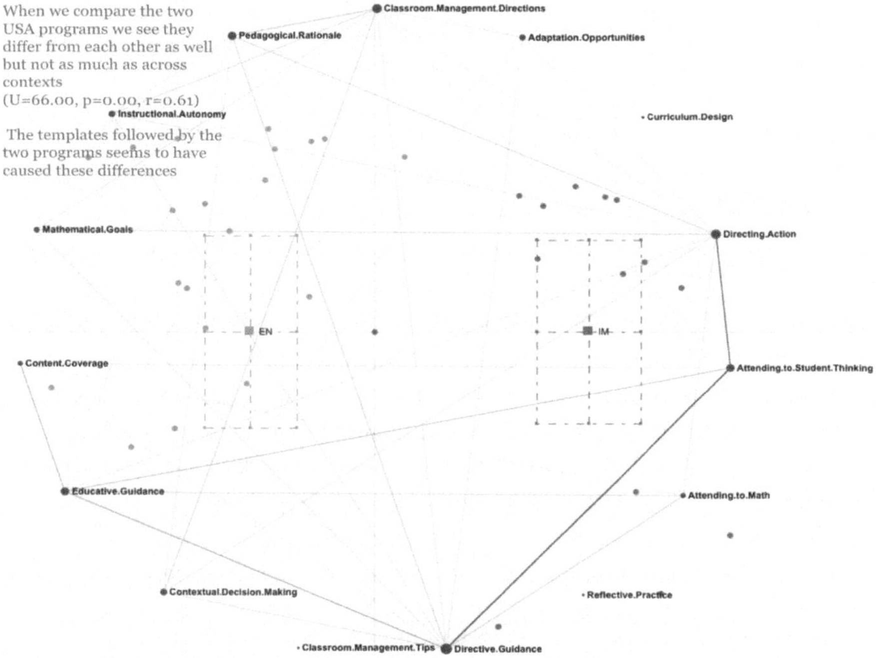

Fig. 6. Network Graph 2: Within USA (IM-EN) Network Difference Graph

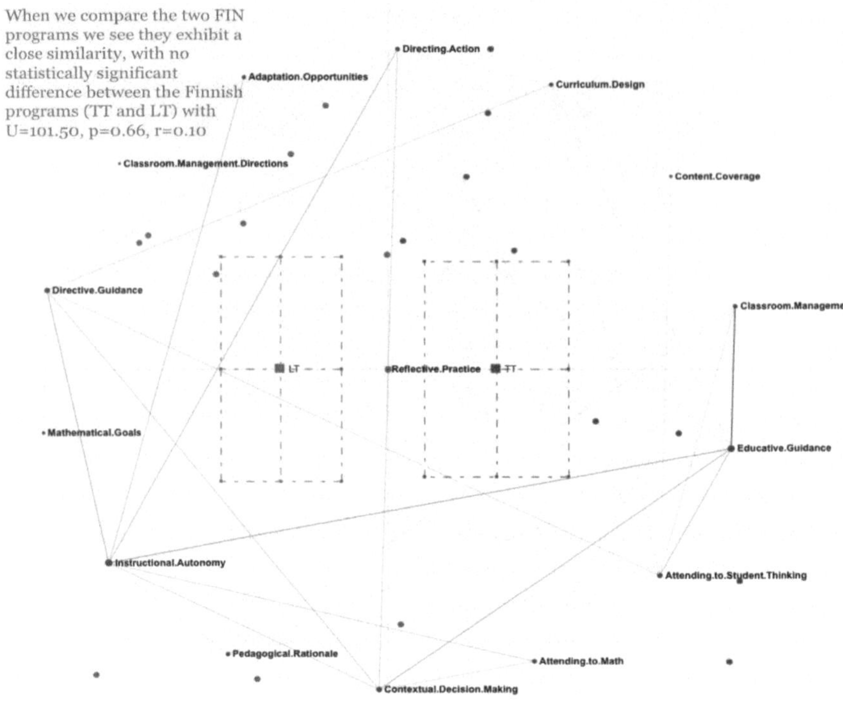

Fig. 7. Network Graph 3: Within FIN (TT-LT) Network Difference Graph

5 Discussion

5.1 Summary Assertions

From the analysis above, three tentative assertions are derived that merit further exploration with further research:

Assertion 1: Differences in Autonomy and Guidance: While American programs often scripted teacher actions, reducing autonomy, Finnish programs supported teacher-led pedagogical decisions. This approach is reflected in the strong associations between IA and EG, suggesting a system that supports pedagogical innovation and teacher-led decision-making.

Assertion 2: Curricular Templates Dictate Teacher Positioning in the USA Curriculum materials. The data suggests that in the USA, the consistent shift away from the 'professional-expert' quadrant across various programs and lessons indicates a system-wide reliance on curricular templates. The examined American programs demonstrate this reliance on curricular templates that appear to standardize curricular positioning of teachers, often at the expense of pedagogical freedom.

Assertion 3: Finnish Programs Achieve Consistent Teacher Positioning Through Cultural Pedagogical Values Rather Than Templates. The Finnish data points to a national pedagogical alignment that facilitates teacher positioning within the 'professional-expert'

quadrant, without the rigidity of templates. This suggests that the Finnish education system supports a culture that inherently values and encourages teacher autonomy and professionalism, allowing for a more organic and culturally embedded approach to teaching.

5.2 Contextual Comparisons

Positioning theory [9] provides a lens through which the positioning of teachers, as delineated in our study, reflects broader societal and pedagogical narratives. The consistent positioning of Finnish teachers towards the 'professional-expert' quadrant, as opposed to the more varied positioning away from it in the U.S., suggests that the Finnish educational context effectively empowers teachers, fostering environments where their professional judgment and expertise are valued and promoted. This aligns with observations that the Finnish system [27] prioritizes teacher autonomy and is reflective of a cultural ethos that values deep pedagogical understanding and innovation. The Finnish approach, characterized by high levels of trust in teachers and minimal prescriptive guidelines, supports a flexible and teacher-driven pedagogy [23].

Conversely, the data from the USA presents a more complex scenario where the reliance on standardized curricular templates appears to create a uniformity that paradoxically leads to greater variability in how teachers are positioned. This finding echoes critiques of the American educational system's focus on standardization [10] and suggests a potential disconnection between the intention of standardized curricula—to ensure consistency and quality across educational outcomes—and the actual impact on teacher autonomy, and professional identity. The U.S. emphasis on control and accountability reflects a cultural logic that prioritizes measurable outcomes over pedagogical freedom, contributing to the variability in teacher positioning observed in this study. This is problematic because the development of teacher expertise is crucial to educational success [3]. Teachers' ability to navigate and adapt curriculum materials critically affects the implementation of educational reforms and ultimately, student outcomes. Such findings invite further scrutiny of standardized practices such as curricular templates and raise questions about their effectiveness in fostering environments that truly enhance teacher professionalism and autonomy. It remains unclear to what extent the templating process overrides the curricular developers' intentions, highlighting a critical area for future research.

6 Conclusion

This inquiry into the positioning of teachers by curriculum materials in the USA and Finland points to significant differences in the positioning of teachers across these systems and highlights the need for further research to understand the full implications of these practices. This research can serve as a call for curriculum companies to reconsider the extent of templatization in their educational materials. By allowing curriculum developers more freedom to craft their content according to pedagogical best practices rather than rigid frameworks, educational programs may better cater to the varying needs of classrooms. Further investigation is also warranted to understand the gap (if any) between the positioning of teachers by curriculum developers and the positioning enforced by the templates themselves.

It is important also to note some of the limitations of this study. The examination of only two curriculum programs warrants further research into standardized curricular templates in the USA, given the vast heterogeneity and size of the country compared to Finland. Moreover, the exclusive reliance on teacher guides excludes potential insights from other curriculum materials directly addressing students. Also, it is important to note that this analysis does not take into account differences in the mathematical aims or approach of the content in the curriculum programs. Given the U.S. tendency to use adopted curriculum programs to shape instructional practice, U.S. materials are likely to include more novel mathematical content and more guidance. Our findings must be understood within this cultural difference.

As we move forward, it is essential to approach educational reform with a focus on enhancing the professional lives of teachers, respecting their expertise, and providing them with the tools and freedoms necessary to implement effective pedagogical strategies. Future studies should explore more deeply the impact of curricular structures on teacher autonomy and professional identity and consider the broader cultural and policy contexts that influence these dynamics. This ongoing dialogue is vital for developing educational systems that not only improve student outcomes but also foster a supportive and enriching environment for teachers.

References

1. Remillard, J.T., Heck, D.J.: Teachers as consumers of curriculum materials: an exploration of teacher agency. Teach. Teach. Educ. **99**, 103293 (2014)
2. Stein, M., Remillard, J., Smith, M.: How curriculum influences student learning. In: Lester, F.K., Jr. (ed.) Second handbook of research on mathematics teaching and learning, pp. 319–369. Information Age, Gweenwich, CT (2007)
3. Darling-Hammond, L., Bransford, J.: Preparing Teachers for a Changing World: What Teachers Should Learn and be Able to do. Jossey-Bass, San Francisco (2005)
4. Kennedy, M.: How does professional development improve teaching? Rev. Educ. Res. **86**(4), 945–980 (2016)
5. Berliner, D.C.: Describing the behavior and documenting the accomplishments of expert teachers. Bull. Sci. Technol. Soc. **24**(3), 200–212 (2004)
6. Hammerness, K., Darling-Hammond, L., Bransford, J.: How teachers learn and develop. In: Preparing teachers for a changing world: What teachers should learn and be able to do, pp. 358–389. Jossey-Bass, San Francisco (2005)
7. Ball, D.L., Cohen, D.K.: Reform by the book What is—or might be—the role of curriculum materials in teacher learning and instructional reform? Educ. Res. **25**(9), 6–8, 14 (1996)
8. Priestley, M., et al.: Teacher Agency: An Ecological Approach. Bloomsbury, London (2015)
9. Harré, R., van Langenhove, L.: Positioning Theory: Moral Contexts of Intentional Action. Blackwell Publishers Ltd, Oxford (1999)
10. Porter, A.C.: Measuring the content of instruction: uses in research and practice. Educ. Res. **31**(7), 3–14 (2002)
11. Schleicher, A.: Preparing Teachers and Developing School Leaders for the 21st Century: Lessons from Around the World. OECD Publishing, Paris (2012)
12. Rezat, S., Straesser, R.: From the didactical triangle to the socio-didactical tetrahedron. J. Math. Teacher Educ. **15**(1), 3–34 (2012)

13. Remillard, J.T., Herbel-Eisenmann, B.A., Lloyd, G.M. (eds.) Curriculum materials in mathematics education reform (2009)
14. Pishghadam, R., Golzar, S., Miri, F.: The relationship between identity and teacher agency. J. Lang. Identity Educ. **21**(1), 48–64 (2022)
15. Remillard, J.T., Kim, O.: Elementary Mathematics Curriculum Materials. Routledge (2020)
16. Davis, E.A., Francis, K.: Discourse and development in science education: the role of teacher guidance in curricular materials. J. Res. Sci. Teach. **60**(3), 377–401 (2023)
17. Davis, E.A., Krajcik, J.: Designing educative curriculum materials to promote teacher learning. Educ. Res. **34**(3), 3–14 (2005)
18. Van Steenbrugge, H., Remillard, J.T.: The multimodality of lesson guides and the communication of social relations. ZDM – Math. Educ. **55**(3), 579–595 (2023). https://doi.org/10.1007/s11858-023-01479-2
19. Hiebert, J., Gallimore, R., Stigler, J.W.: The new heroes of teaching: how teachers learn to teach. J. Staff. Dev. **26**(4), 46–51 (2005)
20. Erss, M., Kalmus, V., Autio, T.H.: A study of Finnish teachers. J. Educ. Policy **31**(5), 567–586 (2016)
21. Simola, H., Rinne, R.: Finnish education as a paradox: the case of curricular policies and teacher autonomy. J. Curric. Stud. **43**(5), 625–640 (2011)
22. Hemmi, K., Lepik, M., Viholainen, A.: Analysing mathematics curriculum materials: a Finnish perspective. J. Curric. Stud. **49**(4), 530–553 (2017)
23. Krzywacki, H., Condon, L., Remillard, J.T., Machalow, R., Koljonen, T., Van Steenbrugge, H.: Emergency remote teaching as a window into elementary teachers' mathematics instructional systems in Finland and the U.S. Int. J. Educ. Res. Open **5**, 100286 (2023). https://doi.org/10.1016/j.ijedro.2023.100286
24. Supovitz, J.A.: Can high stakes testing leverage educational improvement? J. Educ. Change **10**(2–3), 211–227 (2009)
25. Remillard, J., Reinke, L.: Mathematics curriculum in the United States: New challenges and opportunities (2017)
26. Darling-Hammond, L.: The Flat World and Education: How America's Commitment to Equity will Determine our Future. Teachers College Press, New York (2010)
27. Sahlberg, P.: Finnish Lessons: What Can the World Learn from Educational Change in Finland? Teachers College Press, New York (2011)
28. Koljonen, T.: Finnish mathematics curriculum programs: Usage and teacher perceptions. Helsinki Stud. Educ. **17**, 150–165 (2014)
29. CEMD: Comparative Educational Material Database: Annual Report. Center for Education and Media Design, New York (2023)
30. Remillard, J., Condon, L., Koljonen, T., Krzywacki, H., Sayuj, R.: Teacher agency and the use of curriculum materials across cultural contexts. In: Proceedings of the 47th Annual Meeting of the International Group for the Psychology of Mathematics Education (PME-47), Massey University (2023)
31. Shaffer, D.W., Collier, W., Ruis, A.R.: A tutorial on epistemic network analysis. J. Learn. Anal. **3**(3), 9–45 (2016)
32. Ruis, A.R., et al.: Epistemic Network Analysis Version 1.7.0: Advanced user's guide. Learning Analytics Workbench, Madison, WI (2019)
33. Riessman, C.K.: Narrative Methods for the Human Sciences. Sage Publications, Thousand Oaks, CA (2008)

Como Las Mareas Del Océano: A Quantitative Ethnography of Caribbean Latino and Afro-Latino Identity and Education in *El Norte De* Philadelphia

Amalia Dache(✉), Jonathon Sun, and Dennis Espejo

University of Pennsylvania, Philadelphia, PA 19104, USA
adache@upenn.edu

Abstract. AfroLatin American populations living in the United States are difficult to identify and count. This demographic conundrum creates challenges for public and education policy. How can policymakers assess the social, economic, and educational needs of a population that is as racially, ethnically, and geographically diverse as the tides of an ocean? Our research study of a North Philadelphia publicly subsidized housing community consisting of predominantly Caribbean Latinos and AfroLatinos, finds that using a cultural ecological framework through a quantitative ethnography, provides conceptual insights that support safe, sustainable, culturally-based and family-oriented educational housing programs and interventions.

Keywords: Afro-Latin · Cultural Ecology · Publicly Subsidized Housing

1 Introduction and Literature Review

According to a 2023 study, an estimated 2.2 million Latinos identify as Black [1]. However, there are believed to be around 6 million AfroLatinos in the United States. The Pew Research Center highlighted the complexities of AfroLatino identity and the low percentage of Latin American and African descent individuals marking the Black category in the U.S. Census. Their survey found that 6 million AfroLatino adults reside in the U.S. [2]. This leaves 3.8 million, more than 63% of the AfroLatino population, undercounted in the U.S. Census. Our current study, through a neighborhood-specific research inquiry, explores how the landscapes of education and identity are experienced by a largely Caribbean Latino and AfroLatino housing community.

Although there is a scarcity of higher education access and opportunity research on AfroLatino populations in the U.S., research reveals that they are more likely than White Latinos to live in cities in the Northeast United States, be foreign-born, live in neighborhoods with higher populations of Black Americans, have higher rates of poverty, unemployment, and lower household incomes [3]. Yet, a 2023 national study found that Latinos who also identify as Black in the U.S. Census "have higher education levels than non-Black Latinos: 26% of Afro-Latinas completed a college degree, compared to 18%

Y. J. Kim and Z. Swiecki (Eds.): icqe 2024, CCIS 2279, pp. 144–158, 2024.
https://doi.org/10.1007/978-3-031-76332-8_12

of non-Black Latinas. Similarly, 20% of Afro-Latinos completed a bachelor's degree or more, compared to 15% of non-Black Latino men [1]." Paradoxically, the Pew Research survey found that only 15% of AfroLatinos had earned a college degree, while 17% non-Black Latinos, and 29% of U.S. adults had college degrees.

Our current study finds that Latinos who also identify as Black based on U.S. Census data, while present at 2.8% in the El Norte neighborhood, a statistical measurement that as the Pew Center survey revealed does not represent the majority of Latinos with African descendancy residing in the United States, is also an undercount of AfroLatinos living in a North Philadelphia neighborhood. Through a quantitative ethnography of North Philadelphia's Latino housing community, 43.3% of the 72-person study were AfroLatino using "Street Race" [4] to guide the researcher's racial categorization of participants.

We find that the largely Caribbean Latino and AfroLatino populations have unique cultural ecological attributes that contribute to understanding how they engage in informal and formal educational environments based on their migration and national origin history.

1.1 Hispanic-Latinos in Publicly Subsidized Housing and Community Education Initiatives

In Philadelphia, as in many other American cities, the challenges facing Latinos are deeply shaped by immigration and historical exclusion from housing and homelessness assistance. Among the factors affecting access to affordable housing and homeless services for Hispanics are language barriers, immigration status, geographic location, and poverty. Research on neighborhood revitalization initiatives, culture, and change revealed how local small business owners and Latino leaders in North Philadelphia have attempted to address social determinants of Latino inequality through efforts such as increasing neighborhood cultural programming, engaging in economic rebranding, and creating housing initiatives [5]. Thanks to the grassroots efforts led by the Hispanic population in North Philadelphia, nonprofit organizations have succeeded in providing affordable housing for lower-income families. One of these organizations, Hispanic Association of Contractors & Enterprises (HACE), a Latino organization in North Philadelphia that was founded in 1982 as a community development nonprofit 501(c)(3), centers on vitalization projects aiming for a "just and equitable" neighborhood [6]. HACE is the research site where this study takes place.

A small number of federal housing initiatives and housing authority programs address the postsecondary educational needs of public and affordable housing residents. These programs provide resources such as wraparound services, assistance with financial aid forms, and college scholarships in an effort to increase postsecondary attainment for housing residents [7]. In terms of current public housing educational initiatives in Philadelphia, a postsecondary scholarship program called PhillySEEDS provides scholarships for Philadelphia Housing Authority residents [8]. However, PhillySEEDS is not research-based and it does not provide insight into the generational educational experiences within and outside of publicly subsidized housing resident local education environments. Focusing on the largely understudied Latino and AfroLatino residents, our paper will allow for a more robust understanding of the cultural ecological factors and networks of AfroLatin and Caribbean Latino publicly subsidized housing resident and staff educational trajectories within El Norte Philadelphia.

1.2 Neighborhood Factors

North Philadelphia is a predominantly Latino neighborhood whose residents cope with numerous place-based barriers, including lack of investment, poor public transportation, few public services, and high rates of violence and illegal drug use. The exceptionally stratified educational system in Philadelphia and unequal distribution of resources hinder residents' access to educational and employment opportunities, thus hindering their social mobility and community participation [9].

North Philadelphia is one of the Philadelphia neighborhoods most heavily affected by illegal drug use, homelessness, and physical and gun violence [9–11]. AfroLatino and Latino youth are more frequently exposed to community violence than their white counterparts, but only limited attention has been given to the impact of neighborhood violence on these youth and families [12–14]. Dache et al. [9] and others have shown that exposure to violence and fear of violence are critical factors shaping place-bound experiences of marginalized students [15, 16]. Most studies on community violence focused on urban African Americans [17, 18], with only limited attention given to the impact of neighborhood violence on Latinos [14] and their education and workforce trajectories. Place-based and neighborhood-specific barriers and opportunities such as experiencing high rates of violence and living in public housing—part of the environments and local ecology of Latinos [19]—have not been studied as factors of college inaccessibility.

1.3 Educational Opportunities

Research on community colleges, the largest higher education sector serving U.S. Latinos, shows that the main reasons for the low college access and completion rate of Hispanics living in urban and nonurban contexts are largely the same. These factors include financial obstacles, insufficient institutional support, lack of educational readiness, psychosocial factors, and familial and cultural challenges. Within Latino and urban community college student retention research, scholars agree that for institutions to be more effective, additional funding and resources is required to effectively support place-based students [20–23].

Community-based and informal education frameworks can act as potential spaces that create stability, support their wellbeing and learning, and also help residents living in public housing create social connections with others and develop their "right to the city" [24]. We know very little about AfroLatino resident's access to and participation in these forms of education and the cultural-ecological and geographical barriers associated with them as determining factors for participation.

2 Theoretical Framework: Geographic Cultural Ecologies

Several critical geographic educational access studies [25–27] have identified a connection between external environmental factors, such as racial disparities in local college student enrollment demographics and the historical and contemporary racial composition of the surrounding city neighborhoods [28]. These external environments and racial disparities not only contribute to how much physical access students have to local colleges, it contributes to their engagement of their home, school and neighborhood. Bronfenbrenner's [29, 30] model of nested ecological systems is central in understanding the layered lived experiences of individuals and is comprised of five layers: the microsystem (individuals' engaging home, family and schooling environments), mesosystem (the engagement of microsystems to each other), exosystem (transportation and neighborhood contexts), macrosystem (broad institutional structures from the culture and subculture, including the legal, economic, educational, and political systems), and chronosystem (incorporates the dimension of time across and individual's lifespan).

While traditional cultural-ecological theories have explored the nested nature of individual learners and their external environments [29, 31], geographic and cultural ecology research focusing on college access and attainment has not investigated environments such as public and affordable housing in Latino neighborhoods and how racialization and identity are experienced by largely immigrant and Caribbean residents. Within cultural ecology, at the microsystem level the individual engages with their proximal environments such as their parents, children, siblings and in the case of a housing community, the staff and their neighbors within their building. How individual's identify and are identified based on *reciprocity* within the ecological research, includes both the researcher and the participant engaging in categorizing themselves and each other [29]. Specifically with racial-ethnic identity, Roth [32] explains that Latino populations engage in identity in the U.S. through forms of acculturation that are part of a larger Latin American culture, depending on their home countries and migration to the U.S. She finds that Dominicans and Puerto Ricans living in New York City, in Puerto Rico and Dominican Republic, created multiple racial schemas based on their migration status and postsecondary education attainment. These racial schemas are cognitive and cultural, and do not adhere strictly to official classification systems, such as the U.S. census. People can hold multiple racial schemas at any point in time. They acquire them through life and they can be inconsistent between them. There are 3 primary racial schemas: (1) Continuum racial schema, which includes terms that capture gradations of skin color and phenotype within the home country context. (2) Nationality racial schemas, which includes the national home country identity primarily and can additionally include the term Latino/Hispanic in conjunction with the primary terms. (3) U.S racial schemas, that primarily include the terms White and Black, and can include the term Latino and Hispanic in conjunction with the primary terms. These racial schemas contribute to how individual's experience learning, accessibility and development and are situated within broader migratory histories.

To comprehend urban college access and attainment within a predominantly Caribbean Latino (predominantly Puerto Rican and Dominican) and Afro-latino housing community and the complex role of identity and educational experiences, a cultural ecological design approach is essential in guiding institutional outreach and local, state and national policy initiatives.

3 Methodology and Research Design

To evaluate the nested cultural-ecological relationships between the North Philadelphia housing community and their local environments of informal and formal learning, cultural knowledge, we used Quantitative Ethnography [33], a methodological approach that combines ethnography with mathematical tools to extract profound insights from an extensive dataset. The statistical analysis component enables the identification of unexpected patterns within large datasets and the assessment of the strength of associations among variables. The ethnographic analysis component facilitates the interpretation of the meanings underlying resident and staff qualitative data, enabling the narration of their experiences. Based on Ruis's [34] reasoning for studying policy ecosystems, which are challenging due to their complex interactions and extensive data, quantitative ethnography offered an initial approach to mapping a policy ecology providing theoretical and methodological insights. In this endeavor, we interpreted small-d resident and staff discourse data. We documented the cultural ecology of the educational experience of housing residents and staff. Subsequently through an Epistemic Network Analysis (ENA) method, we interpret and derive meaning from the discourse data, aiming to comprehend the broader big-D Discourses related to Latino-AfroLatino resident and staff cultural ecology, learning and self-efficacy.

3.1 Data Collection

From 2020 to 2022, we conducted an exploratory sequential mixed-method study of the educational and workforce experiences of a public/affordable housing community affiliated with the HACE. We collected qualitative data from residents and staff through (A) 73 participant hand-drawn maps (1 participant drew 2 maps) of Philadelphia, where they lived, were employed, and attended schooling, (B) 21 Focus Groups (consisting of 73 participants; 60 residents and 13 staff), (C) 8-weeks of HACE Livability Academy observations. The Livability Academy program assists a diverse group of residents in learning principles of SafeGrowth and Crime Prevention Through Environmental Design, enabling them to collaborate on projects that tackle neighborhood priorities. Participant ages ranged from approximately 21 to over 60. Women represented 68% of the sample. A majority (68%) of participants were first-generation immigrants/migrants from outside the continental United States; ethnically Puerto Ricans consisted of 75%, Dominicans 12%; racially, Afro-Latinos were 43% and African Americans 7%. Additionally, (D) we conducted individual interviews—a total of six—with local college admissions officers for the Community College of Philadelphia, Esperanza College, University of the Sciences, Drexel University, Penn State Brandywine, and Penn State Philadelphia Office. (E) Quantitative data was collected from 5-year 2021 American Community Survey and Philadelphia Depart 2018 crime data.

As an AfroLatin identifying woman and being familiar with the complexity of identifying as such across generations with her own familial experience, the researcher used the "streetrace" measure developed by Dr. Nancy Lopez [4], to draw conclusions on what an individual's perceived race or "streetrace" would be based on phenotypically Black or "Afro" features. Participants who were ethnically Latino with Afro features were included as Afrolatino within the data along with those who verbally identified as

Afrolatin (n = 2). Due to the age, generation status and lack of awareness of Afrolatinidad as a racial-ethnic category, led to a decreased number of participants who self-identified themselves as such.

3.2 Site of Study: El Norte

When comparing the El Norte area to the other Latino black group, El Norte, has a higher population of people who have less than a high school education (39% compared to 29%), and a low population of people who have completed any college degree (12% compared to 18%). Compared to other Latino-identified block groups, El Norte has half the college enrollment that other Latino-identified block groups have across Philadelphia. Comparatively, 42.47% of participants in this study did not complete high school; however, when comparing residents (excluding staff), 51.6% did not. In contrast, the staff all have some experience in a postsecondary institution. Related to violence, El Norte, had a higher incidence of violent crime in comparison to Philadelphia, and specifically, it's almost 50% higher than all other majority Latino groups and double that of other block groups.

3.3 Data Analysis and Current Study

For this study, we will interpret the qualitative focus group dataset as it is resident/staff-focused and generated. To analyze the results of the coded data, we utilize Epistemic Network Analysis (ENA), a tool designed to assess and illustrate the connections among codes present in the data [33, 35]. ENA identifies when and how frequently residents and staff establish connections between domain-relevant elements within the study, such as links between residents' and staff's cultural knowledge, moving and experiences of violence (what type and frequency), within the North Philadelphia cultural ecology. It identifies the simultaneous occurrences of coded elements and represents them in weighted network models. As either a resident or staff repeatedly establishes a connection between elements in a cultural ecology, the strength of the link between those elements increases. Additionally, ENA enables researchers to visually compare networks and utilize summary statistics that reflect the weighted structure of connections.

3.4 Code Development and Coding Process

We used Dedoose qualitative software to code all interviews, focus groups and r to conduct statistical analysis for census and crime data. Additionally, Code development went through a three-step process of open, axial, and selective coding based on (Merriam & Tisdell [36] and incorporating QE methods such as ENA and network analysis to select groupings of codes[37]. The research team anticipated uncovering themes related to neighborhood impact on higher education access and the role of public transportation in college accessibility. Codes were then narrowed down to the following codes: (1) movement, (2) domestic violence, (3) violence, (4) religion and morals, (5) personal education, (6) family education, (7) racism and discrimination, and (8) cultural identity. In addition to these codes, a set of deductive codes was made based on Bronfenbrenner's framework, which included: microsystem, mesosystem, exosystem, macrosystem, and chronosystem. For the second coding round, research team members held three training sessions to ensure coders understood the context of the project and inner-coder reliability measured through Shaffer's rho.

4 Findings

4.1 Cultural Ecological Differences Between HACE Staff and Resident Focus Groups

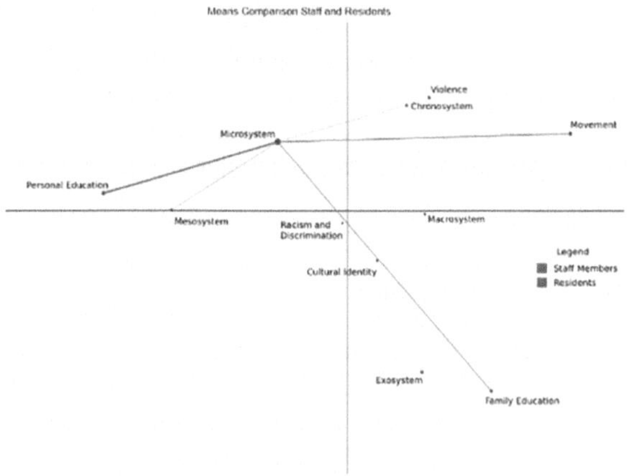

The first model shows the means difference between the residents and the staff using a mixture of inductive and deductive codes. Of note in this network is the relationship that staff interview has to the codes, personal education, mesosystem and microsystem. Between the staff and residents, generally, staff had completed more education beyond high school, although did not have degrees. In focus groups with younger staff, many of them were working on completing their undergraduate degrees at the local community college. Additionally, in this network, there is a relationship that each of these codes have with the mesosystem. The code mesosystem captures when participants expressed a relationship between two microsystems. This is salient because it highlights the role that HACE staff serve in facilitating and experiencing community with residents and the neighborhood.

> "I think it's a societal thing too because when you get here, like [referencing another HACE Staff Member, Misael] said, there's growing up, I mean, all my friends sell drugs and it's much-- at 17, you see somebody driving a Beamer, it seems really appealing when it's such easy money. And you do very little to earn it. I mean, it's like there's no-- no not only are there no repercussions for it, there's somewhat a level of praise where it's like, "Yeah, you're doing good, you're making money, you don't have to do a lot," and very little praise for going to school and attaining an education." (HACE Staff FG2).

This quote comes from a staff member Roberto, who was born and raised in El Norte. Roberto was mentored by one of HACE's leaders who is also from the neighborhood (and is AfroLatino), to work at HACE. Roberto in this quote is talking about his perspective of societal norms established in the neighborhood. He explains that growing up, many people within his network sold drugs because of the appeal and ease, compared to other forms of work which lacked the appeal and monetary benefits. While selling drugs is an individual choice, it is connected to broader urban and neighborhood cultural system and institutions, in this case, the lack of repercussions is tied to law enforcement and how drug crime is under penalized. Thus, this quote presents a case where one individual's microsytem is connected to the mesosytem in his role as staff member, and the crucial role HACE can play in understanding the experiences of families within El Norte.

In contrast participants often had strong relationships between family education and microsystem and migration. For example,

> "I have two grandchildren, a girl and a boy, one is seven and the other is four. And I'm happy with them. And thank God, despite being humble and poor, I taught my son that he has to fight to survive. What I didn't do, he has to strive for."

A focus on microsystems within participant data is supported by the line "despite being humble and poor, I taught my son that he has to fight to survive. What I didn't do, he has to strive for," demonstrating how participants within the HACE community are focused on themselves, their home, their family, and survival thus increasing the prevalence of microsystems and decreasing the prevalence of other systems within the data. Also this quote focuses on family as the mechanism to combat environmental conditions of violence, danger and struggle.

Finally, a unique finding to this study is the lack of connections and the lack of frequency to the theme (code) of racism and discrimination. While Fig. 1, is a means difference network, racism and discrimination was not a salient point for the staff or the residents. Rather residents and staff focused on neighborhood violence and immediate issues within their microsphere.

4.2 Cultural Ecological Differences Between Majority African American and Majority AfroLatin Focus Groups

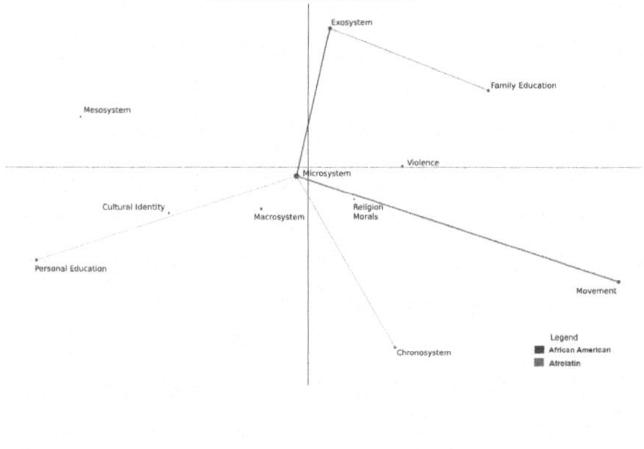

The mean difference network between African American majority focus group residents, in comparison to AfroLatino focus majority groups, reveals some differences between these groups based on a U.S. racial schema categorization (Roth, 2012). This is evidenced by stronger networks between the microsystem, exosystem and family education for African American participants, and stronger networks between microsystems, personal education, movement, macrosystem and chronosystem for AfroLatino majority focus groups.

Due to a longer history in Philadelphia – in comparison to Latino focus group participants who either migrated themselves, or are first generation – African-American communities are more likely to be familiar with the resources and challenges in the city from a generational standpoint (exosystem), and have family members (microsystem) who not only went to school within the city (family education) but also work within the city, broadening both the network and the scope of the exosystem for African-American participants. African Americans speak English as their primary language which also assists in navigating their experiences. The links between these three codes of microsystem, exosystem and family education within African-American participants is best exemplified by an African-American participant's mention of her mother who works at Jefferson Hospital. "She does the respiratory unit. …She goes to school so much for everything. Training…….She goes to school. She's always training for something? And upgrading her education." Throughout the focus groups African American participants shared generational history of parents and grandparents entering Philadelphia postsecondary education institutions and professional employment.

The AfroLatino network reveals a more extensive cultural ecology that includes their mentioning more systems within their lived and informal and formal educational experiences. Themes related to the history of El Norte's Caribbean Latino musical history, were specific to solely the Afrolatino participants in the study. Afrolatino participants had a connection to Afrlotainidad and its ancestral roots through music in multiple countries and its presence in its roots across El Norte. The connection between Afrolatino participants and music was seen within multiple participants throughout separate focus groups. The following quotes are from two Afrolatino participants, one is a Puerto Rican Guitarist Juanito, who is called Dominic[an] by his housing neighbors, the other Ana is a wise Puerto Rican woman, who has a cross-cultural understanding about identity and fluidity. Ana is "all [racial/ethnic]identities, depending on how she feels". She also is a painter/artist and learned these skills in her employment at a factory near her home decades ago.

> Juanito: "I worked there [factory] making guitar cases, and that's where I learned to play guitar and everything.
>
> Ana: Yes, he plays, he sings.
>
> Juanito: My whole family, all of them played. And it came easy to me. Playing was already in my blood. Until three years ago when I retired from music.
>
> Researcher: And was there a community of musicians in Philadelphia? [crosstalk].
>
> Juanito: Yes, I worked with Foto Rodriguez.
>
> Ana: He played in the clubs.

Juanito: Playing around there, we played there.

Ana: In the clubs. He played in all the clubs."

Connections to the chronosystem, which is characterized by time and the lifespan, for the guitarist were based in the development of a community of musicians within the changing music scene in Philadelphia and his strong family musical roots in Puerto Rico. The change in history and urban culture in El Norte, was a topic Latino participants brought up within focus groups, as demonstrated by the increased presence of chronosystems within Afrolatino data. The connection with cultural identity, which is a byproduct of migration as most participants either are children of migrants or migrated themselves, and the chronosystem are highlighted by instances such as the previously mentioned guitarist with the historic past of the Caribbean Latino music scene in Philadelphia, which no longer exists in El Norte.

In reference to why AfroLatinos may have less networked relationships to the exosystem may be explained by the tendency of Latino communities in Philadelphia to "self-isolate", and not get involved with others in the neighborhood as a safety precaution, in comparison to African-American communities who have increased familiarity with one another and may rely on their neighbors to keep a "second eye" out for one another [38]. This was evident across our larger dataset, especially in the Liveability Academy observations, where African Americans were the majority of participants, in comparison to Latinos who did not participate in this educational program designed to respond to crime and violence within the neighborhood.

Cultural Ecological Group Differences Between Puerto Rican Majority and Dominican Majority Focus Groups.

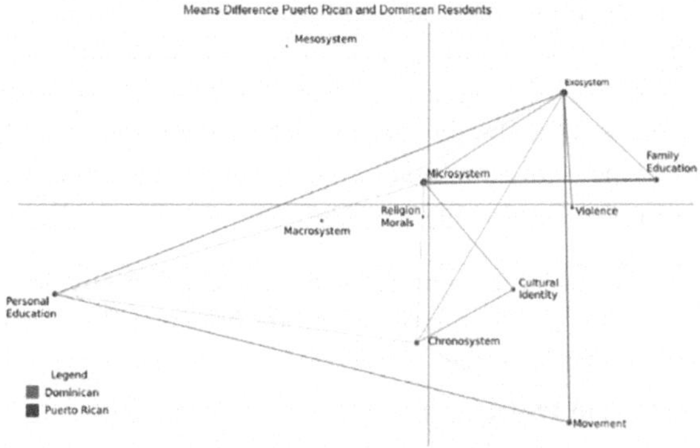

As was evident in our cultural ecological model differences between African American and Afrolatino majority focus groups, AfroLatinos have more dispersed networks across the cultural ecology of the HACE housing community. Since the AfroLatino model consists largely of Puerto Rican and Dominican ethnic groups, and the study population did not have higher education attainment, they self-identified primarily with their nationality racial schemas supporting Roth's 2012 findings associating no postsecondary education attainment with Domincans and Puerto Ricans identifying with their nationality racial schema. When divided across nationality racial schema ethnic groups instead of using U.S. racial schemas, differences emerge between the educational experiences of El Norte Dominicans and Puerto Ricans.

Puerto Ricans have a much longer history in Philadelphia than Dominicans, but not as large as the African American population. This model illustrates how Puerto Ricans have more networks across the cultural ecology supported by years of research documenting this neighborhood history (Whalen, 2006). The Puerto Rican network is more expansive and reveals how the rooted history of Puerto Ricans in El Norte, has an existing larger culture that includes an individual's cultural identity, in experiencing the cultural ecology. The strong Puerto Rican network is best displayed by Oscar, a drummer who spoke of his experience as a musician in El Norte. Oscar arrived in Philadelphia from Puerto Rico to live with his mother and her husband. He was 12 in Puerto Rico playing drums, within a year, Oscar was playing in Philadelphia within the social network of his uncle.

> "Yes. A year after I got here, I started meeting musicians."
>
> Researcher: "Here, in Philadelphia?"
>
> "Yes."
>
> Researcher: "And were there groups of musicians like--?"
>
> "There were too many groups."

Like the guitarist, Juanito, Oscar also experienced the musical mecca of North Philadelphia's Latino community. Later in his life, as he was now a senior, Oscar taught a youth to play drums at his church and gifted him his bongo drums. The large Puerto Rican cultural presence facilitated Oscar's involvement with the community, and in the social scene across Philadelphia and beyond, further displaying the increased network that Puerto Ricans have in the city in comparison to that of Dominicans.

Furthermore, when Puerto Ricans are compared to Dominican majority focus groups, different networks emerged for Dominicans in relation to microsystem, family education and cultural identity. One participant makes note of this in response to the researcher, inquiring if the Dominican community has a large presence in *El Norte*.

> "I don't think so, it's not large. Here [HACE], I know that guy, his mom, and us Dominicans. No one else. There must be more, but since I don't know anyone here—well, just him and his mom.
>
> Researcher: And here in Philadelphia?
>
> No. Just my sisters and that's it. Because I don't leave here. You see that I don't leave here? [laughter]. Here [in Philadelphia], I'm far from my home [laughter].

This response provides evidence that Dominican HACE residents in particular feel isolated, and thus have an increased reliance on family members as their social network (microsystem).

Within the HACE housing community, out of the 72 participants interviewed for our study, only one was currently enrolled in a 4-year institution and was on track to graduate with his 4-year degree a month after our interview. This participant, Antonio was a Dominican immigrant, who was also AfroLatino. Although like most other people of African descent from the Spanish-speaking Caribbean, Antonio did not identify using a U.S. racial schema. However, his mother, who was in a separate focus group and one of only 2 self-identified Afro-Latins, did.

When the PI met Antonio for the first time in his housing building, he quickly stated how much he hated living in the projects and could not wait to move. PI in her memo wrote the exact words that Antonio shared when she informed him that the focus of her study was on the educational experiences of HACE residents and staff. He responded "My English is not good, but I am a Computer Science Major." He was entertaining several job offers, working at private companies in Philadelphia that were seeking to hire him. His mother also participated in a separate focus group and said in a separate interview, "I teach my children that you have to get an education in this country in order not to work like me as a maid cleaning hotel rooms in Philadelphia". Moreover, when asked about Anotnio's educational attainment he said "You know what? Since nobody from my family has a college degree, i think [a] college degree can take me-- I can go further with it." Once again, Dominican interactions are centered on family, showing the tendency of Dominican participants' experiences within the family education theme.

5 Discussion and Implications for Quantitative Ethnography and Future Research

Just as tides rise and fall based on the gravitational pull of the moon and the sun, the identity and educational experiences of Caribbean Latinos and AfroLatinos in a publicly subsidized housing community illustrate the interdependent relationships within their cultural ecology. How they experience migration, crime, poverty and learn and teach their families and communities to survive and be self-determined can inform publicly-subsidized housing programs focused on college accessibility [39]. Local colleges can provide outreach to residents and staff addressing place-based barriers of isolation due to high incidents of violence, and learn more about the migration experiences of this racially-ethnically complex underserved urban population in order to increase their access and retention. Through a quantitative ethnography of the cultural ecology of the HACE housing community, we provide empirical evidence of the overrepresentation of AfroLatinos in publicly-subsidized housing in Philadelphia. This overrepresentation provides a more nuanced perspective in interpreting the U.S. Census statistic, that there are only 2.8% of Latinos who are also Black in *El Norte*. Since immigration status does influence how this group identifies racially, policymakers should collect data from this population in a manner that is place-specific. Future research in quantitative ethnography should explore participatory approaches [40] employing epistemic networks to inquire further into the experiences of school aged children and adults specific to their STEM cultural learning and engagement. Publicly subsidized housing interventions and policy-making should be tailored to address the specific educational needs of place-based adult residential communities such as HACE, providing empirical evidence of the strengths of the cultural foundations of Caribbean Latino history, family support and community advocacy [41, 42].

References

1. Galdámez, M., et al.: Ventering Black Latinidad: A Profile of the U.S. Afro-Latinx Population and Complex Inequalities. UCLA Latino Policy & Politics Institute (2023)
2. Gonzalez-Barrera, A.: About 6 million U.S. adults identify as Afro-Latino. https://www.pewresearch.org/short-reads/2022/05/02/about-6-million-u-s-adults-identify-as-afro-latino/. Last accessed 25 March 2024
3. Logan, J.R.: How race counts for Hispanic Americans. In: The Afro-Latin@ Reader: History and Culture in the United States. Duke University Press (2010)
4. López, N., Vargas, E., Juarez, M., Cacari-Stone, L., Bettez, S.: What's your "street race"? leveraging multidimensional measures of race and intersectionality for examining physical and mental health status among latinxs. Sociol. Race Ethn. **4**, 49–66 (2018). https://doi.org/10.1177/2332649217708798
5. Wherry, F.F.: The Philadelphia Barrio: The Arts, Branding, and Neighborhood Transformation. University of Chicago Press, Chicago, IL (2011)
6. HACE CDC: 2019 Annual Report. Hispanic Association of Contractors & Enterprises (2019)
7. Council of Large Public Housing Authorities: The Kresge Foundation: Eliminating Barriers to Postsecondary Success: Cross-sector Collaborations to Improve Postsecondary Achievement for Students Served by Public Housing Authorities. Council of Large Public Housing Authorities, Washington, D.C. (2019)
8. PhillySEEDS: PhillySEEDS 2024 Annual Update. PhillySEEDS, Philadelphia, PA (2024)
9. Daché, A., Stolper, H., Pickenpack, A., Sun, J., Tay Kearney, L.: Neighborhood Violence and Latino Postsecondary Access in "El Norte" Philadelphia. Journal of Urban Affairs. (In Press)
10. Chiang, H., Gill, B.: Student Characteristics and Outcomes in Alternative and Neighborhood High Schools in Philadelphia. Mathematica Policy Research, Inc. (2010)
11. Gottfried, M.A.: Chronic absenteeism in the classroom context: effects on achievement. Urban Education. **54**, 3–34 (2019). https://doi.org/10.1177/0042085915618709
12. Crouch, J.L., Hanson, R.F., Saunders, B.E., Kilpatrick, D.G., Resnick, H.S.: Income, race/ethnicity, and exposure to violence in youth: results from the national survey of adolescents. J. Community Psychol. **28**, 625–641 (2000). https://doi.org/10.1002/1520-6629(200011)28:6%3c625::AID-JCOP6%3e3.0.CO;2-R
13. Fowler, P.J., Tompsett, C.J., Braciszewski, J.M., Jacques-Tiura, A.J., Baltes, B.B.: Community violence: a meta-analysis on the effect of exposure and mental health outcomes of children and adolescents. Dev. Psychopathol. **21**, 227–259 (2009). https://doi.org/10.1017/S0954579409000145
14. Mora, A.S., Ceballo, R., Cranford, J.A.: Latino/a adolescents facing neighborhood dangers: an examination of community violence and gender-based harassment. Am. J. Community Psychol. **69**, 18–32 (2022). https://doi.org/10.1002/ajcp.12556
15. Cordes, S.A.: Charters and the common good: The spillover effects of charter schools in New York city. Educ. Next. **18**, 60+ (2018)
16. Schwartz, A.E., McCabe, B.J., Gould Ellen, I., Chellman, C.C.: Public schools, public housing: the education of children living in public housing. Urban Affairs Rev. **46**, 68–89 (2010). https://doi.org/10.1177/1078087410367780
17. Schneider, A., Gudiño, O.G.: Predicting avoidance symptoms in U.S. Latino youth exposed to community violence: the role of cultural values and behavioral inhibition. J. Trauma. Stress **31**(4), 509–517 (2018). https://doi.org/10.1002/jts.22313
18. McBride Murry, V., Berkel, C., Gaylord-Harden, N.K., Copeland-Linder, N., Nation, M.: Neighborhood poverty and adolescent development. J. Res. Adolesc. **21**, 114–128 (2011). https://doi.org/10.1111/j.1532-7795.2010.00718.x

19. Mendoza, P., Suarez, J.D., Bustamante, E.: Sense of community in student retention at a tertiary technical institution in bogotá: an ecological approach. Community Coll. Rev. **44**, 286–314 (2016). https://doi.org/10.1177/0091552116659538
20. Burshnick Genthe, C., Harrington, C.: Low completion rates of Latinx community college students. IE. **7**, 32–38 (2022). https://doi.org/10.5195/ie.2022.205
21. Camacho, A.: Successful models in community college STEM education. In: 2015 ASEE Annual Conference and Exposition Proceedings, p. 26.1439.1–26.1439. 16. ASEE Conferences, Seattle, Washington (2015). https://doi.org/10.18260/p.24776
22. Crisp, G., Nora, A.: Overview of hispanics in science, mathematics, engineering and technology (STEM): K-16 representation, preparation and participation. Hispanic Association of Colleges and Universities (2012)
23. Shadduck, P.: Comprehensive cocurricular support promotes persistence of community college STEM students. Community College J. Res. Pract.. **41**, 719–732 (2017). https://doi.org/10.1080/10668926.2016.1222506
24. Harvey, D.: Spaces of capital: Towards a Critical Geography. Taylor & Francis, New York, NY (2001)
25. Daché, A.: Bus-riding from barrio to college: A qualitative geographic iInformation systems (GIS) analysis. J. Higher Educ. **93**, 1–30 (2022). https://doi.org/10.1080/00221546.2021.1940054
26. Daché, A., Sun, J., Krause, C.: A post-ferguson spatial analysis of black resistant and white fortressing geographies. Urban Educ. **59**(5), 1619–1648 (2022). https://doi.org/10.1177/00420859221086511
27. Daché-Gerbino, A.: Mapping the postcolonial across urban and suburban college access geographies. Equity Excellence Educ. **50**, 368–386 (2017)
28. Longerbeam, S.D.: Developing openness to diversity in living-learning program participants. J. Div. High. Educ. **3**(4), 201–217 (2010). https://doi.org/10.1037/a0021277
29. Bronfenbrenner, U.: Contexts of child rearing: problems and prospects. Am. Psychol. **34**, 844 (1979). https://doi.org/10.1037/0003-066X.34.10.844
30. Bronfenbrenner, U.: The ecology of Human Development: Experiments by Nature and Design. Harvard University Press, Cambridge, Mass (1981)
31. Bronfenbrenner, U., Morris, P.A.: The bioecological model of human development. In: Damon, W., Lerner, R.M. (eds.) Handbook of Child Psychology. Wiley (2007). https://doi.org/10.1002/9780470147658.chpsy0114
32. Roth, W.D.: Race Migrations: Latinos and the Cultural Transformation of Race. Stanford University Press, Stanford, California (2012)
33. Shaffer, D.W.: Quantitative Ethnography. Cathcart Press, Madison, Wisconsin (2017)
34. Ruis, A.R., et al.: Thin data, thick description: Modeling socio-environmental problem-solving trajectories in localized land-use simulations. In: Irgens, G.A., Knight, S. (eds.) Advances in Quantitative Ethnography: 5th International Conference, ICQE 2023, Melbourne, VIC, Australia, October 8–12, 2023, Proceedings, pp. 349–364. Springer Nature Switzerland, Cham (2023). https://doi.org/10.1007/978-3-031-47014-1_24
35. Shaffer, D.W., Ruis, A.R.: Epistemic network analysis: a worked example of theory-based learning analytics. In: Lang, C., Siemens, G., Wise, A., Gasevic, D. (eds.) Handbook of Learning Analytics, pp. 175–187. Society for Learning Analytics Research (SoLAR) (2017). https://doi.org/10.18608/hla17.015
36. Merriam, S.B., Tisdell, E.J.: Qualitative Research: A Guide to Design and Implementation. Wiley (2015)
37. Sun, J., Dache, A., Pickenpack, A.: Integrating QE methods into a Qualitative workflow: Using Co-Occurrence Matrices and ENA in Code Selection. International Conference on Quantitative Ethnography. Melbourne, Victoria (2023)

38. Clampet-Lundquist, S.: Finding and keeping affordable housing: analyzing the experiences of single-mother families in North Philadelphia. J. Socil. Social Welfare (2003). https://doi.org/10.15453/0191-5096.2941
39. DiDimenco, M., Johnson, R.: Evaluation of the Project SOAR Demonstration Final Report. U.S. Department of Housing and Urban Development (2020)
40. Vega, H., Irgens, G.A.: Constructing interpretations with participants through epistemic network analysis: towards participatory approaches in quantitative ethnography. In: Wasson, B., Zörgő, S. (eds.) Advances in Quantitative Ethnography: Third International Conference, ICQE 2021, Virtual Event, November 6–11, 2021, Proceedings, pp. 3–16. Springer International Publishing, Cham (2022). https://doi.org/10.1007/978-3-030-93859-8_1
41. Gutiérrez, K.D.: 2011 AERA presidential address: designing resilient ecologies: social design experiments and a new social imagination. Educ. Res. **45**, 187–196 (2016). https://doi.org/10.3102/0013189X16645430
42. Gutiérrez, K.D., Jurow, A.S.: Social design experiments: toward equity by design. J. Learn. Sci. **25**, 565–598 (2016). https://doi.org/10.1080/10508406.2016.1204548

Building a Theory of Teacher Knowledge with ENA

Chandra Hawley Orrill[1,2(✉)] and Rachael Eriksen Brown[1,2]

[1] Rethink Learning Labs, Fall River, MA 02720, USA
chandra.orrill@rethinklearning.com, reb37@psu.edu
[2] Pennsylvania State University Abington, Abington, PA 19011, USA

Abstract. In this paper, we talk about how we are using Epistemic Network Analysis to build a theory of how teachers use their mathematical knowledge to solve novel proportional reasoning tasks. The data for this paper were collected from 32 in-service middle grades teachers across four states. They each completed a think-aloud interview on their own as well as a face-to-face interview that involved both pencil and paper items and items that relied on dynamic sketches. We relied on ENA to analyze the data using Knowledge in Pieces as our theoretical framework. This analysis is uncovering not only what key knowledge resources are for teachers, but also highlighting some of the differences between different groups of teachers.

Keywords: ENA · teacher knowledge · proportions · mathematics education · middle school

1 Introduction

We started this work with the goals of understanding the knowledge teachers need to teach proportional reasoning and what differentiates weaker teachers' knowledge from stronger teachers' knowledge. Our interest was a practical one: we wanted to understand what effective professional development for teachers should include. This is important because so much professional development is viewed as a waste of time by teacher, but at the same time, students' mathematics achievement has remained basically stagnant for decades. This suggests that the professional development teachers have available to them does not offer enough support to meet the goal of supporting teacher learning with an eye toward improving student learning.

Our initial conjecture was that teachers need to develop a coherent understanding of mathematics. This is an idea mentioned throughout the literature (e.g., [1]) on teacher knowledge, but one that is rarely operationalized. In fact, "coherence" is a word used in the literature as if there is a consensus for what it means, when, in fact, there is not. This is one gap we are working to address in the literature.

Another gap in the literature is that little work has been done on in-service teachers' proportional reasoning. The work that has been done suggests that teachers, like students, struggle with proportional reasoning and solving proportions (e.g., [1, 9, 11, 14, 18,

Y. J. Kim and Z. Swiecki (Eds.): icqe 2024, CCIS 2279, pp. 159–166, 2024.
https://doi.org/10.1007/978-3-031-76332-8_13

19, 23, 24]) Our own work has identified ways in which teacher knowledge may lack coherence, suggesting that there are opportunities to better support student learning (e.g., [5, 15]). For example, we have found that, like students (e.g., [7, 22]), teachers are inclined to use proportional reasoning when other kinds of reasoning would be more appropriate (e.g., [5, 24]).

Given these gaps, we have been working to create a theory of teacher knowledge for teaching proportional reasoning that relies on Knowledge in Pieces [8] as a theoretical lens that is operationalized through Epistemic Network Analysis [20]. We have published the set of knowledge resources teachers use [24]. In this paper, we examine how teachers identified as being "strong" in their ability to reason proportionally might differ from those of their more typical peers. By identifying these differences, we refine our ability to support all teachers to move their understandings forward. To this end, we report on new analysis of the dataset in which we answer the following question: Is there a difference in knowledge resource use between teachers who are perceived as being particularly strong mathematically and those who are not?

To answer this question, we first situate the reader in our conceptual framework, which focuses on a theoretical and analytical framework uniquely paired to allow this analysis. We then introduce details of the study and the kinds of mathematics tasks the teachers were asked to solve. We present our data and findings and end with implications for teacher development based on our emerging theory of teacher knowledge for proportional reasoning.

2 Conceptual Framework

2.1 Knowledge in Pieces

Our work is grounded in the knowledge in pieces (KiP) epistemology [8] and is informed by the research on experts and novices (e.g., [4]). KiP posits that any learner, in this case a teacher, has many fine-grained understandings. We refer to these understandings as knowledge resources [10]. Learning, and thus developing expertise, occurs as new knowledge resources are developed, existing knowledge resources are refined, and/or connections are made between and among the resources. The connections are at the heart of a "coherent" understanding—allowing teachers to draw on a wide array of knowledge resources in the moment as they analyze students' novel solutions to mathematics problems. Thus, our conjecture about teacher knowledge, from a KiP perspective is that stronger teachers will have access to more resources in more connected ways than more typical teachers. This is supported by research on expertise which shows that experts not only exhibit more understanding of the topic in which they are experts, but also that their knowledge is organized in a fundamentally different way than novices in the same area [4].

2.2 Epistemic Network Analysis

While KiP provides a lens through which to examine teacher knowledge, it does not provide a means for enactment. Thus, we turned to Epistemic Network Analysis (ENA;

[20]) as our analytical lens. ENA is a computational modeling for analyzing aspects of individuals' cognition [2]. ENA was developed to model connections between knowledge resources and to show the strength and association among elements in a network [20]. ENA's allows us to see connections between and among understandings and to examine the knowledge teachers exhibit across a set of novel tasks.

3 Methodology and Data

3.1 Participants

This research relied on data collected from a convenience sample of 32 in-service middle school mathematics teachers from five states. The teachers taught at a variety of schools (public, private, and charter in urban, suburban, and rural areas). Six of the teachers had been recommended by mathematics educators external to the project as being "strong" in their proportional reasoning. We included these teachers in the sample specifically to understand differences between teachers who were considered typical or whose strength was unknown and those who were identified as being strong.

3.2 Data

Each teacher participated in two interviews. The first was a think-aloud protocol mailed to the teacher. They completed the protocol using a Livescribe™ pen. The pens captured both talking and inscriptions to create a movie recreating their solution paths. The second interview was an in-person interview conducted by the first author. It included both paper-and-pencil tasks and tasks supported by dynamic geometry "toys" that allowed the teacher to work with a variety of scaling and similarity situations [3] in real-time as they solved the tasks. This second interview was videorecorded using two cameras – one trained on anything the teacher was writing or pointing to and the other focused on the teacher. Each interview took about an hour for the teachers to complete. The interviews were transcribed verbatim. Analysis started from transcripts, but also relied on the recordings.

Both interviews relied on novel situations designed to engage teachers in the work of teaching. While some tasks asked teachers to solve a mathematics problem, others asked them to make sense of someone else's thinking or to provide guidance to someone. In this way, we intended to engage teachers in the work they regularly do. Further, we included a number of tasks that pushed beyond calculating answers to instead reason about the situation [11]. The goal was to create a comprehensive picture of the knowledge resources teachers used in their engagement with proportions.

To categorize teachers into ability groups, we administered the Learning Mathematics for Teaching form for Proportional Reasoning (LMT-PR, [12]). While this assessment of teacher knowledge has limitations (c.f., [16]), it was the only validated instrument available to us for measuring teachers' proportional reasoning. Scores reported below are set to 0 being the national mean according to the assessment developers [12]. The score indicates the number of standard deviations above or below the mean a teacher or scored. Throughout the findings, the mean graph for that group is shown rather than a graph for a specific teacher.

3.3 Analysis

To create the nodes for the ENA analysis, we first conducted a qualitative analysis of the interviews to identify the knowledge resources used. The interviews were broken into utterances, in which one utterance was the response to one math task. We relied on a combination of preidentified codes from the literature taken from both prior research and materials specifically generated to support teachers in conceptualizing the domain of proportions [11, 13, 17] and emergent codes found in the data [6]. This process is more fully addressed in Weiland et al. [23].

Using a constant comparative approach, we used binary scoring for each knowledge resource to indicate whether it was present or not present in an utterance. This led to a spreadsheet that was then uploaded into the webENA tool (available at https://app.epistemicnetwork.org/). We treated the teachers as the individual units. The utterances served as the conversation units. The identified knowledge resources served as the codes. We interrogated each ENA map as it was generated to determine whether there were patterns emerging and pursued additional questions by limiting the codes we were analyzing and by grouping participants in particular ways.

4 Findings

We found that regardless of LMT score or recommendation by others as being strong, that all the teacher groups were able to use all four calculation-focused knowledge resources. As shown in Table 1, when looking knowledge resources, there are differences between groups. Most notably, the group scoring below 0 appears to have the fewest connections among their knowledge resources, while those above 0 appear to have more connections for each knowledge resource. There are also shifts in the most relied-upon resources. For the below 0 group, there are strong ties between Unit Rate, Equivalence, and Scaling as well as using Between measure space thinking with Scaling Up and Down. This suggests only minimal attention to the actual structures of proportions, with the most notable structure being ensuring the relationship between the numerator and denominator remains intact.

As the scores increase, we see a shifting reliance as those scoring between 0 and 1 bring in Ratio as Measure, thus suggesting attention to the ratio as an expression of two quantities (e.g., ice cream and milk) that create a new quantity (milkshake) rather than as two separate things. The group scoring between 1 and 2 adds slightly more connection to the idea of Ratio as Measure, which is the most robust and versatile of the knowledge resources. Then, moving into the highest scoring group, we can see that the structural codes are beginning to have a primary role in the teachers' reasoning. The connections between Covary and Scaling and between Between and Scaling become more important for this group. The connections between structures become stronger with Covary and Between being more connected in addition to relative thinking and Ratio as Multiplicative Comparison showing some stronger connections to other codes.

As scores increased on the assessment, the connections between the structural knowledge resources were more frequent. In the group that scored below 0, there is little interaction between the knowledge resources at all. Then, in scores between 0 and 1, we begin to see a pattern emerge as Between thinking is used in coordination with Covary

Table 1. Teachers' general pattern of knowledge use across all nine knowledge resources according to performance on LMT-PR.

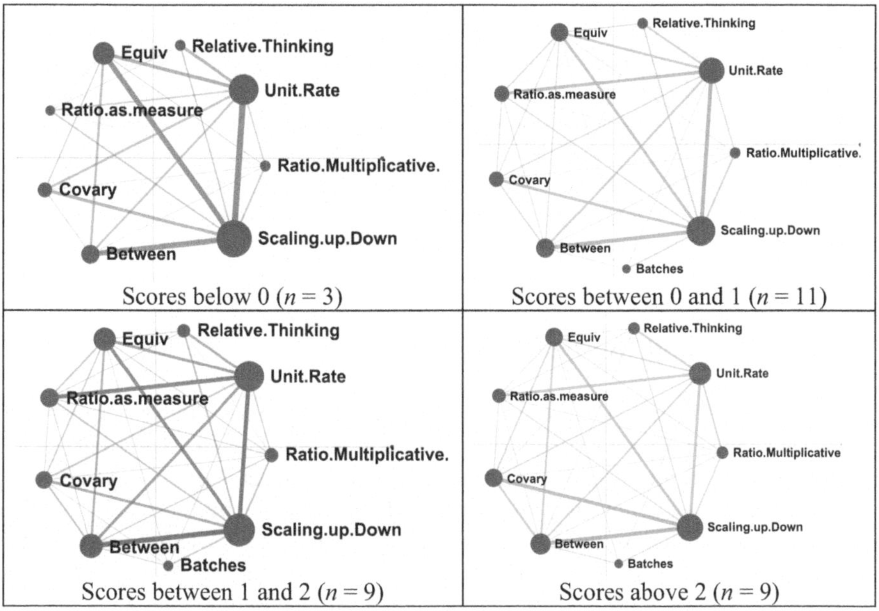

and Ratio as Measure. For teachers scoring more than one standard deviation above the mean, all five of the knowledge resources are used in ways that are connected to each other, however Relative Thinking is still only used in limited connections. Those connections are include working only in coordination with Ratio as Measure for the group scoring between 1 and 2, while Relative Thinking is connected to Between space reasoning for the highest-scoring group.

Analysis of Teachers Identified as Strong. The "strong teachers" all scored above 1.5 on the LMT assessment. We wanted to explore whether this group had any other differences from the overall population, so we conducted the same analyses as above with data from these participants. We collapsed all teachers scoring one standard deviation or more above the mean into a single group and then created a separate group that included only those teachers specifically identified as being strong. When looking at all 9 knowledge resources, there are few differences between the two groups.

This trend remained intact when we examined the teachers' use of structural knowledge resources as well (Table 2). This suggests that the mathematics educators were in agreement with the LMT on which teachers were stronger. Further research would need to be done to determine the reasons the mathematics educators identified the six teachers as being particularly strong. We suspect that, whether consciously or not, the mathematics educators were seeing the attention to structures that these strong teachers exhibited.

Table 2. ENA graph of the structure-focused knowledge resources for all teachers scoring above 1 as well as just those who were identified before this study as being strong.

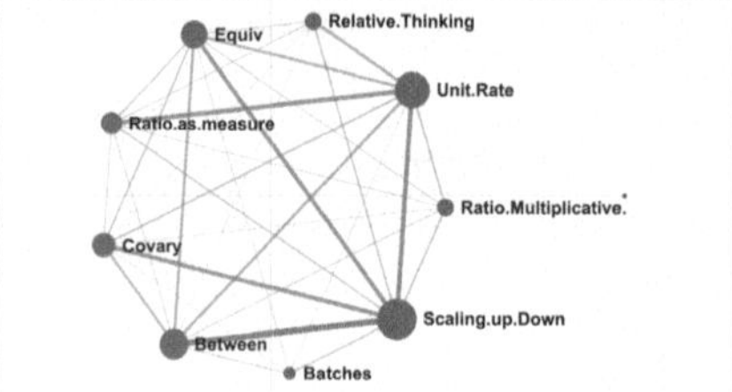	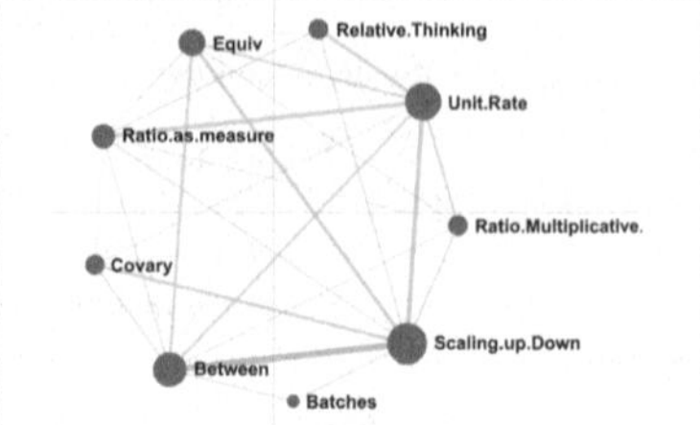
Teachers scoring above 1 ($n = 18$)	Teachers IDed as strong ($n = 6$)

5 Conclusion and Implications

In this study, we sought to demonstrate how ENA is being used to move our theory of teacher knowledge for proportions forward and present new findings about that teacher knowledge. We were able to show a difference between stronger teachers and less strong teachers when we look at how they use their knowledge resources in connected ways. Our initial assertion was that stronger teachers would rely on more knowledge resources and more connections between and among those knowledge resources. The data presented here supports that conjecture. It refines it by specifically highlighting the importance of structure-focused knowledge resources for stronger teachers and their near-absence in less strong teachers.

The implications of this study are most important for teacher development. It seems clear that both assessments of teacher knowledge and mathematics educators value the kinds of thinking exhibited by stronger teachers. And it is equally clear that those teachers rely more on connections between knowledge resources and on structure-focused resources than their more "typical" peers. From a KiP perspective, this would include both building additional structure-focused resources for some teachers and supporting all teachers in building stronger connections between their structural knowledge resources for proportions.

Acknowledgments. The work reported here has been supported by the National Science Foundation through grant numbers 1054170, 1621290, and 2331742. The opinions expressed here are those of the authors and may not reflect those of the National Science Foundation.

Disclosure of Interests. The authors have no competing interests to declare that are relevant to the content of this article.

References

1. Akar, G.: Different levels of reasoning in within state ratio conception and the conceptualization of rate: a possible example. In: Brosnan, P., Erchick, D.B., Flevares, L. (eds.), Proceedings of the 32nd annual meeting of the North American Chapter of the International Group for

the Psychology of Mathematics Education, vol. 4, pp. 711–719. The University of Ohio, Columbus, OH (2010)
2. Bagley, E., Shaffer, D. W.: The epistemology of urban and regional planning 912: Appropriation in the face of resistance. In: Gomez, K., Lyons, L., Radinsky, J. (eds.) Learning in the disciplines: Proceedings of the 9th International Conference of the Learning Sciences, pp 81–88. Chicago: International Society of the Learning Sciences (2010)
3. Beckmann, S., Izsák, A.: Two perspectives on proportional relationships: extending complementary origins of multiplication in terms of quantities. J. Res. Math Educ. **4**, 17–38 (2015)
4. Bédard, J., Chi, M.T.H.: Expertise. Curr. Dir. Psychol. Sci. **I**, 135–139 (1922)
5. Brown, R.E., Weiland, T., Orrill, C.H.: Mathematics teachers' use of knowledge resources when identifying proportional reasoning situations. Int. J. Sci. Math. Educ. **18**(6), 1085–1104 (2020). https://doi.org/10.1007/s10763-019-10006-3
6. Charmaz, K.: Constructing grounded theory, 2nd edn. Sage Publications Ltd. (2014)
7. de Bock, D., Van Dooren, W., Janssens, D., Verschaffel, L.: Improper use of linear reasoning: an in-depth study of the nature and the irresistibility of secondary school students' errors. Educ. Stud. Math **50**, 311–334 (2002)
8. diSessa, A.A., Sherin, B.L., Levin, M.: Knowledge analysis: an introduction. In: diSessa, A.A., Levin, M., Brown, J.S. (eds.) Knowledge and interaction: A synthetic agenda for the learning sciences, pp. 30–71. Routledge, New York (2016)
9. Greer, B.: Overview of the papers: Why is linear thinking so dominant? Math. Think. Learn. **12**(1), 109–115 (2010). https://doi.org/10.1080/10986060903465996
10. Harlow, D.B., Bianchini, J.A., Swanson, L.H., Dwyer, H.A.: Potential teachers' appropriate and inappropriate application of knowledge resources in a model-based physics course: a "Knowledge in Pieces" perspective on teacher learning. J. Res. Sci. Teach. **50**, 1098–1126 (2013). https://doi.org/10.1002/tea.21108
11. Lamon, S.: Rational numbers and proportional reasoning: toward a theoretical framework for research. In: Lester, F.K. (ed.) Second Handbook of Research on Mathematics Teaching and Learning, pp. 629–667. National Council of Teachers of Mathematics (2007)
12. Learning Mathematics for Teaching: Survey of Teachers of Mathematics: Form LMT PR-2007. University of Michigan, Ann Arbor, MI (2007)
13. Lobato, J., Ellis, A.: Developing Essential Understanding of Ratios, Proportions & Proportional reasoning: Grades 6–8. National Council of Teachers of Mathematics, Reston, VA (2010)
14. Modestou, M., Gagatsis, A.: Students' improper proportional reasoning: a result of the epistemological obstacle of "linearity." Educ. Psychol. **27**(1), 75–92 (2007). https://doi.org/10.1080/01443410601061462
15. Orrill, C.H., Brown, R.E.: Making sense of double number lines in professional development: exploring teachers' understandings of proportional relationships. J. Math Teacher Educ. **15**(5), 381–403 (2012). https://doi.org/10.1007/s10857-012-9218-z
16. Orrill, C.H., Cohen, A.S.: Why defining the construct matters: an examination of teacher knowledge using different lenses on one assessment. Math Enthusiast **13**(1), 7 (2016)
17. Pitta-Pantazi, D., Christou, C.: The structure of prospective kindergarten teachers' proportional reasoning. J. Math. Teacher Educ. **14**(2), 149–169 (2011)
18. Post, T., Harel, G., Behr, M., Lesh, R.: Intermediate teacher's knowledge of rational number concepts. In: Fennema, E., Carpenter, T.P., Lamon, S.J. (eds.) Integrating Research on Teaching and Learning Mathematics, pp. 177–198. State University of New York Press (1988)
19. Riley, K.R.: Teachers' understanding of proportional reasoning. In: Brosnan, P., Erchick, D.B., Flevares, L. (eds.) Proceedings of the 32nd annual meeting of the North American Chapter of the International Group for the Psychology of Mathematics Education, vol. 6, pp. 1055–1061. The Ohio State University, Columbus, OH (2010)

20. Shaffer, D.W., Collier, W., Ruis, A.R.: A tutorial on epistemic network analysis: analyzing the structure of connections in cognitive, social, and interaction data. J. Learn. Anal. **3**(3), 9–45 (2016). https://doi.org/10.18608/jla.2016.33.3
21. Smith, J.P.: Competent reasoning with rational numbers. Cogn. Instr. **13**(1), 3–50 (1995)
22. Van Dooren, W., De Bock, D., Janssens, D., Verschaffel, L.: The linear imperative: An inventory and conceptual analysis of students' overuse of linearity. J. Res. Math. Educ. **39**(3), 311–342 (2008)
23. Weiland, T., Orrill, C., Brown, R.E., Nagar, G.: Mathematics teachers' ability to identify situations appropriate for proportional reasoning. Rsch. Math. Ed. **21**(3), 233–250 (2019). https://doi.org/10.1080/14794802.2019.1579668
24. Weiland, T., Orrill, C.H., Nagar, G.G., Brown, R.E., Burke, J.: Framing a robust understanding of proportional reasoning for teachers. J. Mah. Tchr. Educ. (2020). https://doi.org/10.1007/s10857-019-09453-0

Strategies for Doctoral Students to Publish Articles in Social Sciences and STEM: A Comparison Between China and the U.S

Tianshi Hao(✉) and Danielle P. Espino

Pepperdine University, Malibu, CA 90263, USA
tianshi.hao@pepperdine.edu

Abstract. The "publish or perish" paradigm significantly impacts doctoral students' career progression, employability, and academic contributions. Navigating academic publishing involves challenges such as ethical dilemmas, predatory journals, and rigorous peer review. This study explores effective strategies and common challenges faced by doctoral students in publishing across various disciplines and regions. Through quantitative ethnography, it analyzes interviews with nine doctoral students, using Epistemic Network Analysis (ENA) to compare themes across disciplines and locations. Key findings highlight the importance of collaboration, strategy implementation, and mentorship. Social sciences students focus on strategic journal selection, while STEM students emphasize collaborative research. Geographic differences include access to digital resources and familiarity with IRB processes. Universal strategies for publishing success include goal-oriented preparation, efficient literature search techniques, and proactive manuscript enhancement. The study provides valuable guidance for doctoral students navigating academic publishing.

Keywords: Academic Publishing · Doctoral Students · Publish or Perish · Quantitative Ethnography · Publication Strategies · Global Academic Practices

1 Introduction

A significant proportion of doctoral research remains unpublished [1]. For those pursuing an academic career, the quantity and type of journal publications have emerged as pivotal factors in shaping career progression. However, the path to publication has become increasingly challenging, necessitating extensive data collection and additional time dedicated to Ph.D. training [2]. Publications play a crucial role in academic career transitions, promotions, and employability [3].

To get publish or better results, researchers in different field, such as 2.3% researchers in psychology would falsifying the data and 18.7% claim they have witnessed such misconduct [4]. In the current academic landscape, data fabrication remains an issue, with students now targeting predatory publications to pass their graduation requirements [5]. The rise of predatory journals has added another layer of complexity to the academic publishing landscape. These journals, which often lack rigorous peer-review processes,

Y. J. Kim and Z. Swiecki (Eds.): icqe 2024, CCIS 2279, pp. 167–179, 2024.
https://doi.org/10.1007/978-3-031-76332-8_14

can be particularly enticing to faculty members seeking publication, especially after multiple rejections from reputable journals [6]. Despite the pressure encapsulated in the phrase "publish or perish," the proportion of Ph.D. students and post-doctoral fellows getting published in peer-reviewed publications in general remains relatively low [7].

This study aims to identify the most effective strategies for doctoral students seeking to publish academic articles, as well as pinpoint common challenges they face. This study's significance lies in its potential to offer guidance to doctoral students who aspire to publish more or face difficulties during the publication process.

2 Literature Review

2.1 "Publish or Perish"

[8] identified significant discrepancies between traditional academic evaluation metrics and the actual time professors are able to dedicate to research. This gap highlights the prevalent publish or perish culture, which pressures faculty to prioritize frequent publication, often at the expense of long-term research projects and meaningful educational contributions, particularly among tenured faculty. Additionally, [9] noticed that such pressures will intensify when resources are limited and the relevance of research topics to local needs is crucial. The over-emphasis on publishing frequency risks diminishing both the relevance and quality of research, and suggest to the need for broader academic success metrics that reflect diverse academic roles and contributions. Publish or perish was a phenomenon that was observed around the year 2000, as a term to express the metrics that were used to gauge academic career advancement at that time [10]. This emphasis places a lot of pressure on scholars facing high-pressure in competitive academic research environments that prioritize publishing in top-ranked journals and receiving citations from other scholars, while undervaluing or failing to address important societal questions through activities that benefit the larger community or policy engagement [11]. [11] further argue that current ranking metrics, including journal prestige and citation counts, might not accurately reflect the value and impact of academic contributions. This emphasis on rankings could lead to a narrow focus on quantifiable success measures and be detrimental to the broader mission of academic institutions to generate and disseminate knowledge that benefits society. This critique of academic ranking systems raises important questions about the values and priorities of the academic community, challenging institutions to reconsider how they measure and reward scholarly achievements in a way that truly advances knowledge and serves the public good.

Despite the increasing severity of this phenomenon, there are few tutorials for faculty or graduate students to rely on, resulting in an instruction gap [12]. Studies indicate that publishing pressure is not limited to higher education faculty and postdoctoral scholars, but also extending this pressure to graduate students, expecting them to publish before graduation [13–16]. Given this situation, doctoral students should receive more formal training in their early careers [17]. [18] observed that there is a growing expectation for higher-degree research students in Australia to publish during their studies, as a higher publication rate often correlates with increased university funding and improved career prospects. However, Australian universities currently provide insufficient institutional guidance for students aiming to meet these publishing expectations.

2.2 Obstacles in Publishing

Many scholars are aware of the difficulties associated with publishing, and a large number of them have expressed curiosity about the factors that contribute to graduate students having difficulties publishing. Some articles suggest that Ph.D. students struggle because they assume a dual role as both scholars and students, leading to pressure to publish their research [19]. Multiple studies [20, 21] identify students who struggle with writing [20], knowing the rules to participate in the academic community [22], and lacking confidence in their abilities [19].

In addition is the pressure to write that comes from roles, a lack of writing skills, confidence, support [19]. Language barriers are causing problems for Ph.D. students whose first language is not English, making it more difficult for them to publish [19, 23] due to the dominance of the English language in high-ranking academic journals [24].

3 Methodology

This study involved nine doctoral students from diverse academic disciplines including education, leadership studies, engineering, and materials science, spanning two geographical regions: the United States and China. A summary of demographic information of participants is seen in Table 2. Recruitment utilized social media and snowball sampling techniques to form a representative cohort, the study concentrated on a detailed exploration of how academic discipline and geographical location influence publishing outcomes, informed by the qualitative data provided by the participants.

Table 1. Study participant information

Participant	Location	Subjects	Publication Experience
P1	U.S	Social Science (SS)	Proceedings
P2	U.S	SS	Proceedings & Journals
P3	U.S	SS	Journals
P4	U.S	SS	Proceedings
P5	China	SS	Journals
P6	China	STEM	Journals
P7	China	STEM	Journals
P8	China	STEM	Journals
P9	U.S	SS	Journals

Quantitative Ethnography (QE) was employed as the methodology, integrating ethnographic and statistical techniques to examine patterns of human interaction within academic publishing [25]. Data was collected through open-ended online interviews then transcribed. To ensure accuracy and consistency in data interpretation, two independent researchers coded the interviews, maintaining inter-rater reliability, and resolving any differences [26].

The coding was initiated using an inductive, grounded approach, for key constructs to emerge organically from the data. Initial familiarization with the data led to the generation of codes, which were refined and grouped into broader thematic categories based on similarities in meaning [27]. The resulting codebook developed for the analysis is seen in Table 1 below.

Table 2. Codebook of constructs identified for the study.

Code		
Knowledge	Definition	Developing or exited knowledge related to the publication or article
	Example Utterance	"I was learning with a profession in linguistic field at that time and while discussion we felt this negative prefix and adverb could be an interesting topic that is why we decided to work on this topic."
Efficiency & Strategy	Definition	Strategies that participant believes will benefit or expedite the publication process
	Example Utterance	"I used the schimago ranking system for journals to find where to publish"
Synergy	Definition	collaborative efforts and various forms of communication that enhance the publication process by facilitating effective teamwork and idea exchange."
	Example Utterance	"use software to check grammar, discuss with co-authors, and i have no support from anyone else."
Co-authors	Definition	Participants select co-authors based on past achievements or by contacting mentors, determine the order of names based on contribution levels or through other-determined or alphabetical conventions, and engage in discussing literature review techniques to find articles
	Example Utterance	"As for finding a co-author, my approach is pragmatic, given my limited network. I primarily reach out to professors who have previously taught me, leveraging existing relationships built on trust and mutual respect."
Find Articles	Definition	The discussion of literature review techniques
	Example Utterance	"Use of the keywords, I will first think the common keywords that are pertinent to the study, and input those into the databases or Google Scholar, and while reading the results I can often find the keywords that related to the study yet was ignored."

(*continued*)

Table 2. (*continued*)

Code		
Innovation	Definition	The participant takes about the manuscript needs to be innovative enough
	Example Utterance	"Being innovative enough to work on problems that have not yet been solved by current theoretical developments."
Support Systems	Definition	The participants developed their support networks by typically seeking guidance from mentors or senior students and received assistance through software and financial support from organizations or their mentors
	Example Utterance	"have friends that have and colleagues that have published before guide you and help you through the process my friend was that for me"
Lack of Support	Definition	Participants discussed the general lack of support during the publishing process
	Example Utterance	"I don't have any support"
Exempt/Unfamiliarly	Definition	During the process of creating a manuscript, IRB was not involved because it was considered exempt, did not exist, or had a different name in the participant's country or region
	Example Utterance	"I don't understand what you mean. It's an ethical review, right? There is no ethical review in the country."
Publication Preparation	Definition	The action to prepare the manuscript for publication
	Example Utterance	"An editor reviews the content, identifying which sections may not meet the publication's standards and which parts are effective. "

Epistemic network analysis (ENA) was utilized to create a visual and statistical representation of how various publishing strategies and obstacles are interconnected among doctoral students. A minimum edge weight of 0.03 and scaling factor of 1.5 were applied to enhance visibility and emphasis on the most significant connections within the data. Models were generated to compare insights among those in social sciences versus STEM fields, and geographic differences of US and China to uncover patterns and insights relevant to academic success in publishing. A summary of the participants can be seen in Table 2.

4 Results

The resulting ENA models are seen in the following sections, first comparing by fields of study and followed by geographic region. Constructs are represented by nodes on the model. The space is defined by Exempt/Unfamiliarity on the left, Synergy and on the right, Publication Preparation at the top and Co-Author at the bottom. The lines indicate connections between constructs, with the thickness corresponding with the strength of that connection.

4.1 Comparing Social Science (SS) and STEM

The ENA models for SS, STEM, and subtracted are showed below (See Fig. 1).

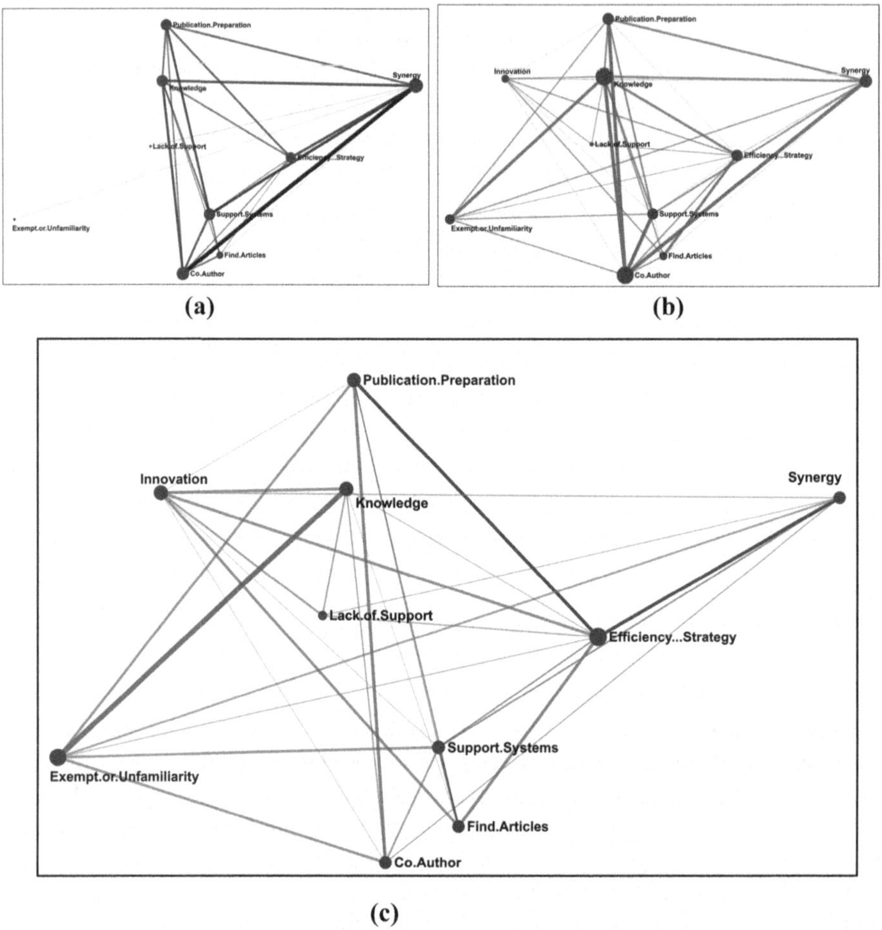

Fig. 1. Above left in blue (a) is the model for STEM participants; above right in red (b) is model for SS participants; bottom is a subtracted model of both

When examining the subtracted model, the STEM participants had the strongest connections between Knowledge and IRB Exempt or Unfamiliarity, Finding Articles and Efficiency & Strategy, and Publication Preparation and Co-author. In contrast, the SS participants had more connections relating to Publication preparation and Efficiency &

Strategy, as well as Efficiency and Strategy with on Synergy. Along the X axis (MR1), a Mann-Whitney test showed that SS ($Mdn = -0.21, N = 6$) was statistically significantly different at the alpha = 0.05 level from STEM ($Mdn = 0.49$, $N = 3$, $U = 18.00$, $p = 0.02$, $r = -1.00$).

4.2 Comparing Geographic Locations

The following section presents ENA models for two geographic regions, the U.S. and China. This category was made based on the program location of each participant. Figure 2 presents the U.S., China ENA model, and subtracted model between two locations.

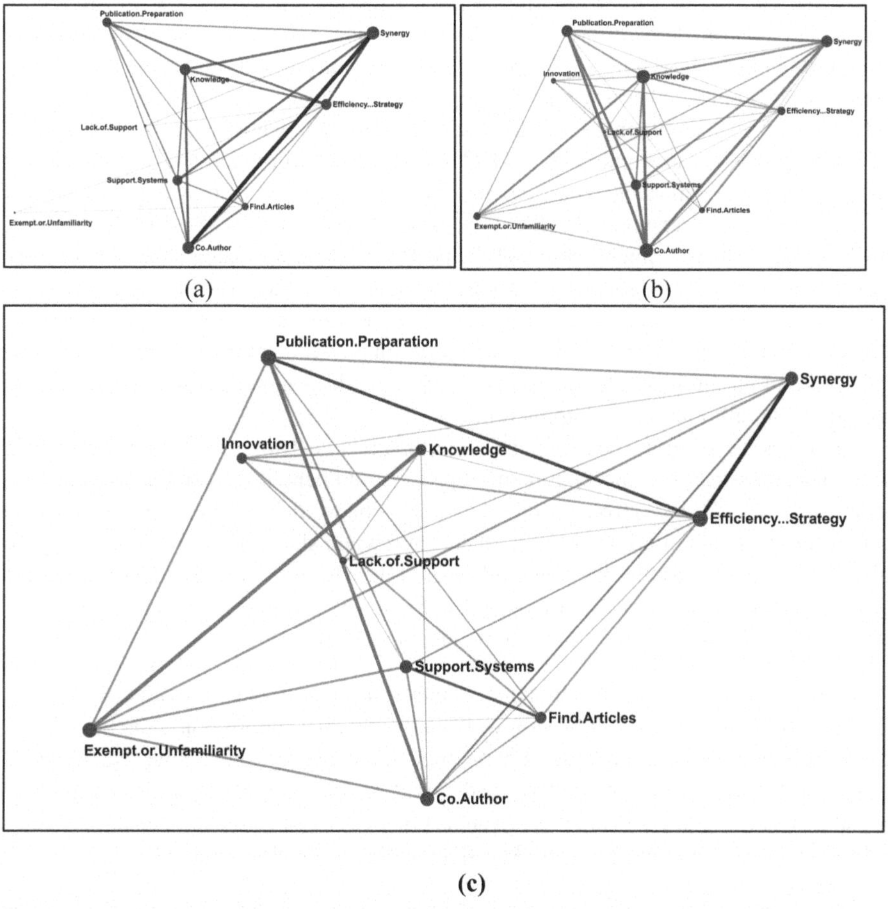

Fig. 2. Above left in blue (a) is the model for China participants; above right in red (b) is model for US participants; bottom is a subtracted model of both

When examining the subtracted model, the U.S. had the strongest connections between Synergy and Efficiency & Strategy, Publication Preparation and Co-author,

Efficiency & Strategy and Publication Preparation, and Find Article and Support System. In contrast, Chinese participants had more connections relating to Knowledge and IRB Exempt or Unfamiliar. Along the X axis (MR1), a Mann-Whitney test showed that the U.S. ($Mdn = -0.30$, $N = 5$) was statistically significantly different at the alpha = 0.05 level from China ($Mdn = 0.31$, $N = 4$, $U = 0$, $p = 0.02$, $r = 1.00$).

5 Discussion

5.1 SS and STEM

The network graph displays several trends in looking at the overall model: the first are knowledge and Exempt or Unfamiliarity, then Efficiency & Strategy with three constructs: Publication Preparation, Synergy, and Finding Articles. These strong connections could indicate how much efficiency and strategy play an important role where most constructs are connected as a whole. When comparing those in SS to those in STEM, all STEM participants comment related the constructs between Knowledge and IRB Expect or Unfamiliarity. For example", P6 (STEM, China)said, "Sorry, don't know much about IRB," and some social science participants also acknowledge that they are not aware of or that they are IRB exempt; P1 (SS, U.S.) said, "IRB is not involved in the process, and I do not know too much about IRB," and P5 (SS, China), when asked about IRB, commented, "I don't understand what you mean. It's an ethical review, right? There is no ethical review in the country." It appears that IRB or ethical review could be U.S. specific, as suggested by P9 (SS, U.S.) who work in the U.S. yet acknowledge their time in Canada: "I am in the context of Canada; what we do is not call it the "IRB," but we normally just call it an 'ethics' application."

Strategies are central to participants in both subjects. Those diverse strategies help participants to streamline their publication process and benefit their publication efforts. For instance, P2 (SS, U.S.) from social science says she would use "the Schimago ranking system for journals to find where to publish," and when she prepares the manuscript to submit, she will "always look at the guidelines if they follow, let's say, Harvard citation style and APA citation time, and that will help you not get rejected immediately." P3 used a similar strategy without mentioning any specific ranking list:

> (When trying to increase the efficiency of publication) A strategy is to identify a list of potential journals for submission well in advance. If a submission is declined by one journal, it's important to quickly proceed to the next option on your list. When rejection comes with constructive feedback, take the opportunity to revise your paper accordingly. … Persisting through rejections and refining your approach based on actionable feedback are key steps in the publication process.

This strategy is recurring in the social science field. P4 (SS, U.S.) commented on something similar when talking about better ways they found to publish their article: "choose the right journal, see if the article fits what the journal wants, and plan what you want to submit first." It seems that goal-setting techniques are quite popular among social science participants in this dataset.

Working with others is also a great strategy to ensure the success of a publication. This was again mostly mentioned by social science participants; for instance, when identifying the best place to submit the article, P1 (SS, U.S.) said, "find a senior doctoral student and ask her opinion on which conference to submit to." In essence, she provides supplementary assistance to complement the previously mentioned strategy. This does not mean that STEM participants do not value synergy; rather, they focus on synergy and co-authors. Despite this connection being more evident in the STEM ENA graph than the subtractive graph, their responses do mention aspects of working with co-authors, or rather, what kind of co-author they want to collaborate with. For instance, P6 hopes the co-authors are those who "research in a similar field or provide unique insights that enhance the paper." Or those who have contributed to the "revision of the paper", the "development of the experimental program", and the "execution of the experiments," according to P7 (STEM, China). In this sense, to a degree, working with others, especially capable others, is a key factor in being successful in publishing.

The strategies also pertain to finding articles; for example, P3 (SS, U.S.) searches databases for articles using keywords and limiters: "I primarily rely on Google Scholar, using keywords related to my study to find relevant literature. ... for more targeted searches, especially when looking for articles from specific years, I employ the advanced search feature."

Other participants (#4 – SS, U.S., #5 – SS, China., #6 – STEM, China, #8 – STEM, China) used similar keywords and reference strategies to find articles; however, P7 (China) from the STEM field commented on some other approaches. They suggest understanding the field holistically, not just related to the topic of the paper, but "papers in related fields should be reviewed." Those comments suggest that learning how to systematically search the literature related to the topic is a key factor in publication success.

Lastly, there is a weak connection to Synergy from STEM participants compared to SS participants, mainly attributed to the small sample size. However this difference still can be indicative of how STEM doctoral students do not really talk to others in selecting their writing topics. For instance, P1 (SS, U.S.), P3 (SS, U.S.), and P5 (China) from SS find topic by discussion "to achieve this, I reached out to my mentor and co-author to discuss the possibility of contributing to this significant topic," or draw inspiration from past experiences "(I found topics) related to my personal experience because I have had a lot of cross-cultural learning experience especially after I went to university at the age of 18, so my passion is whether students' learning experience matches their learning expectations" (P4, SS, U.S.). STEM participants would follow the direction of the group (lab) "usually based on the direction and needs of the subject group" (P6, STEM, China), or they would have their topic assigned by essentially following the group (lab): "based on research direction such as precision hot blanking, springback behavior, and modeling of large plastic compression deformation, the topic is based on the direction of the group." Which in turn affects the criteria for choosing the co-authors. Unless we talk about contribution in general in SS, STEM participants would want someone who "contributed to the revision of the paper, the development of the experimental program, and the execution of the experiments" (P7, STEM, China).

5.2 Locations

The network graph showed several trends. First, it appears the participants in the U.S. would talk more about Synergy and Efficiency & Strategies, discuss various strategies to prepare the manuscript for publication, and talk more about strategies to finding articles and support systems that benefit them in publication. On the contrary, Chinese participants talk more about co-authors and manuscript preparation, they value field related knowledge yet they were unfamiliar with the IRB process. Because there is heavy overlap between SS and the U.S. and STEM and China, the data might be similar to the previous comparison between SS and STEM. For instance, P1a doctoral student in the U.S., talks about her strategy of dividing up work with her collaborators and working together for a full manuscript:

> I came up with the idea, and I took majority of the work, … decide which negative words that we are going to use, and teach those who are not so familiar with the corpus on how to use those. … I in charge of roughly 60–70% of the literature gathering and organizing, write 70% of the manuscript, in charge of the data analyzing, and tell what each co-authors must do during the process.

The participants in the U.S. would leverage more digital services than their Chinese counterparts when finding articles and staying in loop of research trends; for instance, P3 (SS, U.S.) mentioned:

> For practical aspects of research and writing, tools like Grammarly are essential for proofreading, while platforms such as Google Scholar and ResearchGate are pivotal for conducting literature reviews and staying informed about recent studies.

It is understandable that none of the Chinese participants mentioned those services, because all of them are inaccessible in mainland China. Another thing that may be lacking from the Chinese context is the IRB process. Unlike U.S. participants, who acknowledge the IRB: "IRB is not involved in the process and I do not know too much about IRB" (P1; SS, U.S.) or have a different name (P9; SS, U.S.), Chinese participants sometimes acknowledge it but state that "there is no ethical review in the country." While it is not certain if all Chinese universities do not have this or similar practices, this could mean Chinese scholars could pursue a topic faster because they can just go and collect data without being "limited" by the IRB. On the contrary, U.S. participants had to go through the review process, where their strategy to pass that faster is usually to avoid vulnerable populations (P9; SS) or just be succinct and provide just enough details (P2 – SS and P4 – SS). Manuscript preparation is important to both U.S. and Chinese participants; for instance, Chinese participants would hire an editor to enhance the manuscript suggested by P5 (SS): "They (editors) input ranges from suggesting pertinent citations to refining phrases, enhancing the overall quality and depth of the work. "

During the drafting of the manuscript, the U.S. participant would also look for tutorials online to prepare their manuscript for publication. For example, P3 (SS) said:

> YouTube is a surprisingly rich resource; by searching for videos on how to structure a journal publication in education, you can find numerous tutorials and advice that address common questions and challenges in the field.

6 Conclusion

Despite some variations by geographical limitations and subject, there are some commonalities in strategy for publication among doctoral students. For example, creating a clear goal for publication prior to the writing, using keywords, limiters, and advance searches to find relevant articles, and enhancing the manuscript and trying to reduce common errors and issues before submission. The most important variation is created when dividing the participants by geographic locations, where U.S. participants focus on synergy and strategies for manuscript preparation, including digital tools for literature review and IRB navigation. They emphasize collaborative work distribution and utilize services like Grammarly and Google Scholar for research and manuscript enhancement. In comparison, Chinese participants focus on manuscript enhancement through professional editing and bypassing a lengthy IRB process, which is sometimes nonexistent in China. This potentially speeds up their research process compared to their U.S. counterparts, who must navigate IRB reviews. Knowing the common practices from those who already published can be a great help for early career professionals such as Ph.D. student. This knowledge can be used as a practical guide, helping them navigate the complexities of academic publishing and strategically plan their research trajectory. Recognizing these practices can be crucial in effectively managing expectations and aligning their efforts with the established norms and requirements of their respective fields.

While this study successfully created insights from a compact dataset, the current sample's limited diversity may restrict the depth of analysis regarding academic publishing strategies across different academic contexts. There was significant overlap with SS subject participants being from the US, and STEM subject participants being from China. To build on these findings, future research will aim to encompass a broader spectrum of doctoral students from a variation in subject and geographic regions. Expanding the sample to include diverse educational systems and cultural backgrounds would help determine whether the observed differences in publication strategies between countries such as the U.S. and China are unique or pervasive across other regions as well. Further studies should also investigate how these publication strategies correlate with student success, offering a richer perspective on the challenges and strategies doctoral students face in academic publishing.

References

1. Evans, S.C., Amaro, C.M., Herbert, R., Blossom, J.B., Roberts, M.C.: "Are you gonna publish that?" Peer-reviewed publication outcomes of doctoral dissertations in psychology. PLoS ONE **13**(2), e0192219 (2018). https://doi.org/10.1371/journal.pone.0192219
2. Vale, R.D.: Accelerating scientific publication in biology. Proc. Natl. Acad. Sci. U.S.A. **112**(44), 13439–13446 (2015). https://doi.org/10.1073/pnas.1511912112
3. Nihalani, P.K., Mayrath, M.C.: Publishing in educational psychology journals: comments from editors. Educ. Psychol. Rev. **20**(1), 29–39 (2008). https://doi.org/10.1007/s10648-007-9062-3
4. Stricker, J., Günther, A.: Scientific misconduct in psychology: a systematic review of prevalence estimates and new empirical data. Zeitschrift für Psychologie **227**(1), 53–63 (2019). https://doi.org/10.1027/2151-2604/a000356

5. Tang, G., Jia, J.: Why do master's students of humanities and social sciences publish papers in Chinese-language predatory journals? A qualitative study based on Grounded Theory. Accountability Res: Policies Qual. Assur. (2021). https://doi.org/10.1080/08989621.2021.1960164
6. Longyhore, D., Zagar, B.: The predator and prey of publishing research. Am. J. Pharm.Educ. **79**(8), 128 (2015). https://doi.org/10.5688/ajpe798128
7. Rørstad, K., Aksnes, D.W.: Publication rate expressed by age, gender and academic position – A large-scale analysis of Norwegian academic staff. J. Informet. **9**(2), 317–333 (2015). https://doi.org/10.1016/j.joi.2015.02.003
8. Rand, B.: Publish or Perish: What the Research Says About Productivity in Academia. HBS Working Knowledge (2024). http://hbswk.hbs.edu/item/publish-or-perish-what-the-research-says-about-productivity-in-academia
9. Amutuhaire, T.: The reality of the 'publish or perish' concept, perspectives from the global south. Publ. Res. Q. **38**(2), 281–294 (2022). https://doi.org/10.1007/s12109-022-09879-0
10. Feller, I.: Performance measurement redux. Am. J. Eval. **23**(4), 435–452 (2002). https://doi.org/10.1177/109821400202300405
11. Adler, N.J., Harzing, A.-W.: When knowledge wins: transcending the sense and nonsense of academic rankings. Acad. Manage. Learn. Educ. **8**(1), 72–95 (2009)
12. Knievel, J.E.: Instruction to faculty and graduate students: a tutorial to teach publication strategies. portal: Libr. Acad. **8**(2), 175–186 (2008). https://doi.org/10.1353/pla.2008.0020
13. Hangel, N., Schmidt-Pfister, D.: Why do you publish? On the tensions between generating scientific knowledge and publication pressure. Aslib J. Inf. Manag. **69**(5), 529–544 (2017). https://doi.org/10.1108/AJIM-01-2017-0019
14. Haven, T.L., Bouter, L.M., Smulders, Y.M., Tijdink, J.K.: Perceived publication pressure in Amsterdam: Survey of all disciplinary fields and academic ranks. PLoS ONE **14**(6), 1–12 (2019). https://doi.org/10.1371/journal.pone.0217931
15. Huang, Y.: Doctoral writing for publication. High. Educ. Res. Dev. **40**(4), 753–766 (2021)
16. Lei, S.A., Chuang, N.-K.: Research collaboration and publication during graduate studies: evaluating benefits and costs from students' perspectives. Coll. Stud. J. **43**(4), 1163–1168 (2009)
17. Trau, R.N.C.: Review of the publish or perish book: your guide to effective and responsible citation analysis. Acad. Manag. Learn. Educ. **11**(2), 314–315 (2012). https://doi.org/10.5465/amle.2012.0070
18. Jackson, D.: Completing a PhD by publication: a review of australian policy and implications for practice. High. Educ. Res. Dev. **32**(3), 355–368 (2013)
19. Lei, J., Hu, G.: Doctoral candidates' dual role as student and expert scholarly writer: an activity theory perspective. Engl. Specif. Purp. **54**, 62–74 (2019). https://doi.org/10.1016/j.esp.2018.12.003
20. Badenhorst, C., Guerin, C.: Post/graduate research literacies and writing pedagogies. In: Badenhorst, C., Guerin, C. (eds.) Research Literacies and writing Pedagogies for Masters and Doctoral Writers, pp. 3–28. BRILL (2016). https://doi.org/10.1163/9789004304338_002
21. Brabham, D.C.: Within reach: publishing as a graduate student. Rocky Mt. Commun. Rev. **3**(2), 42–46 (2007)
22. Habibie, P.: Writing for scholarly publication in a Canadian higher education context: a case study. In: Badenhorst, C., Guerin, C. (eds.) Research Literacies and Writing Pedagogies for Masters and Doctoral Writers, pp. 51–67. BRILL (2016). https://doi.org/10.1163/9789004304338_004
23. Snowball, J.D., Shackleton, C.M.: Factors enabling and constraining research in a small, research-intensive South African University. Res. Eval. **27**(2), 119–131 (2018)
24. Dahler-Larsen, P.: Making citations of publications in languages other than English visible: on the feasibility of a PLOTE-index. Res. Eval. **27**(3), 212–221 (2018)

25. Shaffer, D.W.: Quantitative ethnography (2017)
26. Armstrong, D., Gosling, A., Weinman, J., Marteau, T.: The place of inter-rater reliability in qualitative research: an empirical study. Sociology **31**(3), 597–606 (1997)
27. Thomas, D.R.: A general inductive approach for analyzing qualitative evaluation data. Am. J. Eval. **27**(2), 237–246 (2006)

Examining Shifts in Elementary Teachers' Collective Connection Making Between Perspectives When Scoping Ill-Structured Engineering Design Problems

Sinead Meehan[1](✉) and Christopher G. Wright[2]

[1] Ball State University, Muncie, IN 47306, USA
sinead.meehan@bsu.edu
[2] Drexel University, Philadelphia, PA 19104, USA

Abstract. Using quantitative ethnography and epistemic network analysis, this study examined video observation data to identify shifts in elementary teachers' connection making between perspectives (i.e. environmental, historical, political/organizational, etc.) as they scoped ill-structured engineering-design problems throughout a critical, engineering focused professional development (PD) program. Results from Mann-Whitney U tests showed statistically significant differences in teachers' connection making from Module 1 to Module 2 ($p = 0.02$), Module 2 to Module 3 ($p = 0.03$), and Module 3 to Module 4 ($p = 0.02$). Despite these differences, the behavioral/social perspective remained a central lens through which participants scoped ill-structured problems across all four modules. Stakeholders should consider the nature of teachers' connection making between perspectives as they design engineering PD, specifically in terms of the design problems selected.

Keywords: problem scoping · K-12 engineering · professional development

1 Introduction

Practicing engineers are tasked with scoping design problems and deciding on the most efficient and effective solutions within their localized contexts. The way an engineering design problem is scoped and eventually solved has real implications for people, multispecies, and the planet, benefitting some and burdening others. Unfortunately, technological advancements and solutions are often prioritized, ignoring the underlying social, political, and systemic aspects of design problems, which in turn, perpetuates injustices. Therefore, recognizing and addressing the socio-political context of engineering design problems is essential, as it can help prevent the reinforcement of inequities and lead to the creation of more holistic, just, and sustainable solutions.

While practicing engineers have opportunities to scope and solve complex, ill-structured problems daily, professional development (PD) opportunities, specifically at the elementary level, tend not to highlight the social and political aspects of engineering.

Y. J. Kim and Z. Swiecki (Eds.): icqe 2024, CCIS 2279, pp. 180–194, 2024.
https://doi.org/10.1007/978-3-031-76332-8_15

Instead, PD opportunities tend to align with existing standards, frameworks, and curricula which perpetuate dominant views of engineering as a strictly technocratic endeavor, thus decentralizing issues of social justice and ignoring the sociopolitical foundations of most problems [1].

This study argues that incorporating critical pedagogies into engineering-focused PD for elementary educators is crucial. Critical pedagogies challenge the dominant view of engineering as an objective and politically neutral field by encouraging educators to investigate disparities in existing engineering design products and systems and supporting teachers in scoping engineering design problems from multiple perspectives. By employing a critical lens, engineering PD can help teachers "recognize and question how certain designs [and the multidisciplinary practices engineers engage in to produce them] promote the welfare and interests of some, while remaining inaccessible [or harming] others" [2]. Furthermore, this study contends that K-12 PD seeking to counteract prevailing notions of engineering should emphasize problem scoping, as it lays the foundation for the rest of the EDP and provides teachers an opportunity to thoroughly examine design problems from multiple perspectives.

2 Literature Review

2.1 Engineering Focused Professional Development

Although the formation and adoption of the *Framework for K-12 Science Education* [3] and the *Next Generation Science Standards* [4] have increased the visibility of engineering in K-12 settings, opportunities for elementary educators to engage in engineering-focused PD remain limited, leaving many teachers unprepared to engage students in engineering activities [5]. To address this gap, schools, universities, and curriculum developers have designed, implemented, and evaluated various forms of engineering-focused PD. Most of these PD programs have focused on expanding teachers' knowledge of the engineering design process [6, 7], their understanding of engineering and the work of engineers [8, 9], and their ability to integrate engineering into their instruction [10–12]. These PD programs have employed a wide range of instructional strategies including (a) engaging teachers in engineering design challenges [6, 7]; (b) providing direct instruction [6, 7]; (c) placing elementary teachers in close proximity to practicing engineers [6, 13, 14]; (d) granting teachers access to engineering facilities [14]; (e) providing exemplar lessons or units [11]; (f) supporting teachers collaborative lesson planning [10, 12]; and (g) offering ongoing coaching and feedback [10].

Findings from these studies have demonstrated that engineering-focused PD for elementary educators can positively impact their confidence for teaching engineering [15], skills in and attitudes toward design thinking [16], engineering pedagogical content knowledge [17], understanding of the work of engineers [12], and the ability to recognize and understand engineering in the world around them [13].

2.2 Critical Approaches to Engineering Education

Researchers, aware of the dominant approach to engineering education have actively advocated for reform [1, 18–20]. As Claris and Riley stated over a decade ago,

> We have long ago reached a certain 'situation critical' in engineering, in which engineers may have abundant logical thinking skills but no practice of thinking critically about problem framing, power relations within the profession, hegemonic epistemologies of the discipline, or reproductive practices of engineering education. This leaves society with technologies that replicate power relations of the status quo, and the profession with intractable problems around underrepresentation of white women and women and men of color, and few tools for understanding or talking about these problems, let alone acting effectively for change" (p. 102).

While designed systems and artifacts are central to engineering, K-12 students and teachers of engineering are rarely challenged to critically examine the social, political, economic, and environmental implications of existing and future designs. To address this "situation critical," researchers contend that we must consider issues of harm, power, and equity when engaging in the engineering design process [1].

For example, McGowan and Bell put forth an instructional framework for engineering education that focuses on the development of learners' critical socio technical literacy [19]. They argue that one dimension of engineering is the ability to "read" the designed world, understanding the history and values embodied in systems and artifacts and the impact these artifacts and systems have on their own communities and everyday lives [19]. Beyond merely "reading" the designed world, they argue for the incorporation of "practices and pathways for imagining and redesigning future possibilities" that are more equitable and just [19]. Likewise, Wilson-Lopez asserts that we must provide opportunities for individuals to practice reading the designed world, as well as the multidisciplinary practices that produced that world, in order to "recognize and question how certain designs promote the welfare and interests of some, while remaining inaccessible to others" [3].

To mitigate the potential effects of a technocratic and utilitarian view of engineering, Gunckel and Tolbert assert that engineering education should draw on feminist theory by reframing engineering education to prioritize an ethos of empathy and care [1]. One way in which teachers can add a dimension of care to their engineering instruction is by helping students "develop more in-depth understandings of the structural inequalities that play a role [in] how the problem is defined and delimited, as well as what solutions might be beneficial, relevant, and accessible, to whom and for whom" [1]. For this reason, the present study and accompanying PD program centered problem scoping, a phase of the EDP that is critical, yet often overlooked by students, teachers, and novice engineers [21–23].

2.3 Problem Scoping

Problem scoping, also referred to as problem framing, is the first phase of the EDP and is often considered a critical component of high-quality solutions [24]. Problem scoping can be described as "the process of discovering and understanding aspects of the problem [and potential solutions] that need consideration" [21]. Problem scoping is the aspect of a design activity which involves identifying the criteria, constraints, and requirements of a project, framing the goals or issues to be addressed, gathering information, and stating any assumptions [22].

To work towards the eradication of systems of injustice and inequity, engineers must scope design problems from as many perspectives as possible and identify the causes underlying the issue at hand [1]. The purpose of this study was to design and evaluate an engineering-focused PD program that would support elementary teachers in developing mindsets resembling that of critical, practicing engineers. Problem scoping in this manner calls for K-6 educators to develop their critical consciousness and apply a "dimension of care" [1], so they can eventually model such practices in their work with students. In this study, ENA was used to explore the nature of teachers' connection making between multiple perspectives (i.e. environmental, historical, political/organizational, etc.) with the expectation that their connection making would shift and expand as they learned about problem scoping, examined existing engineering designs, explored and utilized problem scoping tools, and engaged in the act of scoping ill-structured problems.

3 Methods

3.1 Participants

This study involved four (4) lower elementary teachers from a non-denominational Montessori school in a small city in the Mid-Atlantic region of the United States. All four teachers, whom identify as White females, co-teach in mixed aged group classrooms with students in 1st, 2nd, and 3rd grade. They all hold bachelor's or master's degrees, as well as certification to teach at the elementary level by the American Montessori Society.

3.2 Design of the Professional Development Program and Data Collection

Inspired by Rodriguez and Shim's sociotransformative constructivism framework [20], this PD drew upon constructivism as a learning theory [25] and critical pedagogy as a theory of social justice [26] to engage elementary teachers in the exploration of the problem scoping phase of the engineering design process. In both critical pedagogy and constructivism, dialogic conversation [27], reflection [28], and praxis [29] are considered imperative to the construction of knowledge, therefore, these three participation structures were centered throughout the PD. The year-long course utilized a blended, flipped classroom model, with each of the four modules having one asynchronous session and one in-person session. Table 1 provides an overview of each module.

Data were collected in the form of semi-structured interviews, concurrent think alouds, video observations, teacher generated artifacts, and researcher memos. The present study utilized the video observation data from each of the four in-person PD sessions. These video recordings were transcribed verbatim using Trint software and then cleaned by the researcher. All four video observation transcripts were then uploaded into an Excel sheet, with each line representing a turn of talk.

3.3 Coding

Gunckel and Tolbert argue that "students need to be prepared to conceive of engineering design challenges as a complex intersection of sociocultural, material, biological, political, economic, historical contexts—versus the technocratic, utilitarian, and neoliberal

Table 1. Brief Overview of the Eight PD Sessions

Module/ Topic	Session	Activities
1. An Introduction to Problem Scoping	Online	• Watched YouTube videos on the engineering design process • Read problem scoping/problem framing articles • Read *Engineering Design in the NGSS* • Engaged in individual reflection
	In-Person	• Engaged in collective reflection • Generated a list of problems identified in a self-selected children's book • Scoped one (1) problem in the text from multiple perspectives
2. Examining Existing Engineering Designs	Online	• Read and took notes on an excerpt from *Design Justice: Community-Led Practices to Build the Worlds We Need* by Sasha Costanza-Chock • Engaged in individual reflection
	In-Person	• Engaged in collective reflection • Examined existing engineering designs (i.e. park benches, EV charging station, crash test dummies, and bridges) • Engaged in dialogic conversation around key themes in their responses
3. Problem Scoping Tools	Online	• Listened to *Tehya's Pollution Solution* on YouTube (Sects. 1, 2, 3 and 4) • Watched YouTube videos on Stakeholder Analysis and Five Whys • Completed a stakeholder analysis and five whys analysis for the oil spill problem in the video
	In-Person	• Engaged in collective reflection • Compared the completed stakeholder analysis and five whys worksheets • Introduced and completed a KWL chart for the oil spill problem • Introduced to storyboarding • Engaged in dialogic conversation around each tools' limitations and affordances

(*continued*)

Table 1. (*continued*)

Module/ Topic	Session	Activities
4. Scoping Self-Identified Problems and Reflecting on Problem Scoping Practices	Online	• Generated a list of problems that can be solved through engineering • Selected one problem • Scoped the problem and wrote a problem statement • Engaged in individual reflection
	In-Person	• Reflected on their approaches to problem scoping by examining their individual and collective ENA models for Modules 1, 2, and 3 • Shared their problem statements with the group • Considered which perspectives were dominant and how they might approach problem scoping more holistically moving forward

approach that has dominated engineering in the science curriculum" [p. 949]. Based on these assertions, I developed an initial set of eight deductive codes representing various perspectives or contexts educators might attend to when scoping ill-structured engineering design problems, some of which are outlined in the quote above and others that emerged throughout the rest of the article [1].

As this initial set of codes was applied to the video observation transcripts, it became evident that some codes were too similar, leading to high rates of co-occurrence (i.e. behavioral and social), consequently the researchers decided to merge these codes (i.e. behavioral/social). Other codes were used infrequently (i.e. generational) and therefore eliminated. Finally, one inductive code emerged as the teachers engaged in the act of problem scoping (i.e. geographical). In total, the first author coded 1,891 lines of data for the absence (0) or presence (1) of the nine codes (see Table 2). To enhance the trustworthiness of the analysis, the first author engaged in intracoder reliability, ensuring the consistent application of the coding scheme across the data.

3.4 ENA Model Generation

The ENA web tool, under the researchers' direction, created a series of models illustrating teachers' collective connection making between perspectives as they engaged in problem scoping activities during the in-person PD sessions [30]. The *module* and *participant* variables were selected as the unit of analysis. Since each module consisted of discrete activities, the *module* and *line break* variables were used to define the conversation. The *line break* variable was created by the researcher to delineate distinct conversations in each module, ensuring connections were only made between related conversations. A moving stanza window of four (4) was selected, directing the ENA

Table 2. Codebook

Code	Definition	Example
Social/Behavioral	The interactions, attitudes, and actions of individuals or groups within a given context	"So people who are just like *aren't paying attention* or *see that the trashcan is full and just leave their trash right next to the trash can.*"
Cultural	The values, beliefs, traditions, and practices of a particular group or society, which significantly influence how individuals perceive, interpret, and engage with the issue or proposed solution	"The *development centered verses tribal centered.*"
Economic	The financial implications, resource allocation, and cost-benefit analysis associated with addressing the issue or implementing the solution	"But my guess is that it is a *considerable expense* for them. That's why I looked it up. I don't think that that's like something *readily available.*"
Environmental	The impact of the problem or potential solution on the environment, ecosystems, and natural resources	"Minimizing *plastic pollution* will minimize the *loss of biodiversity.*"
Historical	Past events, trends, and cultural contexts relevant to the issue at hand, providing valuable insights into its origins, evolution, and systemic patterns	"That was a crazy side effect of *COVID* to, was everything was disposable."
Political/ Organizational	Government policies, regulations, and bureaucratic processes, while also considering the political climate, priorities, and agendas of relevant government agencies, politicians, NGOs, or corporations	"And they [Hilton Head] even have *rules* about, you know, like your buildings can't be taller than the tree line and they have to be a particular color so everything looks natural."
Technical/ Structural	Engineering principles, technological capabilities, and/or architectural frameworks to devise efficient and functional solutions	"So something in the [airport scanners] *algorithm.*"

(*continued*)

Table 2. *(continued)*

Code	Definition	Example
Geographical	The geographical context where the issue occurs or the solution is implemented	"So does this have to do with their *geography*...the *geography of the two places*? So, *Nepal* is *next to the mountains*...do they experience *Monsoons*? And *Bangladesh?*"
Materials/ Materiality	The selection, composition, and properties of physical substances utilized in the solution's construction or implementation; Descriptive characteristics of an engineered design	"If they're using a lantern, it is probably one of those like *battery operated* Coleman lanterns over a *kerosene* lamp."

web tool to draw connections between each line and the three (3) previous lines within a given conversation. Finally, the nine (9) codes outlined in Table 2 were selected as the code variables. A total of seven models were generated and compared including one model for each module, as well as a difference model between Modules 1 and 2, 2 and 3, and 3 and 4. This paper primarily shares the difference models to illustrate shifts in elementary teachers' connection making as they progressed through the PD program.

4 Findings

Epistemic networks visualized patterns of connection between the nine perspectives across the four in-person sessions. Additionally, a series of Mann-Whitney U tests identified statistically significant differences in teachers' connection making between perspectives as teachers progressed through the PD program.

4.1 Module 1

In Module 1, the behavioral/social dimension was central to teachers' problem scoping practices (see Fig. 1). Teachers drew connections between the behavioral/social perspective and all other perspectives, but the strongest connections were made between the behavioral/social and environmental (0.48), behavioral/social and economic (0.43), and behavioral/social and material (0.31) perspectives.

To illustrate a connection made between the behavioral/social and environmental perspectives we can look at an excerpt from Ms. Jane's conversation around the text *Rocket Says Clean Up.* As Ms. Jane scoped the problem of plastic pollution in her selected text she shared, "It did say in the book that....a third or half of all the trash that's on the beach...it comes from negligent people. So, people who are just like aren't paying attention or see that the trashcan is full and just leave their trash right next to the trash can." This statement from Ms. Jane illustrates the connection she made between the environmental issue of plastic pollution and the behavioral characteristics of humans, namely their negligence in finding an appropriate receptacle to put their trash.

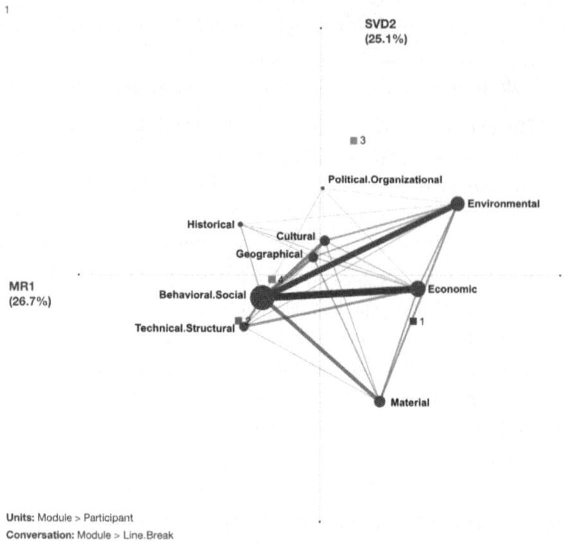

Fig. 1. ENA Model of Teachers' Connection Making in Module 1

4.2 Module 2

A Mann-Whitney test showed a statistically significant difference ($p = 0.02$) in teachers connection making from Module 1 (red) to Module 2 (blue). Like Module 1, teachers drew the greatest number of connections between the behavioral/social dimension and all other dimensions of care. However, during Module 2's in-person session, teachers made stronger connections between the behavioral/social and technical/structural (0.58), behavioral/social and geographical (0.35), and behavioral/social and historical (0.30) perspectives (see Fig. 2).

To demonstrate teachers' connection making between the behavioral/social, technical/structural, and historical perspectives, we share this conversation which occurred between the first author and two of the participants. For context, the teachers were asked to look at existing design products and consider how each design might benefit some and burden others. When looking at the crash test dummy example, Mrs. Austin wrote that people who assume safety without understanding they are at risk, may be burdened. When asked to elaborate on what she meant, the following conversation unfolded.

Mrs. Austin: Like back in the day, when we went from the lap belt to the...

Sinead: The crossover.

Mrs. Austin: The three-point...whatever you want to call that, they like, they assumed that they're going to be safer. So they might take, not necessarily different risks, but maybe, you know.....

Mrs. Singh: So just like the, like on the part of the people using the seatbelts, now they have this, like, false sense of security where they could take more risks.

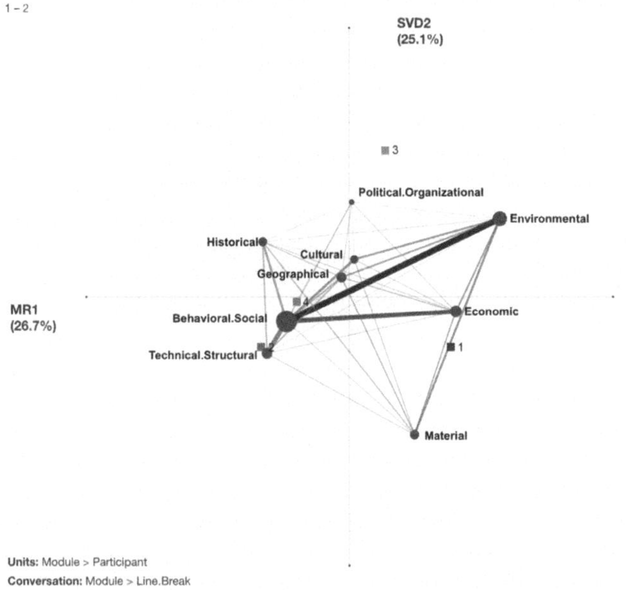

Fig. 2. Difference Model of Teachers' Connection Making Between Perspectives from Module 1 (red) to Module 2 (blue)

In this example, the elementary teachers shed light on how the technological development of seatbelts may have inadvertently made driving less safe by giving people a false sense of security leading to more risk taking on the part of the driver.

4.3 Module 3

A Mann-Whitney test indicated a statistically significant difference ($p = 0.03$) in teachers connection making from Module 2 (blue) to Module 3 (purple). Like the first two modules, teachers drew connections between the behavioral/social perspective and all other perspectives. However, when comparing the nature of connections (see Fig. 3), teachers drew stronger connections between the behavioral/social and political/organizational (0.50) and behavioral/social and environmental (0.43) perspectives in Module 3 than Module 2.

Behavioral/Social and Environmental. For example, teachers drew connections between the behavioral/social, environmental, and technical/structural perspectives as they scoped the oil spill problem in *Tehya's Pollution Solution.* When suggesting steps that might be taken to better understand the oil spill problem, Mrs. Austin suggested that Thomas use models and interpret data to determine which areas of the river had been affected, as well as the best method for cleaning up the oil, without causing further harm to the ecosystem. Mrs. Austin stated, "I mean, he was talking about, like, using a boom, like, to collect and not spread and like, if it's, if we're moving the oil to a place that's clean, we're making more problems." She then proceeded to consider an additional variable, the time it would take the engineers and volunteers to mobilize explaining, "It's

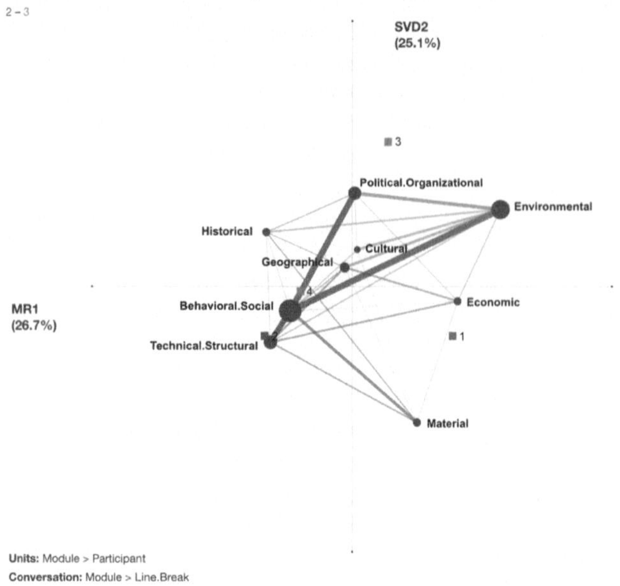

Fig. 3. Difference Model of Teachers' Connection Making Between Perspectives from Module 2 (blue) to Module 3 (purple)

going to take us 8 hours to get organized and now we've got different current patterns." In this example, Mrs. Austin drew connections between the three perspectives by considering the ever-changing and unpredictable nature of both humans and the environment, describing the problem-scoping process as cyclical, requiring engineers to move back and forth between generating models, analyzing data, and developing solutions in real time.

4.4 Module 4

In terms of teachers' connection making, a Mann-Whitney test indicated a statistically significant difference (p=0.02) between teachers' connection making from Module 3 to Module 4. Figure 4 is a difference model which illustrates the variance in teachers' connection making from Module 3 (purple) to Module 4 (green). In Module 4, teachers made stronger connections between behavioral/social and material (0.30), behavioral/social and geographical (0.28), and geographical and technical/structural (0.21) perspectives.

Connections between the behavioral/social and material perspective emerged as Mrs. Miller scoped the issue of missing pencils in her classroom. While Mrs. Miller initially contended that the only problem was that students were not returning pencils to the bin, scoping the problem from multiple perspectives led her to consider the physical properties of the pencils and how they may be attributing in part to the problem. For example, she hypothesized that maybe because the pencils were round, they were rolling off table tops easily. Other underlying problems such as the lack of sharp pencils also emerged. Using their shared frustration and personal experiences, the group collectively brainstormed

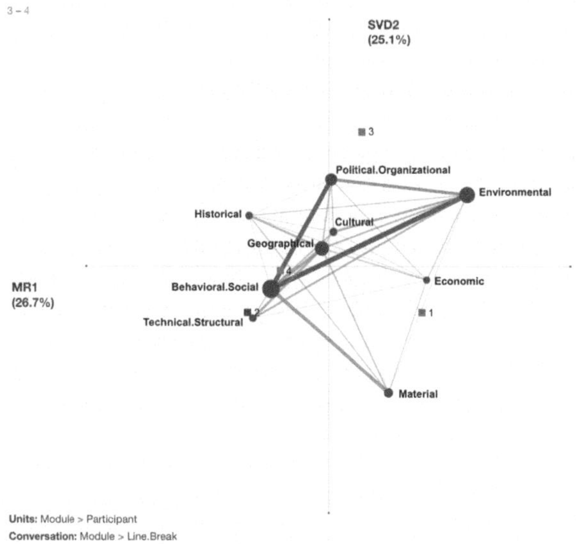

Fig. 4. Difference Model of Teachers' Connection Making from Module 3 (purple) to Module 4 (green)

how the physical properties of the pencil could be changed to decrease students' (and teachers') frustrations and increase productivity. Product solutions included mechanical pencils and colored pencil grips, while systems solutions entailed increasing the time students had to do their classroom jobs (i.e. cleaning up the classroom and sharpening pencils) and writing students names on pencils, making each student responsible for maintaining their own belongings.

5 Discussion and Conclusion

The goal of this study was to understand potential shifts in elementary teachers' connection making between perspectives as they scoped ill-structured engineering-design problems over the course of a four module PD program. Engineers seeking to dismantle systems of injustice and inequity consider design problems from a diverse range of perspectives and apply a systems thinking approach by recognizing the relationships between them. Thus, a key goal of this PD was to broaden the range of perspectives teachers considered and deepen the connections between these perspectives as they engaged in problem scoping activities. ENA illustrated a significant difference ($p < 0.05$) in teachers connection making from Module 1 to Module 2 ($p = 0.02$), Module 2 to Module 3 ($p = 0.03$), and Module 3 to Module 4 ($p = 0.02$).

Some of the differences observed between modules may be attributed to the types of problems the teachers scoped in each session. For example, participants drew stronger connections between the behavioral/social and environmental perspectives in Modules 1 and 3, compared to Modules 2 and 4. As a reminder, in Module 1, one pair of teachers scoped the problem of plastic pollution, while the other pair scoped the kerosene lamp problem. In Module 3, participants scoped the oil spill problem. All three of these problems would traditionally fall into the realm of environmental engineering, thus increasing the likelihood that teachers would attend to the environmental aspects of the problem.

Despite changes from one module to the next, the elementary teachers continuously centered the behavioral/social perspective in their problem scoping practices, regardless of the type of problem they were scoping. In fact, teachers drew connections between the behavioral/social perspective and each of the eight other perspectives across all four modules. In reflecting on the centrality of the behavioral/social dimension to both their individual and group ENA models, the teachers contended that since they are "in the people business" they may be more attuned to the social and behavioral aspects of problems, compared to individuals from other fields. This, along with other conversations, demonstrated their awareness of the impact of an engineer's identify and positionality on their approach to problem scoping.

The results from this study suggest that engineering PD programs that engage teachers in a wide variety of ill-structured problems can support shifts in teachers' problem scoping conversations and activities. In addition, scoping a wide range of problems from texts, pictures, videos, and personal experiences provides opportunities for teachers to attend to multiple perspectives and reinforces the importance of understanding how both the problem and potential solutions impact people, multispecies, and the planet differently. Finally, ENA models can serve as an innovative reflection tool, allowing teachers to identify potential biases in their approaches by recognizing which perspectives they are attending to and drawing connections between, and which ones they were not.

References

1. Gunckel, K.L., Tolbert, S.: The imperative to move toward a dimension of care in engineering education. J. Res. in Sci. Teaching **55**, 938–961 (2018). https://doi.org/10.1002/tea.21458
2. Wilson-Lopez, A., Minichiello, A.: Disciplinary literacy in engineering. J. Adolesc. Adult Literacy **61**, 7–14 (2017). https://doi.org/10.1002/jaal.658
3. National Research Council: A framework for K-12 Science Education: Practices, Crosscutting Concepts, and Core Ideas. National Academies Press, Washington, D.C. (2012)
4. NGSS Lead States: Next Generation Science Standards: For States, By States. The National Academies Press, Washington, D.C. 17226/18290 (2013)
5. Katehi, L., Pearson, G., Feder, M.: Engineering in K-12 education: Understanding the Status and Improving the Prospectus. National Academies Press, Washington, D.C. (2009). https://doi.org/10.17226/12635
6. Deniz, H., Kaya, E., Yesilyurt, E., Trabia, M.: The influence of an engineering design experience on elementary teachers' nature of engineering views. Intl. J. Tech. and Des. Edu. **30**, 635–656 (2020). https://doi.org/10.1007/s10798-019-09518-4
7. Stohlmann, M., Maiorca, C., DeVaul, L.: Elementary teachers' engineering design activities from a state without engineering standards. Sci. Educator **26**, 48–59 (2017)
8. Antink-Meyer, A., Meyer, D.Z.: Science teachers' misconceptions in science and engineering distinctions: reflections on modern research examples. J. Sci. Teacher Edu. **27**, 625–647 (2016). https://doi.org/10.1007/s10972-016-9478-z
9. López, C.C.C., Echeverria, M.J.G., López-Malo, A., Palou, E.: Eliciting Yucatan peninsula teachers' images of engineering and engineers. In: 2012 Frontiers in Education Conference Proceedings, pp. 1–6. IEEE (2012). https://doi.org/10.1109/FIE.2012.6462221

10. Cook, K., Bush, S., Cox, R., Jr., Edelen, D.: Development of elementary teachers' science, technology, engineering, arts, and mathematics planning practices. Sch. Sci. and Math. **120**, 197–208 (2020). https://doi.org/10.1111/ssm.12400
11. Guzey, S.S., Moore, T.J., Harwell, M.: Building up STEM: an analysis of teacher-developed engineering design-based STEM integration curricular materials. J. Pre-College Eng. Edu. Res. **6**, 11–29 (2016). https://doi.org/10.7771/2157-9288.1129
12. Hammack, R., Gannon, P., Foreman, C., Meyer, E.: Impacts of professional development focused on teaching engineering applications of mathematics and science. School Sci. Math. **120**, 413–424 (2020). https://doi.org/10.1111/ssm.12430
13. Duncan, D., Diefes-dux, H., Gentry, M.: Professional development through engineering academies: an examination of elementary teachers' recognition and understanding of engineering. J. of Eng. Edu. **100**, 520–539 (2011). https://doi.org/10.1002/j.2168-9830.2011.tb00025.x
14. Yoon, S.Y., Diefes-Dux, H., Strobel, J.: First-year effects of an engineering professional development program on elementary teachers. Am. J. Eng. Edu. **4**, 67–84 (2013)
15. Parker, M., Ficklin, K., Mishra, M.: Teacher self-efficacy in a rural K-5 setting: quantitative research on the influence of engineering professional development. Contemp. Issues in Tech. Teacher Edu. **20**, 704–729 (2020)
16. Arrington, T.L., Willox, L.: "I need to sit on my hands and put tape on my mouth": improving teachers' design thinking knowledge, skills, and attitudes through professional development. J. Form. Des. Learn. **5**, 27–38 (2021). https://doi.org/10.1007/s41686-021-00054-w
17. Perkins Coppola, M.: Preparing preservice elementary teachers to teach engineering: impact on self-efficacy and outcome expectancy. Sch. Sci. Math. **119**, 161–170 (2019). https://doi.org/10.1111/ssm.12327
18. Claris, L., Riley, D.: Situation critical: critical theory and critical thinking in engineering education. Eng. Stud. **4**, 101–120 (2012). https://doi.org/10.1080/19378629.2011.649920
19. McGowan, V.C., Bell, P.: Engineering education as the development of critical sociotechnical literacy. Sci. Edu. **29**, 981–1005 (2020). https://doi.org/10.1007/s11191-020-00151-5
20. Rodriguez, A.J., Shim, S.W.: Addressing critical cross-cultural issues in elementary STEM education research and practice: a critical review essay of Engineering in elementary STEM education. Cult. Stud. Sci. Edu. **16**, 1–17 (2021). https://doi.org/10.1007/s11422-020-09993-5
21. Watkins, J., Spencer, K., Hammer, D.: Examining young students' problem scoping in engineering design. J. Pre-College Eng. Edu. Res. **4**, 43–53 (2014). https://doi.org/10.7771/2157-9288.1082
22. Atman, C.J., Adams, R.S., Cardella, M.E., Turns, J., Mosborg, S., Saleem, J.: Engineering design processes: a comparison of students and expert practitioners. J. Eng. Edu. **96**, 359–379 (2007)
23. Wendell, K.B.: Design practices of preservice elementary teachers in an integrated engineering and literature experience. J. Pre-College Eng. Edu. Res. **4**, 29–46 (2014). https://doi.org/10.7771/2157-9288.1085
24. Basadur, M., Graen, G.B., Green, S.G.: Training in creative problem solving: effects on ideation and problem finding and solving in an industrial research organization. Org. Behav. and Hum. Perf. **30**, 41–70 (1982). https://doi.org/10.1016/0030-5073(82)90233-1
25. Richardson, V.: Constructivist teacher education: building new understandings. Psychol. Press (1997). https://doi.org/10.4324/9780203973684
26. Freire, P.: Pedagogy of the Oppressed. Penguin Random House, New York (1970)
27. Arnett, R.C.: Dialogic Education: Conversation About Ideas and Between Persons. Southern Illinois University Press, Carbondale, Illinois (1992)
28. Ryan, A., Walsh, T.: Reflexivity and Critical Pedagogy. Brill, Leiden, Netherlands (2018)

29. Rodriguez, A.J., Morrison, D.: Expanding and enacting transformative meanings of equity, diversity and social justice in science education. Cult. Stud. Sci. Edu. **14**, 265–281 (2019). https://doi.org/10.1007/s11422-019-09938-7
30. Elmoazen, R., Saqr, M., Tedre, M., Hirsto, L.: A systematic literature review of empirical research on epistemic network analysis in education. IEEE Access **10**, 17330–17348 (2022). https://doi.org/10.1109/ACCESS.2022.3149812

The Influence of Different Measurement Approaches on Student Affect Transitions Using Ordered Networks

Nidhi Nasiar[1](✉), Andres Felipe Zambrano[1], Jaclyn Ocumpaugh[1], Alex Goslen[2], Jonathan Rowe[2], Jessica Vandenberg[2], Jordan Esiason[2], and Stephen Hutt[3]

[1] Graduate School of Education, University of Pennsylvania, Philadelphia, PA, USA
nasiar@upenn.edu
[2] North Carolina State University, Raleigh, NC, USA
[3] University of Denver, Denver, CO, USA

Abstract. Affect detection is integral to creating affect-sensitive learning systems, but the impact of measurement methods needs further research. This paper uses ordered network analysis (ONA) to compare the affect dynamics of two suites of affect detectors trained on complementary data (i.e., labels from an in-the-moment self-reporting (SR) tool vs labels from field observations) in game-based learning. We then use ONA difference models to assess how divergence in learning and motivational measures impact affect dynamics.

Keywords: Affect Dynamics · Epistemic Network Analysis · Transition Analysis

1 Introduction

Epistemic emotions emerge during cognitive activities and play a vital role in learning [1]. Typically, learning analytics research has focused on 5 emotions: boredom, confusion, frustration, engaged concentration, and delight [1, 3, 4]. Prior work explores the cumulative effect of each emotion [2], its distribution across the learning experience, and the effect of different transitions [1]. However, affect dynamics results have been difficult to interpret even when data is reanalyzed to correct for sampling biases and align methodological choices [4].

One methodological concern that has not been fully studied concerns the ground truth labels that train affect detectors. Exceptions exist [5], but types of labels are rarely compared. Other understudied concerns relate to duration effects and the effects of student-level characteristics (e.g., motivational factors, learning indicators). For example, highly anxious students undergo longer frustration bouts [6], which may mean that common practices of removing self-transitions [7] obscure results.

This study addresses these gaps with a study of Crystal Island, a game-based learning system for middle school microbiology. First, we compare the dynamics of affect detectors [9] trained with ground-truth labels collected using BROMP observations [8]

Y. J. Kim and Z. Swiecki (Eds.): icqe 2024, CCIS 2279, pp. 195–203, 2024.
https://doi.org/10.1007/978-3-031-76332-8_16

to detectors trained on data from a self-report tool employed during those observations. Specifically, we use an ordered network analysis (ONA), a type of epistemic network analysis (ENA) that accounts for directionality, to compare the networks from each set of detectors. We then use ONA difference models to explore how learning gains and situational interest, change affect transitions in these models. We do this to address two research questions (RQ): **RQ1**: Which affective sequences emerge as methodological consequences of ground truth labels (i.e., SR vs. BROMP-based detectors)? **RQ2:** Which sequences emerge due to participant sampling (i.e., differences in students with respect to (a) learning gains and (b) situational interest)?

2 Related Work

Detecting student affect helps us to understand its impact on learning, engagement, and motivation [1, 10]. The development of affective detectors often relies on supervised machine learning (ML) [3], which requires ground truth labels from either the subject (self-report) or a third party (observer), each with strengths and weaknesses. Self-reports can be hampered by self-presentation effects and metacognitive difficulties but have been used to create effective affect detectors in education. Observation-based measurements—like Baker Rodrigo Ocumpaugh Monitoring Protocol (BROMP; [8])—have informed the development of affect detectors in many learning systems [10] but are limited to what coders can discern.

In addition to concerns about labeling strategies, there have also been concerns about what different affective states (or combinations thereof) might mean for learning. [1] hypothesized two main affective pathways, which have been explored using L statistic and ENA [15]. These studies show connections between those pathways and learning, but the hypothesized pathways occur infrequently. Other studies [11] find that the rates of occurrence and recurrence of affect are important. Finally, research suggests that affect dynamics differ for different groups of students. Pathways are different among those with high and low learning [1] and differences are also associated with trait-anxiety [6]. It seems reasonable that we should expand these efforts to other motivational constructs linked to students' emotions, like situational interest, and also learning gains.

3 Methods

This study investigates learning in Crystal Island (CI), an open-world, game-based learning system aligned to 8th-grade microbiology state standards. Students act as investigative scientists to identify a mysterious disease spread on the remote island, interacting with NPCs, reading educational materials, and testing in-game items, while tracking their hypotheses and results. This study uses data from 124 middle schoolers who played CI during their regular science class in the southeastern US. Students are well-balanced for male (N = 53) and female (N = 66), with 5 others who prefer to describe themselves. They include a large share of students from historically marginalized communities (46% Black, 16% Hispanic, 5% Asian, 5% Multiracial, 1% Native American). Students answered a series of pre-surveys (i.e., a demographic questionnaire, knowledge pre-test, and situational interest scale). After 2 days of gameplay, they answered post-surveys (i.e., knowledge post-test and several other motivational measures). While interacting with the game, affect was simultaneously labeled using 2 distinct methods: BROMP observations [8] and a self-report.

3.1 Measures Used in the Study

Affect Detectors using Self-report and BROMP-based Data. This study uses previously published [9], cross-validated, interaction-based detectors of epistemic affective states developed from labels generated from (a) in-game self-reports (SR) and (b) BROMP-based observations. Interaction-based detectors model what students do within a system when they are experiencing an emotion, allowing us to infer these emotions in real-time (see reviews in [12, 13], including a review of BROMP [8]). Students self-reported 1 of 6 affective states: boredom, focused, confusion, happiness, frustration, and nervousness [9]. BROMP classroom observations [8] included boredom (BOR), engaged concentration (ENG), confusion (CON), delight (DEL), and frustration (FRU), but not nervousness, which is hard to observe directly. Corresponding SR labels were aligned with standard BROMP labels adopting a child-friendly language (i.e., focus for engaged concentration; happiness for delight).

BROMP and SR detectors were developed independently from one another. Each set of affective data was used to train a distinct set of ML-based affect detectors, cross-validated to ensure generalization to new populations. As in prior work using BROMP [10], both suites of detectors are trained using 20-s clips of students' log files. Then, each suite is applied and analyzed separately, assigning 2 labels to each clip—from the SR-based detector and BROMP-based detector with the highest probability. Previous work suggests that SR- and BROMP-based detectors capture complementary information about students' affective states [9]. Hence, the differences produced by each are likely to be meaningful.

Learning Gains (LG) and Situational Interest (SI). Students completed identical pre and post-tests of domain knowledge. Normalized learning gains, which scale from 1- to 1, were calculated. Of 124 students, 46 answered both and we excluded students within a standard deviation of the mean (avg = −.10, SD = .35). By ensuring that the groups are distinct, this approach contrasts students with the lowest ($LG < -.45$, $N = 9$) and highest ($LG > .25$, $N = 6$) LGs, avoiding spurious results that can occur when splitting at the mean. SI surveys were adapted for middle school science from [14], featuring 9 items rated on a 7-point scale. Of 124 students, 122 completed this scale, and we excluded students within a standard deviation of the mean (avg = 3.78, SD = 1.05), comparing those with high ($SI > 4.83$, $n = 20$) and low SI ($SI < 2.73$, $n = 16$).

3.2 Ordered Network Analysis (ONA)

We study affective sequences using Ordered Network Analysis (ONA; [16]), building on work using ENA to explore affect transitions [4] and in-game behaviors. We chose ONA for its ability to capture directionality and self-transitions. In *standard uses of ONA*, codes are visualized as nodes in a network, and edges have line weights (LW) of 0 to 1, representing connection strength. Self-transitions are shown with increased node size and LWs. In *ONA difference models,* LWs from one model are subtracted from another (referred to as LW_{diff}). This study selects *ONA parameters* to best understand affective transitions, including self-transitions. Each line of data corresponds to 20-s of gameplay, with 2 labels are applied to each line, one from each suite of detectors. Interrater reliability is unnecessary here as validated detectors provided codes. The *conversation* variable is the full gameplay session (avg = 41.6 min, SD = 15.6) and a *moving stanza window* of size one, meaning only connections between the current and previous line (i.e., affective state) are considered, as standard when analyzing affective transitions [15].

4 Results

4.1 Comparing SR-Based and BROMP-Based Affect Detectors Using ONA

We first use ONA to assess differences in the affective transitions identified by the 2 sets of detectors across all students. Figure 1 shows SR-based models (1a, left) and BROMP-based models (1b, right). Line weights (Table 1) determine node size for self-transitions (e.g., BOR → BOR).

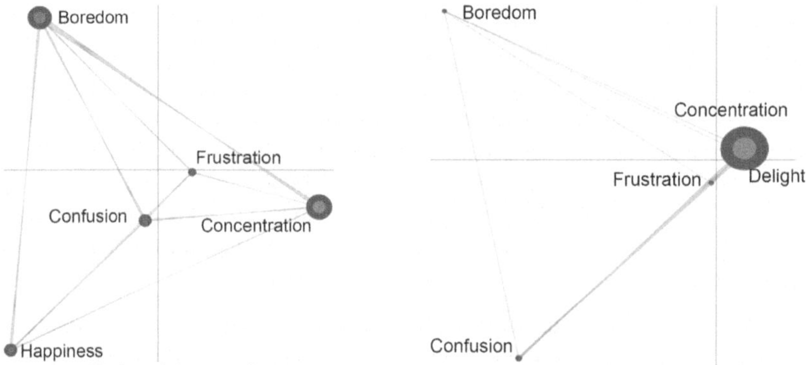

(a) SR-based detector data (b) BROMP-based detector data

Fig. 1. Ordered network of affect transitions for SR-based and BROMP-based detectors.

For both sets of detectors, self-transitions (where the affective state repeats across two 20-s clips) are most common. For SR models, boredom (LW = .51) is followed by concentration (LW = .43), confusion (LW = .21), happiness (LW = .21), and frustration (LW = .12). For BROMP models, the distribution is more skewed towards concentration (LW = .95) than the other four states (LW = .01 to .07).

Within the SR models, common pathways *between different* affective states are much rarer. Pathways between boredom and concentration (BOR → ENG: LW = .04; ENG → BOR: LW = .03) occur slightly more often than pathways involving concentration, confusion, and happiness (LW = .02 for ENG → CONF, CONF → ENG, HAP → ENG, and ENG → HAP). All other transitions have lower LWs. Similarly, in BROMP models, self-transitions (LW = .01 to .95) effectively mute other possible transitions and only shifts between engaged concentration and confusion occur above .01 (CONF → ENG: LW = .03; ENG → CONF: LW = .02).

Table 1. Line Weights for ONA Models shown in Fig. 1. LW > = .10 are in bold.

Self-Transitions	SR	BROMP	Other Transitions	SR	BROMP
BOR → BOR	**0.51**	0.05	BOR → ENG	0.04	<.01
ENG → ENG	**0.43**	**0.95**	ENG → BOR	0.03	<.01
DEL/HAP → DEL/HAP	**0.22**	0.01	DEL/HAP → ENG	0.02	<.01
CONF → CONF	**0.21**	0.07	CONF → ENG	0.02	0.03
FRU → FRU	**0.12**	0.05	ENG → DEL/HAP	0.02	<.01
			ENG → CONF	0.02	0.02

4.2 ONA Difference Models for Learning Gains (LG)

Figure 2 uses ONA difference models to compare students with high and low LG, with models for SR (2a) and BROMP (2b) data. Here, LWs indicate the difference between the two student groups. Transitions that are most common among those with high LG are shown in blue, with low LG in red. Network variability (confidence interval) is shown as a rectangle surrounding a point that represents the average network position (mean). Mann-Whitney U tests show statistically significant differences for LG in SR models but not in BROMP models ($U = 9.0$, $p = .04$, $r = .67$ vs $U = 13.0$, $p = .11$, $r = .52$).

In SR models, sustained states show the largest differences. Low LG learners are more likely to sustain boredom (BOR → BOR: LW = .35 for high vs LW = .45 for low, producing $LW_{diff} = .25$) or confusion (CONF → CONF: LW = .09 vs LW = .32, producing $LW_{diff} = .23$). Six other transitions have LW $\geq$ .02 (ENG → CONF, CONF → ENG and ENG → HAP) or LW $\geq$ .01 (BOR → HAP, CONF → HAP, and HAP → BOR) (Table 2).

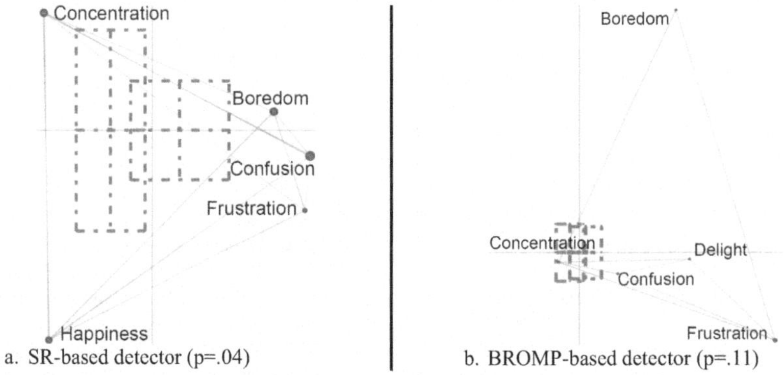

Fig. 2. Difference models for students with high (blue) and low LG (red) for each set of data.

In BROMP models, the largest differences are also for sustained states. High LG students spent less time in sustained frustration or boredom (FRU → FRU: LW = .01 vs LW = .08, $LW_{diff} = .06$; BOR → BOR: LW = .06 vs LW = .09, $LW_{diff} = .03$), and less

Table 2. LWs for ONA difference models in Fig. 2. LW and LW_{diff} > = .10 are in bold.

	SR			BROMP			SR				BROMP		
Self-Trans	HiLG	LoLG	$\lvert$Diff$\rvert$	HiLG	LoLG	$\lvert$Diff$\rvert$	Other Trans	HiLG	LoLG	$\lvert$Diff$\rvert$	HiLG	LoLG	$\lvert$Diff$\rvert$
BOR	**0.25**	**0.45**	**0.25**	0.06	0.09	0.03	BOR → ENG	0.02	0.02	<.01	<.01	<.01	-
ENG	**0.66**	**0.49**	**0.17**	**0.98**	**0.97**	0.02	ENG → BOR	0.01	0.01	<.01	0.01	<.01	<.01
DEL/HAP	**0.38**	**0.24**	**0.14**	<.01	0.02	0.02	DEL/HAP → ENG	0.03	0.01	0.02	<.01	<.01	-
CONF	0.09	**0.32**	**0.23**	0.04	0.05	0.02	CONF → ENG	0.03	0.01	0.02	0.02	0.02	<.01
FRU	0.03	**0.13**	**0.10**	0.01	0.08	0.06	ENG → DEL/HAP	0.03	0.01	0.02	<.01	0.01	<.01
							ENG → CONF	0.03	0.01	0.02	0.02	0.03	0.01
							CONF → FRU	<.01	<.01	<.01	-	0.01	0.01

time in sustained happiness (HAP → HAP: LW < .01 vs LW = .02, yielding LW_{diff} = .02). Differences in 2 other transitions are small but at .01 (ENG → CONF: LW = .02 vs LW = .03, LW_{diff} = .01; CONF → FRU: LW = 0 vs. LW = .01, LW_{diff} = .01).

4.3 ONA Difference Models for Situational Interest (SI)

ONA is also used to examine how affect transitions differ based on SI, and detector type influences these results. High and low SI groups are statistically different in SR models but not in BROMP models (Mann Whitney $\alpha = .05$, U = 68.0, p = .00, r = .56 vs U = 115.5, p = .16, r = .28). In Fig. 3, blue lines show the transitions most common among high SI learners, while red show those for low SI learners (Table 3).

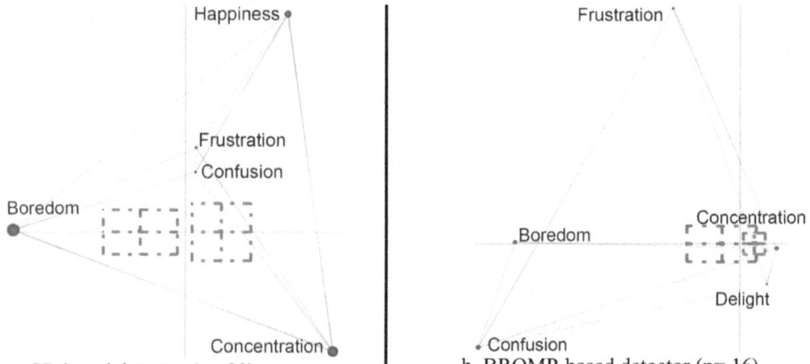

a. SR-based detector (p=.00)   b. BROMP-based detector (p=.16)

Fig. 3. Difference models for high SI (blue) vs. low SI (red) for SR and BROMP data.

Within SR models, the largest differences are again related to self-transitions. High SI learners are less likely to sustain boredom (BOR → BOR: LW = .37 vs LW = .72, LW_{diff} = .35) and more likely to sustain concentration and happiness (ENG → ENG: LW = .59 vs LW = .32, LW_{diff} = .27; HAP → HAP: LW = .25 vs LW = .1, LW_{diff} = .15) and even frustration and confusion (FRU → FRU: LW_{diff} = .04; CONF → CONF LW_{diff} = .02). Differences in transitions between distinct affective states are also found

Table 3. Line weights for ONA difference models in Fig. 3. LW and LW_{diff} >= .10 are in bold.

	SR			BROMP				SR			BROMP		
Self Trans	HiSI	LoSI	|Diff|	HiSI	LoSI	|Diff|	Other Trans	HiSI	LoSI	|Diff|	HiSI	LoSI	|Diff|
BOR	**0.37**	**0.72**	**0.35**	-	0.07	0.07	BOR → ENG	0.03	0.05	0.02	-	<.01	<.01
ENG	**0.59**	**0.32**	**0.27**	**0.98**	**0.9**	0.08	ENG → BOR	0.02	0.04	0.02	-	0.01	0.01
DEL/HAP	**0.25**	**0.10**	**0.15**	0.01	<.01	<.01	DEL/HAP → ENG	0.03	0.01	0.01	<.01	<.01	<.01
CONF	**0.20**	**0.18**	0.02	0.06	**0.16**	**0.10**	CONF → ENG	0.02	0.03	0.01	0.02	0.02	<.01
FRU	**0.13**	0.09	0.04	0.06	0.09	0.03	ENG → DEL/HAP	0.03	0.01	0.02	0.01	<.01	<.01
							ENG → CONF	0.02	0.02	<.01	0.02	0.02	<.01

in the SR models. High SI learners are more likely to transfer from engaged concentration to happiness (e.g., ENG → HAP: LW = .03 vs. LW = .01) and less likely to transfer back and forth between boredom and engagement (BOR → ENG: LW = .03 vs. LW = .05; ENG → BOR: LW = .02 vs LW = .04). Likewise, high SI learners are less likely to show two transitions involving confusion (BOR → CONF: LW = .01 vs. LW = .02; CONF → ENG: LW = .02 vs. LW = .03).

In BROMP models, the largest differences are also in self-transitions, but sustained confusion (i.e., not the most common code, ENG) shows the largest difference. High SI learners are less likely to sustain confusion (CONF → CONF: LW = .06 vs LW = .16, LW_{diff} = .1) and boredom, which was notably absent among high SI learners (BOR → BOR: LW_{diff} = .07). Instead, they are more likely to sustain concentration (ENG → ENG: LW = .98 vs LW = .9, LW_{diff} = .08). Smaller differences are driven by absent transitions among high SI learners, including the only transition between 2 different states with LW_{diff} > .01 (CONC → BOR), and 5 transitions with LW_{diff} < .01 (BOR → ENG, BOR → CONF, CONF → BOR, CONF → DEL, and FRUS → DEL).

5 Discussion and Conclusions

Since affect modeling is key to supporting learning and motivation, it is important to examine the effects of methodological differences. This study uses 2 sets of cross-validated, interaction-based affect detectors, trained with self-reports and BROMP observations, to examine differences in affective dynamics using ONA. Further, ONA difference models are used to study how affect dynamics are shaped by two student-level characteristics, learning gains and situational interest.

Results from RQ1 show that self-transitions are more common regardless of detector type, but the SR-trained data are far more distributed (LW = .51 to .12, BOR and FRU) than the BROMP-trained data, where sustained concentration is markedly more common (LW = .95) than other self-transitions. That is, even though self-transitions are important in both sets of detectors, there are still major persistence-rate differences that could significantly impact intervention design.

Results from RQ2 show the relevance of student-level characteristics in affect dynamics research. Specifically, we compare students at the extreme ends of normalized learning gains (LG), and situational interest (SI). For LG, SR-trained data produced large differences. All 5 self-transitions showed LW_{diff} > .1, with boredom and confusion more likely for low LG students. In BROMP-trained data, self-transitions were also more common than transitions between 2 distinct states. Sustained frustration has the largest difference, with low LG learners experiencing the most frustration. For SI, similar patterns emerge when comparing the 2 sets of detectors. Differences are larger (a) in SR models than BROMP models and (b) for self-transitions, chiefly boredom and concentration. In SR models, low SI learners undergo sustained boredom at twice the rate of others. BROMP models show similar patterns: sustained boredom is entirely absent in high SI learners. High SI learners also exhibit higher rates of concentration, though this effect is strongest in SR models.

More generally, we emphasize the need to study differences related to learning and motivation. Combined with results from the initial ONA analyses, the difference models show the relative importance of self-transitions, often excluded in previous work. We hope that these results motivate similar future investigations.

Acknowledgments. This study was funded by NSF Grants IIS-2016943 and IIS-2016993.

Disclosure of Interests.. The authors have no competing interests to declare for this article.

References

1. D'Mello, S., Graesser, A.: Dynamics of affective states during complex learning. Learn. Instr. **22**(145–157), 9 (2012)
2. Cloude, E.B., Wortha, F., Dever, D.A., Azevedo, R.: How do emotions change during learning with an intelligent tutoring system? metacognitive monitoring and performance with MetaTutor. In: CogSci (2020)
3. Calvo, R.A., D'Mello, S.K.: Affect detection: an interdisciplinary review of models, methods, and their applications. Affective Comput., IEEE Trans. **1**(1), 18–37 (2010)
4. Karumbaiah, S., Baker, R.S., Ocumpaugh, J., Andres, A.: A re-analysis and synthesis of data on affect dynamics in learning. IEEE Trans. on Affective Computing (2021)
5. Kai, S., et al.: A comparison of video-based and interaction-based affect detectors in physics playground. In: International Conference on Educational Data Mining, pp. 77–84 (2015)
6. Andres, J.M.A.L., Hutt, S., Ocumpaugh, J., Baker, R.S., Nasiar, N., Porter, C.: How anxiety affects affect: a quantitative ethnographic investigation using affect detectors and data-targeted interviews. In: International Conference on Quantitative Ethnography (2021)
7. Karumbaiah, S., Andres, J.M.A.L., Botelho, A.F., Baker, R.S., Ocumpaugh, J.: The implications of a subtle difference in the calculation of affect dynamics. In: 26th International Conference for Computers in Education (2018)
8. Ocumpaugh, J., Baker, R.S., Rodrigo, M.M.T.: Baker Rodrigo Ocumpaugh Monitoring Protocol (BROMP) 2.0 Technical & Training Manual. Working Paper (2015)
9. Zambrano, A., et al.: Says Who? How different ground truth measures of emotion impact student affective modeling. In: Proceedings of the 17th International Conference on Educational Data Mining (2024)
10. Jiang, Y., et al.: Expert feature-engineering vs. deep neural networks: Which is better for sensor-free affect detection? Proceedings of the 19th Conference of AIED, pp. 198–211 (2018)

11. Baker, R.S., D'Mello, S.K., Rodrigo, M.M.T., Graesser, A.C.: Better to be frustrated than bored: the incidence, persistence, and impact of learners' cognitive–affective states during interactions with three different computer-based learning environments. Int. J. Hum. Comput. Stud. **68**(4), 223–241 (2010)
12. Baker, R.S., Ocumpaugh, J., Andres, J.M.A.L.: BROMP quantitative field observations: a review. In: Learning Science: Theory, Research, and Practice, pp. 127–156 (2020)
13. Baker, R.S.J.d., Ocumpaugh, J.: Interaction-based affect detection in educational software. In: Calvo, R.A., D'Mello, S.K., Gratch, J., Kappas, A. (eds.) The Oxford Handbook of Affective Computing. Oxford University Press, Oxford, UK (2014)
14. Linnenbrink-Garcia, L., et al.: Measuring situational interest in academic domains. Educ. Psychol. Measur. **70**(4), 647–671 (2010)
15. Karumbaiah, S., Baker, R.S.: Studying affect dynamics using epistemic networks. In: Ruis, A.R., Lee, S.B. (eds.) ICQE 2021. CCIS, vol. 1312, pp. 362–374. Springer, Cham (2021). https://doi.org/10.1007/978-3-030-67788-6_25
16. Tan, Y., Ruis, A., Marquart, C., Cai, Z., Knowles, M., Shaffer, D.: Ordered Network Analysis. In: Damşa, C., Barany, A. (eds.) Advances in Quantitative Ethnography. ICQE 2022. Communications in Computer & Information Science, vol. 1785 (2023)

Conceptualizing and Understanding Mathematics Teaching Identity in Early-Career Elementary Teachers

Lara Condon(✉)

University of Memphis, Memphis, TN 38152, USA
lcondon@memphis.edu

Abstract. Many elementary teachers enter the profession with anxieties about teaching mathematics that can impact their approaches to math instruction. Though teacher education programs often strive to alleviate these anxieties, the process of learning to teach math is complex, and novice teachers often enter the field with little support for continued learning. This study proposes a dynamic systems model of mathematics teaching identity and applies it to understand how early-career teachers negotiate their identities in the first years of teaching. Using Epistemic Network analysis along with qualitative case studies, this study seeks to surface the complex dimensions of early-career elementary teachers' experiences with mathematics instruction. Findings from this study offer research and teacher educators a meaningful framework to understand mathematics teaching identity and better support early-career teachers.

Keywords: Mathematics Teaching Identity · Epistemic Network Analysis · Early-Career Teachers

1 Introduction

Brittany walked into her classroom to prepare for her math lesson. She felt the same familiar anxiety begin to build, just like she'd experienced her math methods class, during every single math class growing up, and every time her dad sat and quizzed her on her multiplication tables when she was growing up. She took a deep shaky breath, and thought to herself, I never managed to master my times tables. I mean, it's like math just left me behind. How am I supposed to teach math to my students?

This vignette, a compilation of Brittany's experience and those of several other early-career teachers, is far from uncommon, as many individuals enter into elementary teaching with significant anxieties about teaching math [1]. These anxieties, and the way they impact early-career teachers' (ECTs) approaches to mathematics instruction, are complex. How ECTs reflect on and approach their math instruction stems from the deeply intwined nature of their cognition (e.g. their knowledge and vision) and their affect towards mathematics (e.g. their math identity and self-efficacy. For the past several decades, researchers have sought to understand the complexities of what pre-service

Y. J. Kim and Z. Swiecki (Eds.): icqe 2024, CCIS 2279, pp. 204–216, 2024.
https://doi.org/10.1007/978-3-031-76332-8_17

teachers bring with them into teacher education by decomposing these into distinct characteristics like knowledge [2] attitudes, beliefs, emotion, and identity [3] influence approaches to mathematics instruction once teachers enter into the classroom. I argue that understanding answering these questions requires adopting a complex dynamic systems approach to understanding teachers' identities as individuals by conceptualizing of a distinct mathematics teaching identity. Rather than decomposing each of these constructs into separate characteristics for analysis, I argue that the interrelationship of several individual characteristics is what ultimately drives teachers' approaches to mathematics instruction. Informed by recent advances in frameworks of identity and prior research on factors that inform teachers' approaches to mathematics instruction, I adapt Kaplan & Garner's *dynamic systems model of role identity* to create a framework for *mathematics teaching identity (MTI)*. Using interview data from 16 early-career teachers, I use Epistemic Network Analysis to explore the affordances of this model as a tool for researchers and teacher educators to better understand and support the identity development of ECTs. The research questions guiding this study are:

1. What are the primary factors that interact to inform early-career teachers' mathematics teaching identity?
   a. Are there differences in the elements and configurations of factors within each individuals' descriptions of their MTI?
   b. How does each dimension of MTI relate to how ECTs think about their mathematics instruction?
2. How can a dynamic systems model of MTI serve as a valuable lens for understanding early-career teachers' approaches to mathematics instruction?

This paper explores these questions by examining research on the nature of teacher characteristics that comprise teachers' MTI from a dynamic systems model of role identity (DSMRI). I incorporate both qualitative and quantitative ethnographic approaches to explore the complexities of the interrelation of the dimensions of mathematics teaching identity. By approaches to mathematics instruction, I refer to how each individual teacher reflects on and describes the factors that influence their instructional decision-making during mathematics lessons. This approach adds important nuance to the field's understanding of mathematics teaching identities. Further, this paper is situated in the unique space of understanding early-career teachers' MTI as they transition from teacher education into the first years of teaching.

2 Background and Framing Concepts

This study brings together literature from four key areas of scholarship around factors that influence teachers' approaches to mathematics instruction: (1) mathematics identity, (2) mathematical knowledge in and for teaching, (3) mathematics instructional vision, and (4) mathematics self-efficacy. These dimensions are not only the most researched, but they also align with the overarching constructs that comprise Kaplan and Garner's (2017) dynamic systems model of role identity [4]. In this section, I provide a brief overview of research on each individual construct and its impact on approaches to mathematics instruction as well as how those constructs align with DSMRI to create a distinct and ever-changing mathematics teaching identity (MTI).

2.1 Research on Characteristics that Inform Approaches to Mathematics Instruction

Mathematics Identity. Although specific definitions of math identity vary slightly across research literature, most studies adopt a Meadian concept of identity [5], viewing identity as multiple, evolving, and socially constructed—simply put, it is the story we tell ourselves about our relationship to mathematics in different contexts based on our experiences [6]. In this view, identity is not static, but is instead "an ongoing process of negotiating and interrelating multiple I-positions in such a way that a more or less coherent and consistent self is maintained throughout various participations" [7, p. 315]. Research suggests that mathematics identity can shape teachers' approaches to instruction [1]. Those elementary teachers who perceive themselves as "not math people" or who possess an aversion to mathematics as a subject more often approach mathematics instruction defined by rote procedures and convey lower expectations for student achievement [8]. Further, teachers' own mathematics anxiety and negative self-concept can often be transferred to their students [1], perpetuating a cycle of individuals coming into pre-service teaching with negative mathematics identities.

Mathematical Knowledge in and For Teaching. Researchers have employed many different terms and approaches to understanding that knowledge, whether it be knowledge for teaching, or a more dynamic conceptualization of knowledge in teaching [9], including the importance of contextual factors as well as cognitive processes that occur in action and on action [10]. For the purposes of this study, I use both conceptions of knowledge for teaching and in teaching, as both represent important cognitive processes and dimensions for understanding how teachers approach mathematics instruction. The most prominent conception of mathematical knowledge for teaching was developed by Ball and colleagues [2]. This framework divides MKT along two interrelated dimensions: *subject matter knowledge* and *pedagogical content knowledge*, each having multiple sub-dimensions included within them. Importantly, the authors note that strict boundaries do not exist between the definitions of each dimension and sub-dimension, but rather, they interact with one another in ways that help teacher educators and researchers to understand how teachers can and should respond to students' thinking.

Vision of High-Quality Math Instruction. A less explored dimension of the proposed model for mathematics teaching identity is the construct of instructional vision. Vision consists of images of what teachers hope could be in their classrooms, their schools, their communities, even society [11, p. 145]. In short, instructional vision encompasses the type of mathematics practices a teacher aspires to use in their classroom under ideal circumstances. It is developed based on a combination of teachers' knowledge of a subject as well as their beliefs about how and what children should be learning [11]. Definitions of instructional vision within educational research are consistently inclusive of notions of teachers' aspirations, often reflecting the goals for instructional practice that teachers strive to attain [11, 12]. Operationalized, researchers view vision as the way teachers describe, either through written or spoken form, their view of the type of teaching that they believe to represent high-quality instruction [12, 13]. The very nature of instructional vision as aspirational positions it as a powerful potential mechanism to help drive growth in teachers' practice.

Mathematics Self-efficacy. Each of the dimensions described thus far in this review contribute to and are influenced by a key component of what drives teachers' practices: mathematics self-efficacy. Understanding and finding ways to increase self-efficacy are important, as many elementary teachers enter into pre-service teacher education with significant mathematics anxiety from their prior learning experiences [1]. According to Bandura [14], an individual's sense of efficacy determines how the individual will respond in specific situations. Self-efficacy theory thus argues that "people process and synthesize feedback information from sequences of events over long intervals about the situational circumstances…that are necessary to produce given outcomes" (p. 192). In other words, a person's beliefs about how certain behaviors, in this case approaches to math instruction, will lead to specific outcomes develops from the accumulation of their past experiences.

Dynamic Systems Model of Mathematics Teaching Identity. Figure 1 depicts an adapted version of Kaplan & Garner's (2017) dynamic systems model of role identity that illustrates the overlapping and interrelated nature of the components of mathematics teaching identity described in previous sections. This framework of mathematics teaching identity allows for a nuanced understanding of the factors that drive teachers' actions in their role as elementary and middle-years mathematics teachers.

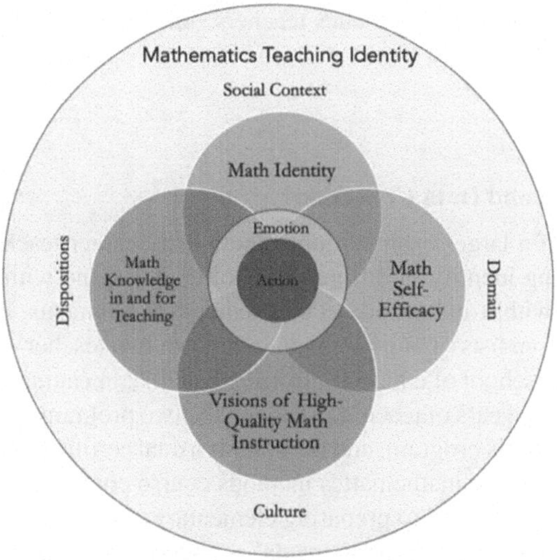

Fig. 1. Dynamic Systems Model of Mathematics Teaching Identity

As illustrated by this figure, this study focuses primarily on interrelationship between the individual-level factors that teachers describe as influencing their approaches to and beliefs about mathematics instruction. However, as teachers are necessarily working within institutional settings, the study also incorporates analysis of how external factors impact participants on an individual level. Each dimension within the dynamic system is contextually constructed and constitutes its own unit of analysis, however the overlapping and interactive nature of those dimensions play an important role in the networked system. Ultimately, these interactions then drive the action of the individual in a particular role. For teachers, this means that enactment of classroom instruction is driven by the interaction of each role-specific dimension, and that action then provides feedback to the teacher that "influences future iterations of the role identity system through its manifestation to the self and to others of commitments, or lack thereof, to certain meanings in the role" [4, p. 2040].

Understanding the complexities of an individual's role identity in this way provides important considerations for how an individual will behave and respond in any given environment. Further, it highlights the importance of internal alignment of each element in the system. Individuals with an aligned role identity will feel more empowered to engage in actions that demonstrate that identity. Importantly, however, the model highlights how DSMRI is context specific, existing within a sociocultural context that can alter the meanings and perceptions of the individual, thus potentially influencing a change in the internal dimensions of the individual's identity. In this way, Kaplan & Garner [4] posit that the DSMRI framework helps scholars to consider more deliberately the unit of analysis they wish to study. For the purposes of this review, it allows for a better understanding of the dimensions that drive a teacher to enact specific approaches for mathematics instruction. Further, prompting teachers to reflect and consider the individual components of their mathematics teaching identity provides a more holistic and thorough approach for identity exploration processes that researchers have used previously to help reshape elementary mathematics teachers' identities and support opportunities for teacher learning [15].

3 Methods

3.1 Study Context and Data Collection

This study is part of a larger examination of how early-career teachers negotiate their mathematics teaching identity in different school contexts and with different learning supports from both within and outside of their school environments. Participants for this study were drawn from lists of alumni graduating from two teacher education programs in the same graduate school of education from 2020–2022, meaning that all participants were in their first three years of teaching. Though the two programs differ slightly in that one is a full-time master's program, and the other is a dual certification/master's program for in-service teachers, the mathematics methods course contain the same components and share the same approaches to preparing elementary mathematics teachers. As such, I use purposive sampling to keep participants' pre-service teacher education constant. I conducted interviews lasting approximately one hour with 16 alumni working in a variety of contexts of school contexts (public, charter, and private schools). These interviews focused on developing and understanding of participants' background, including their own perceptions of their mathematics identity, their instructional vision and goals, their mathematical knowledge for teaching, and their mathematics self-efficacy.

3.2 Data Analysis

Epistemic Network Analysis (ENA) is a technique developed to help model associations that develop over time as participants engage with and learn from complex social and interactional systems [16]. Though relatively nascent in its use and originally developed to address challenges in learning analytics, ENA has a history of helping researchers to develop understanding about teachers' and students' growth in knowledge and beliefs over time [17], individual identity [18] as well as collaborative learning in communities of practice [19]. The key assumption that underscores this method is that there is meaning within the structure of connections in the data. As such, it is a valuable tool for understanding how these internal processes related to ECTs mathematics teaching identity are interconnected and developing over time. By applying a set of codes and subcodes related to each of the four constructs of mathematics teaching identity, I use ENA to illustrate patterns and connections in participants' interview data that may not otherwise be observed.

Once data were sorted according to the most prevalent code in each utterance, they were then structured chronologically with each participant's interview constituting a conversation. In other words, the associated models visualize the co-occurrence, or connection between codes, but only looking at connections across each individual participant. Since utterances were excerpted from throughout the interviews, I selected a whole conversation window size for the analysis, meaning that connections were only made when codes co-occurred within an utterance for that participant. As such, the data was structured with a primary parent code from Phase 1 of data analysis and then coded for the other elements of MTI that co-occurred when the participant was speaking about that particular topic in relation to their mathematics instructional approaches. The full set of codes (see Table 1) were applied to the data using 0 to 1 binary deductive coding, indicating 1 if the code was present and 0 if it was not. For example, the following excerpt from Madison, a second-year teacher who moved schools, was coded with a parent code of Math Self-Efficacy, and also was coded with a 1 for including both math self-efficacy (MSE) and mathematical knowledge in and for teaching (MKT):

> I think, I think I want to like be better about like thinking about like an entire unit. I think it's been really challenging this year, because I'm like, basically a first year teacher. And I'm just kind of like, I was just like swimming and hoping that I floated at the beginning of the year. And so, like that long term planning piece was just kind of like one day at a time when that time.

The main emphasis in this utterance is Madison's challenges with self-efficacy in terms of finding time to plan more longitudinally, however it indicates elements of her mathematical knowledge for teaching in relation to planning and knowledge of the curriculum.

Once coded, the resulting networks for each participant were then aggregated using a binary summation in which the networks for a given line reflect the presence or absence of the co-occurrence of each pair of codes. Networks were visualized using network graphs where nodes correspond to codes, and edges reflect the relative frequency of co-occurrence, or connection, between two codes. The result is two coordinated representations for each unit of analysis: 1) a plotted point which represents the location of that unit's network in the low-dimensional projected space, and 2) a weighted network. The positions of the network graph are fixed, and those positions are determined by an optimization routine that minimizes the difference between plotted points and their

Table 1. Dimensions of Mathematics Teaching Identity Codes.

Code	Definition
Mathematics Identity	Emotions and beliefs about one's personal and social characteristics in relationship to mathematics in context
Mathematics Knowledge in and for Teaching	Knowledge held as true about mathematics and the ways a teacher responds to students' learning based on that knowledge
Mathematics Instructional Vision	The ideal mathematics classroom practice, including the role a teacher should play, the nature of classroom discourse, and the types of mathematical tasks given
Mathematics Teaching Self-Efficacy	Future-oriented perception of a teacher's ability to enact tasks related to mathematics teaching based on perceptions of their own competence and contextual factors

corresponding network centroids. Because of this co-registration of network graphs and projected space, the positions of the network graph nodes and the connections that they define can be used to interpret the dimensions of the projected space and explain the positions of plotted points in space.

Several networks were constructed using meta data during on this phase of analysis in order to understand different aspects of participants' MTI. Each comparative model is described in more detail in the Results section that follows. These varied models provide for a more in-depth examination of the dynamic nature of the proposed framework of mathematics teaching identity. Once the various models were created, I returned to the original interview data to close the interpretive loop and highlight the meaning of the connections visualized in the ENA models using illustrative quotes from participants. By using these different methodological lenses in conjunction with one another to unpack the complexities of MTI, this study highlights important nuances of the interaction between cognitive and affective characteristics of early-career teachers.

4 Results

Participants' reflections on elements of their mathematics teaching identity—and by extension their perspectives on approaches to mathematics instruction—confirm affordances of adopting a dynamic systems framework of mathematics teaching identity. This lens allowed for consideration of the unique and complex interplay between dimensions of MTI, while surfacing the ways in which certain dimensions can play a more apparent role than others.

4.1 The Interrelationship of Dimensions of MTI

Each participant exhibited a unique distributions of dimensions MTI. Relative frequencies of data suggested that cognitive dimensions (knowledge and vision) played a more prominent role in ECTs' descriptions of their approaches to mathematics instruction than more affective dimensions (identity and self-efficacy). However, epistemic network analysis allowed for a more nuanced understanding of how each dimension is inextricably related to one another.

Although the affective dimensions were less often the focus of participants' reflections, epistemic network analysis of the interview data illustrates how those elements of those dimensions were frequently connected to how they understood their MTK and MV (see Fig. 2). This model had co-registration correlations of 1(Pearson) and 1(Spearman) for the first dimension and 0.99 (Pearson) and 0.99 (Spearman) for the second, indicating a strong goodness of fit. In the mean model depicted in Fig. 2, each individual point shows the location of each participant's network in relation to the mean. The model shows that participants made connections across all four dimensions of MTI, and importantly that the connections between both affective dimensions and MKT. Further, the varying distribution of each participants mean shows how different teachers exhibited notably different interrelationships between dimensions of their MTI.

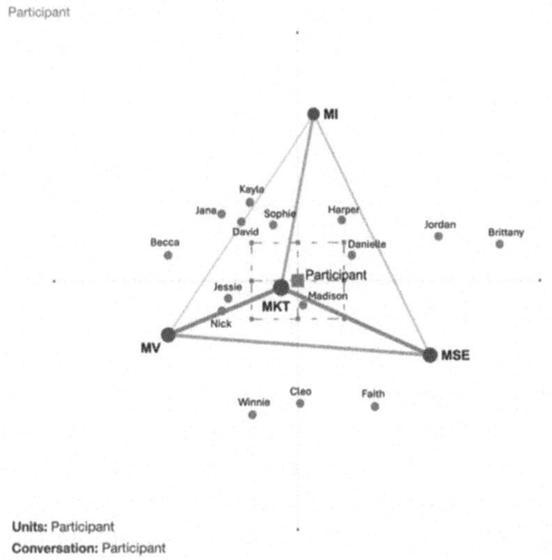

Fig. 2. Mean Epistemic Network Analysis Model of Participants' MTI

To further illustrate the meaning of this ENA analysis, I provide further discussion of two participants' networks, demonstrating the affordance of this approach in understanding the factors that drive ECTs mathematics instruction. Understanding these factors offers insights and considerations for more deliberate strategies for supporting ECTs to enact high-quality mathematics instruction.

Case Analysis of MTI Using ENA Visualizations. Both Becca and Brittany worked as self-contained classroom teachers, teaching all subjects, in 3rd and 2nd grade, respectively. Both teachers are also in their second year of teaching in an urban school setting, however Brittany began her teaching in conjunction with her certification and master's program. As shown in the network visualizations for each teacher (Figs. 3 and 4), all of the hypothesized dimensions of mathematics teaching identity played a significant role in how they reflected on and described their mathematics instruction. The configurations and connections illustrated by each network, however, highlight each teacher's MTI is driven by different connections between those dimensions.

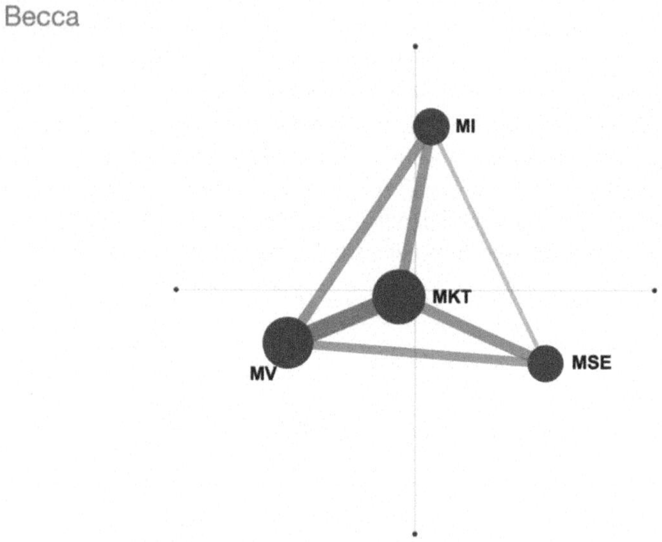

Fig. 3. Epistemic Network Model of Becca's MTI

Becca's network shows a high frequency of co-occurrences between her mathematical vision (MV), her mathematical knowledge in and for teaching (MKT), and her math identity (MI), most specifically as a person who loves math and views it as her favorite subject to teach. Throughout her schooling and her teaching experience, Beca viewed mathematics as her favorite subject, and this identity drove her to learn more about effective strategies for mathematics instruction. These dimensions underly her overarching vision of mathematics as the practice of identifying patterns and determining different ways to solve problems. These connections are illustrated in her response to the question of how she sees herself as a math teacher:

> I love it so much because I feel like I'm teaching them all the foundational skills, the multiplication division, the fractions. And I think the kids in my class they know my bias is my favorite subject to teach is math. And I think the reason I like it so much is that there's so many different activities and centers, and there's just so many different ways that you could solve something not like when we're writing an essay that we we're trying to follow in the format.

In this segment of the interview, what is most apparent is Becca's vision of what math is and how it's taught. However, it is clear that this vision is deeply intertwined with her own identity as someone who loves math as well as her knowledge of the fundamental skills that are key to students' mathematics learning in the third grade. However, what Becca's network also shows is that her self-efficacy, or what she feels she needs to be the most effective math teacher she can be, is most prominently connected to her vision and her knowledge, and not her identity as a "math person." This relationship can be seen in Becca's explanation of what she thinks makes an effective math teacher:

> I even think like the, understanding why, sometimes things work, even when I was teaching the distributive property, it was like the first time I understood, like actually why it worked. And I remember learning about like the area model and all these other things. So I really thinking about, even for me, just understanding. Okay, why do these processes work? And having that deeper understanding in those areas.

This excerpt focused teacher efficacy is deeply grounded in Becca's mathematical knowledge in and for teaching, as well as her vision of mathematics as relational. This vision can be seen her emphasis on instructional strategies that highlight *why* mathematical procedures and concepts operate in specific ways.

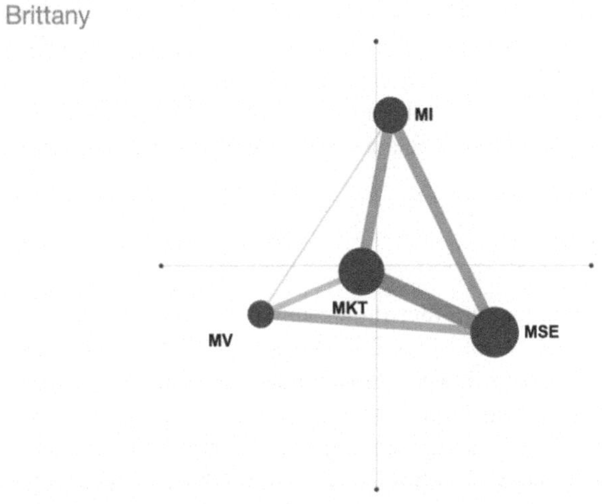

Fig. 4. Epistemic Network Model of Brittany's

For Brittany, her network (Fig. 4) illustrates how her perceptions of her mathematics self-efficacy were the strongest dimension in her descriptions, illustrated by the size of the node for mathematics self-efficacy (MSE). Further, MSE shows frequent co-occurrences with her mathematical knowledge in and for teaching, and her mathematics identity, both of which constitute a high frequency of code occurrences.This network of connections stems from Brittany's negative self-perceptions about her ability to teach mathematics, related to her own identity as not being a math person and her self-described lack of common and specialized content knowledge:

> I didn't like math in school. I don't really like teaching math. I don't like the curriculum we have. I have a hard time explaining things to kids like, it's the thing that I struggle with the most.

It is important to note that the connections between dimensions of Brittany's MTI network are driven primarily by the challenges she faces as a math teacher, reflected in statements similar to the above excerpt. Importantly, Brittany also describes a vision of high-quality mathematics instruction that aligns with best practices [13] when reflecting on how she wants to be able to teach that connects to knowledge she hopes to gain as well as a current lack of self-efficacy in being able to enact those practices:

> Ideally, I would want to be able to like conference with them and ask them what they were thinking when they did something, and because I feel like that's where the learning really happens... Sometimes I see something, and it takes me like a while to figure out what, exactly, where did they go wrong? But ideally, I would be able to like, see it right away, and kind of also be able to anticipate, like, what are they going to do so that it can be like more of a quick fix than like a oh, they did it wrong.

Examining Brittany's MTI network provides insights into the strong role that self-efficacy plays in her approaches to mathematics instruction. Combining this approach to visualization of MTI with excerpts from the qualitative data adds an important interpretive lens to surfacing the complexities of cognitive and affective dimensions of MTI that inform Brittany's actions in relation to her mathematics instruction.

5 Discussion

As shown in the findings, the four dimensions within the dynamic systems model of mathematics teaching identity play a significant and interrelated role on early-career teachers' perspectives regarding their mathematics instruction. Based on these findings, there are several important implications for the affordances of effectively leveraging a dynamic systems lens to understanding MTI to support early-career teachers. Most importantly, the affordances this framework suggest that by examining these dimensions in conjunction with one another rather than as distinct constructs, researchers and teacher educators can provide more nuanced and specific support for early-career teachers.

Namely, this initial application of a dynamic systems approach to MTI highlights how viewing vision and self-efficacy are distinctly interrelated and could be seen as driving forces in the evolution of ECTs' mathematics teaching identity. Development of a strong vision of high-quality mathematics instruction helps support teachers in working towards aligning the other dimensions of their MTI, giving them motivation to gain more knowledge and develop self-efficacy towards reaching those instructional goals. Similarly, a lack of self-efficacy can impede teachers' ability to feel that they can enact high-quality mathematics instruction. As shown by Becca's example, although she possessed a clear vision of high-quality mathematics instruction, her doubt in her own knowledge and related lack of self-efficacy as a mathematics teacher made it hard for her to feel she could enact these approaches to mathematics instruction. Recognizing these interrelated dimensions, however, provided Brittany with important insights into how to address them and thus work to improve her mathematics teaching identity overall.

6 Conclusion

As mentioned in the introduction to this paper, little configural research exists examining the interrelated dimensions of mathematics teaching identity. This study provides a model that allows researchers, teacher educators, and those who design professional learning within schools and districts with opportunities to consider more multifaceted approaches to understanding and therefor meeting the professional learning needs of early-career teachers. However, one strength and limitation of this study is that all participants attended the same institution for their preservice teacher training.

I describe this as both a strength and a limitation because of the specific affordances and constraints of how the program potentially informed participants' MTI. Because all participants were prepared to teach using the same approaches of responsive mathematics teaching, their vision of mathematics instruction was very consistent regardless of their prior experiences or orientations towards mathematics. This similarity in learning experience could potentially contribute to the lack of differences between the epistemic networks for each of the dimensions of MTI when compared across years of experience and subject-matter focus. Further research should consider exploring the mathematics teaching identities of teachers coming from different educational backgrounds, as well as those working within individual schools and districts.

Another limitation of this study is that it is based solely on interview data, thus it only confirms the interaction of the four dimensions of the framework. Since teachers' descriptions of their instructional actions are self-reported, this study cannot confirm that teachers' MTI does, in fact, lead to their instructional actions in the classroom. Further research should classroom observations in addition to self-report to determine if and how MTI informs teachers actions.

References

1. Brady, P., Bowd, A.: Mathematics anxiety, prior experience, and confidence to teach mathematics among pre-service education students. Teachers Teach. **11**(1), 37–46 (2005)
2. Ball, D., Thames, M.H., Phelps, G.: Content knowledge for teaching: what makes it special? J. Teach. Educ. **59**(5), 389–407 (2008)
3. Hannula, M., Kaasila, R., Laine, A., & Pehkonen, E.: Structure and typical profiles of elementary teacher students' view of mathematics. In: Chick, H., Vincent, J. (eds.) Proceedings of the 29th PME Conference, vol. 3, pp. 89–96. University of Melbourne (2005)
4. Kaplan, A., Garner, J.K.: A complex dynamic systems perspective on identity and its development: the dynamic systems model of role identity. Dev. Psychol. **53**(11), 2036–2051 (2017)
5. Darragh, L.: Identity research in mathematics education. Educ. Stud. Math. **93**(1), 19–33 (2016)

6. Sfard, A., Prusak, A.: Telling identities: in search of an analytic tool for investigating learning as a culturally shaped activity. Educ. Res. **34**(4), 14–22 (2005). https://doi.org/10.3102/0013189X034004014
7. Akkerman, S.F., Meijer, P.C.: A dialogical approach to conceptualizing teacher identity. Teach. Teach. Educ. **27**(2), 308–319 (2011)
8. Drake, C., Spillane, J.P., Hufferd-Ackles, K.: Storied identities: teacher learning and subject-matter context. J. Curric. Stud. **33**(1), 1–23 (2001)
9. Rowland, T., Huckstep, P., Thwaites, A.: Elementary teachers' mathematics subject knowledge: the knowledge quartet and the case of Naomi. J. Math. Teacher Educ. **8**(3), 255–281 (2005). https://doi.org/10.1007/s10857-005-0853-5
10. Schön, D.A.: Educating the Reflective Practitioner: Toward a New Design for Teaching and Learning in the Professions. Jossey-Bass, San Francisco (1987)
11. Hammerness, K.: Teachers' visions: the role of personal ideals in educational reform. J. Educ. Change **2**, 143–163 (2001)
12. Jansen, A., Gallivan, H.R., Miller, E.: Early-career teachers' instructional visions for mathematics teaching: Impact of elementary teacher education. J. Math. Teacher Educ. **23**(2), 183–207 (2020)
13. Munter, C.: Developing visions of high-quality mathematics instruction. J. Res. Math. Educ. **45**(5), 584–635 (2014)
14. Bandura, A.: Self-efficacy: toward a unifying theory of behavioral change. Psychol. Rev. **84**(2), 191–215 (1977)
15. Lutovac, S., Kaasila, R.: Pre-service teachers' future-oriented mathematical identity work. Educ. Stud. Math. **85**(1), 129–142 (2014)
16. Shaffer, D.W., Collier, W., Ruis, A.R.: A tutorial on epistemic network analysis: analyzing the structure of connections in cognitive, social, and interaction data. J. Learn. Anal. **3**(3), 9–45 (2016)
17. Scianna, J., Gagnon, D., Knowles, B.: Counting the game: visualizing changes in play by incorporating game events. In: Ruis, A.R., Lee, S.B. (eds.) Advances in Quantitative Ethnography, Communications in Computer and Information Science, pp. 218–231. Springer International Publishing, Cham (2021)
18. Fan, Y., Barany, A., Foster, A.: Possible future selves in STEM: an epistemic network analysis of identity exploration in minoritized students and alumni. IJ STEM Ed **10**, 22 (2023)
19. Rolim, V., Ferreira, R., Lins, R.D., Gǎsević, D.: A network-based analytic approach to uncovering the relationship between social and cognitive presences in communities of inquiry. Internet High. Educ. **42**, 53–65 (2019)

Model Based Analysis to Explore the Patterns of Thinking in an Interactive Learning Environment for Problem-Posing

Yusuke Hayashi[1](✉), Ayano Ohsaki[2], Tatsuki Yamamoto[3], and Tsukasa Hirashima[1]

[1] Hiroshima University, Hiroshima 08544, Japan
hayashi@lel.hiroshima-u.ac.jp
[2] Shinshu University, Nagano, Japan
[3] The Ministry of Education, Culture, Sports, Science and Technology (MEXT), Tokyo, Japan

Abstract. This study investigates the causes of impasses in Monsakun, an arithmetic problem-posing learning platform. We analyzed learners' cognitive processes using epistemic networks generated from learning logs. Results revealed two main factors: (1) lack of awareness about task setting variability and (2) insufficient understanding of arithmetic word problem structure. These findings aim to contribute to future interactive learning environment development and enhance learner engagement.

Keywords: Interactive learning environment · Impasse · Ordered Network Analysis · Automated Codes · Interaction Log

1 Introduction

Failures in learning cause an impasse and have traditionally been viewed as outcomes to be avoided. However, recent research has revealed that failures provide valuable opportunities for promoting deep learning and understanding [8]. Impasse-driven learning [15] facilitates learners' identification and resolution of obstacles, emphasizing the importance of environments that support this process. Interactive digital learning environments (IDLEs), widely utilized for their diverse task offerings, can provide contexts where learners engage in repeated attempts, sometimes struggling with impasses caused by failures on various tasks. However, the lack of a standardized method for extracting features of attempts and failures from log data and aligning them with target competencies impedes stakeholders' ability to interpret and respond to the data effectively [10]. This limitation presents a significant challenge in maximizing the potential of IDLEs for learning from failure.

In this paper, as a concrete example of the analysis of learners' attempts in IDLEs, we explore the patterns of decisions that lead to successful and unsuccessful problem-posing within Monsakun [7,13], an interactive digital learning environment for problem-posing as sentence-integration. To visualize and interpret

Y. J. Kim and Z. Swiecki (Eds.): icqe 2024, CCIS 2279, pp. 217–224, 2024.
https://doi.org/10.1007/978-3-031-76332-8_18

learners' problem-posing process, we utilize Orderd Network Analysis (ONA) [14], a quantitative ethnographic technique that can illustrate connection patterns between concepts or behaviors in large, complex datasets. Our study builds upon previous research that used IDLE log data to uncover players' actions and understand how learning and decision-making processes evolve.

2 Literature Review

One effective method for analyzing problem-solving processes is visualizing the sequences of learners' actions. Sequence analysis (SA), in particular, goes beyond simple classification by frequency and has demonstrated value as an effective approach for identifying individual differences among learners and patterns within the community as a whole [9]. Techniques such as Hidden Markov Models (HMM) and sequence clustering are commonly used for sequence analysis. However, as the data volume increases, HMMs present the dual challenge of modeling behavior based on observable actions while also making it difficult to derive meaning from the output results [3,5].

An increasing amount of work with the Quantitative Ethnography (QE) approach highlights the value of these logs for examining complex behaviors across different contexts and over time in human-computer interactions. Wu et al. [16] propose the measurement of cognitive behavior from the perspective of self-regulated learning (SRL) with the QE approach. They demonstrate the potential for measuring cognitive behavior by coding log files recorded by an online learning application based on an SRL model with the help of two raters. Liu et al. [11] investigate the causes of players giving up during gameplay by analyzing the in-game events recorded in the log data of a puzzle game with the QE approach. By defining codes for in-game events, they are able to code the log data automatically.

3 Context

In this study, we explored user actions enacted in Monsakun as a concrete example of analyzing learners' attempts in IDLEs. It is an IDLE for learning arithmetic word problems by problem-posing. Problem-posing is an effective method for developing a conceptual understanding of mathematical relations [4]. With Monsakun, users can pose problems by setting sentences into the slots, and then request to check them, as shown in Fig. 1(a). If the answer satisfies the requirements, they can do the next exercise. However, if the answer is incorrect, Monsakun provides feedback on the mistake, as shown in Fig. 1(b), and encourages the users to try again.

This study uses three levels of problem-posing tasks based on the differences in requirements. Figure 2 shows examples of the level setting. The settings consist of two elements: the *displayed mathematical formula* and the *consistency* between the formula to get the solution and the required story. Regarding the *displayed mathematical formula*, Levels 1 and 2 are story-based, while Level 3 is

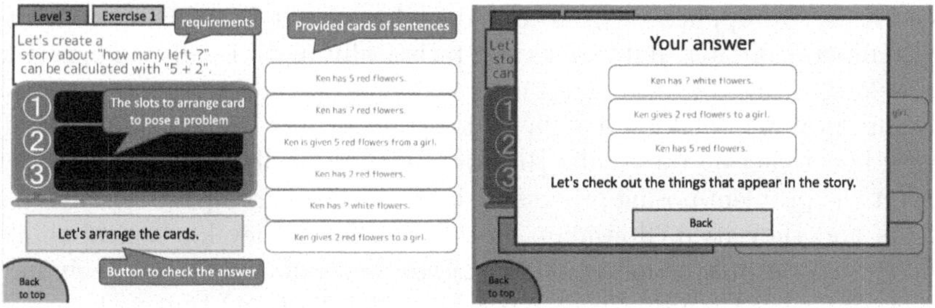

(a) Problem-posing in Monsakun (b) Feedback from Monsakun

Fig. 1. Monsakun

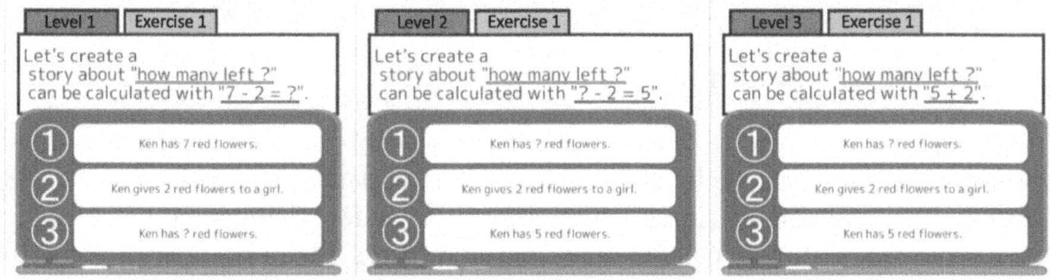

Fig. 2. Examples of the required problems at each level.

solution-based. The story-based formulas align with the required narrative flow. The solution-based formulas are the ones to get the solution. Regarding the *consistency*, the setting at Level 1 is consistent, and the others are inconsistent. At Levels 2 and 3, the mathematical formulas to get the solution are "5 + 2," which is inconsistent with the implied mathematical formula for subtraction from the decreasing story type represented by "How many left?"

Previous study [17] has shown that elementary students have a higher incidence of failures at Level 3 although not at Levels. The same trend is observed among adults [6]. This suggests that they lack conceptual understanding of arithmetic word problems because traditional arithmetic word problems typically focus on applying operational rules [1]. The role of Monsakun is to draw such learners' attention to conceptual understanding. Moreover, to provide comprehensive support to learners, we must develop an approach for clustering problem-posing patterns that surpasses simple frequency-based classification methods.

4 Method

The goal of this study is to investigate what kind of impasse they reach and overcome in their problem-posing process in Monsakun, especially at Level 3. If we can identify the learners' impasse and explain it, we can consider comprehensive support to the learners who are at an impasse and excessively struggle to resolve it. We applied ONA to our data because it is a QE approach that is for temporal ordered data and can statistically and visually analyze them, preferable to other sequence analysis [14]. While many SA techniques are not easily interpretable, making it difficult for stakeholders to understand the data or know how to act on the results [10], we can statistically compare and visually interpret the problem-posing process with ONA. The participants are university students and they used Monsakun as the exercise to develop logical thinking in the lecture on programming. This exercise is conducted at the beginning of the lecture for six lecture times in six weeks. The first and last weeks are used to measure their problem-posing performance as pre- and post-tests. Between them, the students use Monsakun for each story type. Each week, they pose problems about only one type of story: "combination," "decrease," "increase," or "comparison."

4.1 Participant Sampling

This study uses the log data of the problem-posing exercise of the "decrease" story conducted in the third week. This week, 42 participants attended, of which 38 completed all tasks at all three levels. Figure 3a shows the change of steps by users. From this data, we can see that there are users whose number of steps to reach the correct answer increases or decreases for each task. To identify the patterns of steps to complete, We use R for hierarchical clustering of the completed participants by the change of steps to reach the correct answer through all the tasks. The number of clusters was determined with the NbClust package [2]. As a result, they were divided into four clusters, with the number of individuals in clusters 1 through 4 being 20, 6, 10, and 2, respectively. Figure 3 shows the overview of the four clusters.

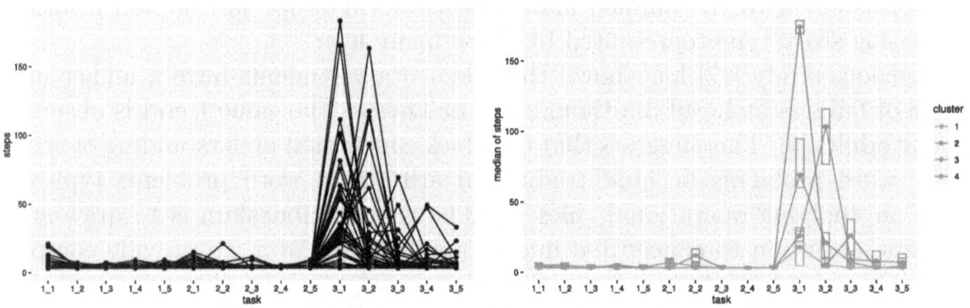

(a) by users (b) by clusters

Fig. 3. Numbers of Steps to complete in each task

Cluster 1 does not take many steps to reach the correct answer throughout. Similar to Cluster 1, Cluster 2 does not require many operations to reach the correct answer in the first task of Level 3. However, for the second task, Cluster

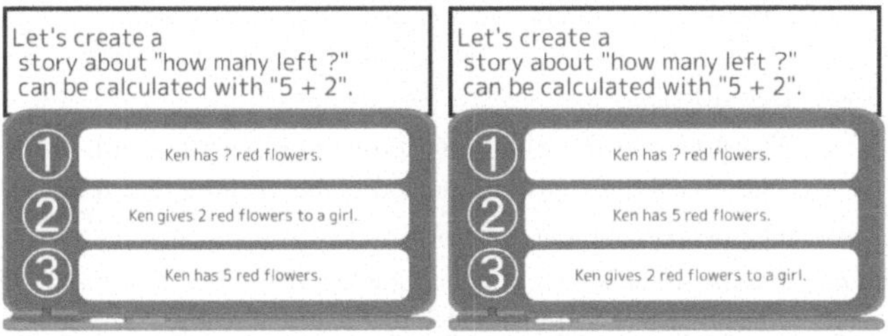

(a) An example of `F.x_S.S` (b) An example of `F.x_S.x`

Fig. 4. Examples of posed problems with codes

2 requires the highest number of operations to reach the correct answer among all clusters. Clusters 3 and 4 have a considerably high number of steps in the first problem-posing task of Level 3, and then the steps decrease in subsequent tasks. Here, we focus on the difference between Cluster 1 and Cluster 2. While the number of steps in the first task of Level 3 is not significantly different, there is a significant difference in the second task. If we only look at the first task of Level 3, both clusters could be considered to have no impasse and to be approaching the correct understanding. However, from the results of the second task, Cluster 2 appears to lack correct understanding. Is it possible to identify this difference from the data for the first task?

4.2 Coding Scheme

Our investigation focuses on identifying the differences in the problem-posing process among users who find it difficult to complete the problem-posing tasks and those who do not, seeking to explore the reasons why some users are at an impasse while others may not. We use ONA to our data with the ENA Web Tool (version 1.7.0) [12]. The window size was set as four lines for transition between codes in the problem-posing process in Monsakun. Our ONA model included the following codes: `C`, `E`, `F.e_S.e`, `F.F_S.S`, `F.F_S.u`, `F.F_S.x`, `F.x_S.s`, `F.x_S.S`, `F.x_S.u` and `F.x_S.x` (Fig. 2). The codes `C` and `E` represent actions related to posed problem verification, and the others represent the state of the problem during the problem-posing process as a combination of state related to the formula and the required story type in Table 1. Based on the definition of each code primitive, coding can be automatically done

5 Results

As shown in Fig. 3, while Clusters 1 and 2 have almost similar numbers of steps in task 3_1, they are different in task 3_2. The left of Table 2 shows the statistical test result of the comparison between Cluster 1 and 2 by the Wilcoxon rank sum test. There is no significant difference in the steps to the correct answer between

Table 1. The coding primitives for log data.

Type	Code	Definition
Check	C	The user requests the posed problem to check, and it is incorrect
	E	The user requests the posed problem to check and it is correct
Formula	F.e	The posed problem is empty
	F.x	The posed problem is not following the order of numbers in the mathematical formula
	F.F	The posed problem is following the order of numbers in the mathematical formula
Story	S.e	The posed problem is empty
	S.x	The posed problem is not following the sentence order for any type of story
	S.s	The posed problem is following the sentence order different from the requested type of story
	S.S	The posed problem is following the sentence order for the same type of story requested
	S.u	The story type of the posed problem cannot be identified because the posed problem is in progress (less the three sentence cards) and does not include any relational sentences

Table 2. the difference between clusters 1 and 2 at Level 3

	median of steps				ONA			
					x-axis		y-axis	
task	c1	c2	p-value	ES (r)	p-value	ES (r)	p-value	ES (r)
3_1	18	26	0.259	0.25	0.005	0.783	0.648	0.133
3_2	5	103	<0.001	1.03	<0.001	0.983	0.259	0.317
3_3	3	9	0.143	0.33	0.210	0.342	0.347	0.258
3_4	3	8	<0.001	0.77	0.005	−0.750	0.048	0.533
3_5	3	7	<0.001	0.88	0.001	0.883	0.009	0.700

Cluster 1 and 2 in the tasks 3_1 and 3_3. From this data, we cannot find the difference between the clusters.

Figure 5a and 5b shows ONA graphs of Cluster 1 and 2 in task 3_1, and Fig. 5c shows the difference between them. The right of Table 2 shows the comparison results between Cluster 1 and 2 at each task. There are significant differences in the tasks other than 3_2. ONA identifies the difference between task 3_1, where there is no significant difference between them in the comparison of steps.

From Fig. 5b Cluster2 users are in the loop among `F.x_S.x`, `F.x_S.u` and `C`. This loop is considered their impasse in which they repeat to cause failures (represented by `C`) with posed problems failing to make both formula and story valid (represented by `F.x_S.x` or `F.x_S.u`). This loop is very weak in the ONA graph of Cluster 2, as shown in Fig. 5a; that is, they did not have such a trend.

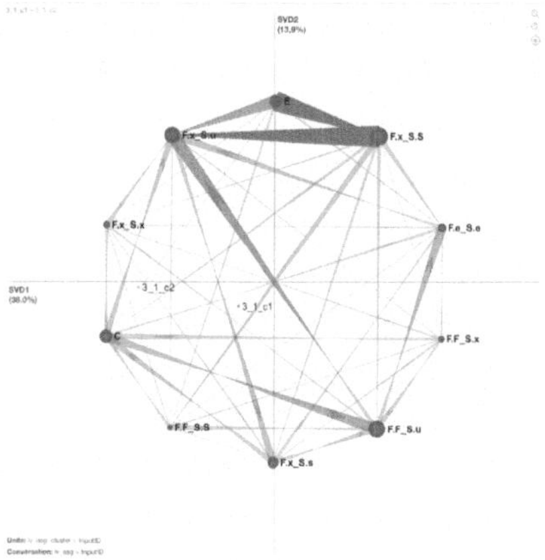

(a) ONA graph of Cluster 1

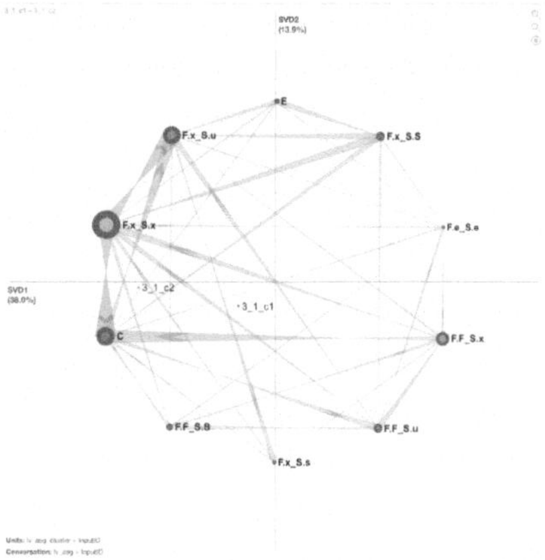

(b) ONA graph of Cluster 2

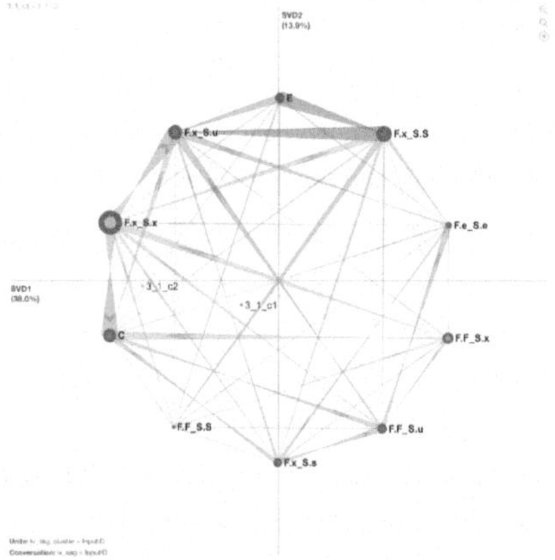

(c) Difference of ONA graph between Cluster 1 and 2

Fig. 5. ONA graph of the task 3_1

This result suggests that the QE approach could be used to distinguish between learners who are learning effectively and those who are not within problem-posing tasks, where differences cannot be seen by step count alone.

6 Discussion

This research explored possible reasons for the difficulty in successful and unsuccessful problem-posing within MONSAKUN, an IDLE for learning by problem-posing as sentence-integration, by visualizing and interpreting users' problem-posing process using ONA. The analysis revealed that merely counting the steps required to complete the required problem is insufficient to infer users' understanding when investigating problem-posing performance and learning.

These results indicate that applying the QE approach to investigating users' actions in IDLEs is a promising way to deepen our understanding of how students learn and interact with complex systems.

Acknowledgments. This work was supported by JSPS KAKENHI Grant Number 23K11357.

References

1. Bonotto, C.: Artifacts as sources for problem-posing activities. Educ. Stud. Math. **83**(1), 37–55 (2013)
2. Charrad, M., Ghazzali, N., Boiteau, V., Niknafs, A.: NbClust: an R package for determining the relevant number of clusters in a data set. J. Stat. Softw. **61**, 1–36 (2014)
3. Doleck, T., Basnet, R.B., Poitras, E.G., Lajoie, S.P.: Mining learner-system interaction data: implications for modeling learner behaviors and improving overlay models. J. Comput. Educ. **2**, 421–447 (2015)
4. English, L.D.: The development of fifth-grade children's problem-posing abilities. Educ. Stud. Math. **34**(3), 183–217 (1997)
5. Eichmann, B., Greiff, S., Naumann, J., Brandhuber, L., Goldhammer, F.: Exploring behavioural patterns during complex problem-solving. J. Comput. Assist. Learn. **36**, 933–956 (2020)
6. Hasanah, N., Hayashi, Y., Hirashima, T.: Posing arithmetic word problems in a sentence integration learning environment in English and Indonesian: A utilization analysis. J. Inf. Syst. Educ. **18**(1), 51–62 (2019)
7. Hirashima, T., Yokoyama, T., Okamoto, M., Takeuchi, A: Learning by problem-posing as sentence-integration and experimental use. In: Proceedings of of AIED2007, pp. 254–261 (2007)
8. Kapur, M.: Productive failure. Cogn. Instr. **26**(3), 379–424 (2008)
9. Kinnebrew, J.S., Biswas, G.: Identifying learning behaviors by contextualizing differential sequence mining with action features and performance evolution. Proc. EDM **2012**, 57–64 (2012)
10. Kleinman, E., et al.: Analyzing students' problem-solving sequences. Learn. Anal. **9**, 138–160 (2022)
11. Liu, X., Hussein, B., Barany, A., Baker, R.S. Chen, B.: Decoding player behavior: analyzing reasons for player quitting using log data from puzzle game baba is you. In: Proceedings of ICQE 2023, pp. 34–48 (2023)
12. Marquart, C. L., Hinojosa, C., Swiecki, Z., Eagan, B., Shaffer, D. W.: Epistemic network analysis (Version 1.7.0) (2021). http://app.epistemicnetwork.org
13. Nakano, A., Hirashima, T., Takeuchi, A: An evaluation of intelligent learning environment for problem posing. In: Proceedings of ITS2002, pp. 861–872 (2002)
14. Tan, Y., Ruis, A.R., Marquart, C., Cai, Z., Knowles, M.A., Shaffer, D.W.: Ordered network analysis. In: Proceedings of ICQE 2023, pp. 101–116 (2023)
15. VanLehn, K.: Toward a theory of impasse-driven learning. In: Mandl, H., Lesgold, A. (eds.) Learning Issues for Intelligent Tutoring Systems, pp. 19–41 (1988)
16. Wu, M., Zhang, J., Barany, A.: Understanding detectors for SMART model cognitive operation in mathematical problem-solving process: an epistemic network analysis. In: Proceedings of ICQE 2023, pp. 314–327 (2023)
17. Yamamoto, S., Kanbe, T., Yoshida, Y., Maeda, K., Hirashima, T.: A case study of learning by problem-posing in introductory phase of arithmetic word problems. In: Proceedings of ICCE2012, pp. 25–32 (2012)

How We Code Code: Leveraging GPT and Ordered Networks for Understanding Introductory Programming Education

Maciej Pankiewicz, Andres Felipe Zambrano(✉), Amanda Barany, and Ryan S. Baker

University of Pennsylvania, Philadelphia, PA, USA
{mpank,azamb13}@upenn.edu

Abstract. University-level computer science (CS) courses can be particularly challenging for students with limited programming backgrounds. To support novice learners, instructors often employ automated assessment systems for programming assignments. These systems provide students with feedback on demand as they work through problems online. Outcomes remain mixed, perhaps due to differences in the strategies learners use to address different types of coding errors after receiving feedback. In this study, we used Ordered Network Analysis (ONA) to explore data from an automated assessment platform used iteratively by students in an introductory CS course. We employed a GPT-based approach to automate the process of qualitative coding on this dataset. Our analysis revealed behavioral differences in how high performing and low performing novice learners changed their code over time, particularly when disaggregated by the types of errors they faced (compiler versus non compiler errors). By understanding these patterns, instructors can create interventions that guide students through challenges, improving their chances of success in programming tasks.

Keywords: Computer Science Education · Automated Assessment · Ordered Network Analysis · Large Language Models · ChatGPT

1 Introduction

Computer Science (CS) skills have gained attention in education research and practice, leading to global efforts to broaden and improve CS education [1, 2]. As part of this effort, automated assessment tools have been widely used in CS education to offer personalized on-demand feedback, which can be helpful when students need multiple attempts to master programming concepts [3, 4]. Although studies generally suggest that automated assessments can support learning [3], the benefits often vary, depending on how students approach and interact with these tools. However, it is not yet clear precisely how different behaviors and strategies influence learning outcomes, underscoring the need for more research into the specific activity patterns associated with success and failure in programming tasks.

Y. J. Kim and Z. Swiecki (Eds.): icqe 2024, CCIS 2279, pp. 225–240, 2024.
https://doi.org/10.1007/978-3-031-76332-8_19

We investigate this by using Ordered Network Analysis (ONA) to analyze data from an automated programming assessment system used in an introductory CS course, where students iterate on specific coding goals while intermittently using the assessment system. By investigating the emergent patterns during their work, we aim to contribute to a deeper understanding of how student actions influence their learning outcomes in university-level CS education.

Specifically, we investigate whether we can automatically detect fine-grained and meaningful changes in student behavior during programming in a scalable fashion, compose them into patterns using ONA, and then investigate which of these patterns are associated with better learning outcomes. By doing so, we seek to identify behavior patterns in debugging that could inform targeted interventions to support students in achieving programming success.

2 Related Work

2.1 Automated Assessment in Computer Science Education

Systems for automated assessment of programming code have become increasingly prevalent in computer science education assisting students in many different introductory programming courses and providing support for a wide range of programming languages [5, 6].

The availability of data originating from such systems has resulted in increased research on areas such as the impact of syntax (compiler) errors on student progress [7], automated generation of hints and feedback [8, 9], or early prediction of student performance in a programming course [10]. In contrast to some quantitative research on learning to program, qualitative research in this domain has been limited to small sample sizes [11], as the extensive volume of available data often surpasses the capacity for traditional human coding. However, the advent of Large Language Models (LLMs) now enables the automated execution of some qualitative research processes at increasingly high quality [12, 13], thereby suggesting a potential for a more thorough analysis of programming code and detecting valuable insights at larger scale.

In CS automated assessment systems, program correctness is checked using a set of predefined tests, assuming there are no syntax errors (which makes it possible for the code to be compiled and executed). If the code does not compile, compiler errors may provide insights into student struggle. For a more detailed analysis of how learners attempt to improve across attempts, programming code can be examined using an Abstract Syntax Tree (AST), which is a simplified representation of the code structure [14]. ASTs allow tracking of precise changes between different versions of the code [14]. However, ASTs are often not useful until the student is able to produce code that compiles without errors, a challenge for many novice students in introductory programming courses who struggle with code syntax. Since an AST represents the syntactic structure of code, any part of the code that doesn't adhere to the language's syntax might not be correctly represented in the tree, or the tree generation might fail entirely. This issue is often addressed by including only compiled code in the analysis [15], which offers an incomplete picture of novices' CS understanding. Regular expressions are another alternative for examining changes in students' attempts by searching for specific sequences of characters in those lines where changes are detected [16]. However, examining such changes based on a mere identification of fixed sequences of characters can also offer a limited understanding of those students who struggle with code syntax because those types of errors might result in the specific known sequences not being present in their code. Therefore, these types of automated approaches can be insufficient for fully understanding how students improve their code across attempts.

2.2 QE Approaches for CS Education

Given the challenges with existing approaches to automated assessment for studying CS learning, some programming education researchers have instead used manual labeling of programming code [17]. This often involves researchers coding data sources for the presence of relevant qualitative constructs to understand, for example, students' thought processes when creating code comments [18], the acquisition of data science skills [11] or patterns of debugging behaviors [19].

Research in computer science education has also recently begun to employ Quantitative Ethnography techniques such as Epistemic Network Analysis (ENA) to investigate patterns in coding practices, with a particular focus on collaborative learning. In K-12 settings, Su et al. [20] and Vandenberg et al. [21] have used ENA to analyze interactions within pair programming and across course topics. At the university level, ENA has also been utilized to compare computational thinking strategies among novice learners, distinguishing between low- and high-performing students during collaborative problem-solving sessions in CS courses [22]. Data sources from these examples consisted of transcripts of discourse or student written reflections, which offer insights on student mindset, but not direct assessment of programming skill development.

To address this limitation, Pinto and colleagues [23] qualitatively coded programming actions directly, building epistemic networks to explore debugging patterns in code submissions and revealing distinct approaches between experienced and novice programmers. The codebook contained constructs describing changes between two subsequent code submissions: a) code changes (e.g. changing variable name, massive deletion), b) results of the compilation event (new error detected in the compilation process), and c) combination of both: code changes and result of the compilation event (line with an error deleted). Although their results from the use of these codes highlighted differences between experienced and novice students' debugging behaviors, coding novices' data for more nuanced constructs as those constructs emerge across repeated programming attempts might reveal further insights into complex CS learning processes.

Therefore, we develop and apply a set of qualitative codes regarding students' fine-grained modifications to programming code, processed efficiently by an LLM. We then employ Epistemic Network Analysis (ENA) and Ordered Network Analysis (ONA) techniques to delve into the debugging behaviors of novice programmers. By doing so, we aim to discern the strategies that correlate with high and low outcomes on final examinations, providing deeper insights into the learning processes of students engaged with these automated systems.

3 Methods

3.1 Data Collection and Research Context

The data for this study was gathered during the fall 2022/2023 semester as part of a CS1 course, a required first-semester class for computer science students at a large European university. The dataset includes 1) responses to a questionnaire completed at the start of the semester, 2) results from a pre-test taken immediately after the questionnaire, 3) logs of activity on an online platform for automated programming assessment throughout the semester, and 4) scores from the final test, which was a graded assignment at the semester's end. All participants (N = 198) provided consent before their data was included in the study.

An automated assessment platform for programming assignments was provided as a learning tool within the course. Use of the tool was optional and did not count towards the final grade. During the study, 169 students submitted code 44,448 times through the platform. They uploaded their C# code for evaluation across 146 tasks, which spanned basic programming topics introduced during the semester including types and variables (33 tasks), conditional statements (25 tasks), recursion (28 tasks), and arrays and loops (60 tasks).

Directly after each submission, the code was automatically compiled. If compiler errors were detected at this stage (which means the code cannot be executed and tested), students were presented with a feedback message that listed the detected compiler errors. If compilation succeeded, the code was executed against a set of unit tests that verified if the students' code met the assignment requirements. In this case, students were presented with a list of all tests executed on their code. Each test was marked with fail or success. To retrieve details about the test execution, students had to click on a selected test. As correcting the submitted code requires understanding which test requirements were not met, we only included clicks checking the details of tests that failed.

3.2 Knowledge Self-reports and Tests

In this work, we examine the debugging behaviors of learners who self-reported having little to no programming experience prior to joining the course. The level of prior programming experience was determined based on student responses to a survey item deployed during the first class sessions: "On the scale 1–5, where 1 is zero experience, and 5 is a lot of experience, please rate your basic programming knowledge (types, variables, conditional statement, recursion, loops, arrays)." We considered students who responded with a 1 or 2 (N = 110 out of total 198) in the questionnaire to be novices, as in past use of this instrument [24], and included them in our analyses. We also excluded students who did not use the online platform to solve conditional statements tasks (69 experienced and 100 novices solved at least one conditional statement task in the platform).

We validated students' self-reports of expertise by asking students to take a pre-test assessing their general programming knowledge (see Table 2). This test was administered immediately after students submitted the questionnaire. At the end of the semester, a final test was administered to evaluate student knowledge of the introductory programming concepts taught in the course. Within the novice group, we further categorized students based on their performance. 40 novices with final test scores within the highest quartile were assigned to the high-performing group (hp-novices). 28 novices with scores in the lowest quartile were assigned to the low-performing group (lp-novices). The two quartiles were different sizes due to students with the same score on the final test.

In this research, we focus on submissions made on conditional statements tasks, for which 10,673 code submissions (7,136 from novices) have been collected on the platform. We chose this specific set of tasks because they are the first module in the semester that requires a basic understanding of both syntax and programming logic. By examining the correctness of submissions and debugging behaviors to solve errors in this set of tasks, instructors could recognize early in the semester whether some students still need to learn some key initial concepts that are critical for future success in programming learning.

3.3 Qualitative Coding Procedures

When coding student data, our objective was to identify and characterize the changes made across all pairs of consecutive student submissions for the same task. For a task of this detail and a dataset of this size, human qualitative coding of changes across submissions is time-consuming, and the regular expression automated approach often used in QE (e.g. [25, 26]) is challenging to apply reliably because novice students' code often does not follow syntax rules. With increased availability of large language models (LLMs), however, training tools such as GPT-4 to emulate human qualitative coding procedures at scale has become more feasible for automated qualitative coding of text (e.g., [12]).

To achieve this, we first employed a difference algorithm (diff) to generate changes between all pairs of subsequent code submissions. We created a tool that presents these changes in HTML format, incorporating additional fields that allow for labeling each identified change (Fig. 1). Two human coders used this tool and initially performed qualitative coding on a set of 100 examples of consecutive submissions with differences that indicate the actions taken by students to solve the corresponding errors (Table 1).

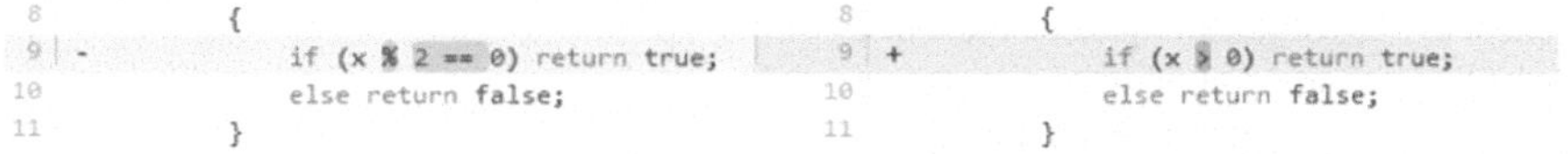

Fig. 1. A sample of two consecutive pieces of programming codes submitted by a student with changes across submissions highlighted.

Next, we used a prompt engineering approach and employed GPT-4 (gpt-4-turbo-2024-04-09) for the automated coding of the remaining submissions. Our analysis focused only on submissions for tasks involving conditional statement ("if"), as this area has been previously identified as one of the earliest where differences between high and low-performing students become apparent [24, 27].

During prompt engineering, GPT's performance increased when it was presented with the results of the difference algorithm (e.g., the lines affected by a change as highlighted in Fig. 1) along with the code. We designed a set of prompts that achieved

Table 1. Codebook with definitions, accuracy and reliability metrics.

Code	Definition	Human 1 - GPT		Human 1 - Human 2	
		Accuracy	K	Accuracy	K
If Header	Student submission contains modifications to the if condition/ header	0.907	0.808	0.981	0.959
Function Return	Student submission contains modifications inside the return statement	0.928	0.814	0.916	0.748
Commenting	Student commented at least one line in a submission	0.990	0.852	1.000	1.000
Code Added	Student added new code lines in a submission	0.979	0.905	0.972	0.854
Code Removed	Student removed code lines in the submission	0.961	0.779	0.991	0.955
Testing	Student modified code inside the Main function (section of the code used for testing)	0.918	0.784	0.963	0.907
No Change	Student submission is identical to the previous submission	*	*	*	*
Other Change	Student submission contains changes other than those identified above	*	*	*	*
Compiler Error	Student submitted code containing a compiler error	*	*	*	*
Unit Test Failed	Student submitted compiling code but failing to pass at least one unit test	*	*	*	*
Feedback Clicked	Student requested feedback after submitting code that failed to pass all unit tests	*	*	*	*

* Did not require coding procedures

a Cohen's Kappa over 0.7 with human coders in the initial subset of 100 examples (See Table 1). Finally, we applied GPT-based coding to the remaining submissions for the "if" set of tasks.

Several codes included in the analysis did not require qualitative coding techniques. Instances of no change across submissions were identified using the diff algorithm; changes identified by the diff algorithm that did not fall under the human-identified coding categories were grouped into "Other change". Student responses marked as having compiler errors or unit tests that failed were pulled directly from the log data from student use of the automated platform, as were instances in which students chose to access the platform's feedback.

3.4 Data Analysis Procedures

To compare the debugging behaviors between the two groups (hp-novices vs. lp-novices), we used Ordered Network Analysis (ONA), which accounts for the order of appearance of constructs. This technique helped us identify which actions followed an unsuccessful submission and what the subsequent steps taken to rectify coding mistakes were. Additionally, ONA examines self-transitions within each construct, enabling us to determine whether students repeatedly test a particular debugging strategy and if they persist in making the same type of changes when submission contains a compiler error or unit tests that failed [7].

Using ONA, we conducted a two-stage analysis. First, using a difference model, we examined the primary distinctions between high-performing and low-performing groups based on all their submissions. This model included the two types of unsuccessful submissions as constructs, as well as the student's choice to click on feedback, helping us understand how students react to different error types.

Recognizing that the results of epistemic networks can be influenced by some categories being much more frequent than others (in this case, submissions with compiler errors and failed unit tests), we conducted a second-stage analysis where we compared the debugging behaviors specific to each type of an unsuccessful submission. For this, we developed separate difference models for 1) submissions immediately following a submission with a compiler error and 2) submissions immediately following a submission containing unit tests that failed. We analyzed the actions taken in the submission immediately after an unsuccessful one because these actions represent the students' direct responses to resolve the problem. For the same reason, we used a moving stanza window of size one for all models, pairing only two consecutive submissions to identify the actions that followed each unsuccessful submission in the primary analysis and the action that followed the previous unsuccessful attempt for the same type of error in the secondary analysis.

4 Results

4.1 Descriptive Statistics

Table 2 shows descriptive statistics for total submissions, the number of tasks attempted and correctly solved, incorrect submissions due to a compiler error and failed unit tests, and initial and final scores for 4 groups of students: Experienced, Novices, Novices with the highest final test score (top quartile) and Novices with low performance in the final test (bottom quartile).

Students who self-reported being novices had much lower pretest scores (Mdn = 16%) than the other students (Mdn = 65%), $p < 0.001$, $U = 452$ for a Mann-Whitney U test. The primary distinction between these groups in their use of the online platform was in the number of submissions, which was statistically significantly different, U = 2214, $p < 0.001$, despite these two groups having a nearly identical total number of attempted and correctly completed tasks. This difference is the result of the higher number of submissions containing compiler errors (Mdn = 19.0) and failed unit tests (Mdn = 20.0) that novices made compared to experienced students (Mdn of 11.0 and 10.0 for compiler errors and failed unit tests, respectively).

The difference between experienced and novice students is reduced in the final scores at the end of the semester, although still statistically significant (Mdn of 67% and 56%, respectively, $p < 0.001$, U = 2228.5 for a Mann-Whitney U test). This result indicates that even though they started the semester with lower prior knowledge, some novices were able to close that knowledge gap, while other novices had much poorer learning (the low-performing group of novices had a Mdn of 22% on the final exam). This sharp contrast between outcomes for the novice groups underscores the importance of recognizing the differences in the interaction with the platform that might help explain these differences in the learning outcome.

Though the two groups of novice students (high-performing and low-performing) achieved different outcomes on the post-test (by definition, given how the two groups were selected), the two groups started with a similar pre-test score (Mdn of 18% and 16%, $p = 0.15$, U = 444.5 for a Mann-Whitney U test). This indicates that the difference in their final score is not a consequence of having different levels of prior knowledge of the course content.

Table 2. Descriptive statistics comparing experienced students and novice students with high and low learning gains.

Variable	Experienced (N = 69)		Novices (N = 100)		Novices High Score (N = 40)		Novices Low Score (N = 28)	
	Mdn	Avg (SD)	Mdn	Avg (SD)	Mdn	Avg (SD)	Mdn	Avg (SD)
Submissions	46.0	51.0 (27.3)	64.0	71.3 (41.0)	57.0	64.3 (31.6)	73.0	79.8 (49.4)
Comp. Errors	11.0	14.7 (12.7)	19.0	26.6 (24.8)	16.0	21.1 (18.6)	26.0	35.4 (32.4)
Tests failed	10.0	13.7 (11.7)	20.0	21.7 (15.7)	17.5	20.0 (14.3)	21.5	22.7 (15.6)
Tasks	25.0	21.4 (6.6)	25.0	21.9 (5.8)	25.0	22.5 (5.0)	25.0	21.4 (6.5)
Correct Tasks	24.0	21.0 (6.5)	24.0	21.2 (5.9)	25.0	22.1 (4.9)	24.0	20.3 (6.6)
Pre-Test	65%	64% (0.21)	16%	20% (0.18)	18%	25% (0.20)	16%	16% (0.13)
Final Test	67%	67% (0.2)	56%	51% (0.22)	67%	73% (0.09)	22%	21% (0.1)

4.2 Differences Between High and Low-Performing Novices

Figure 2 shows the ONA model of the most commonly occurring codes for all the 100 novices (left) and a difference model comparing the actions of the two groups of novices described in the previous section (right). Table 3 shows the line weights (lw) of the highest differences found when comparing these two groups (differences higher than 0.02). Along the X axis (MR1), a Mann-Whitney U test showed significant differences across both groups ($U = 319$, $p = 0.005$). The most substantial difference between the two groups of novices is observed for the compiler errors code. The difference model indicates that low-performing novices are more likely to repeatedly submit code with compiler errors (lw = 0.27) than their high-performing counterparts (lw = 0.18). This association reverses for submissions with failed unit tests, where high-performing novices (lw = 0.17) seem to have a slightly higher tendency to submit another code with a failed unit test compared to the low-performing group (lw = 0.14). It is worth noting that this difference in the line weights for submissions with failed unit tests does not imply that high-performing students make more errors of this type (See Table 2). It instead indicates that these students require fewer attempts to reach a correct submission, and therefore, these students have a higher percentage of submissions with failed unit tests than the low-performing novices do.

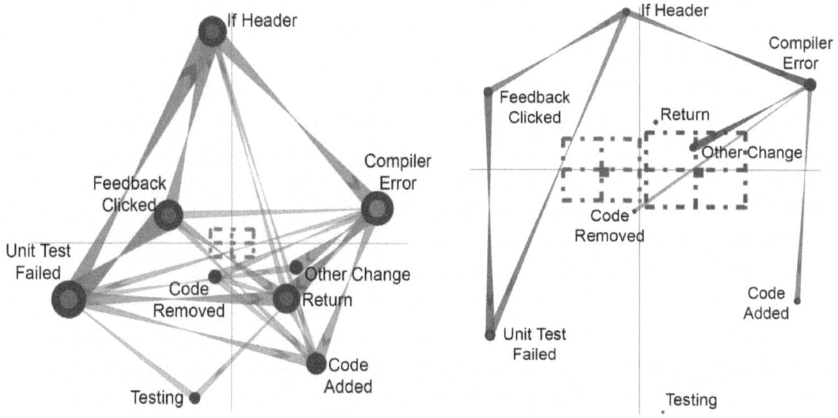

Fig. 2. A summary ordered network considering all novices (left) and a difference model comparing novices with high (blue) and low (red) final test scores (right). Only connections with weights over 0.02 are shown to enhance the clarity of the visualization.

This contrast in the base rates of submissions with a compiler error and submissions with failed unit tests influences most of the observed differences in the Ordered Network. Although both groups of novices frequently edit the *If Header* following submissions containing a compiler error or failed unit tests (lw = 0.14 and lw = 0.21, respectively), this behavior is more pronounced among low-performing novices for compiler errors (lw = 0.16) and among high-performing novices for failed unit tests (lw = 0.23). In both cases, this temporal association with the *If Header* construct is bidirectional mainly because students' subsequent submissions after experiencing a compiler error also often

Table 3. Line weights for the summary model and the difference model contrasting novices with high and low scores in the final test. Associations are listed based on the magnitude of the difference between the two groups.

Association	Summary Model	Difference Model		
		High	Low	Diff
Compiler Error → Compiler Error	0.22	0.18	0.27	−0.08
Feedback Clicked → Unit Test Failed	0.26	0.29	0.22	0.07
Unit Test Failed → Feedback Clicked	0.25	0.28	0.22	0.06
If Header → Compiler Error	0.14	0.12	0.18	−0.06
Compiler Error → Other Change	0.13	0.11	0.17	−0.06
Feedback Clicked → If Header	0.17	0.19	0.14	0.05
If Header → Unit Test Failed	0.16	0.18	0.13	0.05
If Header → Feedback Clicked	0.13	0.15	0.10	0.05
Unit Test Failed → If Header	0.21	0.23	0.19	0.04
Compiler Error → If Header	0.14	0.12	0.16	−0.04
Compiler Error → Code Added	0.11	0.10	0.14	−0.04
Unit Test Failed → Unit Test Failed	0.16	0.17	0.14	0.03
Code Added → Compiler Error	0.10	0.09	0.12	−0.03
Feedback Clicked → Feedback Clicked	0.10	0.11	0.08	0.03
Other Change → Compiler Error	0.10	0.08	0.11	−0.03
Code Added → Code Added	0.04	0.03	0.05	−0.03
Compiler Error → Code Removed	0.08	0.07	0.09	−0.02
Compiler Error → Return	0.19	0.18	0.20	−0.02

contain compiler errors. Also, in the event that a submission contains a failed unit test, it usually takes several attempts until fully correct code is submitted (as also shown by the self-transition weights of these two constructs).

Following compiler errors, low-performing novices often make additional changes to their code that do not involve the *If Header*, *Return Statement*, *Testing*, or *Adding* or *Removing* lines of code (lw = 0.17), unlike their high-performing counterparts (lw = 0.11). Additionally, low-performing novices are more likely to *Add code* (lw = 0.14) or *Remove code* (lw = 0.09) compared to high-performing novices (lw = 0.10 and lw = 0.07, respectively), although these differences are weaker than the former. Both behaviors are unexpected responses to compiler errors and suggest that these students may have a misunderstanding of what a compiler error means.

Across all novice students, there is a stronger connection between a submission containing a failed unit test and consulting feedback to identify which unit test failed in the previous submission (lw = 0.25). This behavior suggests that students frequently request feedback, but, as also demonstrated by the self-transitions of both error-related constructs, students' submissions containing a compiler error are often followed by another submission with a compiler error. Also, when a student makes a submission with failed unit tests, subsequent submissions often also contain failed unit tests. Although all novices show this behavior (requesting feedback after a submission with failed unit tests), the difference model reveals that high-performing novices (lw = 0.28) engage in this action more frequently than their low-performing counterparts (lw = 0.22). This indicates that students in the low-performing group may sometimes avoid or forget to request detailed feedback about the failed unit tests from their last submission.

4.3 Specific Differences Between High and Low Performing Students for Each Type of Error

To account for the specific differences in the frequency of submissions containing a compiler error and failed unit tests between each group, we conducted a secondary analysis and developed separate difference models for each error type, as shown in Fig. 3 and Table 4. Along the X axis (MR1), the two groups were statistically significantly different for submissions following a compiler error ($U = 270$, $p < 0.001$) and for submissions following failed unit tests ($U = 334$, $p = 0.009$). For compiler errors, the difference model shows that high-performing novices tend to repeatedly modify the *Return statement* more frequently (lw = 0.31) than low-performing novices (lw = 0.24), although this is still the strongest association for both groups. Additionally, high-performing novices more often adjust the *If Header* after modifying the *Return statement* (lw = 0.15) and alter the *Return statement* following other types of code changes (lw = 0.12) more than the low-performing groups (lw = 0.12 and lw = 0.08, respectively).

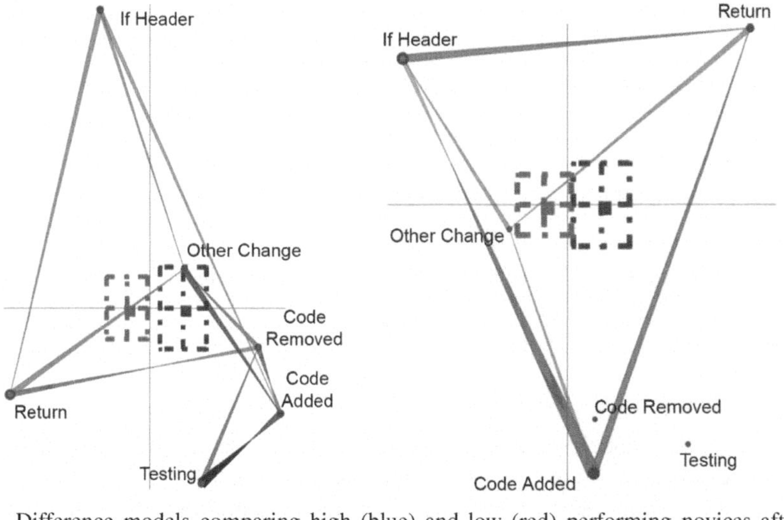

Fig. 3. Difference models comparing high (blue) and low (red) performing novices after the submission containing compiler errors (left) and failed unit tests (right). Only connections with weights over 0.02 are shown to enhance the clarity of the visualization.

Table 4. Line weights of difference models contrasting behaviors after the submission containing compiler errors and failed unit tests of novices with high and low scores in the final test. Associations are listed based on the magnitude of the difference between the 2 groups for compiler errors. Differences greater than 0.03 are shown in bold.

	Compiler Errors			Failed Unit Tests		
Association	High	Low	Diff	High	Low	Diff
Return → Return	**0.31**	**0.24**	**0.07**	**0.18**	**0.22**	**−0.04**
Code Added → Testing	**0.03**	**0.10**	**−0.07**	0.05	0.06	−0.01
Other Change → Return	**0.12**	**0.08**	**0.04**	**0.03**	**0.06**	**−0.03**
Testing → Code Added	**0.05**	**0.09**	**−0.04**	0.05	0.06	−0.01
Return → If Header	**0.15**	**0.12**	**0.03**	**0.20**	**0.24**	**−0.04**
Code Removed → Return	**0.12**	**0.15**	**−0.03**	0.08	0.09	−0.01
Code Added → Code Removed	**0.11**	**0.14**	**−0.03**	0.09	0.10	−0.01
Code Added → If Header	**0.13**	**0.10**	**0.03**	0.18	0.16	0.03
Code Added → Code Added	**0.08**	**0.11**	**−0.03**	0.08	0.10	−0.02
Code Removed → Testing	**0.01**	**0.04**	**−0.03**	0.02	0.02	0.00
Other Change → Code Removed	0.05	0.07	−0.03	0.02	0.02	0.00
Code Removed → Code Added	0.12	0.14	−0.03	0.08	0.09	−0.01
Other Change → Other Change	0.13	0.15	−0.02	**0.06**	**0.03**	**0.03**
Return → Code Removed	0.10	0.12	−0.02	0.09	0.10	−0.01
Other Change → If Header	0.09	0.11	−0.02	0.07	0.06	−0.01
Return → Code Added	0.20	0.21	−0.01	**0.15**	**0.20**	**−0.04**
If Header → Code Added	0.10	0.11	−0.01	**0.23**	**0.15**	**0.07**
If Header → Other Change	0.11	0.10	0.01	0.05	0.07	−0.02
Other Change → Code Added	0.08	0.09	0.01	0.04	0.06	0.02
If Header → If Header	0.21	0.21	0.00	**0.44**	**0.34**	**0.10**

The difference model for submissions with compiler errors shows that the primary action more prevalent among low-performing novices than high-performing ones is modifying the *Testing* section of the code after *Adding* more lines (lw = 0.10 for low-performing vs. lw = 0.03 for high-performing). Similarly, low-performing novices are more likely to alter the *Testing* section after *Removing Code* (lw = 0.04) and exhibit more frequent fluctuation between *Adding* and *Removing Code* (lw = 0.14 for removing after adding, and lw = 0.11 for adding after removing). Low-performance novices also modify the *Return statement* more frequently (lw = 0.15) than the high-performance group (lw = 0.12), particularly after *Removing Code.*

In summary, high-performing novices are more likely to act upon an apparent understanding that the most frequent sources of compiler errors (at least for the specific tasks considered here) are the *If Header* and *Return statements*, which are the sections they primarily modify in their submissions. While low-performing students also focus on these two code sections, they are more inclined to also add or remove code within the function body, testing, or other sections of code that are less likely to resolve a compiler error.

For submissions containing failed unit tests, the high-performing group predominantly focuses on recurrently modifying the *If Header* (lw = 0.44), possibly recognizing it as the primary section of the code where a mistake in logic could appear and cause their submissions to fail some unit tests. This is particularly true for the tasks considered in this study, which focus on conditional statements. High-performing novices also more frequently add lines of code after adjusting the *If Header* (lw = 0.23) when failed unit tests have been identified in the submission, which is typical debugging behavior for addressing issues in conditional statement tasks.

Although low-performing novices also frequently modify the *If Header* (lw = 0.34) and add lines of code afterward (lw = 0.15), they do so less often than their high-performing counterparts. Occasionally, they shift to other types of changes (lw = 0.07) such as introducing new variables or modifying existing expressions. They also sometimes choose to first modify the *Return statement* and then adjust the *If Header* (lw = 0.24) or add new lines of code (lw = 0.20). Given the cumulative nature of programming learning across tasks, it is possible that low-performing novices were trying to apply actions from prior coding tasks that they had not yet mastered. Although high performers also engage in these behaviors (lw = 0.20 and lw = 0.15, respectively), their strategies tend to focus more directly on the *If Header*.

Examination of the two difference models reveals contrasting behaviors for each novice group when they encounter failed unit tests versus compiler errors. When dealing with compiler errors, the transition from modifying the *Return statement* to the *If Header* is more prevalent among high-performing novices, indicating their recognition that many of these errors may stem from simple typos in the *Return statement* (e.g., missing a semicolon, improper operator usage, etc.). For submissions with failed unit tests, high performers recognize that primary logic issues can often be resolved by adjusting the *If Header*. Low-performing novices instead tend to make this transition from modifying the *Return statement* to the *If Header* more frequently for submissions with failed unit tests. This suggests that they might not have the same level of discernment between the types of errors as their high-performing peers, leading them to adopt strategies that may not be as effective in resolving the issues in their program code.

5 Discussion and Conclusion

In this study, we investigated patterns of fine-grained changes in novice learners' debugging behaviors when using an automated assessment tool, and the association between these changes and learning outcomes. Given that manually labeling a complete dataset with thousands of submissions is highly time-consuming to do manually, we used GPT-4 turbo to automate the process of identifying differences in students' programming code across multiple submissions. Next, we employed these automatically labeled examples to track code modifications made by students and used ONA to identify the differences in coding behaviors between groups of novice programmers who ultimately achieved high final scores and those who performed poorly.

Our findings indicate that both groups began the course with similar incoming knowledge, and both groups demonstrated similar rates of activity, correctly solving approximately the same number of tasks involving conditional statements. When examining the complex patterns of behaviors using ordered networks, however, we observed nuanced differences in how each group interacted with the code. These differences became apparent early in the semester.

In particular, students who eventually scored well on the final exam tended to make changes involving key concepts relevant to the current stage of the learning path, such as conditional statements and the use of the return keyword. In contrast, students who scored low on the test frequently made changes unrelated to these core topics. This pattern suggests that, already at an early stage, the lower-performing students likely had a weaker grasp of key initial topics such as types and variables.

Although future research still needs to investigate how these differences in debugging behaviors also manifest for more advanced tasks throughout the semester (such as loops or recursion), they appeared to have a lasting impact on students' progress. Despite visible engagement with the tasks, these foundational misunderstandings seemed to propagate throughout the course, culminating in lower final scores. This study highlights the critical role of early diagnostic and intervention strategies in programming courses where early foundational understanding is crucial for later success. Scaffolds could include tailored messages that can help indicate where errors can originate, or hints or notes to remind students of key concepts.

GPT-based models have previously been employed to generate personalized feedback for students by analyzing the submissions that led to their most recent errors [9]. These models have demonstrated promising results in helping students learn to produce correct solutions, even after the feedback is turned off. Our findings suggest that these types of interventions can be further refined to not only consider students' recent errors, but also to scaffold the behaviors they adopt while addressing compiler errors or failed unit tests, specifically helping them learn to focus on modifying the right sections of their programs. Additionally, it may be beneficial for instructors to analyze the individual ordered network models for each student as well as the overall classroom model to identify whether certain students or a significant portion of the class lacks foundational knowledge. By supporting students in learning to focus their debugging in the right areas, and addressing foundational knowledge gaps promptly, we may be able to mitigate the difficulties that students encounter later in the semester.

Acknowledgments. Andres Felipe Zambrano thanks the Ministerio de Ciencia, Tecnología e Innovación and the Fulbright-Colombia commission for supporting his doctoral studies through the Fulbright-MinCiencias 2022 scholarship.

The authors have no competing interests to declare that are relevant to the content of this article.

References

1. Ou, Q., Liang, W., He, Z., Liu, X., Yang, R., Wu, X.: Investigation and analysis of the current situation of programming education in primary and secondary schools. Heliyon **9**(4), e15530 (2023)
2. Vegas, E., Hansen, M., Fowler, B.: Building skills for life: how to expand and improve computer science education around the world (2021)
3. Paiva, J.C., Leal, J.P., Figueira, Á.: Automated assessment in computer science education: a state-of-the-art review. ACM Trans. Comput. Educ. **22**, 1–40 (2022)
4. Pankiewicz, M., Baker, R., Ocumpaugh, J.: Using intelligent tutoring on the first steps of learning to program: affective and learning outcomes. In: International Conference on Artificial Intelligence in Education. pp. 593–598. Springer (2023)
5. Lobb, R., Harlow, J.: Coderunner: a tool for assessing computer programming skills. ACM Inroads. **7**, 47–51 (2016)
6. Edwards, S.H., Murali, K.P.: CodeWorkout: short programming exercises with built-in data collection. In: Proceedings of the 2017 ACM Conference on Innovation and Technology in Computer Science Education, pp. 188–193. (2017)
7. Jadud, M.C., Dorn, B.: Aggregate Compilation Behavior: Findings and Implications from 27,698 Users. In: Proceedings of the Eleventh Annual International Conference on International Computing Education Research, pp. 131–139. Association for Computing Machinery, New York, NY, USA (2015)
8. Rivers, K., Koedinger, K.R.: Data-driven hint generation in vast solution spaces: a self-improving python programming tutor. Int. J. Artif. Intell. Educ. **27**, 37–64 (2017)
9. Pankiewicz, M., Baker, R.S.: Large language models (GPT) for automating feedback on programming assignments. In: International Conference on Computers in Education. pp. 68–77 (2023)
10. Pereira, F.D., et al.: Explaining individual and collective programming students' behavior by interpreting a black-box predictive model. IEEE Access **9**, 117097–117119 (2021)
11. Theobold, A.S., Wickstrom, M.H., Hancock, S.A.: Coding code: qualitative methods for investigating data science skills. J. Stat. Data Sci. Educ. **32**, 161–173 (2024)
12. Zambrano, A.F., Liu, X., Barany, A., Baker, R.S., Kim, J., Nasiar, N.: From ncoder to chatgpt: From automated coding to refining human coding. In: Irgens, G.A., Knight, S. (eds.) Advances in Quantitative Ethnography: 5th International Conference, ICQE 2023, Melbourne, VIC, Australia, October 8–12, 2023, Proceedings, pp. 470–485. Springer Nature Switzerland, Cham (2023). https://doi.org/10.1007/978-3-031-47014-1_32
13. Barany, A., et al.: ChatGPT for education research: exploring the potential of large language models for qualitative codebook development. In: Olney, A.M., Chounta, I.-A., Liu, Z., Santos, O.C., Bittencourt, I.I. (eds.) Artificial Intelligence in Education: 25th International Conference, AIED 2024, Recife, Brazil, 8–12 July 2024, Proceedings, Part II, pp. 134–149. Springer Nature Switzerland, Cham (2024). https://doi.org/10.1007/978-3-031-64299-9_10
14. Falleri, J.-R., Morandat, F., Blanc, X., Martinez, M., Monperrus, M.: Fine-grained and accurate source code differencing. In: Proceedings of the 29th ACM/IEEE International Conference on Automated Software Engineering. pp. 313–324 (2014)
15. Liu, K., Kim, D., Bissyandé, T.F., Yoo, S., Le Traon, Y.: Mining fix patterns for FindBugs violations. IEEE Trans. Software Eng. **47**, 165–188 (2021)
16. Ade-Ibijola, A., Ewert, S., Sanders, I.: Abstracting and narrating novice programs using regular expressions. In: Proceedings of the Southern African Institute for Computer Scientist and Information Technologists Annual Conference 2014, pp. 19–28 (2014)
17. De Lucia, A., Di Penta, M., Oliveto, R., Panichella, A., Panichella, S.: Labeling source code with information retrieval methods: an empirical study. Empir. Softw. Eng. **19**, 1383–1420 (2014)

18. Mohammadi-Aragh, M.J., Beck, P.J., Barton, A.K., Reese, D., Jones, B.A., Jankun-Kelly, M.: Coding the coders: a qualitative investigation of students' commenting patterns. In: 2018 ASEE Annual Conference & Exposition. ASEE Conferences, Salt Lake City, Utah (2018)
19. Lewis, C.M.: The importance of students' attention to program state: a case study of debugging behavior. In: Proceedings of the Ninth Annual International Conference on International Computing Education Research. pp. 127–134. (2012)
20. Su, Y.-S., Wang, S., Liu, X.: Using epistemic network analysis to explore primary school students' computational thinking in pair programming learning. J. Educ. Comput. Res. **62**, 559–593 (2024)
21. Vandenberg, J., Lynch, C., Boyer, K.E., Wiebe, E.: "I remember how to do it": exploring upper elementary students' collaborative regulation while pair programming using epistemic network analysis. Comput. Sci. Educ. **33**, 429–457 (2023)
22. Wu, B., Hu, Y., Ruis, A.R., Wang, M.: Analysing computational thinking in collaborative programming: a quantitative ethnography approach. J. Comput. Assist. Learn. **35**, 421–434 (2019)
23. Pinto, J.D., Liu, Q., Paquette, L., Zhang, Y., Fan, A.X.: Investigating the relationship between programming experience and debugging behaviors in an introductory computer science course. In: Irgens, G.A., Knight, S. (eds.) Advances in Quantitative Ethnography: 5th International Conference, ICQE 2023, Melbourne, VIC, Australia, October 8–12, 2023, Proceedings, pp. 125–139. Springer Nature Switzerland, Cham (2023). https://doi.org/10.1007/978-3-031-47014-1_9
24. Zambrano, A.F., Pankiewicz, M., Barany, A., Baker, R.S.: Ordered network analysis in CS education: unveiling patterns of success and struggle in automated programming assessment. In: International Conference on Innovation and Technology in Computer Science Education, pp. 443–449. Association for Computing Machinery (2024)
25. Cai, Z., Siebert-Evenstone, A., Eagan, B., Shaffer, D.W., Hu, X., Graesser, A.C.: NCoder+: A Semantic Tool for Improving Recall of nCoder Coding. In: Eagan, B., Misfeldt, M., Siebert-Evenstone, A. (eds.) ICQE 2019. CCIS, vol. 1112, pp. 41–54. Springer, Cham (2019). https://doi.org/10.1007/978-3-030-33232-7_4
26. Dubovi, I., Tabak, I.: Interactions between emotional and cognitive engagement with science on YouTube. Public Underst. Sci. **30**, 759–776 (2021)
27. Izu, C., Denny, P., Roy, S.: A resource to support novices refactoring conditional statements. In: Proceedings of the 27th ACM Conference on Innovation and Technology in Computer Science Education, vol. 1. pp. 344–350 (2022)

Cultural Discourse

Detecting Differences in Community Conversations with Epistemic Network Analysis

Lisa Lundgren[1(✉)] and Brock Couch[2]

[1] Utah State University, Logan, UT, USA
Lisa.Lundgren@usu.edu
[2] Loyola University of Maryland, Baltimore, MD, USA
bcouch@loyola.edu

Abstract. Current research around science education and communication on social media sites, particularly Twitter (also known as X), lacks holistic exploration and explanation of three key aspects: determining who is involved in conversations, the content people are communicating about, and reach of that content. To integrate these aspects and gain a holistic understanding of connections between learners, content, and the online social world, we used Epistemic Network Analysis (ENA). ENA is well-used in research on discussion boards where a) learners have an impetus for posting and b) there are fewer conversations which creates dense networks with low topic variation. We use ENA in a real-world setting where multiple conversations, large numbers of learners, and the voluntary nature of engagement create sparse networks with high topic variability. We use a pre-existing Twitter dataset from a community focused on paleontology. Data were collected from July 2017 through August 2018. Nearly 8,000 tweets were created by 1,290 entities. Findings indicate differences in individuals, conversation structure, and reach of conversations that were originally hidden when analyzed with social network analysis. With this research, we provide an integrated view of connections between learners, content, and their online social world. We highlight a need for employing ENA within real-world settings that include large numbers of users, variable topics, and multiple conversations.

Keywords: Twitter · affinity space · communication · social media · informal STEM education

1 Introduction

Open, online social networks allow anyone with an internet connection to share opinions and gather information. Such open, online social networks can encourage diverse communities who are interested in varied topics, including those related to STEM, to communicate about their interests, leading to scientific discoveries, friendships that turn into collaborations [1], and varied forms of interest-based, social learning [2]. This interest-based social learning is important as people can choose what they are interested in learning about and respond to those who share interests. Indeed, communicating and

Y. J. Kim and Z. Swiecki (Eds.): icqe 2024, CCIS 2279, pp. 243–257, 2024.
https://doi.org/10.1007/978-3-031-76332-8_20

learning from others on online social networks is a popular pastime, with 83% of Americans reporting that they use at least one social networking site [3]. Within such networks, people create massive amounts of digital trace data in the form of posts, comments, replies, and links to external sources. Researchers from across disciplines have sought to understand how people use these social networks; educational researchers especially have found compelling evidence that social learning occurs within these spaces [4–6]. Such social learning can be represented as learning within an affinity space [7]. We now describe the framework of affinity spaces to provide the theoretical underpinning of our study before discussing related literature.

2 Theoretical Framing

Gee's [8] influential research on affinity spaces concerned video games, where players played, discussed strategies, created video game-adjacent content, and shared knowledge collectively. Current research around affinity spaces is most often based in online environments and concerns peoples' thoughts, beliefs, values, actions, and social relationships. Most importantly, the theory of affinity spaces is concerned with people and the ways they interact with one another. In contrast to other social learning theoretical frameworks such as Communities of Practice [9], community membership within affinity spaces is secondary, as the concept of community can surface tensions related to belonging and formal membership requirements [8].

Researchers can identify an affinity space through applying 11 indicators: a common primary endeavor, space is shared by those from varied expertise, some portals act as strong generators, interactional organization transforms content organization, intensive and extensive knowledge is encouraged, individual and distributed knowledge is encouraged, dispersed knowledge is encouraged, tacit knowledge is honored, multiple routes and forms of participation exist, there are many routes to status, and leadership is porous [10]. Previous research into online STEM education affinity spaces has found that such spaces do not fulfill all 11 indicators [11]. However, other researchers have determined the context and content within online affinity spaces. [12] found that affinity spaces on Reddit varied in contributions by individuals, content interaction, and social interaction. Similarly, [13] examined two subreddits, determining that participation patterns changed over time. Within both these studies, the emphasis is on people holistically, however, we find it fruitful to explore how interactions and contributions to such spaces can be further characterized through the application of novel methods. Additionally, while emphasizing this content connection is important, characterizing the people and their connections within an affinity space is of equal importance, yet has not been fully explored. The limited research that explores people and their connections within an affinity space is limited to health science research, specifically to work on an online forum dedicated to supporting people with diabetes [14, 15]. To better understand interest-based interactions within an online affinity space centered on paleontology, we turned to Epistemic Network Analysis (ENA).

3 Literature Review

3.1 Epistemic Network Analysis

ENA provides researchers with the ability to quantify connections among people or ideas and represent them as a network [16]. This method has been used to analyze formal learning environments, especially how students conceptualize STEM content within those classrooms [e.g. 17–19]. Within STEM education contexts, studies that feature ENA as a data analysis technique mostly focus on formalized classrooms and students [20]. Within these studies, group sizes are small [21], focus on chat logs [22], and often examine school-specific topics (e.g. photomicrographs) [23, 24]. Expanding ENA's use to informal learning settings is valuable learning in formal and informal settings differs [25, 26]. Researchers have already started expanding ENA's use to other learning settings, such as lifelong learning [27], Twitter [28], and military training [29]. We add knowledge about the use of ENA to understand informal, interest-based STEM learning with a case study of learning within a Twitter affinity space.

3.2 Twitter as a Learning Space

Twitter has been extensively examined as a space for learning. For instance, [30] collated databases of tweets to study learning on Twitter. Two lines of work emerge for Twitter-based learning: research on how formal classroom teachers and learners use Twitter to connect to one another and inquiries into how Twitter is an informal learning environment. Twitter has been extensively studied to determine how it acts to support teachers as a space for professional development, networking, or support [31–34]. Twitter has also been used to supplement online or face-to-face learning at the high school [35] and college levels by asking students to create Twitter posts and respond to one another [36]. When examining Twitter as an informal learning environment, users' original tweets, mentions, retweets, hashtags and replies supply researchers the ability to understand learning. [37] discussed how message design (e.g. including hashtags, URLs, and replies) related to informal science learning. These studies show ways that Twitter can be considered a learning environment and especially how like-minded individuals find one another to have conversations about topics in which they have interest and expertise. With our summary of affinity spaces, review of ENA, and description of Twitter as a learning space, our research question is: To what degree can ENA detect differences in community conversations?

4 Methods

4.1 Context for the Study

@projectFOSSIL was the Twitter handle for The FOSSIL Project which focused on building connections and practice among a community of paleontologists [38]. Social media for the project was built around Hoadley and Kilner's [39] design principles for learning which included interpersonal connections and conversation around domain-specific problems (i.e. paleontology). Previous Twitter-specific research that has emerged from The FOSSIL Project includes classifying Twitter users who interact with scientific hashtags [40] and a review of message design elements for social media engagement [37]. All data associated with the project's social media research is open-access which provides the ability for other researchers to recompile, remix, and reinterpret data [41]. We make use of the open-access dataset where [42] used content analysis, social network analysis, and topic modeling to analyze the project's annual cycle of activity on Twitter.

4.2 Data Collection

We conducted social network analysis (SNA) and ENA on a Twitter-based dataset collected from July 2017 through August 2018. The open-access dataset had all identifying information removed from tweets (i.e. handles, mentions). [42] used Netlytic [43] to sample the Twitter public search API every 15 min. Duplicate tweets were removed, then the authors employed the Paleontological Identity Taxonomy [44] to classify user biographies based on users' self-identified interest in the domain of paleontology. This classification system included categories of Public, Scientist, Education and Outreach, and Commercial (reported herein as proper nouns). Public entities were those who expressed an interest in paleontology; Scientist entities indicated in their biography they were some kind of scientist (e.g. paleobotanist, geophysicist); Education and Outreach entities were affiliated with K-12 or universities, but not in research positions; and Commercial entities were those that sought to profit off the science of paleontology (e.g. through selling fossils or leading guided fossil collecting trips). Lundgren and colleagues originally also employed topic modeling, specifically, the Gibbs sampling Dirichlet mixture model, a form of Latent Dirichlet Allocation (LDA), to determine topics of conversation [45], finding 38 distinct topics, ranging from General Discussion of Paleontology, Citizen Science, Microfossils, and Paleontological Fieldwork (see Table 2 in Supplemental Material). For a full review of data collection processes used in the original research, see [42]. For this study, we used the originally collected, de-identified data and conducted new analyses on that dataset. We describe these analyses below.

4.3 Data Analysis

For SNA, our nodes were individuals who interacted with the @projectFOSSIL Twitter space with connections being an interaction between individuals within the space. We removed all nodes that did not have a connection to another node from the dataset, as well as those connections where the nature of the tweet was a retweet. We decided to remove retweets to avoid any bias in assuming connections between entities, instead focusing on more direct interactions (i.e., tweets, mentions, and replies to). For this study, we define communities as entities with connections to one another on Twitter. To detect communities within the network, we tested several detection algorithms (Clauset Newman Moore, Leiden Clustering, Louvain, Spinglass) and found that the Louvain detection algorithm had the best modularity (0.50). For the created communities, we assessed the different groups of individuals to understand the composition and influential interactions within the community. Using the created communities, we conducted ENA [46, 47] for each community to understand what individuals were communicating about on Twitter. Our nodes for ENA were the topics produced from the topic analysis and the connections were the presence of two codes in the same community. We utilized the 38 topics categorized in the original dataset and then created connections between topics based on the nature of the tweet (i.e., original tweet, reply, mention). Once connections were created, we visualized the differences between the types of conversations and frequency of topics being discussed within communities.

4.4 Limitations

This study is not without limitations. One limitation is the use of Twitter data itself–Twitter users at the time of this study comprised 22% of the US population [48]. Additionally, in 2022, Twitter moved from a publicly traded entity to a private site that discourages scientific research through instituting cost-prohibitive expenses to accessing Twitter API data. Thus, there is little ability to recreate this study with post-2022 datasets.

5 Results

We now describe the entities and their communities broadly, followed by the reach of topics across communities, and then indicate how topics were discussed within communities.

5.1 Describing Communities

The affinity space contained 1,290 entities which belonged to 20 distinct communities (Table 1). Such entities were not evenly distributed across communities, with Community 1 having the largest number of entities (n = 487, 37.75% of all entities) (Fig. 1). Additionally, we detected five communities that had fewer than nine entities (Community 15 = 3 entities, Community 17 = 4 entities, Community 18 = 8 entities, Community 19 = 3 individuals, Community 20 = 3 entities), which is less than 1% of all entities. When looking at our Paleontological Identity Taxonomy (PIT) categories, Scientists were the most represented category (n = 504), followed by Public (n = 461), Education and Outreach (n = 302), and Commercial (n = 13). Within the communities, Public entities were a part of every community. Scientists and Education and Outreach entities were in 18 of the 20 communities. Commercial entities were only represented in five of the 20 communities. When focusing on the distribution of PIT categories within the communities, there was an even distribution of Scientists, Education and Outreach, and Public across communities, although some communities tended to have a disproportionate amount of one of the three PIT categories. For example, Commercial entities always made up a small proportion of the communities they occupied.

5.2 Reach Across Communities

All communities, except for 15, 17, 18, 19, and 20, were densely connected between each other (Fig. 2). For communities 15, 17, 19, and 20, the connections were only between them and Community 1, and connections were unidirectional (either going to or from Community 1). When looking at individual communities, Community 1 had the

Table 1. Number of Entities Within Each Community

Community	Number of Entities	Percent of Whole Community
1	487	37.75
2	77	5.97
3	70	5.43
4	55	4.26
5	61	4.73
6	78	6.05
7	69	5.35
8	31	2.40
9	30	2.33
10	73	5.66
11	46	3.57
12	38	2.95
13	45	3.49
14	63	4.88
15	3	0.23
16	46	3.57
17	4	0.31
18	8	0.62
19	3	0.23
20	3	0.23
Total Number of Entities = 1290		

largest reach by having interactions with all other communities. Community 1 also had a relatively large number of incoming interactions from other communities, highlighting the central role they played within the affinity space. Another community of interest was Community 14. Community 14 had the second highest number of interactions (~ 600) within the community, with only 62 entities (7th largest community) and most entities being scientists (73% of community) (Fig. 1). This is around half of the amount of connections Community 1 had, despite only 12% of the members. Although Community 14 had a relatively large number of connections within the community, they had a much lower number of interactions with entities outside of their community.

5.3 Content Being Discussed

Eighteen of the twenty communities were further analyzed using ENA. Communities 15 and 20 were not included because they did not meaningfully engage with a particular paleontology topic. We analyzed what the topic modeled content communities

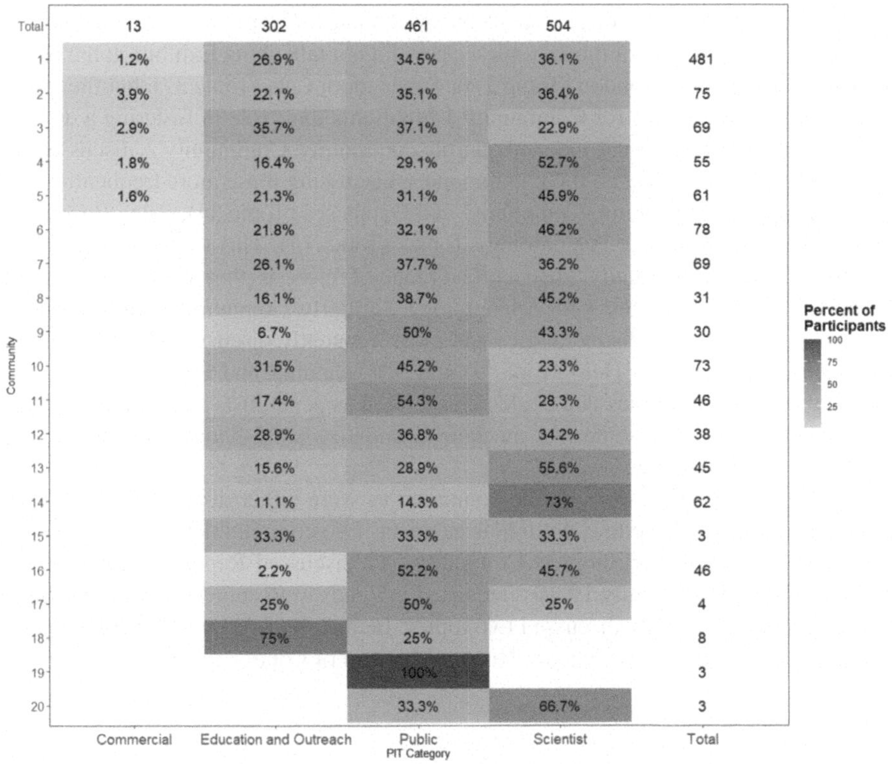

Fig. 1. Percentage of PIT categories within each community

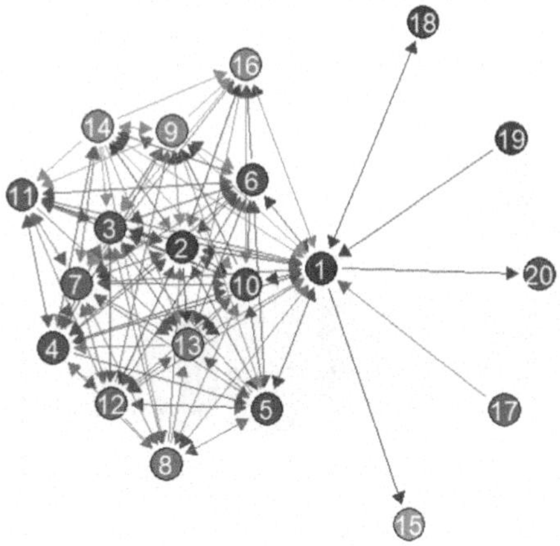

Fig. 2. Network of community interactions

communicated about (Fig. 3). We divided communities by quartiles: The top quartile communities (Q1 and Q2) discussed 12 or more topics (Fig. 3). The lower quartile communities (Q3 and Q4) discussed 11 or fewer topics. Community 1, a top quartile community, discussed 36 of the 38 topics. They did not talk about Exhibits at the Natural History Museum of London (Topic 2) or Saber-tooth Cats (Topic 37), but the broad depth of discussion topics for Community 1 highlights their role in fostering a diverse conversation on paleontology. One top quartile community, Community 2, discussed 25 topics, but focused interest on three main topics, discussing these more frequently than any other topics: 3D Printing, Community and Databases (Topic 34), Paleo Resources (Topic 13), and Lists about Paleontology Topics (Topic 15). This shows that although the entities within Community 2 had a broad range of interests, they were most focused on community-based resources for paleontology. Similarly, Community 4 ranged in discussions surrounding 21 distinct topics, but most frequently discussed Complimenting Specimens & Preparation Help (Topic 9) and 3D Scanning and Printing (Topic 21). Thus, although communities that could be described as generalists as they talked about many topics, also seemed somewhat specialized, and they had 2–3 topics that they talked about more often than other topics.

On the other hand, lower quartile communities were either distinct specialists, or those who seemed to have few, dissimilar interests. Two communities (17 and 19) only communicated about single topics: Community 17 discussed Reports or Discoveries (Topic 32) while Community 19 was interested in Leads to Resources (Topic 20). Similarly, Community 18 only discussed two topics: Inclusion of Amateur Paleontologists (Topic 0) and Exhibits at the Natural History Museum of London (Topic 2).

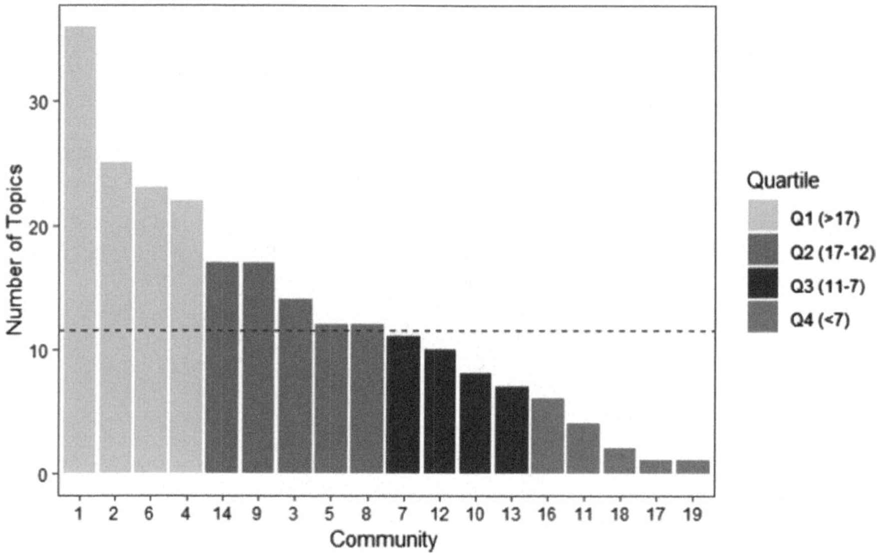

Fig. 3. Number of Topics Discussed by Communities

5.4 Reach of Content Being Discussed

When engaging in discussion of a topic, the most common form of engagement was replies (Fig. 4). We found that five topics, Exhibits at the Natural History Museum of London (Topic 2), An Individual Network Discussion (Topic 22), Reposting of Recent Research Papers (Topic 28), Paleontological Fieldwork (Topic 32), and Saber-tooth Cats (Topic 37), did not have an initial engagement (i.e., tweet) by any of the communities and were only discussed in mentions or replies. When looking across communities, mentions were most often utilized when discussing topics. Community 1 was the community to initiate most of the discussions across topics, with Community 2 and 5 as the only other communities who created tweets. Additionally, when mentioning or replying about topics, Community 1 had an even distribution of engagement in the form of mentions, replies to, and tweets across topics. In contrast, Community 14 had a more specialized engagement in which they focused on using mentions to discuss Women in Paleontology (Topic 11). Because of this specialization on the topic of Women in Paleontology, Community 14 had the highest engagement (i.e., number of connections) on a particular topic (~200 connections). Similarly, Community 4 specialized on two topics (Complimenting Specimens & Preparation Help, Topic 9 and 3D Scanning and Printing, Topic 21) using mentions. Interestingly, as mentioned above, Community 14 had much more conversation about their topics within their community, compared to Community 4. This highlights that Community 4 may have a further reach about their topics than Community 14 because they are engaging more with others outside of their community. Overall, the communities within this interest-based affinity space seemed prone to mentioning and replying to one another versus creating original content (i.e. tweets).

6 Discussion

Other researchers [11] have shown that social media-based affinity spaces sometimes lack the presence of the 11 indicators of affinity spaces. Our research showed that in this affinity space, 4 indicators were present: a common primary endeavor, the space was shared by those from varied expertise, multiple routes and forms of participation existed, and there was encouragement of knowledge disbursement. While some other indicators might have been present, our analyses were not necessarily able to portray them. For example, because we did not focus on tracing individual entities and their content creation, we were not able to assess the indicators of a porous leadership structure, the encouragement of individual and distributed knowledge, or the routes to status within the affinity space.

However, in relation to the composition of this affinity space, we found equal representation of three categories of entities. In other research on online affinity spaces, specifically Massive Open Online Collaboration course discussions on Twitter, the composition of participants did not matter if the participants were able to connect [49]. Our research reifies the notion that any interested entities can participate in an affinity space and that membership defined by boundaries is secondary [8].

From a practitioner perspective, understanding what topics, entities, and conversation structures prevent redundant, siloed communications in online, social worlds can allow

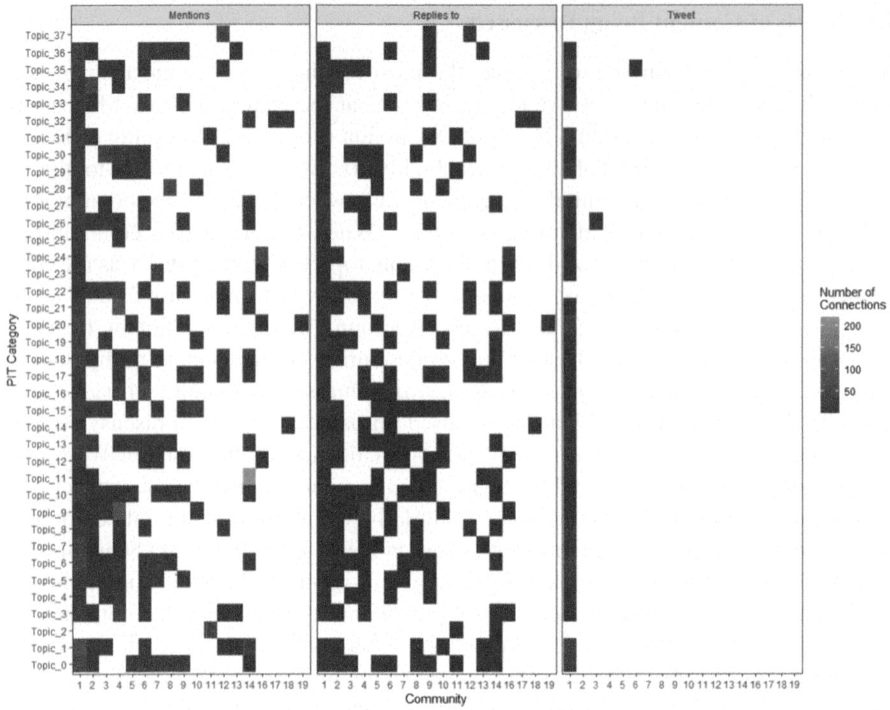

Fig. 4. Engagement strategies used by communities to discuss topics

for better transfer and understanding of information [15]. Related to this concept is the affinity space indicator that intensive and extensive knowledge is encouraged [10]; within our research, we found that communities often communicated about a wide variety of topics (i.e. they were generalists), but other communities were more prone to be specialized, communicating about 2–3 specialized topics, such as exhibits at a natural history museum. Our findings show the prevalence of intensive and extensive knowledge within an affinity space and potentially indicate the ways that knowledge transfer and information sharing occur.

Most ENA studies have focused on understanding formal educational spaces with sample sizes less than 100 individuals [20]. In contrast, this research highlights the potential for working with a large dataset that is not constrained by school-based topics and a limited number of users, which creates a high variation of topic discussion. Because of the undefined boundaries within the space, we found that utilizing community detection in combination with ENA allowed for us to better understand where topics were siloed (i.e., Women in Paleontology within Community 14), as well as widely discussed topics. Additionally, the use of directed social networks allowed us to understand the nature of the discussion between these communities. We were also able to show which communities within the space were driving the creation of new conversations (i.e., Community 1). Gaining an understanding of the nature, direction, and drivers of conversation within an open online community, this analysis could allow researchers to better understand the location and flow of information, which, in turn, could help combat misinformation in online spaces and develop informal learning communities.

This work highlights a need for employing ENA in a wider STEM education context within real-world settings that include large numbers of users, variable topics, and multiple conversations. While this analysis allowed us to see topics within communities and the nature of discussion, it did not allow us to understand the direction of conversations on specific topics (e.g., Community 14 discussing Women in Paleontology with Community 1). Also, within and across communities, we were not able to gain an individual perspective on information creation and flow within the space. Gaining these more fine-grained perspectives may have furthered our understanding of siloed topics and creation of information and should be looked at in future studies.

Appendix

Table 2. List of topics discussed by communities

Topic Number	Topic Description
0	Inclusion of Amateur Paleontologists
1	Citizen Science
2	Exhibits at NHM London
3	Events at Florida Museum
4	Fossils from Various States
5	General Discussion of Paleontology
6	Project Webinars
7	Paleontology Education & News
8	Undefined
9	Compliment Specimens & Prep Help
10	Project Outreach Events
11	Women in Paleontology
12	In-Person Events
13	Paleontology Resources
14	News Stories About Paleontology
15	Lists about Paleontology Topics
16	Microfossils
17	Historical Paleontology

(*continued*)

Table 2. (*continued*)

Topic Number	Topic Description
18	Project Newsletters and Conferences
19	Leads to Resources
20	Multimodal Sharing
21	3D Scanning and Printing
22	Individual Network Discussion
23	Resources for Ind. Fossil Collectors
24	Paleoart
25	News About Paleontology
26	Time Scavengers
27	Paleontology in K12
28	Reposting of Recent Research Papers
29	Natural History, Forams & Ancient Things
30	Project In-person Events
31	Reports or Discoveries
32	Fieldwork
33	Technology and Fossils
34	3D Printing, Community and Databases
35	Ways to Share Paleontology
36	Opportunities
37	Saber-tooth Cats

References

1. Cormier, M., Cushman, M.: Innovation via social media - The importance of Twitter to science. Res. Pract. Thromb. Haemost. **5**, 373–375 (2021). https://doi.org/10.1002/rth2.12493
2. Déchêne, M., Lesperance, K., Ziernwald, L., Holzberger, D.: From research to retweets—Exploring the role of educational Twitter (X) communities in promoting science communication and evidence-based teaching. Educ Sci. **14**, 196 (2024). https://doi.org/10.3390/educsci14020196
3. Gottfried, J.: How Americans Use Social Media | Pew Research Center. https://www.pewresearch.org/internet/2024/01/31/americans-social-media-use/
4. Malik, A., Heyman-Schrum, C., Johri, A.: Use of Twitter across educational settings: a review of the literature. Int. J. Educ. Technol. High. Educ. **16**, 36 (2019). https://doi.org/10.1186/s41239-019-0166-x
5. Malik, Z., Haidar, S.: Online community development through social interaction — K-Pop stan twitter as a community of practice. Interact. Learn. Environ. **31**(2), 733–751 (2020). https://doi.org/10.1080/10494820.2020.1805773

6. Jünger, J., Fähnrich, B.: Does really no one care? Analyzing the public engagement of communication scientists on Twitter. New Media Soc. **22**, 387–408 (2020). https://doi.org/10.1177/1461444819863413
7. Gee, J.P.: Affinity spaces and 21st century learning. Educ. Technol. **57**, 27–31 (2017)
8. Gee, J.P.: Affinity Spaces. Situated Language and Learning. Routledge, London (2004)
9. Wenger, E.: Communities of practice: Learning, meaning, and identity. Cambridge University Press, Cambridge, U.K. (1998)
10. Gee, J.P.: Situated Language and Learning: A Critique of Traditional Schooling. Routledge (2012). https://doi.org/10.4324/9780203594216
11. Rosenberg, J.M., Greenhalgh, S.P., Koehler, M.J., Hamilton, E.R., Akcaoglu, M.: An investigation of State Educational Twitter Hashtags (SETHs) as affinity spaces. E-Learn. Digit. Media **13**(1–2), 24–44 (2016). https://doi.org/10.1177/2042753016672351
12. Staudt Willet, K.B., Carpenter, J.P.: Teachers on Reddit? Exploring contributions and interactions in four teaching-related subreddits. J. Res. Technol. Educ. **52**, 216–233 (2020). https://doi.org/10.1080/15391523.2020.1722978
13. Staudt Willet, K.B., Carpenter, J.P.: A tale of two subreddits: change and continuity in teaching-related online spaces. Br. J. Educ. Technol. (2020). https://doi.org/10.1111/bjet.13051
14. Sharma, P., Li, Q., Land, S.M.: Knowledge sharing discourse types used by key actors in online affinity spaces. Inform. Learn. Sci. **122**(9/10), 671–687 (2021). https://doi.org/10.1108/ILS-09-2020-0211
15. Sharma, P., Land, S.: Patterns of knowledge sharing in an online affinity space for diabetes. Educ. Tech. Res. Dev. **67**, 1–29 (2018). https://doi.org/10.1007/s11423-018-9609-7
16. Shaffer, D.W.: Epistemic network analysis: understanding learning by using big data for thick description. In: Fischer, F., Hmelo-Silver, C.E., Goldman, S.R., Reimann, P. (eds.) International Handbook of the Learning Sciences, pp. 520–531. Routledge, New York, NY (2018)
17. Peters-Burton, E.E., Dagher, Z.R., Erduran, S.: Student, teacher, and scientist views of the scientific enterprise: an epistemic network re-analysis. Int. J. Sci. Math Educ. (2022). https://doi.org/10.1007/s10763-022-10254-w
18. Peters-Burton, E.E., Parrish, J.C., Mulvey, B.K.: Extending the utility of the views of nature of science assessment through epistemic network analysis. Sci. Educ. **28**, 1027–1053 (2019). https://doi.org/10.1007/s11191-019-00081-x
19. Peters-Burton, E., Baynard, L.R.: Network analysis of beliefs about the scientific enterprise: a comparison of scientists, middle school science teachers and eighth-grade science students. Int. J. Sci. Educ. **35**, 2801–2837 (2013). https://doi.org/10.1080/09500693.2012.662609
20. Elmoazen, R., Saqr, M., Tedre, M., Hirsto, L.: A systematic literature review of empirical research on epistemic network analysis in education. IEEE Access **10**, 17330–17348 (2022). https://doi.org/10.1109/ACCESS.2022.3149812
21. Hod, Y., Katz, S., Eagan, B.: Refining qualitative ethnographies using epistemic network analysis: a study of socioemotional learning dimensions in a humanistic knowledge building community. Comput. Educ. **156**, 103943 (2020). https://doi.org/10.1016/j.compedu.2020.103943
22. Nguyen, H.: Exploring group discussion with conversational agents using epistemic network analysis. In: Wasson, B., Zörgő, S. (eds.) Advances in Quantitative Ethnography: Third International Conference, ICQE 2021, Virtual Event, 6–11 Nov 2021, Proceedings, pp. 378–394. Springer International Publishing, Cham (2022)
23. Cheung, K.K.C., Winterbottom, M.: Students' integration of textbook representations into their understanding of photomicrographs: epistemic network analysis. Res. Sci. Technol. Educ. **41**(2), 544–563 (2021). https://doi.org/10.1080/02635143.2021.1920382

24. Cheung, K.K.C.: Exploring the inclusion of nature of science in biology curriculum and high-stakes assessments in Hong Kong. Sci. Educ. **29**, 491–512 (2020). https://doi.org/10.1007/s11191-020-00113-x
25. Committee on How People Learn II: The Science and Practice of Learning, Board on Behavioral, Cognitive, and Sensory Sciences, Board on Science Education, Division of Behavioral and Social Sciences and Education, National Academies of Sciences, Engineering, and Medicine: How people learn II: learners, contexts, and cultures. National Academies Press, Washington, D.C. (2018)
26. Callanan, M., Cervantes, C., Loomis, M.: Informal learning. Wiley Interdiscip. Rev. Cogn. Sci. **2**, 646–655 (2011). https://doi.org/10.1002/wcs.143
27. Prieto, L.P., Rodríguez-Triana, M.J., Ley, T., Eagan, B.: The Value of Epistemic Network Analysis in Single-Case Learning Analytics: A Case Study in Lifelong Learning. In: Ruis, A.R., Lee, S.B. (eds.) Advances in Quantitative Ethnography: Second International Conference, ICQE 2020, Malibu, CA, USA, February 1–3, 2021, Proceedings, pp. 202–217. Springer International Publishing, Cham (2021)
28. Misiejuk, K., Wasson, B., Egelandsdal, K.: Using learning analytics to understand student perceptions of peer feedback. Comput. Human Behav. **117**, 106658 (2021). https://doi.org/10.1016/j.chb.2020.106658
29. Swiecki, Z., Shaffer, D.W.: iSENS: An integrated approach to combining epistemic and social network analyses. In: Proceedings of the Tenth International Conference on Learning Analytics & Knowledge, pp. 305–313. ACM, New York, NY, USA (2020)
30. Banda, J.M., et al.: A large-scale COVID-19 Twitter chatter dataset for open scientific research—an international collaboration. Epidemiologia **2**, 315–324 (2021). https://doi.org/10.3390/epidemiologia2030024
31. Carpenter, J.P.: Twitter's capacity to support collaborative learning. Int. J. Soc. Media Interactive Learn. Environ. **2**, 103 (2014). https://doi.org/10.1504/IJSMILE.2014.063384
32. Carpenter, J.P., Morrison, S.A.: Enhancing teacher education…with Twitter? Phi Delta Kappan. **100**, 25–28 (2018)
33. Carpenter, J.P., Krutka, D.G.: How and why educators use Twitter: a survey of the field. J. Res. Technol. Educ. **46**, 414–434 (2014). https://doi.org/10.1080/15391523.2014.925701
34. Krutka, D.G., Carpenter, J.P.: Participatory learning through social media: How and why social studies educators use Twitter. Contemp. Issues Technol. Teacher Educ. **16**, 38–59 (2016)
35. Chapman, A.L., Marich, H.: Using Twitter for civic education in K-12 classrooms. TechTrends **65**, 51–61 (2021). https://doi.org/10.1007/s11528-020-00542-z
36. Corrales, K.A., Erwin, T.C.: Twitter and reflection: tweeting towards deeper learning. Reflective Pract. **21**, 484–498 (2020). https://doi.org/10.1080/14623943.2020.1779048
37. Lundgren, L., Crippen, K.J., Bex, R.T.: Social media interaction as information science learning: a comparison of message design in two niches. Res. Sci. Educ. **52**, 1–20 (2020). https://doi.org/10.1007/s11165-019-09911-y
38. Crippen, K.J., Ellis, S., Dunckel, B.A., Hendy, A.J.W., MacFadden, B.J.: Seeking shared practice: a juxtaposition of the attributes and activities of organized fossil groups with those of professional paleontology. J. Sci. Educ. Technol. **25**, 731–746 (2016). https://doi.org/10.1007/s10956-016-9627-3
39. Hoadley, C.M., Kilner, P.G.: Using technology to transform communities of practice into knowledge-building communities. SIGGROUP Bull. **25**, 31–40 (2005). https://doi.org/10.1145/1067699.1067705
40. Bex, R.T., Lundgren, L., Crippen, K.J.: Scientific Twitter: the flow of paleontological communication across a topic network. PLoS ONE **14**, e0219688 (2019). https://doi.org/10.1371/journal.pone.0219688
41. van der Zee, T., Reich, J.: Open education science. AERA Open. **4**, 233285841878746 (2018). https://doi.org/10.1177/2332858418787466

42. Lundgren, L., Crippen, K.J., Bauer, J.E., Bex, R.T.: Social paleontology on Twitter: a case study of topic archetypes, network composition, and structure. Soc. Media + Soc. (2022). https://doi.org/10.1177/20563051221080475
43. Gruzd, A.: Netlytic: Software for Automated Text and Social Network Analysis (2016)
44. Lundgren, L., Crippen, K.J., Bex, R.T.: Digging into the PIT: A new tool for characterizing the social paleontological community. In: Proceedings of E-Learn: World Conference on E-Learning in Corporate, Government, Healthcare, and Higher Education, pp. 121–128. Association for the Advancement of Computing in Education, San Diego, CA, USA (2018)
45. Nikolenko, S.I., Koltcov, S., Koltsova, O.: Topic modelling for qualitative studies. J. Inf. Sci. **43**, 88–102 (2017). https://doi.org/10.1177/0165551515617393
46. Shaffer, D.W., et al.: Epistemic network analysis: a prototype for 21st-century assessment of learning. Int. J. Learn. Media **1**, 33–53 (2009). https://doi.org/10.1162/ijlm.2009.0013
47. Shaffer, D.W., Collier, W., Ruis, A.R.: A tutorial on epistemic network analysis: analyzing the structure of connections in cognitive, social, and interaction data. J. Learn. Anal. **3**, 9–45 (2016). https://doi.org/10.18608/jla.2016.33.3
48. Perrin, A., Anderson, M.: Share of U.S. adults using social media, including Facebook, is mostly unchanged since (2018). https://www.pewresearch.org/fact-tank/2019/04/10/share-of-u-s-adults-using-social-media-including-facebook-is-mostly-unchanged-since-2018/
49. Honeychurch, S., Patrick, F.: Massive Open Online Courses as affinity spaces for connected learning: Exploring effective learning interactions in one massive online community. Res. Comparative Int. Educ. **13**(1), 117–134 (2018). https://doi.org/10.1177/1745499918768112

Civil Discourse as a Depolarization Strategy: An Exploration of Gen Z Dialogue Using Epistemic Network Analysis and Reflexive Thematic Analysis

Liane Weintraub(✉)

Graduate School of Education and Psychology, Pepperdine University, Malibu, CA, USA
liane.weintraub@pepperdine.edu

Abstract. This paper investigates the impact of engagement in civil discourse on a group of U.S. college students. To address rising antagonism among groups and individuals with differing ideologies, an intervention was designed to test whether dialogue can be depolarizing. Although dialogic tools have been touted throughout the historical literature, little research exists into the efficacy of such methods in the context of contemporary polarization. Furthermore, the discourse dynamics of Generation Z have not been widely studied. This study employed epistemic network analysis to examine the discourse patterns that emerged in a facilitated group dialogue among 26 students and 19 individual, follow-up interviews. Additionally, reflexive thematic analysis was used to further analyze and interpret patterns and themes within data. The research results indicate that engaging in civil discourse had a substantial effect on subjects' attitudes, beliefs, and behaviors.

Keywords: Polarization · Civil Discourse · Gen Z · Dialogue · Social Media

1 Introduction

This paper explores the effects of a civil discourse intervention intended to test whether dialogue can be depolarized in a group of Generation Z (Gen Z) college students. Animosity between groups and individuals with opposing viewpoints is a long-standing cultural phenomenon that has recently increased dramatically. Today, the level of American polarization is considered pervasive and dangerous [1, 2]. The result is a prevailing culture characterized by widespread antagonism and a breakdown in public and private discourse [3]. In the place of pluralistic conversation intended to increase understanding, ideological adversaries resort to shouting and demeaning each other on and offline. The polarization problem is further fueled by social media algorithms that limit diverse beliefs from broad dissemination [4], thus amplifying tensions among racial, ethnic, economic, and other groups. The breakdown in discourse is evident in recent conflicts erupting across the U.S., particularly on university campuses, prompting scholars and legislators to seek strategies to repair the fraying relationship between opposing groups and, in particular, among Gen Z.

Y. J. Kim and Z. Swiecki (Eds.): icqe 2024, CCIS 2279, pp. 258–272, 2024.
https://doi.org/10.1007/978-3-031-76332-8_21

1.1 Gen Z Discourse Dynamics

Gen Z, born between 1997 and 2012, accounts for 46 million Americans, or 14% of the population [5, 6]. They are more racially and ethnically diverse than previous generations, with a bare majority of non-Hispanic Whites–52% versus 61% of Millennials [7]. Most of the cohort are students, and as today's young adults who have recently or will soon enter the workforce, Gen Z already has a powerful influence on popular culture, social and educational trends, and sociopolitical issues. American Gen Z has lived through global crises, including 9/11, the Great Recession, and the COVID-19 pandemic, and has grown up with routine school shootings and lockdowns. According to generations scholar Twenge [8], these events informed Gen Z's beliefs and behaviors, including their social attitudes and political stances. Gen Z is conspicuously politically active and vocal about social issues and is visibly leading efforts to rethink and redefine many longstanding social norms such as gender, sexuality, mental health, neurotypicality, and religion. Gen Z is also spearheading calls for increased diversity, equity, and inclusion (DEI) initiatives and corporate and government transparency.

The literature on polarization within Gen Z is sparse, perhaps because much of the generation is still in adolescence. One relevant study [9] of 44 college students found that prior to responding to measures of polarization, the subjects reported feeling relatively immune to polarization and undivided in supporting human rights and social issues (e.g., LGBTQ rights, racial issues, and climate change). Their surveys revealed significant affective polarization: 68% reported unfavorable views of the opposing party, 41% felt it was important to live among people with shared values, and 59% are politically aligned with their close friends. However, after learning about the causes and impacts of polarization and engaging in dialogue with fellow subjects, the group reconsidered their positions. Although the sample size is small, the study suggests that when they are aware of the adverse effects of polarization, Gen Z may be open to civil discourse to bridge their divides.

1.2 Digital Nativity

Gen Z is the first *digitally native* generation, with technology—specifically social media—permeating every facet of their lives [10]. Gardner and Davis [11] contended that technology significantly shapes our sense of identity and our relationships, and that Gen Z "thinks of the world as an ensemble of apps" (p. 8). Ropolyi [12] proposed a theory of *web-life* in which the current generation regards technology as their contextual situation rather than a collection of tools. In web-life, Gen Z does not simply use the Internet; they exist online. This seamlessness between online and offline life is a defining characteristic of Gen Z's identity and worldview. Technology is not only Gen Z's chosen source for social interaction, but also for news and information. One third of Americans under age 30 regularly get news from TikTok [13].

Apps alter users' cognitive processes and relational intimacy, a construct that is central to understanding Gen Z social relationships. Because digital technologies reduce face-to-face interactions and reinforce superficial connections, the generation is more likely to feel disconnected and isolated and to approach relationships as transactions. Turkle [14] asserted that the predominance of digital existence has a devastating effect on Gen Z's communication dynamics by reducing authenticity in interactions due to online identities that are curated rather than genuine. This inauthenticity impedes empathic concern. Furthermore, ever-present, distracting apps result in *continuous partial attention* in which individuals divide the focus they should give each other. Consequently, Gen Z's discourse tends to be inattentive, unfocused, and easily diverted.

1.3 Online Tribalism

In 2002, Sunstein [15] posited the *law of group polarization,* which asserted that collective deliberation on an issue–be it gun control, affirmative action, or another policy topic–invariably leads individuals to adopt more extreme positions (i.e., to radicalize) than they held prior to the group discussion. This tendency toward extremist tribal in-group associations prompted Sunstein to caution that such social cascades may become "consequences of the Internet" (p. 1). Indeed, two decades later, research indicates that online tribalism fuels American affective polarization [16].

The human instinct to form tribalistic associations is grounded in evolutionary theory [17]. Early tribes (i.e., ancestral clans) banded together to increase their chances of survival. Such tribal loyalties can have protective qualities, such as fostering a sense of community and belonging and instilling a desire to preserve shared culture and traditions. However, tribalism can also have a negative side, contributing to tribal biases that distort beliefs and intensify animus towards out-groups. Social scientists contend that this deep-rooted impulse to seek homophily underpins the in-group support and out-group scorn that characterizes contemporary society [18]. Polarization over-simplifies social conflicts into an us-versus-them binary, which leads to the false conclusion that disputes are between camps rather than individuals.

Digital platforms are particularly adept at fanning tribal loyalties. Through content-promoting algorithms, finding like-minded others is not left up to users. By design, users receive information that is either consistent with their attitudes [19] or so divergent from their leanings that it provokes fury [20]. In this way, social media capitalizes on the hardwired human drive for belonging by encouraging the curation of homophilic communities. As it happens, Gen Z has a proclivity to homophily that is bolstered by social media *filter bubbles* that cause users to interact only with like-minded others, resulting in intellectual and ideological silos Sunstein [21].

1.4 Discourse and Polarization in the Academy

A large percentage of Gen Z is of college age (the median age of Gen Z is 18.5). Data indicates that they will be the most educated generation on record, with 57% of 18 to 21-year-olds no longer in high school enrolled in college as of 2018 [7]. Therefore, discourse in the academy affects a substantial portion of the Gen Z population. The current state of campus discourse and polarization in higher education has dominated national headlines and sparked widespread debate [22, 23]. Academic freedom protections, the hallmark of educational institutions which should allow students, faculty, and administrators to hold and express opinions without fear of censorship or negative consequences have been increasingly challenged [23]. Instances of disinvited speakers [24], classroom disruptions, and dismissal of faculty with controversial viewpoints [23] underscore the fragile state of free expression on campuses. These conditions stifle intellectual diversity and create an atmosphere of fear and self-censorship [25].

Such practices contribute to a climate of intolerance for critical thought and uncomfortable discourse in favor of safe (but unproductive) consensus. Bordone and colleagues at the Harvard Negotiation and Mediation Clinical Program (HNMCP) detected a noticeable shift in the tone and content of political discussions in law school classes [26]. Whereas future lawyers once engaged in robust debate about polarizing topics (e.g., gender, violence, or rape), current students steer clear of controversy by engaging in self-censorship. HNMCP identified two dynamics contributing to the current state of discourse in higher education. First, that students were unaware of the value of engaging in collective problem-solving. Second, that students were unskilled at navigating conversations about areas of disagreement. Consequently, the quality of dialogue on campuses has deteriorated and undermines the educational mission of universities to cultivate critical thinking and expose students to a variety of perspectives.

2 Theory

2.1 Social Identity Theory

Social identity theory is a psychological framework that seeks to explain how individuals categorize themselves and others into social groups. Proposed by Tajfel and Turner in 1979 [27], the theory explores the cognitive processes that underlie group identification. Social identity theory posits that individuals derive a significant part of their self-concept (i.e., sense of self) from their perceived memberships in social groups such as nationality, religion, and political affiliation. This self-categorization affects how individuals perceive and interact with members of their own groups (i.e., the in-group) and those of other groups (i.e., the out-groups). The theory holds that human beings naturally practice in-group favoritism and reject the out-group with whom we do not identify. While this behavior fosters protective factors such as self-esteem and a sense of belonging, it can also perpetuate prejudice and discrimination.

Intergroup discrimination is the foundation of polarization [28]. When the outcome of in-group affiliation is an "us versus them" mentality marked by excessive punishment or disparagement of the out-group, the societal impact can be intensely harmful. Affiliation can easily morph into tribalism—particularly when it is encouraged by social media algorithms—leading to the sort of animosity that polarization scholars point to as destructive and dangerous [1, 4, 29]. It should be noted that political and social scientists do not point to a lack of consensus as the troubling aspect of polarization, but rather to a divided populace that is increasingly unable to interact conversationally and who no longer agree on fundamental shared values.

2.2 Discourse and Interpersonal Communication Theories

The roots of discourse theory can be traced to ancient Greece. Philosophers Aristotle and Plato explored rhetoric as a tool for persuasion and for shaping public opinion and society. Twentieth-century communication scholars (a selection of whom are cited herein) regarded dialogue as fundamental to effective human relationships. Buber's [30] philosophy of dialogue suggests that verbal encounters between individuals constitute the basis of human existence and that when managed correctly, dialogue brings us closer to each other. Rogers' [31] humanism—the foundation of person-centered psychotherapy—advocated approaching others with unconditional positive regard and restating the other person's beliefs and position (a rhetorical method based on Aristotle). Bohm [32] developed a method of respectful exchange in which each party suspends spoken or unspoken responses or criticism until the speaker has concluded. Gadamer's [33] hermeneutics theory offers a framework for understanding and communication through interpersonal give-and-take. Collectively, discourse theories emphasize civility through tools such as active listening, suspension of judgment and the iterative exchange of ideas to cultivate mutual understanding and social cohesion.

2.3 Civil Discourse as a Depolarization Strategy

Today, incivility pervades both the public and private sectors. Because uncivil rhetoric is characterized by intensity and loudness, acrimonious and hostile discourse is more easily heard above the fray. Therefore, incivility tends to impart a sense of validity through its volume, which may imply that larger numbers hold the viewpoints expressed than is the case (Shaffer, 2020). Today, dozens of organizations committed to depolarization are using civil discourse interventions. They employ dialogic tools rooted in ancient Greek philosophy and informed by modern era discourse scholarship. These organizations focus on convening diverse groups to engage in civil conversation in the hope that ideologically divided individuals will find common ground. In the U.S., Living Room Conversations, Braver Angels, and BridgeUSA (a student-led group) are among the best known. However, little research exists into the impact and efficacy of such methods to restore civil discourse in today's polarized climate. Furthermore, research into the discourse dynamics of Gen Z is especially sparse. Consequently, the present study aimed to explore two research questions:

- **RQ1:** What discourse patterns emerge when Gen Z members engage in respectful dialogue about polarizing topics?
- **RQ2:** How does engagement in respectful dialogue impact Gen Z's preconceived social attitudes?

3 Methods

3.1 Context, Design, and Participants

This study involved two sources of data collected from American Gen Z (18+) university students in 2023. To ensure a diverse representation within the sample, participants were recruited from various types of institutions, including private, public, and faith-based institutions and two-year, four-year, and master's programs. Although 55 students initially volunteered, only the data collected from the 26 students who participated in the intervention are included in the first dataset. Those 26 participants signed informed consent forms prior to attending a two-hour facilitated group dialogue, or "salon," in a private home, during which they discussed social issues that are often polarizing. The contents of the dialogue were video and audio recorded. After the salon, 19 students volunteered to submit to one-on-one, semi-structured interviews that were scheduled between two- and four-weeks post-intervention. The interviews were video and audio recorded, and all 19 transcripts were included in the second dataset.

3.2 Data Collection and Analysis

Salon Dataset Coding. Two codebooks were developed using a priori constructs related to the literature on polarization and Gen Z. The salon codebook contained four overarching thematic constructs (*anxiousness, solidarity, negativity*, and *homophily*) and two codes intended to capture the emotional valence of the discourse (*hopeful* and *hopeless*). The six themes in the salon codebook are seen in Table 1. Every utterance (i.e., turn of talk) was represented by one line of data. Each turn of talk was independently coded by two raters who then engaged in a process of social moderation to reach consensus on the final coding of 201utterances [34].

Interviews Dataset Coding. Twenty-four open-ended interview questions were divided into three temporal frames that addressed the participants' reflections on the time periods before (questions 1–8), during (questions 9–16), and after the intervention (questions 17–24). The 19 interview transcripts were compiled into a dataset. 11 themes were independently coded by two raters and socially moderated to reach consensus on the final coding of 1,053 utterances [34]. The interviews codebook is seen in Table 2.

Six of the interview codes overlapped with the salon codebook (*anxiousness, solidarity, negativity, homophily, hopeful,* and *hopeless*). Five additional codes were unique to the interview dataset (openness *to discourse, wariness or partisanship, civic interest, mindset shift*, and *behavior shift*). The codes *mindset shift* and *behavior shift* were intended to capture statements in which participants indicated a change in attitude or behavior. These two themes were only coded for utterances that were temporally situated during and after the salon (i.e., answers to questions 9–24).

3.3 Epistemic Network Analysis (ENA)

ENA is a quantitative, computational tool that graphically represents patterns or relationships within discourse networks [35]. By expressing and quantifying relationships between coded constructs, the ENA web tool [36] produces a visual output (i.e., a graph or model) representing connections among discourse themes. In this way, qualitative data can be analyzed quantitatively. In ENA models, dots represent nodes (coded constructs), which are labeled. The edges (lines) connecting the nodes illustrate the associations between them, with varying thicknesses indicating the strength and significance of these connections. Thicker lines signify stronger associations suggesting heightened interrelation or increased frequency of co-occurrence, whereas thinner lines denote weaker or less substantial associations. In the present study, ENA was used to was used to address

Table 1. Salon Codebook

Code	Description	Utterance Example(s)
Anxiousness	This code encompasses expressions of: 1. Concern for country (worry over the state of America, democracy, or society) 2. Disparagement of authority (scorn or mocking of older generations, lawmakers, government, or elites) 3. Disapproval of social media (negativity about social media or technology) 4. Worry about the future (generalized concern) 5. Wish for change (wanting different leaders, processes, social behaviors)	1. *"It's impossible to really get anything done or come together and solve any of the big issues plaguing our society"* 2. *"Now it's like theater politics where [politicians] play to their audience and using their unwillingness almost like to score political points."* 3. *"You're either going to see that bubble, that echo chamber, or something that is designed to make you mad. Those are the 2 ways you can engage with it -- agreement or sheer opposition."* 4. *"Is this system still kind of broken, or do people have power behind the vote? And how do we convince people? Because I don't know."* 5. *"If parents aren't really emphasizing that discourse of trying to listen to the other side, you know it becomes difficult to even have a discourse to begin with."*
Solidarity	Expression of caring for another's feelings or well-being	*"People just want to really belong in a community and to fit in. I think that's what it really is about."*
Negativity	This code encompasses expressions of: 1. Frustration, skepticism, or anger (includes unhappiness, disapproval, irritation, or cynical statement) 2. Partisan antipathy (partisan superiority, denigration of another party or political figure) 3. Respectful disagreement (civil dissent with the views/ideas of another)	1. *"Everyone's so angry, so frightened in their corners, that we can't just come together and make a decision to benefit all of us."* *"We can now just be anonymous online and do what? And [one person can have] 1,500 accounts to just spew whatever rhetoric."* 2. *"Everyone's so angry, so frightened in their corners, that we can't just come together and make a decision that's going to benefit all of us."* 3. *"I don't necessarily fully agree with the idea that America was set up to be a true democracy."*
Homophily	This code encompasses expressions of: 1. Agreement or affiliation (accord with another participant's expressed views) 2. Supportive approval (support for another; encouragement)	1. *"That's participation … Right? I mean, it's having the people take the power back."* 2. *"And along the lines of that, I feel like you said it before …"*
Hopeful	Positive outlook/valence (optimism or upbeat attitude toward self & society)	*"Everyone around our age needs to step up and really hold accountability and get involved and share our voices."*
Hopeless	Negative outlook/valence (pessimism or despairing attitude toward self & society)	*"There's a real breakdown in our society of physical meeting spaces ... you can be walking down the street and everyone's wearing headphones, right?"*

both research questions. By constructing network models that captured the structural relationships between themes in the salon data, the software illuminated underlying dynamics in the discourse. For the salon dataset, the unit of analysis was "speaker" and a window size of 7 was used [37]. For the interviews dataset, the unit of analysis was "speaker" grouped by "question number" so that networks were generated for all participants' responses to every question. These networks were then aggregated by "question group" to analyze the networks according to the temporal frames within which the questions were situated. The "whole conversation" option was used because the dataset was monologic. That is, each transcript was from a single participant and did not represent a dialogue [38].

Table 2. Interviews Codebook

Code	Temporal Frame	Description	Utterance Example(s)
Anxiousness	Before, during salon, after intervention	Worry over the state of America, democracy, society, or the future -- this may include scorn or disapproval of authority, government, social systems, or technology tools and a wish for change	*"I don't want to be labeled as such, or labeled as another thing, and say something wrong."* *"Just thinking about what this means for our future, like for future generations."* *"It's like uncertainty, like, what direction are we going in?"*
Solidarity	Before, during salon, after intervention	Expression of respect, concern, connection, curiosity, or caring for the feelings and well-being of others	*"I feel like I learned so much from hearing from other people … it was just a very nice, comfortable environment."*
Negativity	Before, during salon, after intervention	Expression of dissent with the views or ideas of another; anger, unhappiness, disapproval, or cynicism; partisan superiority or denigration of a political ideology or figure	*"I may have disagreed with someone's opinions or been very against them."* *"I think I was a bit exhausted from just a lot of the trauma that came from talking about politics."*
Homophily	Before, during salon, after intervention	Expression of agreement or approval of ideas shared by other participants	*"I think that literally everyone agreed on everything we talked about honestly, maybe even too much."*
Hopeful	Before, during salon, after intervention	Positive outlook/valence – Expression of upbeat attitude toward self & society	*"Everyone can be respectful of each other and their opinions, and that's exactly what it was, so it was great."*
Hopeless	Before, during salon, after intervention	Negative outlook/valence -- Expression of pessimistic attitude toward self & society	*"We have 10 hours of screen time a day and have really been disconnected from each other and like the world."*
Openness to discourse	Before, during salon, after intervention	Habit of positive interactions or desire to engage with others who have different backgrounds, values, or political attitudes	*"I would definitely say that I'm regularly talking about social issues, probably mostly with my parents."*
Wariness or partisanism	Before, during salon, after intervention	Experience of negative interactions or aversion to engaging with others who have different backgrounds, values, or political attitudes	*"Usually when I engage with people who have different opinions, it's less of a debate. Like [it's] non-negotiable, and I need to change your opinion."*
Civic interest	Before, during salon, after intervention	Interest in social issues, engagement in current events; current activism or a desire to participate in the public sphere	*"To me, antisemitism isn't a political issue, it's a human rights issue. People should care about Jewish people."*
Mindset shift	During salon, after intervention	Expression of change in mindset, outlook, or attitude	*"I was so shocked and surprised in the best way possible by so many people, and their kindness."*
Behavior shift	During salon, after intervention	Expression of novel or altered behavior or intention to change behavior	*"I think I have a different interest now in being maybe more involved in the public policy aspect."*

3.4 Reflexive Thematic Analysis (RTA)

RTA offered a helpful complement to ENA to explore participants' experiences of mindset and behavior shifts since the salon [39]. RTA is a way of interpreting qualitative data that emphasizes the active role of the researcher in understanding the data, promoting a thoughtful and reflective engagement with the data and the analytical process. Specifically, RTA was used to further address RQ 2 (how does engagement in respectful dialogue impact Gen Z's preconceived social attitudes?) by exploring participants' direct quotes related to mindset and behavior shifts in the coded data.

4 Results

4.1 Discourse Patterns: ENA Models

Salon Discourse. The complete ENA network model of the salon data in Fig. 1 shows connections in the salon discourse. The model shows the strongest connections between *negativity* and *homophily*, *negativity* and *anxiousness*, and *anxiousness* and *homophily*. It is clear that participants made stronger associations among negative valence codes than positive valence codes. This is reflected in the frequency counts of negative codes such as *anxiousness* (71%) and *negativity* (57.5%) which were far higher than positive codes like *solidarity* (27%) and *hopeful* (17.5%).

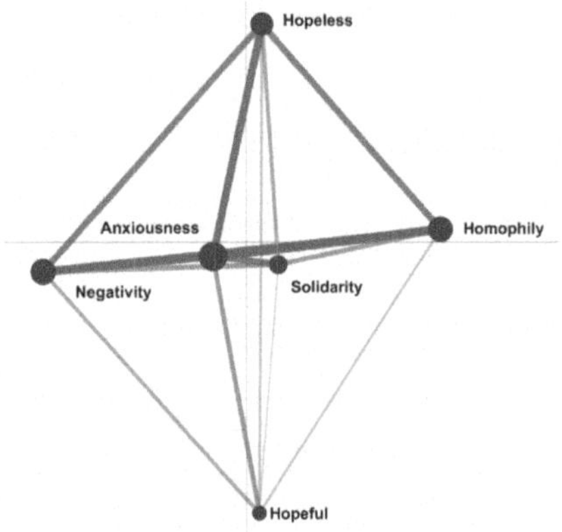

Fig. 1. ENA network model of salon discourse

Participants' Direct Quotes. Anonymized participants' comments—frequently centered on fears and concerns about the state of the country—reflect these findings.

•Jonathan: Our country exists in such a polarized state right now. It's impossible to really get anything done or come together and solve any of the big issues plaguing our society. If people are so up in arms with each other, they can't even have a normal conversation.
•Alex: I also think that the norms of debate and the norms of the legislature are kind of falling apart. There's kind of this idea that you respect and acknowledge what has been said from the opposition, and I think that as we become more polarized, it's really devolved to where people aren't willing to even come to the table.
•James: Unfortunately, the educational system in the US is crumbling a bit, at least cracking. And I think, without repairing that you're not going to get people that are able to converse with the other side.

Interviews Discourse. The complete ENA network model of the 19 interviews is shown in Fig. 2. The most prominent connections depicted in this model are among the positive valence codes. This graph visually reflects the greater frequencies of positive codes such as *openness to discourse* (42.7%), *hopefulness* (34.85%), *civic interest* (32.86%), and *solidarity* (21.08%). In contrast, the model shows weaker connections among more negative codes. This was also reflected in the frequency counts of *negativity* (8.17%), *anxiousness* (16.05%), and *hopelessness* (12.25%).

The ENA models in Figs. 1 and 2 highlight a stark difference in the emotional tones of the salon and interviews discourse. While the data is insufficient to generalize, it suggests that the overall tone of the salon was largely pessimistic whereas the interviews were mainly optimistic.

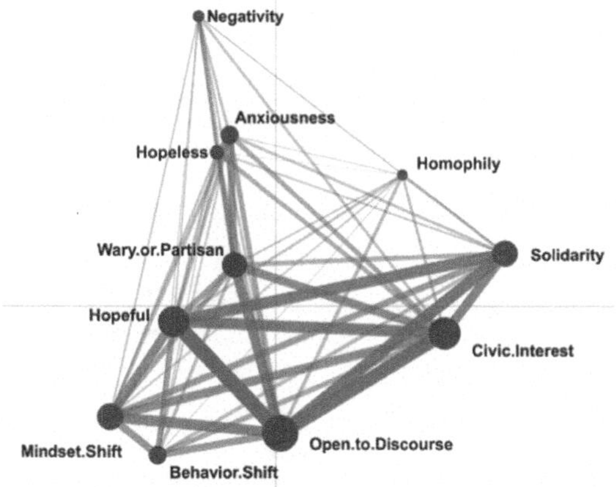

Fig. 2. ENA network model of interviews discourse

Figures 3a-b depict the ENA models of connections participants made when they reflected on different temporal frames related to the salon. Figure 3a shows the model associated with the pre-intervention time period (the network of questions 1–8) minus the network of network of their reflections on their experiences post-intervention (questions 17–24). Figure 3b shows the model related to during the intervention (questions 9–16) subtracted from the post-intervention network (questions 17–24). Both models indicate that participants made wholly different connections when reflecting on their attitudes pre- and during versus the post-intervention time period. They appeared to make strong connections to mindset shift and behavior shift when discussing the post-salon topics, and relatively fewer connections to either of the "shift" themes when answering questions about their pre- and during experiences. Although it is not possible to draw inferences about the details of the discourse, the network representations are compelling and may imply that participants underwent changes in their beliefs and attitudes.

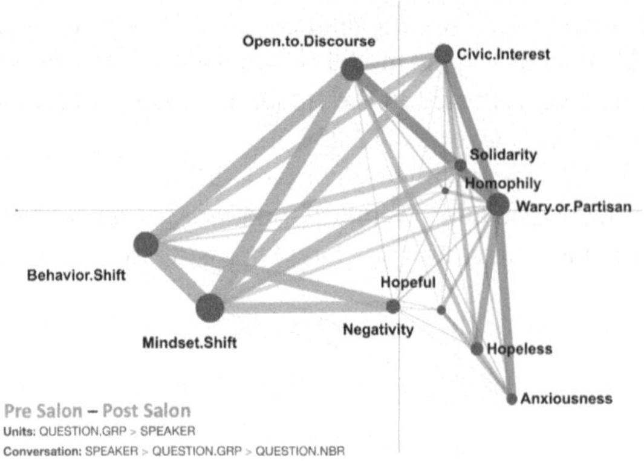

a. Interviews discourse by temporal frame (pre-minus-post)

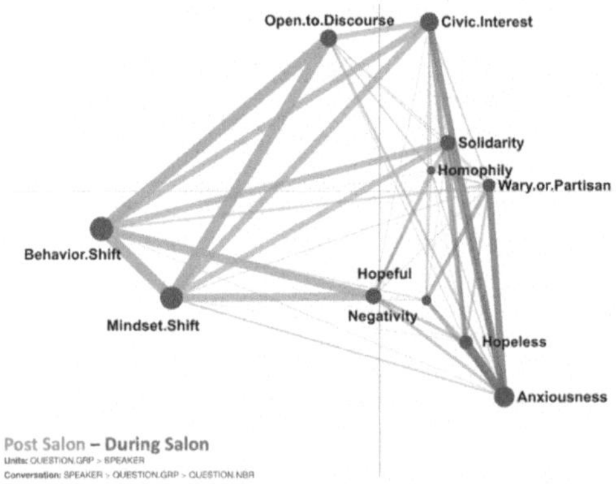

b. Interviews discourse by temporal frame (post-minus-during)

Fig. 3. a. Interviews discourse by temporal frame (pre-minus-post). b. Interviews discourse by temporal frame (post-minus-during).

4.2 Mindset and Behavior Shifts: RTA

RTA was used to delve deeper into the nature of the association between the salon experience and shifts in participants' attitudes and behaviors (highlighted by the ENA models shown in Figs. 3a-b). *Mindset shift* was one of the most frequently occurring codes with every interview participant ($n = 19$) coded for mindset shift. On average, each participant referenced a mindset shift 12.42 times during their interview session. Additionally, all but one ($n = 18$) were coded for *behavior shift* and each of them referenced a behavior shift 6.32 times. These frequencies suggest that participants' thoughts, attitudes, and behaviors were different after the salon. Table 3 provides samples of responses that were coded as mindset or behavior shifts.

Table 3. Mindset and Behavior Shift Sample Utterances

Name	Mindset Shift: Sample Utterance	Behavior Shift: Sample Utterance
Alex Male White Democrat	*I did feel a kind of new sense of emboldment to potentially discuss this, and bold is the wrong word. More maybe comfortability, maybe new hope.*	*I realized with the rush of emotions that come from being on a political side … I knew I had to digest and think carefully about how I respond to make it practical and productive.*
Anamaria Female Hispanic Democrat	*It's allowed me to be more open with my opinions amongst my friends or colleagues or classmates.*	*I felt way more confident to just share my opinion than I think I had weeks prior, months prior.*
Andrew Male White Independent	*The thing is like shifting that starting point for how you see people you know? People can then obviously reveal themselves to be closed-minded or open-minded*	*I was just like, okay, let's just slow down and try to find where the actual disagreement is, because sometimes it's in a different spot than you anticipate*
James Male White Independent	*People want to at the end of the day to agree and make the world a better place ... I think there's a willingness to learn more than potentially I've given people credit for.*	*I think, taking a step further and saying … how do we take this issue and kind of reconcile what we think about and turn it into something productive?*
Lauren Female Black Democrat	Q: Do you feel that those types of conversations are different for you after the salon than prior to the event? A: *Most definitely [...] I feel more educated and I feel like I'm able to have an argument, and I'm able to defend it.*	Q: Do you feel in the future that you will be more likely to engage in those kinds of dialogue? A: Yes … *If anything, I want to hear the opposite of my argument, so I can learn something new.*
Michael Male Asian Democrat	*I think it made me more likely to engage with dialogue, because it was a lot easier in that environment.*	*In the future I'm going to try to like, replicate some of that environment where you kind of just take turns rather than like trying to talk over each other.*
Patty Other White Democrat	*Since then [the salon] I've definitely been wanting to put even more open mindedness forward and I want to put a lot more effort into these conversations.*	*I definitely think that I would be able and more willing to have a dialogue and try to make it a healthy, open dialogue, with the intention of learning.*
Penelope Female Asian Democrat	*I wouldn't say I feel differently about a certain issue, but I am more open minded to other individuals' opinions.*	*I think I would be more I guess, willing to hear it out from the beginning to the end … I would give more time to hear them out on an issue.*
Rosalie Female Other Other	*After [the salon], I feel like I'm very open to hearing why people believe certain things, and that's what I actually really enjoyed … it made me way more open minded.*	*I still want to use my platform to speak up but I want to do it correctly. I don't want to do it with animosity. I don't want to do it with any type of anger or resentment.*
Susie Female White Republican	*Being around other people who were expressing their opinions and watching them, I'm like, oh, they're safe.*	*I would just be so much smarter and more confident with who I am as a person if I was having conversations like that even once a week … I feel ready to talk about the world that I'm a part of.*
Veronica Female Black Republican	*It was a great experience in just having humility and listening to others, and just really getting to know other people and not seeing them as … liberal or conservative*	*It was a nice start to get back into that space, and it made me excited to have conversations like this in the future.*

5 Discussion

The first finding that there was a difference in the emotional tones between the salon discussions and the post-intervention interviews suggest several possibilities. One possibility is that in the collective setting, the participants were more disposed to focus on the negative, sharing their concerns about the state of society while privately maintaining hopes for positive outcomes which they shared only during their interviews. Another possibility is that participants may have experienced a dispositional shift between the salon and the follow-up interviews. In this case, it is possible that participating in a structured dialogue with enforced norms of civility may have had a therapeutic effect on participants' general outlooks. The collective environment may thus serve as a catalyst for more emotionally charged conversations, potentially due to the immediacy of social support and peer influence. The shift in emotional tone from the salon to the post-intervention interviews suggests that the passage of time may have softened participants' outlooks or that the temporal gap could have allowed participants to process and reflect on their experiences.

The second finding of an association between the salon experience and mindset and behavior shifts indicates a possible perceived positive evolution in participants' cognitive and behavioral patterns. While causality cannot be established, the finding suggests the potential of civil discourse not only to facilitate respectful conversation about difficult topics but also to catalyze meaningful personal growth and change.

The RTA of participants' utterance revealed several overarching themes:

- Increased open-mindedness (e.g., "It's allowed me to be more open with my opinions" and "I am more open minded to other individuals' opinions")
- Greater hope and comfort (e.g., "I did feel a kind of new sense of emboldment… Maybe new hope")
- Personal growth (e.g., "I feel more educated and I feel like I'm able to have an argument and I'm able to defend it")
- Increased empathy and understanding (e.g., "People at the end of the day want to agree and make the world a better place" and "I don't want to do it with animosity")
- Increased confidence (e.g., "If you want to make a change, you're the only person who can do that" and "I definitely feel more confident being the young people who are willing to talk about these issues")
- Reflective behavior (e.g., "Moving forward, I will be more mindful of the way I write things or the way I speak" and "I definitely think I would be able to have a dialogue…with the intention of learning")

These self-reported transformations suggest that engaging in structured, respectful dialogue may have served as a catalyst for personal and potentially depolarizing change. Such evidence lends credence to the hypothesis that civil discourse, when facilitated effectively, holds the power to transcend entrenched viewpoints, fostering an environment where shared humanity and understanding can begin to mitigate societal divides. The nature of these shifts—ranging from subtle alterations in perceptions to more pronounced behavioral changes—carries with it the promise of sustained impact. If such transformations can be nurtured and retained over time, the implications for societal polarization are profound. The ripple effects of individual change could collectively contribute to a social fabric that is more resilient to the forces of division and more receptive to diverse perspectives. Collectively, the interpretations of the study's key findings indicate that civil discourse is not just a theoretical ideal, but that it can offer a pragmatic path towards bridging ideological chasms with empathy, respect, and a shared commitment to the common good.

Acknowledgments. The author wishes to recognize the efforts of the research team in coding the data included in the analysis, including Jessica Ariazza and Haille Trimboli.

Disclosure of Interests. The author has no competing interests to declare that are relevant to the content of this article.

References

1. Somer, M., McCoy, J.L., Luke, R.E.: Pernicious polarization, autocratization, and opposition strategies. Democratization **28**(5), 929–948 (2021)
2. Pew Research Center: Americans' feelings about politics, polarization, and the tone of political discourse (2023). https://www.pewresearch.org/politics/2023/09/19/
3. Bougher, L.D.: The correlates of discord: Identity, issue alignment, and political hostility in polarized America. Polit. Behav. **39**(3), 731–762 (2017)
4. Harel, T.O., Jameson, J.K., Maoz, I.: The normalization of hatred: Identity, affective polarization, and dehumanization on Facebook in the context of intractable political conflict. Soc. Media + Soc. **6**(2), 1–10 (2020)
5. Dimock, M.: Defining generations: Where millennials end and generation z begins. Pew Research Center (2019). http://www.pewresearch.org/fact-tank/2019/01/17/
6. Merriman, M., Oktem, C.: Why Gen Z matters and what boards should know. EY Center for Board Matters (2022) https://www.ey.com/en_us/board-matters/
7. Parker, K., Igielnik, R.: On the cusp of adulthood and facing an uncertain future. Pew Research Center (2020). https://www.pewresearch.org/social-trends/2020/05/14/
8. Twenge, J.M.: Generations: The Real Differences Between Gen Z, Millennials, Gen x, Boomers, and Silents-and What They Mean for the Future. Atria Books, New York, NY (2023)
9. McBeth, M.K., Belyea, J., Perry, A.: Dalton and putnam: teaching political polarization to generation Z students. Polit. Sci. Polit. **54**(4), 750–754 (2021)
10. Bhalla, R., Tiwari, P., Chowdhary, N.: Digital natives leading the world: Paragons and values of Generation Z. In: Stylos, N., Rahimi, R., Okumus, B., Williams, S. (eds.) Generation Z Marketing and Management in Tourism and Hospitality, pp. 3–23. Springer, Cham (2021). https://doi.org/10.1007/978-3-030-70695-1_1
11. Gardner, H., Davis, K.: The App Generation: How Today's Youth Navigate Identity, Intimacy, and Imagination in a Digital World. Yale University Press, New Haven, CT (2013)
12. Ropolyi, L.: Toward a philosophy of the Internet. Philos. Comput. **17**(2), 40–49 (2018)
13. Matsa, K.E.: More American are getting news on TikTok, bucking the trend seen on most other news sites. Pew Research Center (2023). https://www.pewresearch.org/short-reads/2023/11/15/
14. Turkle, S.: Alone Together: Why We Expect More From Technology and Less from Each Other. Hachette Book Group, New York, NY (2017)
15. Sunstein, C.R.: The law of group polarization. J. Polit. Philos. **10**, 175–195 (1999)
16. Whitt, S., et al.: Tribalism in America: behavioral experiments on affective polarization in the Trump era. J. Exp. Polit. Sci. **8**(3), 247–259 (2021)
17. Clark, C.J., Liu, B.S., Winegard, B.M., Ditto, P.H.: Tribalism is human nature. Curr. Dir. Psychol. Sci. **28**(6), 587–592 (2019)
18. Hobfoll, S.E.: Tribalism: The Evolutionary Origins of Fear Politics. Palgrave Macmillan, Cham, Switzerland (2018)
19. Cinelli, M., De Francisci Morales, G., Galeazzi, A., Quattrociocchi, W., Starnini, M.: The echo chamber effect on social media. Proc. Natl. Acad. Sci. **118**(9), e2023301118 (2021)
20. Rogers, N., Jones, J.J.: Using Twitter bios to measure changes in self-identity: are Americans defining themselves more politically over time? J. Soc. Comput. **2**(1), 1–13 (2021)
21. Sunstein, C.R.: # Republic: Divided Democracy in the Age of Social Media. Princeton University Press, Princeton, NJ (2018)

22. Carter, . L.: College is all About Curiosity and that Requires Free Speech. The New York Times magazine (2024)
23. Kaufmann, E.: Academic freedom in crisis: punishment, political discrimination, and self-censorship. Center Study Partisanship Ideol. **2**, 1–195 (2021)
24. FIRE: 2021 college free speech rankings. https://www.thefire.org/research/publications/student-surveys/2021-college-free-speech-rankings/. Last accessed 27 May 2024
25. Heterodox: 2022 campus expression survey report. https://heterodoxacademy.org/reports/2022-campus-expression-survey-report/. Last 27 May 2024
26. Bordone, R.C.: Building conflict resilience: it's not just about problem-solving. J. Dispute Resol. **1**, 65–69 (2018)
27. Tajfel, H., Turner, J.C.: An integrative theory of intergroup conflict. In: Hatch, M.J., Schultz, M. (eds.) Organizational Identity: A Reader, pp. 56–65. Oxford University Press, Oxford, UK (1979)
28. Harel, T.O., Maoz, I., Halperin, E.: A conflict within a conflict: Intragroup ideological polarization and intergroup intractable conflict. Curr. Opin. Behav. Sci. **34**, 52–57 (2020)
29. Iyengar, S., Lelkes, Y., Levendusky, M., Malhotra, N., Westwood, S.J.: The origins and consequences of affective polarization in the United States. Annu. Rev. Polit. Sci. **22**(1), 129–146 (2019)
30. Buber, M.: I and Thou. Martino Publishing, Mansfield Centre, CT (2010; originally published in 1923)
31. Rogers, C.R.: On Becoming a Person. Houghton Mifflin, New York, NY (1995; originally published in 1960)
32. Bohm, D.: On Dialogue. Routledge, New York, NY (2004; originally published in 1996)
33. Gadamer, H.G.: Philosophical Hermeneutics. Univ. Cal. Press, Berkeley, CA (1977)
34. Herrenkohl, L.R., Cornelius, L.: Investigating elementary students' scientific and historical argumentation. J. Learn. Sci. **22**(3), 413–461 (2013)
35. Shaffer, D.W., Collier, W., Ruis, A.R.: A tutorial on epistemic network analysis: Analyzing the structure of connections in cognitive, social, and interaction data. J. Learn. Anal. **3**(3), 9–45 (2016)
36. Marquart, C.L., Hinojosa, C., Swiecki, Z., Eagan, B., Shaffer, D.W.: Epistemic network analysis, version 1.7.0 [Computer software] (2021)
37. Ruis, A., Siebert-Evenstone, A., Pozen, R., Eagan, B., Shaffer, D.W.: Finding common ground: a method for measuring recent temporal context in analyses of complex, collaborative thinking. In: Lund, K., Niccolai, G.P., Lavoué, E., Hmelo-Silver, C., Gweon, G., Baker, M. (eds.) A wide lens: Combining embodied, enactive, extended, and embedded learning in collaborative settings. In: 13th International Conference on Computer Supported Collaborative Learning 2019, vol. 1, pp. 136–143. Lyon, France (2019)
38. Zörgő, S.: Segmentation and code co-occurrence accumulation: operationalizing relational context with stanza windows. In: International Conference on Quantitative Ethnography, pp. 146–162. Springer Nature, Cham, Switzerland (2022)
39. Braun, V., Clarke, V.: The ebbs and flows of qualitative research: time, change, and the slow wheel of interpretation. In: Clift, B.C., Gore, J., Gustafsson, S., Bekker, S., Batlle, J.C., Hatchard, J. (eds.) Temporality in qualitative inquiry, pp. 22–38. Routledge, New York, NY (2021)

The Application of ENA to Political Discourse in Taiwan: A Case Study

Jianxing Yu[1], Eric Hamilton[2(✉)], Ching-Hsing Wang[3], and Dongpin Hu[4]

[1] Faculty of Social Science, The Chinese University of Hong Kong, New Territories, Hong Kong, Ma Liu Shui, Hong Kong
yujianxing@ena3d.org

[2] School of Education and Psychology, Pepperdine University, Malibu, CA 90263, USA
eric.hamilton@pepperdine.edu

[3] Department of Political Science, National Cheng Kung University, Tainan, Taiwan
chinghsing@gs.ncku.edu.tw

[4] Hong Kong Centre for the Development of Educational Leadership, The Chinese University of Hong Kong, New Territories, Ma Liu Shui, Hong Kong
hudongpin@ena3d.org

Abstract. This study investigates social media interactions between individuals commenting on Taiwanese social media during a visit by the Speaker of the U.S. House of Representatives to Taiwan It specifically focuses on discourse patterns on the Facebook fan pages of Taiwan's three major parties: the Democratic Progressive Party (DPP), Kuomintang (KMT), and Taiwan People's Party (TPP). Furthermore, it models comments on PTT, the Taiwanese equivalent of Reddit. The discourse is qualitatively coded by two researchers using Hamilton's framework for political discourse analysis. Epistemic Network Analysis (ENA) is used to model connections between codes. Results show that DPP supporters employ civil and supportive language in response to the Speaker's visit, whereas KMT and TPP supporters appear acrimonious and sarcastic. Additionally, TPP supporters tend to be more rational, civil, and supportive than those of the KMT. The supporters' discourse patterns appear to align with the parties' public rhetoric. The PTT model demonstrates general support for the visit but often in acrimonious and sarcastic tones. Nevertheless, alternations between civility and acrimony are observed in the PTT discourse. This study highlights the potential of ENA in analyzing Taiwanese political discourse on social media.

Keywords: Political Discourse. Taiwan · Social Media · Epistemic Network Analysis · Facebook · PTT

1 Introduction

On August 2, 2022, the Speaker of the U.S. House of Representatives, Nancy Pelosi, visited Taiwan as part of an Asia tour despite concern expressed by U.S. President Joe Biden, making her the highest-ranking U.S. official to visit the island since Newt Gingrich in 1997. The Taiwan government and high-ranking officials welcomed her. However,

Y. J. Kim and Z. Swiecki (Eds.): icqe 2024, CCIS 2279, pp. 273–287, 2024.
https://doi.org/10.1007/978-3-031-76332-8_22

in response to the Speaker's visit, the People's Republic of China (PRC), which views Taiwan as an integral part of the country and considered the visit as support from the U.S. to Taiwan's pro-independence camp, launched an unprecedented six-day live-fire military operation around the island and imposed a ban on food imports from Taiwan. This operation drew international attention. It not only worsened the U.S.-China relationship but also had the potential to trigger a war between China and Taiwan [1]. Social media attention to the visit and the PRC's response surged. However, beyond a handful of studies looking at public opinion on social media in China during this event, few researchers have examined the discourse on Taiwanese social media. Taiwan enjoys the highest social media penetration in the Asia-Pacific region [2], with Facebook and PTT (the country's equivalent of Reddit) playing especially crucial roles in Taiwanese political communication. This study explores the discourse patterns of users on Taiwanese social media during this sequence of events.

Studies on the use of social media for political purposes in Taiwan precede this effort. For example, Lu investigated platform differences in political campaigns in Taiwan [3]. Wang studied the difference between opinion structures in political comments on Facebook and PTT [4]. However, Wang's research only modeled comments and senders as nodes and investigated the networks formed by the discussion, not treating questions of underlying emotion. Chang et al. [5] investigated online political participation in Taiwan across major social media in Taiwan, including Facebook, Instagram, Twitter, and PTT. They found that social media platforms differ in the diversity of political opinion related to Taiwan, possibly due to the high-volume misinformation spread from China and the counter-bot mechanism that social media platforms employ. Facebook, YouTube, and Line are among the social media most severely influenced by misinformation, with PTT as a particular target of China. Huang [6] analyzed comments on political news from Taiwanese news organizations on Facebook, concluding that over 25% of comments are uncivil, speculating that acrimonious comments were ways commenters released hostile emotions.

In addition to comparative research on different social media platforms, studies on how Taiwanese political parties use social media in their campaigns have emerged. For example, Tan studied how candidates leveraged their Facebook fan bases, their personal characteristics, and the networks of their friends on the platform to support their election campaigns in Taiwan's 2016 legislative election [7]. Ko analyzed the discourse of Tsai Ing-wen's Facebook page in the 2016 presidential election based on Aristotle's theory of rhetoric and content analysis [8].

However, little research has focused on the interaction between supporters of political candidates and their discourse patterns on social media. This study aims to fill this gap by studying the discourse of supporters of three major parties in Taiwan – DPP, KMT, and TPP – using Quantitative Ethnography (QE) and epistemic frame theory [9]. The study uses Epistemic Network Analysis (ENA), a prominent method in QE, to model discourse [10].

Traditionally, epistemic frame theory [9] has considered the structure of an individual's knowledge, skills, experiences, beliefs, and epistemologies as a unified analytical unit. Hamilton & Hobbs [11] proposed an analytical framework for political discourse analysis by incorporating cognitive appraisal theory, epistemic frame theory, and ENA.

This framework was later extended to include complex adaptive systems (CAS) and neural networks [12].

Other investigations on political discourse in social media and governmental documents apply ENA. For example, Schnaider [13] researched health authorities' responses to the Covid-19 pandemic in Denmark, Norway, and Sweden, focusing on the discourse in their news press releases. There are also studies on cross-parties comparison of discourse. Combining sentiment analysis and ENA, Misiejuk [14] investigated the differences in discourse related to the pandemic between Democrats and Republicans by constructing ENA models based on the COVID-19 Tweets Dataset from March to April 2020. However, few attempts have been made to apply analysis to Taiwanese political discourse on social media, including questions such as how supporters' discourse from the major parties in Taiwan differs from each other. In this study, we examine political discourse in Taiwan by focusing on social media surrounding the Pelosi visit to Taiwan. In addition, we apply ENA to political discourse in PTT, (as noted, a prominent Taiwanese local brand social media platform). The study addresses two research questions (RQs):

RQ1: *What is the partisan difference in political discourse between the supporters of DPP, KMT, and TPP on Facebook in the discussion of Pelosi's visit?*

RQ2: *How can the ENA be used to analyze discursive patterns in PTT?*

Section 2 briefly describes Taiwan's historical background and its main political parties. In addition, we discuss related works on social media in Taiwan and the ENA approach to analyzing political discourse on social media. Section 3 presents the data collection method, the dataset, and the ENA configuration. Section 4 introduces the ENA models and is followed by discussion and conclusions.

2 Relevant Taiwanese Historical and Social Media Context

The independence-unification debate has remained a central issue in Taiwanese politics, primarily dominated by the DPP and KMT. The DPP is pro-independence and liberal on issues like LGBT and women's rights. The KMT advocates for close economic ties and eventual reunification with China, taking a conservative stance. In 2019, Mayor Ko Wen-je established the Taiwan People's Party, proposing alternative approaches to the China issue. China seeks unification with Taiwan, a core national interest [15]. The "1992 Consensus" resulted in different interpretations of "China," causing conflicts. PRC's strategies to incorporate Taiwan include the "One Country, Two Systems" framework, diminishing international recognition, cyber operations, and military threats [16]. Geopolitical tensions could lead to military conflicts between China and the United States, with which Taiwan has close relations [15].

Wang and Tzeng [17] analyzed statements from top Chinese leaders and official documents related to Taiwan before and after Speaker Pelosi's visit, concluding that, despite military threats, China's core strategy remains peaceful reunification. Military threats target Taiwanese independence supporters and foreign interference, not the island's population. Chen et al. [18] studied public opinion on Chinese social media from April 1 to August 13, 2022, collecting around 400,000 data points. Using BERTopic and ALGC algorithms, they found that online opinion shifted over time. Before Pelosi's visit, discussions focused on U.S.–China relations and warnings. During the visit, attention moved to military actions and international relations. After the visit, joint military operations and potential sanctions against Speaker Pelosi dominated. Zha and Jin [19] studied Chinese nationalist sentiments on 4,353 Weibo, finding that nationalist sentiment decreased over time, with regional variations in patterns of change.

Social media is pervasive in Taiwanese politics and public communication. Facebook, PTT, and Line are key platforms for political communication, with candidates' social media presence linked to electoral success [20]. PTT, similar to Reddit, is a vital information source for journalists and a significant public discourse platform in Taiwan [21]. Its sarcastic and critical culture has been studied for hosting misogynistic content [22, 23]. Platform differences could affect users' public discussion and participation. Taiwan frequently faces cyberattacks from Chinese nationalists, who engage in trolling and coordinated attacks on Facebook [21]. Additionally, "cyber armies" hired by politicians spread information to boost candidates' reputations or attack opponents [21].

3 Epistemic Network Analysis for Political Discourse

Quantitative Ethnography (QE) combines qualitative and quantitative methods, with Epistemic Network Analysis (ENA) as a prominent analytic tool [24]. ENA models connections in data, representing meaningful features as codes that appear as graph nodes and relationships between features as graph edges. By modeling connections in the form of network graphs, ENA provides a means to visualize – with reasonable mathematical precision – how constructs of interest emerge in temporal proximity, as a foundation for ethnographic interpretation. ENA has been applied in various fields, including learning analytics, task performance, gaze patterns, team communication, governmental policy, and social media analysis [9, 13, 25]. It has also been applied to political discourse, particularly regarding the pandemic. Kampf [26] furnishes this paper's working definition of political discourse as talk and text in the public square, by politicians and non-politicians alike. Hamilton et al. [11, 27] proposed a schematic (Fig. 1) for political discourse analysis, focusing on social media. It includes Epistemic Frame Theory, an ENA-ready Coding System, Discursive Transactions, and Emotional Grammars. This framework suggests that cognitive appraisals and emotional reactions shape political beliefs and discourse. Hamilton and colleagues then applied this to commentary threads on major news sites and developed a new framework for analyzing dysfunctional discourse using ENA, complex adaptive systems, and neural networks [12].

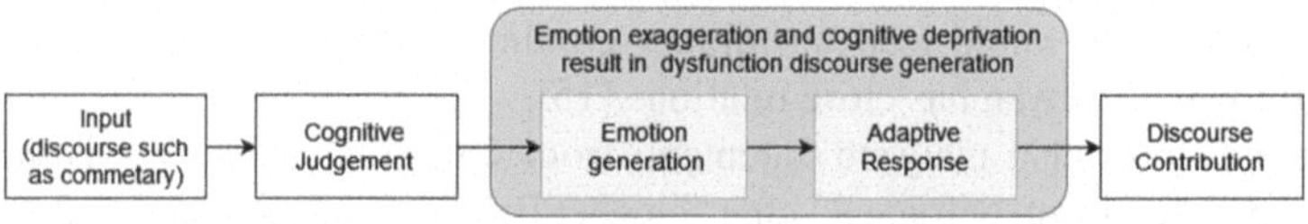

Fig. 1. Five phases of a Discursive Transaction proposed by Hamilton. In this framework, dysfunctional discourse is generated in Phases 3 and 4. Through the lens of ENA, we inference from Phase 5 the epistemic frame in previous phases (Hamilton & Hobbs, 2021)

4 Method

Dataset and Preparation. To address the research questions, our dataset is constructed using the comments on Speaker Pelosi's Taiwan visit, from the Facebook fan pages of the DPP, KMT, and TPP. The Facebook dataset consists of comments from different posts made on **August 3**, welcoming her visit. Facebook provides different options for viewing comments: 1) "All Comments" in which all the comments are displayed, 2) "Most Relevant" where friends' comments and the most engaging comments are shown with priority decided by Facebook algorithms, and 3) "Newest" in which comments are sorted according to Newest to Oldest. Using JavaScript, we scraped the top 150 comments from "All Comments." However, this study omits conversations within reply comments. In total, the Facebook dataset consists of 438 entries of data.

The PTT dataset consists of comments on an **August 1** post which reports the news about the Speaker's upcoming visit. This post was selected for its combination of objectivity and comment saturation. Additionally, the PTT dataset is moderated by user reactions, which serve as an important signifier of users' intentions.

Table 1. Codes, Examples, and Cohen's Kappa Validation Scores.

Code	Example (Working definitions appear in [27])	Kappa
Acrimony	Totally rubbish!	0.88
Moral Distancing	Stick to what's right and don't worry about what the extremists in KMT say…	0.87
Cancel	The reactionary faction of the Kuomintang will be thrown into the garbage heap of history!	0.89
Sarcasm	Is it because you lost a bet game and were forced to post (this)?	0.80
Civic	TPP must clearly express (its stance), otherwise, they will lose ground in the year-end elections	0.83
Civil	Awesome, Love Taiwan	0.88
EF-Held	Support high-level US officials coming to Taiwan! Defend Taiwan's sovereignty!	0.96
EF-Opposed	There's no problem Nancy Pelosi can't make worse	0.77
EF-Held-Justified	Don't care for her in general politics, but I give her props for going after she was threatened	0.95
EF-Opposed-Justified	What is wrong with this administration? You had an opportunity to prevent war in Ukraine, instead you accelerated it. You have the chance to avoid serious troubles with China, yet you are creating the exact situation to provoke more troubles	0.73
Gratitude	Welcome, welcome, the most beautiful and elegant American Speaker, also a great democratic fighter, Pelosi, to Taiwan, thank you, thank you	0.79
Fear	Missiles are ready to launch (crying face emoji)	0.88

The lines with "upvote" reactions are programmatically coded with either `EF-Held` or `EF-Held-Justified`, meaning that the comment aligns with the individual's epistemic frame (either expressing the frame (`EF-Held`) or providing justification (`EF-Held-Justified`)). By contrast, the comments with "downvote" reactions are coded with either `EF-Opposed` or `EF-Opposed-Justified`. Finally, those without directional reactions remain uncoded.

We identified and extracted the HTML elements containing usernames and comments using Python and JavaScript. We collected only plain text in the comments, while multiple media elements, such as images and videos, were ignored. Following the data capture, we translated the non-English posts into English using ChatGPT and subsequently manually edited them for accuracy of expression.

Due to the limited resources, only the top 150 comments from the posts of each party were collected and analyzed. This research is also limited by the method of data collection. In this study, we scrape data directly from the websites, and conversations within a reply thread are omitted, although including these could provide a more comprehensive understanding of discursive patterns on Facebook and PTT.

In this study, we employ a slightly expanded version of the codebook (Table 1) used by Hamilton et al. [11, 27] designed for political discourse analysis using ENA, adding codes for `Gratitude` and `Fear`. The top-down coding method was employed. Two coders discuss the coding and agree on resolving discrepancies between them. Cohen's kappa, a popular measurement in quantitative ethnography, was used to measure the level of agreement between coders. Social moderation is used where all 438 data entries are coded manually by the coders and used in kappa calculation. Therefore, the statistics for the generalization of intercoder reliability, such as Shaffer's Rho, is not necessary.

5 Quantitative Modeling with Epistemic Network Analysis

Epistemic Network Analysis (ENA) was applied to our data using the rENA package and the ENA webtool version 1.7.0 [29], to produce the two models appearing in Fig. 2. Model 1 compares discourse on the Facebook Fan Pages of DPP, KMT, and TPP. Model 2 depicts the discourse patterns on PTT. For Model 1, the units of analysis consist of all lines of data associated with a single value of platform, subsetted by political_leaning and username. In other words, one unit is a comment in a post. For example, one unit consisted of all the lines associated with political_leaning *DPP* and username *Ludwig101,* which means all comments by *Ludwig101* on the *DPP's* post on Facebook that welcomes Pelosi visiting. The reason for this configuration is that the order in which replies display is determined by the platform's algorithms and we cannot conclude that there exists a meaningful relationship between comments. The order and appearance of comments are decided by Facebook's algorithm which could filter out aggressive comments and show comments based on calculated popularity (Table 2).

However, the PTT model has a different configuration in conversation than Facebook. Because the comments in PTT appear in temporal order and are not affected by any algorithmic change, a meaningful relationship between comments can be established. However, due to this difference in model configuration, the PTT model is not comparable to the Facebook models in this study.

Table 2. ENA Models

Model	Groups	Conversation	Codes
1	DPP KMT TPP	Politcal_Leaning -> username (comments from a user)	Acrimony, Cancel, Sarcasm, Civic, Civil, EF.Held, EF.Opposed, and Fear
2	PTT	Platform (the post on PTT)	Acrimony, Cancel, Sarcasm, Civic, Civil, EF.Held, EF.Opposed, and Fear

The ENA software tool uses a moving window to construct a network model for each line in the data, showing how codes in the current line are connected to codes that occurred previously [10, 29]. The window is defined as 4 lines (each line plus the 3 previous lines) within a given conversation. The resulting networks are aggregated for all lines for each unit of analysis in the model. In this model, we aggregated networks using a binary summation in which the networks for a given line reflect the presence or absence of the co-occurrence within the window of each pair of codes.

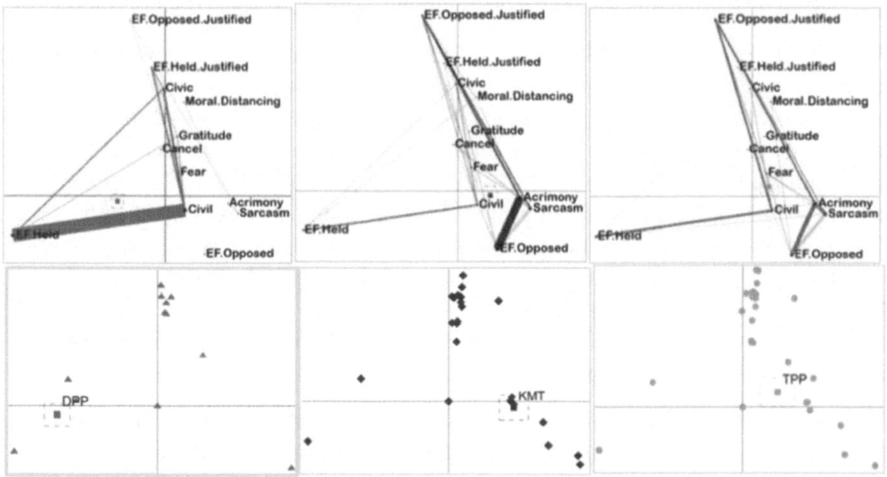

Fig. 2. The ENA models of the discourse of DPP **(left, red color, triangles)**, KMT **(middle, blue color, diamonds),** and TPP **(bottom, purple color, circles)**. The centroid of the KMT model sat very close to the code Acrimony and therefore is hidden by the code in visualization. Thicker lines indicate stronger connections between codes. (Co-registration correlations of 0.97 (Pearson & Spearman) for SVD1 and 0.88 (Pearson) and 0.87 (Spearman) for SVD2.)

Networks were visualized using network gradphs where nodes correspond to the codes, and edges reflect the relative frequency of co-occurrence, or connection, between two codes. The result is two coordinated representations for each unit of analysis: (1) a plotted point, which represents the location of that unit's network in the low-dimensional projected space, and (2) a weighted network graph of nodes and the edges connecting them. The positions of the network graph nodes are fixed and are determined by an optimization routine that minimizes the difference between the plotted points and their corresponding network centroids. Because of this co-registration of network graphs and projected space, the positions of the network graph nodes—and the connections they define—can be used to interpret the dimensions of the projected space and explain the positions of plotted points in the space. Our model had co-registration correlations of 0.96 (Pearson) and 0.95 (Spearman) for the first dimension and co-registration correlations of 0.87 (Pearson) and 0.88 (Spearman) for the second.

ENA can be used to compare units of analysis in terms of their plotted point positions, individual networks, mean plotted point positions, and mean networks, which average the connection weights across individual networks. Networks may also be compared using network difference graphs. These graphs are formed by subtracting each connection weight in one network from corresponding connections in another.

6 Result

ENA models for the comments in DPP, KMT, and TPP Facebook Fan Pages help visualize and compare the discourse patterns of each party's supporters. Additionally, the PTT model depicts the dynamic of conversation on the Taiwanese equivalent of Reddit.

Model 1: DPP, KMT, and TPP: Fig. 3 displays the ENA discourse model in the DPP Facebook Fan Page. The centroid of the network sat close to `EF-Held`. There is a strong connection between `Civil` and `EF-Held` (no justification for support provided in the comments) (0.71), and `Civic` and `Civil` (0.11). However, there was a small association between `Civil` and `EF-Held-Justified` (0.09) and between `Civic` and `EF-Held` (0.07). The code `Gratitude` is predominately associated with `Civil` (0.04) and `EF-Held` (0.02). The epistemic network analysis suggests that the supporters of DPP tend to employ civil language to express their support for Speaker Pelosi's visit, although few supporting comments are accompanied by justification. Moreover, the expression of support and civility is also associated with mentioning civic participation, such as democracy and voting.

By contrast, the connection between `Acrimony` and `EF-Opposed` (that is, no justification is written into the comment) (0.44) dominates the KMT model in Fig. 3. There is a moderate connection between `Acrimony` and `Sarcasm` (0.24) and between `EF-Opposed` and `Sarcasm` (0.21). To a much lesser degree, an association between `Civil` and `EF-Held-Justified` (support with some justifications) emerged (0.07). The centroid of the KMT model occurs close to the code `Acrimony` and `Sarcasm`. KMT supporters, the ENA model suggests, tend to express their opposition to Pelosi's visit using sarcastic and acrimonious language that shows emotions such as anger and contempt. However, the supporters are not inclined to explain their opposition. For instance, one comment from the KMT Fan Page responded to the party's posts that welcomed Pelosi by sarcasm "It feels like your party (KMT) is slowly transforming into a branch of the DPP!" Like the KMT model, the TPP ENA model is dominated by the connections between `Acrimony` and `EF-Opposed` (opposition without justification) (0.23), `Acrimony` and `Sarcasm` (0.22), and `Sarcasm` and `EF-Opposed`

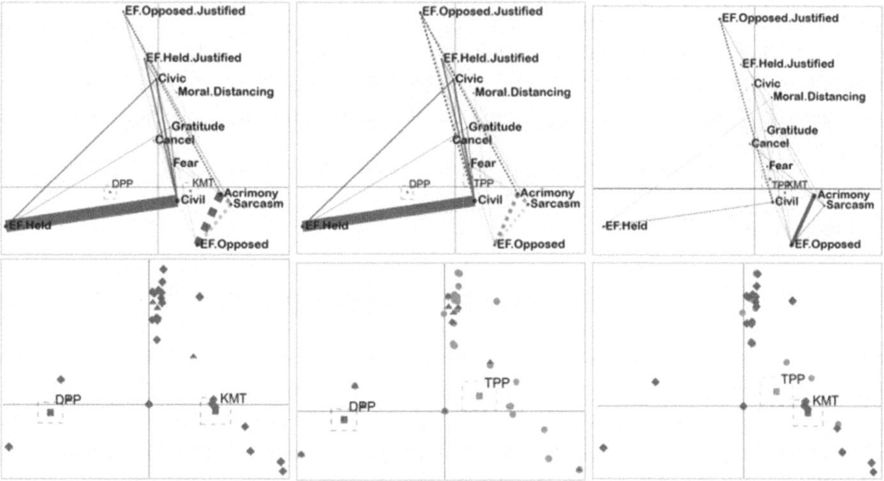

Fig. 3. (Left) Comparison ENA plot of DPP (red line network, triangle points) and KMT (blue dot network, diamond points). (Middle) Comparison ENA plot of DPP (red line, triangles) and TPP (purple dot network, circle points). (Right) Comparison ENA plot of KMT (blue line, diamonds) and TPP (purple dot, circles). Thicker lines represent a stronger connection for that code. Networks appear on the top and points distributions appear on the bottom.

(0.18), as shown in the bottom plot in Fig. 3. The analysis shows that the TPP supporters disapprove of their parties' support for the Speaker's visit. With respect to `EF-Opposed-Justified` (opposition with some justifications), the connection with `Civil` is slightly stronger than `Acrimony` (0.12 vs 0.10). This suggests that when justifying opposition, TPP supporters also tend to display civility rather than hostility. Although outnumbered by the expression of acrimonious opposition, some followers of the Fan Page display their support with civil language, as the connection between `Civil` and `EF-Held` (0.14) also occurred. Nevertheless, there is also a weak connection between `Sarcasm` and `EF-Opposed-Justified` (0.05). The code `Fear` is predominately associated with `EF-Opposed-Justified` (0.04), and weakly associated with `Acrimony`, `Sarcasm`, and `EF-Opposed`. This indicates that TPP supporters are inclined to express their fear using justification statements.

The subtraction models show that DPP discourse more frequently exhibits language that is civil and supportive than KMT and TPP discourse. KMT discourse displays a stronger connection between unjustified opposition and acrimony. Notably, TPP supporters tend to be more civil in voicing their opposition with or without justification.

The Mann-Whitney test suggests that there are statistically significant differences between DPP and KMT, DPP and TPP, and KMT and TPP. Along the X axis (SVD1), a Mann-Whitney test showed that DPP was statistically significantly different from KMT with a large effect size (0.85) and from TPP with a medium effect size (0.74) at the alpha = 0.05 level, as shown in Table 3. There is a statistically significant difference between TPP and KMT with a small effect size (0.23).The PTT model is dominated by the connection between `Sarcasm` and `EF-Held` (0.34), followed by the associations between `Acrimony` and `EF-Held` (0.30), `Sarcasm` and `Civil` (0.29),

Civil and EF-Held (0.26), Acrimony and Civil (0.26), and Acrimony and Sarcasm (0.24). This concurs with the platform's infamous sarcastic and critical comment culture. The codes Gratitude, EF-Held-Justified, Moral Distancing, and EF-Opposed-Justified do not appear in the model because they have no occurrence.

7 Discussion

Using Hamilton's political discourse analysis framework, this study examined the expression of emotional patterns in online comments related to Pelosi's visit on PTT and the Facebook fan pages of three major parties in Taiwan with the ENA model. The finding in this study suggests that discourse on the Facebook fan pages of TPP, KMT, and DPP differ on the topic of Speaker Pelosi's visit. Supporters of the DPP generally express their support for the Speaker in a civil manner, while those aligned with the KMT and TPP are more likely to voice their opposition—both to the parties' stances and the Speaker's visits—using acrimonious and sarcastic language. However, TPP followers appear to be more supportive than those of KMT.

It merits note that the ENA models concur with the political stances of the three parties. DPP is traditionally considered as pro-independence. Indeed, the comments of DPP supporters not only display a frequent use of civil and supporting language but also a frequent mention of the concept of democracy when expressing their support. Speaker Pelosi's visit to Taiwan was seen as a support for democratic values from the United States. Her office explicitly stated that this tour would "focus on mutual security, economic partnership, and democratic governance in the Indo-Pacific region." Contrary to the parties' welcoming messages, both supporters from KMT and TPP use uncivil

Table 3. Non-Parametric Test Result

Axis	Pair	N	Mean	Median	SD	Mann-Whitney		
						U	*p*	*r*
X axis (SVD1)	DPP	100	0.50	0.72	0.32	727.50	<0.05	0.85
	KMT	99	−0.34	−0.52	0.38			
X axis (SVD1)	DPP	100	0.50	0.72	0.32	1275.50	<0.05	0.74
	TPP	99	−0.17	−0.08	0.44			
X axis (SVD1)	KMT	99	−0.34	−0.52	0.38	3770.00	<0.05	0.23
	TPP	99	−0.17	−0.08	0.44			
Y axis (SVD2)	DPP	100	−0.04	−0.21	0.26	6481.00	<0.05	−0.31
	KMT	99	−0.03	−0.23	0.33			
Y axis (SVD2)	DPP	100	−0.04	−0.21	0.33	4786.50	0.68	0.03
	TPP	99	0.07	0	0.36			
Y axis (SVD2)	KMT	99	−0.03	−0.23	0.33	3893.50	<0.05	−0.21

language to express their opposition to Speaker Pelosi's visit and their parties' stances on this issue. However, the opposition from KMT supporters concurs with KMT's traditional pro-unification position which strongly opposes any moves that can anger PRC and worsen the cross-strait relation. However, unlike KMT, TPP supporters also demonstrate some civil support. This concurs with the middle-way stance that TPP claims to take. TPP is not as vigorous in promoting independence as the DPP, which has rejected the "1992 consensus" altogether. Meanwhile, the party is not inclined to maintain a close relationship with China that KMT has been seeking such that KMT party leaders would visit China and shake hands with the president of Chinese Communist Party (CCP). TPP and its supporters enjoy a friendly relationship with China and the U.S., or "take a balancing act on both sides." These ideological differences are quite evident in the ENA models.

The DPP's social media management may also explain the civility observed on the DPP fan page. The party invested heavily in building influence on social media [30]. In addition, Tsai's Facebook posts are mostly concerned with political campaigning and mobilization, avoiding attacks from opponents [39]. Moreover, Tsai frequently employs the pathos rhetorical technique on Facebook, which appeals to the audience's empathy and emotions, such as fear, sadness, joy, and hope.

When examining the accuracy of the models, the influence of misinformation and Facebook's algorithms should also be considered. Taiwanese social media has experienced misinformation spread from both domestic campaigns and cross-strait campaigns from China [21]. In particular, DPP has a scandalous history of recruiting a cyber army to assert its positions [31]. Accordingly, discourse on DPP's Facebook fan page might include comments posted by the cyber army, thus undermining the accuracy of this ENA model in explaining the discourse patterns of actual DPP supporters. Additionally, a cyber army also has its presence in PTT [31]. On the other hand, we should take the algorithm utilized by social media to filter acrimonious comments. Facebook implements systems to stop the spread of harmful content on the platform. Such techniques include filtering aggressive comments or shadow blocking, where threads posted by a user are banned, but the ban is not apparent to the users. In these cases, the "civil or encouraging" comments are prioritized, while the acrimonious comments are somewhat hidden. In this data collection, we addressed the influence of the algorithm by choosing the "Show All Comments" option on Facebook, which allows aggressive comments while prioritizing the most engaging comments.

PTT differs significantly from the Facebook platform. Most importantly, PTT does not determine or moderate content by algorithms, enabling more accurate discursive modeling than Facebook permits. Thanks to the voting system in PTT, we observed the discrepancy between users' intentions and readers' perceptions of the comments. On the PTT forum, what one might perceive as an opposition to another's epistemic frame with uncivil, sarcastic language might turn out to be supporting. This discrepancy might be a factor that contributes to political polarization on social media. Future investigation on the discrepancy between readers' deduced intention of uncivil comments and the actual motivation of the senders merits exploration. Nevertheless, this model is far from a widely applicable model to discourse on PTT. Although PTT is well-known for its sarcastic and critical culture, its positive aspects should not be ignored. For example,

Chang studied online social support in the Psychiatry and Beauty discussion groups on PTT and found that users often provide social and emotional support to those who express health concerns [32].

Considering the historical background, this study quantifies how Facebook supporters of three major parties in Taiwan responded to Speaker Pelosi's visit, an historically significant event in cross-strait relations and U.S.-China relations. Although the three parties welcomed the Speaker officially, their supporters reacted differently. Understanding the discursive patterns in supporters is vital. Violent and acrimonious language, such as disdaining, or the more subtle forms of contempt, such as canceling or being sarcastic, can disrupt political discussion. Given the importance of the cross-strait relations that increasingly draw international attention and could potentially result in a military conflict between two of the most powerful countries in the early 21st century, civil dialogue between different parties in Taiwan is important. A creative and consensus solution to the reunification problem requires civil and rational communication between major political forces in Taiwan, especially given the military dominance of its counterpart.

7.1 Future Research and Conclusion

Future studies can include the systematic investigation of posts on different topics on the Facebook fan pages of DPP, KMT, and TPP with evolving versions of the framework Hamilton originally proposed. Discourse analysis with ENA could also be conducted on different social media platforms in Taiwan, such as private fan groups on Line, a popular private messaging app in Taiwan, or Dcard, a social media platform similar to PTT and popular among young undergraduate students.

Future research could also use trajectory analysis to investigate how ENA could describe changes in political discourse patterns over time. Zha and Jin analyzed the evolution topics during Speaker Pelosi's visit using Bertopic [34] and an abbreviated large-graph clustering (ALGC) algorithm. However, the big data approach only discovers the change of topics but fails to disclose how these emotions are expressed and how the expression has changed over time. The issue of change in patterns of political discourse is intriguing and could be usefully explored in further research (Fig. 4).

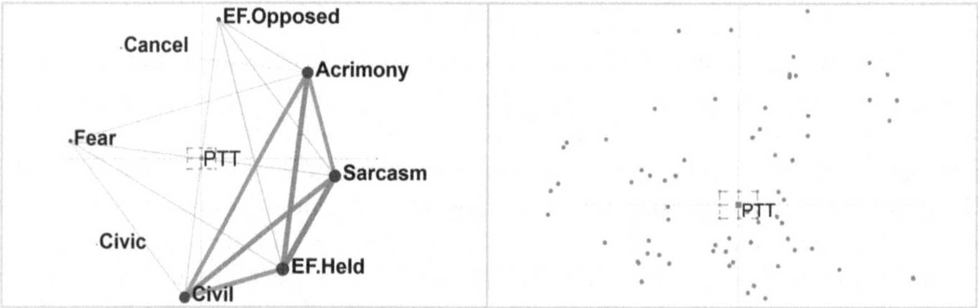

Fig. 4. The ENA model of the PTT platform. The network representation is on the left and the points distribution is on the right.

Additionally, it may be possible to employ grounded theory to develop codes for the social media platform PTT, reflecting the platform's sarcasm and concern-troll culture. The frequent alternation of civility and acrimony in PTT also deserves exploration. Indeed, coders reported difficulty in modeling the PTT discourse using this framework. Such a codebook may benefit the research of PTT-like social media platforms such as Diba in China.

In this paper, we explore reactions on Taiwanese social media during Speaker Pelosi's visit. However, this study does not claim to discover general discursive patterns on these Facebook fan pages or PTT. Indeed, a more accurate and generalizable model, if possible, would need to consider multiple topics instead of focusing on one single event. However, ethnographic research, as Shaffer stated in his foundational book *Quantitative Ethnography*, observes what people do in a specific time and place and seeks to explain why they do it, rather than to predict how everyone, or someone with certain characteristics, would behave [10]. In that spirit, this study focuses on the Speaker's visit and models the discursive patterns of supporters of the three parties on her visit, one of the most significant events in cross-strait relations.

By using ENA, we investigated the supporters' discourse on the Facebook Fan Pages of DPP, KMT, and TPP, in addition to comments on PTT. Discourse models show that DPP supporters employ civil and supportive language in response to the Speaker's visit. While supporters of KMT and TPP appear to be acrimonious and sarcastic, TPP followers tend to use less emotionally charged language; PTT discourse is supportive but also acrimonious and sarcastic and alternates between civility and acrimony. In addition, the PTT model shows a discrepancy between readers' perceptions and users' intentions toward social media comments. Finally, this paper demonstrates the potential of ENA in analyzing Taiwanese political discourse, especially in modeling supporters' discursive patterns on social media.

Acknowledgments. Special thanks to Mr. Zhangjing Zheng, Mrs. Yi-Chen Kuo and Mrs. Hsuan-Ya Huang for their efforts in coding and supporting this work and discussion.

Disclosure of Interests. The authors have no competing interests to declare that are relevant to the content of this article.

References

1. Chen, Y.: Fourth Taiwan strait crisis? examining the implications of PLA exercises following Pelosi's Taiwan visit from the perspective of strategic deterrence. Korean J. Def. Anal. **35**, 293–316 (2023). https://doi.org/10.22883/KJDA.2023.35.2.007
2. Lai, L.T.: Social media in Taiwan – statistics and facts. https://www.statista.com/topics/10374/social-media-in-taiwan (2023)
3. Lu, Y.-C.: 誰是社群選戰贏家? facebook, youtube, instagram 跨平台分析 [Analyzing Taiwanese Politicians Social Media Adoption On Facebook, YouTube, And Instagram. Master's thesis, National Taiwan University]. Airiti Libr., pp.1–115 (2020). https://doi.org/10.6342/NTU202000234

4. Wang, T.J., Wang, J.-C.: Facebook 與 PTT的輿論結構研究 [A Case Study of Facebook and PTT Opinion Structures] (2015). https://doi.org/10.6843/NTHU.2015.00192
5. Chang, H.-C.H., Haider, S., Ferrara, E.: Digital civic participation and misinformation during the 2020 Taiwanese presidential election. Media Commun. **9**(1), 144–157 (2021). https://doi.org/10.17645/mac.v9i1.3405
6. Huang, Y.: 公領域私語化:臺灣社群媒體政治新聞貼文與討論分析 [Privatized discourse in the public sphere: content analysis of Taiwanese news organizations' political posts and user comments on facebook pages]. **38**, 215–252 (2020)
7. Tan, Y., Chou, H.-Y., Lin, R.-J.: 臺灣2016和2020年立委選舉中候選人臉書貼文策略的影響 [The Impact of Political Candidates' Facebook Message Strategies During the 2016 and 2020 Legislative Elections in Taiwan]. Chin. J. Commun. Res. **43**, 199–243 (2023). https://doi.org/10.53106/172635812023060043005
8. Ko, H.-C.: 選戰策略:2016 台灣總統選舉臉書的政治溝通 [Campaign strategy: political communication on facebook in the 2016 Taiwan presidential election]. J. Commun. Cult. **140** (2019)
9. Shaffer, D.W., et al.: Epistemic network analysis: a prototype for 21st-century assessment of learning. Int. J. Learn. Media. **1**, 33–53 (2009)
10. Shaffer, D.W.: Quantitative Ethnography. Cathcart Press (2017)
11. Hamilton, E., Hobbs, W.: Epistemic frames and political discourse modeling. In: Ruis, A.R., Lee, S.B. (eds.) Advances in Quantitative Ethnography: Second International Conference, ICQE 2020, Malibu, CA, USA, 1–3 Feb 2021, Proceedings, pp. 32–46. Springer International Publishing, Cham (2021). https://doi.org/10.1007/978-3-030-67788-6_3
12. Hamilton, E., Williamson, M., Hurford, A.: Theory-building and tool-building for a science of dysfunctional political discourse. In: Arastoopour Irgens, G., Knight, S. (eds.) Advances in Quantitative Ethnography, pp. 275–289. Springer Nature Switzerland, Cham (2023)
13. Schnaider, K., Schiavetto, S., Meier, F., Wasson, B., Allsopp, B.B., Spikol, D.: Governmental response to the COVID-19 Pandemic – a quantitative ethnographic comparison of public health authorities' communication in Denmark, Norway, and Sweden. In: Ruis, A.R., Lee, S.B. (eds.) Advances in Quantitative Ethnography: Second International Conference, ICQE 2020, Malibu, CA, USA, 1–3 Feb 2021, Proceedings, pp. 406–421. Springer International Publishing, Cham (2021). https://doi.org/10.1007/978-3-030-67788-6_28
14. Ka Misiejuk, J., Scianna, R Kaliisa, Vachuska, K., Shaffer, D.W.: Incorporating sentiment analysis with epistemic network analysis to enhance discourse analysis of twitter data. In: Ruis, A.R., Lee, S.B. (eds.) Advances in Quantitative Ethnography: Second International Conference, ICQE 2020, Malibu, CA, USA, February 1-3, 2021, Proceedings, pp. 375–389. Springer International Publishing, Cham (2021). https://doi.org/10.1007/978-3-030-67788-6_26
15. Hu, W., Meng, W.: Geopolitics, domestic politics, and risks of war in the Taiwan strait. China Rev. **23**, 17–39 (2023)
16. Gordon, S.M., Mullen, M.G., Sacks, D.: US-Taiwan Relations in a New Era: responding to a More Assertive China. Counc. Foreign Relat. (2023)
17. Wang, H.-H., Tzeng, W.-F.: No turning back? assessing China's intent to use force to resolve the Taiwan issue after 2018. Issues Stud. (2023). https://doi.org/10.1142/S1013251123400076
18. Chen, T., et al.: Public opinion evolution in cyberspace: a case analysis of Pelosi's visit to Taiwan. IEEE Trans. Comput. Soc. Syst. **11**, 319–329 (2024). https://doi.org/10.1109/TCSS.2023.3239046
19. Zha, Y.-R., Jin, J.W.: Attitude decay, event salience, and emotional reversal: Chinese cyber-nationalism after Pelosi's visit to Taiwan. Issues Stud. **59** (2023)
20. Wang, C.-H., Tsai, C.: Social media as mobilizer and demobilizer: evidence from Taiwan. SAGE Open **13**, 21582440231156810 (2023). https://doi.org/10.1177/21582440231156806

21. Monaco, N.J.: Computational propaganda in Taiwan: where digital democracy meets automated autocracy. Comput. Propag. Polit. Parties Polit. Polit. Manip. Soc. Media. (2017)
22. Chen, L.-W., Chou, P.-N.: A case study on the analysis of posting culture in the web-based community. J. Educ. **34**, 53–79 (2015)
23. Yu, C.-Y.: 「我說妳是妳就是」：從PTT「母豬教」的仇女行動談網路性霸凌的性別階層 [You are what I said: Discussing the gender hierarchy of cyberbullying through the example of misogynistic actions of PTT's Religion of Sows]. Forum Womens Gend. Stud. **105**, 22–29 (2016). https://doi.org/10.6256/FWGS.2016.105.22
24. Shaffer, D.W., Ruis, A.R.: Is QE just ENA? In: Damşa, C., Barany, A. (eds.) Advances in Quantitative Ethnography: 4th International Conference, ICQE 2022, Copenhagen, Denmark, October 15–19, 2022, Proceedings, pp. 71–86. Springer Nature Switzerland, Cham (2023). https://doi.org/10.1007/978-3-031-31726-2_6
25. Hansen, J., Zaki, M., Benna, A., Porter, C.: Epistemic network analysis of reddit comments relating to COVID-19 vaccine news on the r/coronavirus subreddit. In: Third International Conference on Quantitative Ethnography: Conference Proceedings Supplement, p. 81 (2022)
26. Kampf, Z.: Political discourse analysis. In: Tracy, K., Sandel, T., Ilie, C. (eds.) The International Encyclopedia of Language and Social Interaction, pp. 1–17. Wiley (2015). https://doi.org/10.1002/9781118611463.wbielsi096
27. Hamilton, E., Hurford, A.: Political discourse modeling with epistemic network analysis and quantitative ethnography: rationale and examples. In: Damşa, C., Barany, A. (eds.) Advances in Quantitative Ethnography, pp. 359–373. Springer Nature Switzerland, Cham (2023)
28. Marquart, C. L., Hinojosa, C., Swiecki, Z., Eagan, B., Shaffer, D. W.: Epistemic network analysis (Version 1.7.0) (2021). http://app.epistemicnetwork.org
29. Lee Siebert-Evenstone, A., Irgens, G.A., Collier, W., Swiecki, Z., Ruis, A.R., Shaffer, D.W.: In search of conversational grain size: modeling semantic structure using moving stanza windows. J. Learn. Anal. (2017). https://doi.org/10.18608/jla.2017.43.7
30. Wang T.-L.: 「臉書選舉」？ 2012年台灣總統大選社群媒體對政治參與行為的影響 ["Facebook election?" The impact of social media on political participation in Taiwan's 2012 presidential elections]. Soochow J. Polit. Sci. **31** (2013)
31. Ko, M.-C., Chen, H.-H.: Analysis of cyber army's behaviours on web forum for elect campaign. In: Zuccon, G., Geva, S., Joho, H., Scholer, F., Sun, A., Zhang, P. (eds.) Information Retrieval Technology, pp. 394–399. Springer International Publishing, Cham (2015). https://doi.org/10.1007/978-3-319-28940-3_32
32. Chang, H.J., Ho, M., Huang, C.: 線上社會支持類型探討: 以 PTT 精神疾病版及整型美容版為例 [Typology of online social support: a study of bulletin board system in Taiwan]. Mass Commun. Res. 61–105 (2008)
33. Wang, Z., Chen, J., Chen, H.: Identifying interdisciplinary topics and their evolution based on BERTopic. Scientometrics 1–26 (2023)

Navigating Identity Tides: Perceived Identity Threats and Coping Strategies Among Bicultural Hong Kong Citizens

Gemma Salazar, Letitia Lee, and Ying-yi Hong(✉)

The Chinese University of Hong Kong, Hong Kong SAR, China
{gemmasalazar,yyhong}@cuhk.edu.hk, letitialee@link.cuhk.edu.hk

Abstract. This study examines the perceived identity threats among Hong Kong citizens and their coping strategies in relation to their level of Bicultural Identity Integration (BII). By analyzing the interplay between perceived threats and coping strategies within Hong Kong's unique sociopolitical landscape, the study provides valuable insights into how individuals with varying levels of BII respond to identity challenges. Using Epistemic Network Analysis (ENA), we found that individuals with low BII, compared to those with high BII, made significantly different connections among perceived identity threats and coping strategies. Specifically, when faced with various identity threats, low BII participants were more likely to employ homesteading and denial, while high BII participants tended to adopt strategies such as accepting social flaws and making their identities prominent. From the content analysis, we delved deeper into understanding the meaning of these associations. Future studies could benefit from a longitudinal design to better capture the fluidity and complexity of identity integration.

Keywords: Bicultural Identity Integration · Social Identity · Epistemic Network Analysis · Identity Threats and Coping

1 Introduction

In the face of globalization, the identification with two or more cultural knowledge traditions or widely shared systems of beliefs and practices [1], is an increasingly salient issue. Given that cultural identity is one fundamental way in which individuals can define and understand themselves [1], difficulties may arise when multicultural individuals' cultural identities are perceived to be incompatible or conflicting. This can become even more complex when individuals perceive threats in their social environment that challenge or undermine one of their identities. How can individuals manage their multiple cultural identities and cope with threats to their cultural self-concept?

In major reviews of multiculturalism/biculturalism and the negotiation of the relevant cultural identities, scholars have limited their address to cases involving international migration, such that at least one of the cultures is a heritage/home culture, and at least one culture is a receiving/host culture (e.g., [2, 3]). However, this neglects cases of

Y. J. Kim and Z. Swiecki (Eds.): icqe 2024, CCIS 2279, pp. 288–301, 2024.
https://doi.org/10.1007/978-3-031-76332-8_23

biculturalism wherein both focal cultures could be reasonably construed as heritage or host cultures. Non-migrant individuals in previously colonized territories, fluent in various cultural traditions, may have unique experiences of multicultural identity, threats, and coping strategies.

Hong Kong is one such unique context. In 1997, Britain handed Hong Kong's sovereignty back to China, leading to the establishment of the Hong Kong Special Administrative Region (HKSAR). Amongst the cultural identities in Hong Kong, two are particularly salient for locals: the local Hongkonger identity, and the national/ethnic Chinese identity. Some argue that the Chinese identity is superordinate in this case since a myriad of citizens are ethnically Chinese and Hong Kong also has a long, intertwined history with Mainland China [4]. However, for one cultural identity to be subsumed or equivalent to another, their respective knowledge traditions would have to overlap completely [1], and some argue that Hong Kong developed its own distinct indigenous cultural identity as a result of its colonial history [5]. This would suggest that the knowledge tradition of the Hongkonger identity has diverged and is different from that of the Chinese identity.

Arguably, many Hong Kong citizens may be non-migrant bicultural individuals in a unique circumstance where both focal identities can be reasonably construed as either heritage or host cultures, depending on one's perspective. According to Fung [6], Hong Kong residents had shifted towards a more dualistic and hybrid identity by 1999. Researchers have also observed that the proportion of Hong Kong people endorsing dual identities increased in the decade following reunification [7].

In 2019, Hong Kong experienced a wave of social movement sparked by the proposed Anti-Extradition Law Amendment Bill. This bill would have permitted the transfer of fugitives to Mainland China for trial [8]. Amidst the already pre-existing local-national tensions, a sense of blurred national identity, and the governance integration slated for 2047, the introduction of the bill was seen as the latest trigger, creating perceived threats and anxiety among Hong Kong people [9]. Despite the nearly 30 years elapsed since the handover, Hong Kong people continue to grapple with balancing their national and local cultural identities [10]. As Hong Kong and Mainland China continue to integrate socially, politically, and financially, some worry that their local identity is under threat, while others may welcome the integration of the identities or favor the national identity. Indeed, some evidence suggests that while some Hong Kong people may still favor identification with dual identities, the endorsement of a predominantly singular local identity among young people rose from 2016 to 2022 [11].

This study seeks to deepen our understanding of how individuals navigate their multiple cultural identities. Specifically, we examined the identity threats perceived by Hong Kong citizens and the coping strategies they employ in response. To this end, we conducted epistemic network analysis and thematic content analysis of fifteen in-depth semi-structured interviews with Hong Kong citizens. Drawing on the bicultural identity integration (BII) framework [12], we found that the perceived identity threats and coping strategies of Hong Kong citizens vary based on how they perceive and navigate their Hongkonger and Chinese identities—whether they view the two identities as blended or compartmentalized, and as harmonious or conflicted. Understanding Hong Kong citizens' identity threats and coping strategies, in the context of their Hongkonger and Chinese identities, can inform interventions to ease identity tensions and reduce intergroup conflicts.

2 Theoretical Background

2.1 Bicultural Identity Integration (BII)

BII refers to the degree to which individuals perceive their two cultural identities as compatible or conflictual, and as integrated or compartmentalized [12]. BII is characterized by two dimensions: 'Conflict vs. Harmony' and 'Blendedness vs. Compartmentalization'. On one hand, the 'Conflict vs. Harmony' dimension gauges whether individuals perceive their two cultural identities as being in conflict or harmony. In other words, it measures the perceived tension or clashes versus compatibility between the two cultures. On the other hand, the 'Blendedness vs. Compartmentalization' dimension determines whether individuals perceive their two cultural identities as blended into one or as distinct and separate. This dimension measures the degree of dissociation versus overlap perceived between the two cultures [12].

Individuals with low BII tend to perceive their two cultural identities as distinct and often in conflict. They may feel torn between the two cultures and find it challenging to reconcile the differences. Moreover, low BII individuals often feel as if they ought to choose one of the cultures [12]. In the context of Hong Kong, individuals with low BII may struggle with the dichotomy between traditional Chinese values and the more Westernized aspects of Hong Kong society. They might feel a sense of conflict between these two cultural identities and may compartmentalize their behaviors and attitudes depending on the social setting and who they are with.

In contrast, those with high BII see their two cultural identities as compatible and integrated. They are able to blend elements from both cultures and create a unique, cohesive identity. They can navigate both cultures seamlessly, drawing on both cultural repertoires in a flexible and adaptive manner. In Hong Kong, high BII individuals may embrace the fusion of East and West that characterizes Hong Kong. Biculturals with high levels of BII are unconflicted about their two cultural orientations and see them in non-oppositional terms, they will engage in cultural frame-switching fluidly by reacting to external cues in culturally consistent ways [13].

BII is increasingly recognized as a dynamic process that reflects the ongoing negotiation of dual identities, particularly in contexts where cultural distance and conflict are pronounced [12]. While the literature acknowledges the dynamic nature of BII and its impact on identity negotiation, especially in the face of cultural conflict, there is a dearth of empirical data on how individuals with varying levels of BII perceive identity threats and their coping responses. Understanding how experiences of identity threats and coping responses may vary as a function of BII is paramount in understanding individual differences in the navigation of bicultural identities.

2.2 Identity Threat

Social Identity Theory posits that individuals strive for a positive personal identity and a positive social identity, the latter being derived from group membership [14]. This need is fulfilled by inclusion in groups that are distinctively positive compared to relevant outgroups. When this need is unmet or threatened, a state of social identity threat arises [14–17]. This threat could stem from a person's cultural knowledge of how people with certain social identities are perceived in specific settings and activities [18], or it could be triggered by a cue in the environment that suggests potential devaluation [19]. The experience of identity threat is subjective and will be gauged by individuals disparately. It is a continual experience in which people frequently experience challenges to their self-esteem, continuity, self-efficacy, and distinctiveness [20]. Branscombe et al. [15] proposed a taxonomy of four distinct classes of social identity threats: categorization threat, distinctiveness threat, threat to the value of social identity, and acceptance threat.

The socio-political changes in Hong Kong and its gradual integration with Mainland China have led to perceived identity threats among some Hong Kong citizens [10]. For instance, Edwards [21] found that some Hongkongers perceive the Cantonese language as being under threat and view the spread of Putonghua in Hong Kong as an act of political assimilation, potentially eroding the Hong Kong local culture. Such pressures can disrupt the integration process, leading to a conflict between local (Hongkonger) and national or ethnic (Chinese) identities. This may relate to the distinctiveness threat proposed by Branscombe et al. [15].

In the context of Bicultural Identity Integration (BII), individuals with low BII often perceive their two cultural identities as highly dissimilar and incompatible. They may struggle to incorporate both cultures into a cohesive identity. When faced with situations that challenge their cultural identities, such as the example given by Edwards [21], these individuals may feel a heightened sense of conflict or stress, feeling pressured to choose between their cultural identities. In contrast, individuals with high BII have successfully integrated their two cultural identities into a cohesive whole, making them more resilient to identity threats. As a result, they may experience less conflict and threat when faced with identity challenges. It is expected the connections between perceived identity threats and coping strategies would be different among high versus low BII participants.

2.3 Coping Strategies

Coping strategies could be understood as the thoughts or behaviors that individuals use to modify or remove threats to identity [22]. Sharma and Sharma [23] proposed ways of coping related to multiculturalism, such as denial and homesteading. Denial involves refusing to acknowledge the threat or the identity itself, while homesteading is a proactive strategy where individuals mentally construct a political and social space for themselves to cope with discomfort and anxieties when facing identity-related threats, a phenomenon referred to by Kinnvall [24]. In this study, we expand beyond the coping strategies proposed by Sharma and Sharma [23] and introduce additional strategies identified through a deductive approach (see Table 1).

Jaspal et al. [20] suggested that coping strategies are not necessarily inherent to an individual's personality but rather associated with the type of identity threat. They have found that threats to an individual's self-esteem and self-efficacy are often linked to coping strategies focused on the self (e.g., concealment of self and denial), while threats to distinctiveness are associated with coping strategies that involve social engagement and focus on relationships with others [20]. However, the processes underlying these associations remain unclear, as the use of multiple regression in their study primarily identified linear relationships between threats and coping strategies without capturing the complex, interconnected nature of these responses. This study aims to address this gap by capturing the intricate and multifaceted relationships between various coping strategies and identity threats using Epistemic Network Analysis (ENA), which will be further detailed below.

3 Methods

3.1 In-Depth Semi-structured Interviews

Sixteen local-born Hong Kong citizens were recruited through the Centre of Communication and Public Opinion Survey, an interview recruitment service affiliated with a local university. These individuals participated in semi-structured interviews, each lasting between 90 to 120 min, conducted from June to October 2023. One datum was discarded as the participant had already filled in a questionnaire from our previous studies on Hongkonger and Chinese identity. The recruitment process was designed to capture a diverse cross-section of the populace's perspectives on Hongkonger and Chinese identities. The sample was stratified by gender (53% male), age (53% over the age of 50), and educational attainment (60% degree-level). The sample was also stratified by self-reported political stance (one-third identified as "blue", and another third identified as "yellow"), reflective of the divisions during the 2019 social unrest in Hong Kong.[1] Participants received HKD 500 (approximately USD 65) for their contribution.

Each interview was conducted by two interviewers and the interview protocol included four sections, focused on participants' perceptions of Hongkonger identity, Chinese identity, the integration of these identities, and their predictions for the future of Hong Kong. The order in which interviewees were asked about the Hongkonger and Chinese identities was counterbalanced amongst interviewees to mitigate the impact of any anchoring effects that the salience of one identity may have on the other. Given Hong Kong's colonial past, a significant portion of the Hong Kong population are Cantonese-Chinese and English bilinguals. As such, the interviews were predominately conducted in Cantonese-Chinese, supplemented by English. With the interviewees' consent, all interviews were audio-recorded. Participants also completed a structured questionnaire on the contents of Hongkonger and Chinese identity, the integration of the identities, and demographic information after the interview.

3.2 Data Coding

Each interview was transcribed verbatim in Chinese and English. A team of three coders (one lead researcher, and two research assistants trained by the lead) coded the transcriptions using MAXQDA version 24. Each utterance (turn of speech) was coded for its embedded meaning, attitudes, emotions, or concepts related to the Hongkonger and

[1] Details of the comprehensive demographic information can be found at https://osf.io/7ych6/?view_only=02c4fd6bd91a4dc684ed489445a34353.

Chinese identities, as well as the subjective experience of these identities and associated phenomena. The coding process was inherently iterative and collaborative, with the research team revisiting the transcripts multiple times. This led to the development of a comprehensive codebook over the course of three iterations. A mixed indo-deductive approach was used throughout the coding process, with higher-level thematic codes emerging ground-up from grouping lower-level codes, subsequently refined with reference to social psychological theories. Two transcripts (13%) were randomly selected and independently coded by all three coders. The intercoder reliability was quantified using Cohen's kappa; the kappa values between the lead coder and the assistant coders were high at $\kappa = .71$, and $\kappa = .86$, respectively. The scope of this paper is limited to the analysis and discussion of the codes and themes that pertain to the interviewees' perceptions of threats, and their coping strategies in relation to the integration of these identities. The relevant portion of the codebook is detailed in Table 1.[2]

3.3 Epistemic Network Analysis

We conducted epistemic network analysis (ENA) [25–28] using the ENA Web Tool (version 1.7.0) [29] to examine the connections among identity threats and coping strategies that interviewees described when speaking about their Hongkonger and Chinese identities. Given that these concepts were interwoven throughout each interview, we modeled connections across the entirety of each interview (whole conversation window), using participants with high versus low BII as the unit of analysis, with each interview constituting a conversation.

Recognizing that the perceived threats and coping strategies experienced by Hong Kong citizens may vary based on their degree of BII, we conducted a comparative analysis. Specifically, we divided interviewees into two groups using a median split: those with low BII and those with high BII. The BII groups were derived from participants' survey responses on two BII items, considering the dimensions of blendedness versus compartmentalization and harmony versus conflict. The resulting low BII ($n = 7$) and high BII ($n = 8$) groups served as categorical variables in our ENA models, allowing us to compare the network structures of participants with the two BII profiles. Means rotation was applied to the model to maximize the between-group differences on the X-axis dimension.

4 Results

4.1 Perceived Threats and Coping Strategies as a Function of BII

An ENA model was constructed to examine the connections between different perceived threats and coping strategies among individuals with high BII and low BII (see Fig. 1). Along the X-axis, which accounted for 20.1% of the variance, a two-sample t-test assuming unequal variance indicated that the mean of the low BII group (mean = -0.243, SD = 0.129) was statistically significantly different from the mean of the high BII group (mean = 0.213, SD = 0.299; $t(9.783) = -3.914$, $p = 0.003$, Cohen's d = 0.94).

[2] Details of the code book with subcodes and examples can be found at https://osf.io/7ych6/?view_only=02c4fd6bd91a4dc684ed489445a34353.

Table 1. Code Book for Threats and Coping Strategies

Code	Definition
Threats	
Distinctiveness threat	Group distinctiveness is undermined [15]
Categorization threat	Being categorized against one's will [15]
Threat to the value of social identity	The group's value is undermined [15]
Threat to psychological safety	A situation or behavior that undermines an individual's sense of well-being, security, and comfort in expressing themselves within a group
Coping strategies	
Engagement	The active participation and interaction in discussion and argument in order to express their views
Make identification prominent	To make their social identity explicit or easily noticeable, so that they can be recognized or understood without ambiguity
Acceptance	Acceptance of their social identity
Acceptance of social flaws	Recognizing and embracing the imperfections, mistakes, and shortcomings in our social behaviors and interactions
Disengagement from outgroup	The process of withdrawing or distancing oneself from a group that one does not identify with or does not want to identify with
Homesteading	A proactive strategy where individuals mentally construct a political and social space for themselves to cope with uneasiness and anxieties when facing identity-related threats
Avoidance	The act of steering clear from certain actions, thoughts, or situations that are perceived as unpleasant or anxiety-inducing
Denial	Denial of their social identity

In general, compared to high BII participants, low BII participants made more connections between homesteading and all four identity threats (see Fig. 1). Content analysis similarly showed that low BII participants tended to use homesteading as a way to cope with identity threats, wanting to create a space for themselves to only talk to people of similar values. For instance, participant 16 (M/20–29/student) said that "(when someone identifies as a Hongkonger), it allows you to quickly identify certain parts of their values … which makes communication easier or harder. It helps you categorize (whether the person) is someone you want to talk to or not." In this case, knowing someone's identity can help in the assessment of whether the person is like-minded, and therefore an (in)appropriate partner for further homesteading engagement.

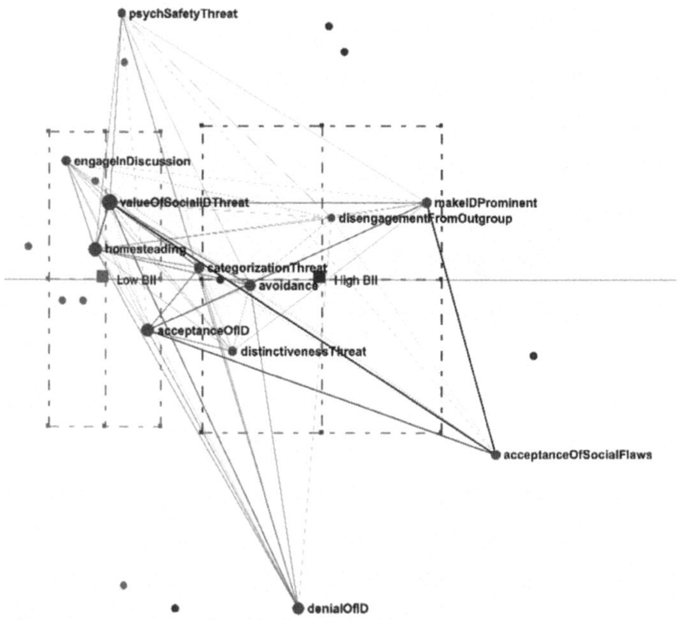

Fig. 1. Subtraction network of means-rotated ENA model of Low BII and High BII participants' perceived threats and coping strategies.

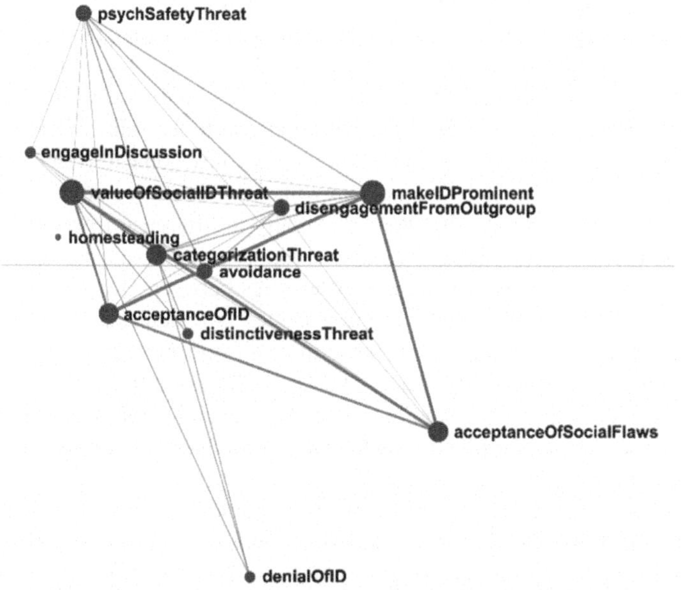

Fig. 2. Means-rotated ENA model of High BII participants' perceived threats and coping strategies.

Fig. 3. Means-rotated ENA model of Low BII participants' perceived threats and coping strategies.

Furthermore, more association was made between denial of their identity and three identity threats (categorization threat, threats to the value of social identity, and psychological safety threat) for those who are low in BII than those who are high in BII, (see Fig. 1). Participant 13 (F/20–29/employed) expressed that more exposure to individuals from Mainland China has made her more alert to threats to the value of her Hongkonger social identity. "Maybe it's because more mainlanders have come to Hong Kong to visit, settle, or live here, so we've had more contact with them, or we see more of these people in Hong Kong. We've realized that there's actually a difference from what we imagined. We find that they don't have the cultural sophistication we expected. And we've also noticed that there really are cultural differences between Hong Kong and China, which leads to conflict easily." Later in the interview, she denies her Chinese identity. "Maybe there's a blood connection because after all, my grandparents are originally from the mainland… Emotionally, though, I don't really feel it (identifying as Chinese), and I don't feel any conflict (between the Hongkonger and Chinese identities). I think the conflict arises when you identify as Chinese. But since I don't have that sense of identification, this conflict doesn't exist."

Threats to the value of one's social identity were mentioned throughout the interviews by both participants low in BII and high in BII. Its importance is reflected in the network diagrams showing each group in isolation (see Figs. 2 and 3). However, when the two groups' networks are subtracted from one another (see Fig. 1), the threat was more associated with the acceptance of social flaws and making one's identity prominent for high BII than low BII participants. "You could say that recently, with the anti-extradition protests, I've felt even more strongly about this. I don't really identify with the social movement or what they are doing. No matter how good their intentions might be, I don't agree with them because they're essentially turning their dissatisfaction with China into something extreme. If you're unhappy with your country, you can express it, but you shouldn't do such things (behaviors during the 2019 social unrest). Because of what they've done, I feel an even stronger sense of identification with being Chinese. The more they act this way, the more I identify with my Chinese identity" (Participant 11/M/60–69/retired). This participant coped with his dissatisfaction with the behaviors of the protestors by making his Chinese identity prominent.

Participant 12 (M/60–69/retired) also expressed discontent towards the 2019 protestors: "It's simple. For example, with the recent actions of the pro-democracy protesters and the violence, most of whom are Hongkongers, I find them extremely repulsive. First of all, do you really need to use these methods to overthrow the government? Secondly, is the Hong Kong government really so bad that it needs to be overthrown?" However, he opted to cope by accepting social flaws even though they threaten his value of social identity. "Every person and country has their flaws. It's like if my family member, my younger brother, broke the law, would you kick him out of the house? Of course not. I would treat him with a loving attitude." (Participant 12).

The statistically significantly different connections made by the two groups suggest that although both low BII and high BII individuals may share some perceived threats, the two groups differ on the connections between identity threats and coping strategies.

4.2 Perceiving no Threats

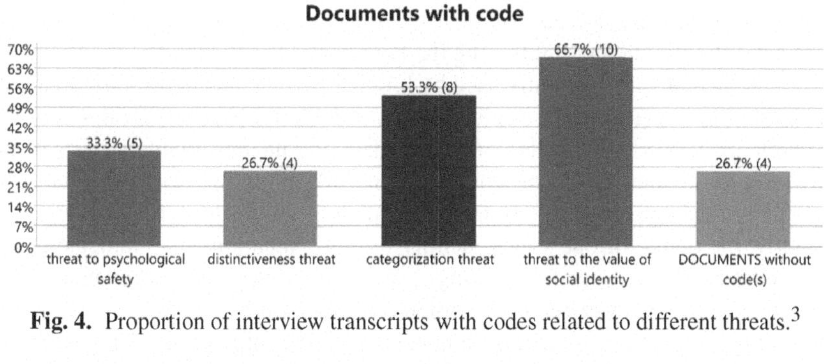

Fig. 4. Proportion of interview transcripts with codes related to different threats.[3]

Participants in both the high and low BII groups recognized the four types of identity threats. However, interestingly, four participants – three (37.5%) from the High BII group and one (14.3%) from the Low BII group – did not mention perceiving any threats to their identity (see Fig. 4). The participant from the Low BII group, who did not perceive threats, viewed Hong Kong as an inseparable part of China and regarded the Hongkonger and Chinese identities as one singular national or ethnic identity. "I think the two identities

[3] The number in brackets indicates the number of participants whose transcripts were coded into each threat; each transcript can be coded into more than one threat. The proportion was calculated by the number divided by 15 (total number of participants).

are one. Because I identify myself as Chinese, there's no point in defining myself by referring to a specific region (Hong Kong), right?" (Participant 6/F/40–49/employed)[4] This viewpoint indicates that for this individual, a broader national identity supersedes the local regional identity. The socio-political changes in Hong Kong had not affected his steadfast Chinese social identity.

In contrast, the three participants from the high BII group, who did not perceive any threats, strongly identified with both the Hongkonger and Chinese identities. They considered these identities integral to their self-concept, regardless of whether they viewed them as distinct or unified. This suggests that they have managed to integrate their dual identities in a way that minimizes conflict and compartmentalization, contributing to a high BII score.

5 Discussion

This study examines the identity threats perceived by high and low BII individuals and their different coping strategies in the context of Hong Kong's unique sociopolitical landscape. Consistent with our prediction, we found that individuals with low (versus high) BII made significantly different connections among perceived identity threats and coping strategies. Specifically, low BII participants were more likely to use homesteading and denial as coping strategies across various identity threats. Homesteading, characterized by creating a space for like-minded individuals, was employed to mitigate feelings of conflict and stress associated with identity threats. Participants expressed that understanding someone's identity helps determine their suitability for interaction, indicating a desire to shield oneself from perceived threats by associating with similar values. In this context, identity becomes a crucial marker for distinguishing ingroups from outgroups, with the act of homesteading reinforcing the boundaries between them.

Similarly, denial was frequently used by low BII participants in response to identity threats related to categorization, social identity value, and psychological safety. This coping strategy allows individuals to avoid confronting uncomfortable aspects of their identity or cultural conflict. Consistent with Benet-Martínez and Haritatos' [12] study, low BII individuals are more likely to feel as if they should just choose one culture. Importantly, the denial of one's own identity in these situations may indicate that the individual has ascribed a specific meaning to the identity they reject when under threat, a nuance that may not have been fully explored in prior work.

In contrast, high BII participants demonstrated different patterns. They were more likely to use strategies such as accepting social flaws and making their identity prominent when facing threats, particularly those related to the value of their social identity. Participants who felt threatened by the 2019 protests affirmed their personal values toward their Chinese identity as a way to express dissatisfaction with the protests. Again, their identities have played a significant role while navigating the challenges of integration.

Moreover, some high BII participants did not perceive any identity threats highlighting the successful integration of their dual identities, allowing them to navigate complex

[4] This participant may not be considered as low in BII as he has not identified with the two identities. Hence, BII may not be applicable to this person according to Benet-Martínez & Haritatos [12].

sociopolitical environments with minimal internal conflict. This suggests that high BII individuals can harmonize their Hongkonger and Chinese identities in a way that reduces the likelihood of experiencing identity-related threats. Theoretically, this supports the notion that high BII is characterized by an ability to reconcile multiple cultural identities and more resilience. Furthermore, for high BII individuals, the integration of dual identities may serve as a protective factor and buffer against the potential stressors associated with identity threats. By successfully merging these identities, high BII individuals are better equipped to maintain a stable self-concept, even in the face of external challenges.

The findings of this study contribute significantly to the existing theoretical frameworks of bicultural identity integration (BII), particularly by expanding upon the work of Benet-Martínez and Haritatos [12]. While previous research has established the broad distinctions between high and low BII individuals, our study delves deeper into how these differences manifest in the specific connections between perceived identity threats and coping strategies. The results suggest that low BII individuals are more inclined to engage in coping strategies such as homesteading and denial, when faced with various identity threats. This contrasts with high BII individuals, who tend to adopt approaches like accepting social flaws and making their identity prominent when facing identity threats. By highlighting these distinct coping strategies, our study provides a more nuanced understanding of how bicultural individuals navigate identity conflicts, thus underscoring the importance of considering the dynamic interplay between identity threats and coping strategies.

One limitation of this study is its cross-sectional design, which captures data only at the time of the interview and restricts the ability to examine changes in BII and coping strategies over time. Without longitudinal data, it is challenging to understand how BII and the use of coping strategies might evolve in response to ongoing experiences or significant life events. Most of the participants mentioned that the 2019 social unrest has significantly impacted their views on their identities, so the results of this study capture specific views in a particular moment. However, as suggested by Benet-Martínez & Haritatos [12], BII is a process, not a fixed state. Given the dynamism of identities and identification and different personal experiences, it is possible that individuals could continue or cease to identify with either identity, seeing the identities as more or less integrated over time. Future research with a longitudinal design may better capture the fluidity and complexity of identity and BII, to examine how threats and coping strategies may develop and change over time as a function of identities and BII.

In conclusion, our study contributes to the literature on bicultural identity integration by shedding light on the interplay between perceived identity threats and coping strategies. It underscores the importance of considering these factors in understanding and supporting bicultural individuals in their identity integration journey.

Acknowledgments. This research was supported by grant funding from the Senior Research Fellow Scheme (Grant No. SRFS2122-4H01) of the Research Grant Council, Hong Kong SAR government, conferred to Y. Hong.

The authors have no competing interests to declare that are relevant to the content of this article.

References

1. Hong, Y., Wan, C., No, S., Chiu, C.: Multicultural identities. In: Kitayama, S., Cohen, D. (eds.) Handbook of Cultural Psychology. The Guildford Press (2007)
2. Schwartz, S.J., Birman, D., Benet-Martínez, V., Unger, J.: Biculturalism: Negotiating multiple cultural streams. In: Schwartz, S.J., Unger, J. (eds.) The Oxford Handbook of Acculturation and Health. Oxford University Press (2016)
3. Meca, A., Eichas, K., Schwartz, S.J., Davis, R.J.: Biculturalism and bicultural identity development: A relational model of bicultural systems. In: Titzmann, P.F., Jugert, P. (eds.) Youth in Superdiverse Societies: Growing Up with Globalization, Diversity, and Acculturation. Routledge (2020)
4. Census and Statistics Department, the Government of the Hong Kong Special Administrative Region (2023). https://www.censtatd.gov.hk/en/scode600.html. Retrieved 30 May 2023
5. Ma, E., Fung, A.: Negotiating local and national identifications: Hong Kong identity surveys 1996–2006. Asian J. Commun. **17**(2), 172–185 (2007). https://doi.org/10.1080/01292980701306555
6. Fung, A.: Postcolonial Hong Kong identity: Hybridising the local and the national. Soc. Identities **10**(3), 399–414 (2004). https://doi.org/10.1080/1350463042000230854
7. Kim, J., Ng, S.H.: Perceptions of social changes and social identity: Study focusing on Hong Kong society after reunification. Asian J. Soc. Psychol. **11**(3), 232–240 (2008). https://doi.org/10.1111/j.1467-839X.2008.00262.x
8. Chan, A.K.W., et al.: Hong Kong's new wave of migration: Socio-political factors of individuals' intention to emigrate. Comp. Migr. Stud. (2022). https://doi.org/10.1186/s40878-022-00323-y
9. Shek, D.T.: Protests in Hong Kong 2019–2020: a perspective based on quality of life and well-being. Appl. Res. Qual. Life **15**(3), 619–635 (2020). https://doi.org/10.1007/s11482-020-09825-2
10. Kit, C.C.: China as "Other": Resistance to and ambivalence toward national identity in Hong Kong. China Perspectives **2014**(1), 25–34 (2014). https://doi.org/10.4000/chinaperspectives.6374
11. Yang, S.: Decoding mixed identities in Hong Kong: a clustering analysis of multiple identity indicators. Soc. Indic. Res. **171**, 585–603 (2024). https://doi.org/10.1007/s11205-023-03248-w
12. Benet-Martínez, V., Haritatos, J.: Bicultural identity integration (BII): components and psychosocial antecedents. J. Pers. **73**(4), 1015–1050 (2005). https://doi.org/10.1111/j.1467-6494.2005.00337.x
13. Benet-Martínez, V., Leu, J., Lee, F., Morris, M.W.: Negotiating biculturalism: cultural frame switching in biculturals with oppositional versus compatible cultural identities. J. Cross Cult. Psychol. **33**(5), 492–516 (2002). https://doi.org/10.1177/0022022102033005005
14. Tajfel, H., Turner, J.C.: An integrative theory of intergroup conflict. In: Austin, W.G., Worchel, S. (eds.) The Social Psychology of Intergroup Relations, pp. 33–47. Brooks/Cole (1979)
15. Branscombe, N.R., Ellemers, N., Spears, R., Doosje, B.: The context and content of social identity threat. In: Ellemers, N., Spears, R., Doosje, B. (eds.) Social Identity: Context, Commitment, Content, pp. 35–58. Blackwell Science (1999)
16. Branscombe, N.R., Schmitt, M.T., Harvey, R.D.: Perceiving pervasive discrimination among African Americans: implications for group identification and well-being. J. Pers. Soc. Psychol. **77**(1), 135–149 (1999). https://doi.org/10.1037/0022-3514.77.1.135
17. Ellemers, N., Spears, R., Doosje, B.: Self and social identity. Annu. Rev. Psychol. **53**, 161–186 (2002). https://doi.org/10.1146/annurev.psych.53.100901.135228
18. Goffman, E.: Stigma: Notes on the Management of Spoiled Identity. Prentice-Hall (1963)

19. Steele, C.M., Spencer, S.J., Aronson, J.: Contending with group image: the psychology of stereotype and social identity threat. In: Advances in Experimental Social Psychology, vol. 34, pp. 379–440. Elsevier (2002). https://doi.org/10.1016/S0065-2601(02)80009-0
20. Jaspal, R., Lopes, B., Wignall, L.: The coping with identity threat dcale: development and validation in a university student sample. Identity **20**(4), 225–238 (2020). https://doi.org/10.1080/15283488.2020.1808469
21. Edwards, J.G.H.: 'I have to save this language, it's on the edge like an endangered animal': perceptions of language threat and linguistic mainlandisation in Hong Kong. J. Multiling. Multicult. Dev. **42**(4), 307–326 (2019). https://doi.org/10.1080/01434632.2019.1691565
22. Breakwell, G.M.: Coping with Threatened Identities, 1st edn.. Psychology Press (1986). https://doi.org/10.4324/9781315733913
23. Sharma, S., Sharma, M.: Globalization, threatened identities, coping, and well-being. Psychol. Stud. **55**(4), 313–322 (2010). https://doi.org/10.1007/s12646-010-0048-8
24. Kinnvall, C.: Globalization and religious nationalism: Self, identity, and the search for ontological security. Polit. Psychol. **25**(5), 741–767 (2004). https://doi.org/10.1111/j.1467-9221.2004.00396.x
25. Bowman, D., et al.: The mathematical foundations of epistemic network analysis. In: Ruis, A., Lee, S.B. (eds.) Advances in Quantitative Ethnography: Second International Conference, ICQE 2020, Malibu, CA, USA, 1–3 Feb 2021, Proceedings, pp. 91–105. Springer (2021)
26. Shaffer, D.W.: Quantitative ethnography. Cathcart Press (2017)
27. Shaffer, D.W., Collier, W., Ruis, A.R.: A tutorial on epistemic network analysis: analyzing the structure of connections in cognitive, social, and interaction data. J. Learn. Anal. **3**(3), 9–45 (2016)
28. Shaffer, D.W., Ruis, A.R.: Epistemic network analysis: a worked example of theory-based learning analytics. In: Lang, C., Siemens, G., Wise, A.F., Gasevic, D. (eds.) Handbook of Learning Analytics, pp. 175–187. Society for Learning Analytics Research (2017)
29. Marquart, C.L., Hinojosa, C., Swiecki, Z., Eagan, B., Shaffer, D.W.: Epistemic network analysis (Version 1.7.0) [Software] (2021). http://app.epistemicnetwork.org

Author Index

Y. J. Kim and Z. Swiecki (Eds.): icqe 2024, CCIS 2279, pp. 303–304, 2024.
https://doi.org/10.1007/978-3-031-76332-8

The manufacturer's authorised representative in the EU is Springer Nature Customer Service Centre GmbH, Europaplatz 3, 69115 Heidelberg, Germany. If you have any concerns regarding our products, please contact ProductSafety@springernature.com

Printed and bound by CPI Group (UK) Ltd, Croydon, CR0 4YY
01/10/2026
02225834-0007